f₂ —

Unequal City

DEPARTMENT OF THE ENVIRONMENT

Unequal City

Final Report of the Birmingham Inner Area Study

Llewelyn-Davies Weeks Forestier-Walker & Bor

LONDON   HER MAJESTY'S STATIONERY OFFICE

Designed by HMSO Graphic Design

ISBN 0 11 751142 0

Foreword

by the Minister of Housing and Construction

This report is the outcome of one of the three studies undertaken by consultants for the Department of the Environment in the inner areas of major cities – Birmingham, Liverpool and London.

For over four years the consultants, in collaboration with the local authority, worked in the Small Heath area of Birmingham carrying out research into a wide range of issues. At the same time they have carried out action projects which in addition to shedding light on the issues have brought some practical benefits to the residents of the study area. Reports on many of the action projects have been published and are available from the Inner Cities Directorate of the Department, together with reports of particular research studies done by the consultants.

It is well over a decade since some of us started to advocate a 'total' approach to urban renewal, urging that this should be brought to the centre of politics rather than continue as a peripheral issue. During these last four years, while the studies continued, concern about the multiple problems and challenges of inner urban areas has grown. Peter Shore's statement in the House of Commons on 6 April 1977 made this a central issue of the Government's social, economic and planning policies. The work of the inner area studies has contributed much to our understanding of these problems. The Summary Reports published in January of this year have already stimulated many valuable comments as to the future directions of urban policy and have contributed to the discussions which led to the Commons statement and then to the preparation of the Government's White Paper. But the Summary Reports could only set out the consultants' arguments and conclusions in outline. The present report sets them out in full, with their supporting evidence, and contains a great deal of additional material.

It has been my privilege during the greater part of the consultants' study to serve as Chairman of the Joint Steering Committee which has guided their work. I am grateful to the members and officers of the Birmingham City Council for their help and co-operation. These studies will prove to be of lasting value to everyone concerned with renewing the conditions and opportunities for life in the old urban areas which lie at the hearts of our cities. I hope this report, and those from the other two studies, will be read widely and closely. They certainly deserve to be.

Reg Freeson

Chairman of the Steering Committee

June 1977

Contents

List of tables

List of figures

Roger Coward

As the bus is going through town, I notice very clean streets and clean shops. We go into Digbeth, I notice the city getting dirtier, and as we enter Small Heath it looks like a slum area.

A Child's Eye View of Small Heath

Introduction

The evidence, conclusions and recommendations presented in this our final report form a synthesis of what we have learned from almost four years' work in Small Heath. They take as their starting-point a substantial programme of study and experimental action centred on Small Heath in its particular city and regional context but mark also our reflection upon that experience in the light of the growing body of published analysis and argument about urban problems, their causes, and the means of their solution or alleviation.

During the course of our work we have prepared many reports, both published and unpublished, dealing with specific aspects of research, policy analysis or experiment. A list of individual projects (some 40 in all) is given in Appendix A and an annotated bibliography in Appendix B. Our more detailed findings and recommendations in any one particular field of activity, such as housing or pre-school provision, are to be found in the individual reports and each constitutes part of our response to the overall study brief. This final report concentrates on the fundamental issues and common themes arising out of our work as a whole and attempts to look beyond Small Heath and Birmingham to draw lessons of more general applicability.

The study brief

The original study brief, set out in a Department of the Environment background paper in August 1972, contained the following four objectives:

1. To discover by study a better definition of inner areas and their problems.
2. To investigate by experiments on the ground the actions affecting the physical environment of these areas which could usefully be undertaken for social and environmental purposes.
3. To examine whether the concept of 'area management' can usefully be developed and what the practical implications would be for the local authority.
4. To provide the basis for general conclusions on statutory powers, finance and resource questions, and techniques.

The main changes in emphasis during the life of the Birmingham study (hereafter referred to as BIAS) have concerned the second and third objectives, those most closely associated with investigation and action on the ground. First, the narrow focus on strictly 'physical' types of experiment quickly gave way to the broader concept of an action programme that would use limited resources in support of any project which responded to a demonstrable or clearly articulated local need in an innovative manner. The whole environment of the community – social, educational and economic as well as physical – was taken to be the study's concern. Second, the investigation of 'area management' was dropped in favour of a more general examination of what might be done to improve the 'coordination of local services'. Both changes were embodied in a reformulated set of objectives ratified by the BIAS steering committee in July 1973, at the start of the main phase of the study. The objectives now read:

1. To define inner areas and their problems.

2. To investigate by experimental action methods of improving the environment of inner areas.

3. To look at the advantages of greater coordination of local services in dealing with the problems of inner areas and to consider its implications for the city concerned.

4. To make recommendations to the Department of the Environment on the need for legal, administrative, financial and technical changes in the current methods for approaching inner area problems.

Since then the formal content of our brief has remained unaltered. The direction of the study has continued, however, to be influenced by a variety of internal and external factors: changes in the personalities involved, in interpretation and political emphasis, in the state of the national and regional economies. Our report inevitably reflects these influences. In particular, the deep recession which marked the final two years of our work in Small Heath (a climate very different from that at the onset of the study) has led to a greater concern with the economic and political obstacles to realising the commitment of resources necessary to tackle the basic causes of inner area decline.

The report structure

Our report is divided into three main parts, broadly following the sequence implicit in the four objectives of the BIAS brief. Part one (The Cause for Concern) describes the challenge. Parts two and three (The Search for Solutions) describe the form we believe the response to that challenge should take, from respectively local (area-specific) and wider perspectives.

Chapters 1 to 3 relate directly to objective one. They are concerned with establishing a general definition and typology of inner areas (1), illustrating the range of problems which our research in Small Heath and knowledge of other research lead us to regard as characteristic of such areas (2), and examining what we take to be the principal causes of these problems (3).

Chapter 4 represents a bridge between the investigation of problems and the consideration of possible means of seeking their solution. It looks at the potential for change inherent within the agencies of urban government and in the relationship between government and the people of inner areas. And it discusses briefly obstacles to change in the present economic and political context.

Chapters 5 to 8 serve as our principal response to objectives two and three of the brief. They treat various strategy approaches amenable to producing change through action at a local level. Chapter 5, concerned with improvement of the residential environment, bears a direct relation to objective two in its original form, though its evidence derives more from research, case study and policy analysis than from BIAS-initiated or sponsored experiment. Chapter 6, dealing with issues of coordination in urban government policy formation and execution, responds to objective three in its revised form. Chapter 7 explores approaches towards community organization and development, aspects of strategy which we see as complementary to those discussed in Chapter 6 and which came to be an increasingly important focus of our study, particularly the action projects, as time progressed. Finally, Chapter 8 examines the question of area-specific compensatory programmes and positive discrimination in general, a theme that underlies not only Inner Area Studies but other government initiatives in the field of urban deprivation from Educational Priority Areas onwards.

Chapter 9 constitutes a second bridge. Its concern is with the vehicle of research itself. It reviews some of the strengths and limitations of area-based initiatives as a means of promoting innovation and suggests the directions that future research and experiment might take.

Chapters 10 to 14 are by way of a response to the more general objective four, both in its original form and as it was later reformulated. They deal with strategy approaches which are open to only little influence from the local level and demand action on a wider front: increasing employment opportunities (10), raising personal incomes (11), the generation and allocation of resources (12), urban planning (13), and education as a means of creating conditions more favourable to change (14).

Composition and presentation of the report

The individual chapters of the report have all been written according to a common outline argument developed out of previous BIAS reports, working papers and discussions involving the full team engaged on the study during its final eighteen months or so. Roughly two-thirds of the text was written by two authors (Peter Walding and Paula Jones) working in very close collaboration. The remainder is composed of contributions by four other team members. Because of the different hands involved there are inevitable differences in style and emphasis from chapter to chapter, particularly in the final part of the report. However, the various contributors have followed an agreed main line of argument, so that in this sense the report represents a 'team view'.

In presenting evidence from research, especially in part one, we have chosen to use data selectively, to build up for the reader a general (and sometimes impressionistic) picture of Small Heath and its people, as they are today and how they have changed over time. We have therefore minimised the use of detailed tables. Much of the information relating to Small Heath is drawn from two sample surveys. The first was a structured questionnaire completed for roughly 1 in 13 households and carried out for us by Social and Community Planning Research (SCPR) in spring 1974. The second was a series of depth interviews (referred to as Circumstances of

Families) recorded on tape mainly in autumn 1975. The majority of the 115 households interviewed were taken from those identified from the SCPR survey as being in poverty, single parent families or families with 4 or more children. The full number was made up by some 20 further interviews with people living in short-life housing in an area scheduled for clearance. Since the numbers in sub-samples are often quite small, quantitative evidence cited in the text should be interpreted in the light of the broad pattern or order of magnitude they reveal rather than as precise measurements. In tables base numbers have always been given to indicate sub-sample sizes. When referring to tables it should be noted that small differences in figures will in some cases fall within the range of a standard error.

The principal recommendations put forward in parts two and three are brought together in a brief summary at the end of the book. The summary also includes a shortlist of priorities for immediate action.

＊

In presenting our final case we cannot claim that our analysis of the evidence is 'scientifically' proven, that our conclusions are demonstrably appropriate to all inner areas, or that our recommendations have been fully tested. But we do believe our experience of the past four years in Small Heath, in research, observation and trying to get a few simple things done for the benefit of the local community, has made us very much more aware of both the realities of urban deprivation and of the strengths and limitations of small-scale intervention than would otherwise have been possible. It has certainly changed our perceptions of many of the problems we have encountered, and strengthened our conviction that there is an urgent need for much greater political commitment to addressing causes as well as symptoms. Securing such commitment would not be a simple matter in times of general prosperity, involving as it does difficult political choices; it will be much harder, but even more necessary, in the current situation of economic and financial stringency.

We hope the argument pursued in this report will make a positive contribution towards the alleviation of inner area problems by stimulating not only thought but action. Otherwise BIAS will be of little value to the people who are most intimately concerned: the residents of inner areas.

January 1977

PART ONE

The cause for concern

John Peverley

Twenty years ago Small Heath was the elite area of the Midlands.

Small Heath has changed infinitely for the worse. In my road there were police inspectors, insurance people. That class of people have all gone.

SCPR Exploratory Study

1 Defining inner areas

Our terms of reference required us to designate an inner area within Birmingham
before we developed a programme of research and experiment on the ground, even
though part of the purpose of that programme, made explicit in the first objective of
our brief, was to 'discover a better definition of inner areas and their problems'. A
study area had therefore to be selected (deductively) on the basis of criteria which
implied some prior understanding of what was generally meant by the term 'inner
area' and of what problems were held to be characteristic of such a locality.
Having selected a study area we then had to proceed (inductively) from analysis of a
specific body of experience to conclusions of general applicability which would permit
more informed judgements about priorities for action and appropriate strategies for
dealing with them.

In practice, the passage from the general to the particular and vice versa went on
continuously throughout the study. We had constantly to draw back from the detail
to look for patterns; and to find these patterns we had to make repeated comparisons
with what we knew about circumstances in other areas, within Birmingham and
elsewhere, now and in the past. In turn, our detailed evidence enabled us to assess
the validity of certain theories of urban form and change. For this reason, in
presenting our conclusions we shall not attempt to follow a strictly linear path,
culminating in the final 'discovery' of a 'better definition'. We shall put forward our
understanding of the concept of 'inner areas' first, next propose a general definition
and broad typology of the kind of localities we take to be the concern of the three
studies (Birmingham, Lambeth, Liverpool), then turn to the specific example of our
own study area, Small Heath, as an illustration of what we have in mind.

The concept of 'inner area'

Use of the term 'inner area' derives from the recognition that many cities have
broadly similar physical patterns. The inner areas are generally understood to be
zones of old residential and industrial development which lie between city centre
and the nearer suburbs and in which is to be found a high incidence of the range of
physical, social and economic problems frequently referred to collectively as 'urban
deprivation'.

A quick glance at some of the maps later in this report will show examples of typical
shapes from the classic models of urban structure (concentric zones, sectors and
multiple nuclei) in Birmingham's physical form and socio-economic composition.
Small Heath before redevelopment of its western end presented an almost perfect
cross-section of concentric residential development distorted only by an equally
characteristic wedge or sector of industrial land following the railway and canal
to the south and spreading along the Cole valley to the southeast. There are however

two important points we would make in relation to patterns of city structure. First, a city's development should not be looked at from a purely physical perspective. The form and character of a city's built environment are a manifestation of that city's changing functions and fortunes over time; and the variations within the city's built environment mirror the diversity of activities those changing functions and fortunes promote. Second, distance from the city centre, size, shape, etc. are of only incidental relevance as far as a practical consideration of policy issues is concerned. In other words, the primary focus of our study is on the phenomenon of 'urban deprivation', wherever it occurs.

We shall not then use the term 'inner area' in a strictly geographic or static sense. The concept we have of inner areas is essentially a historic or dynamic one. It rests on the premise that comparisons between localities can only be meaningful if set within the localities' evolving cultural context (technological, economic, social, political), both at the local or neighbourhood level and at the level of town, city, conurbation, region. The closer the parallel between their respective contexts, the greater will be the similarity between the policy issues they raise and the strategies required to resolve them. While we should have preferred, for the sake of accuracy, to have employed a designation that was linked less to space, such as 'areas of urban deprivation', we shall continue to refer to 'inner areas' in a loose sense. Many, though by no means all, will of course fall within a fairly narrow radius of major city centres.

Small Heath, we shall argue, illustrates a range of problems and issues which are characteristically the concern of inner area policy. Yet it is far from homogeneous. Variations between one part of the area and another on important indicators of deprivation (lack of housing amenities, households without a car, male unemployment, etc) are greater than the variation between the area and city averages. Nor are the parts which show the highest concentration of certain problems necessarily as bad in these respects as individual neighbourhoods to be found elsewhere in the city and in other urban locations. Our purpose, however, is not to prepare league tables or discuss relative scales of intervention to deal with different quantitative intensities of particular problems or sets of problems. Rather, it is to try and illuminate the qualitative nature of the problems and the types of initiative which might be helpful in tackling them. Whether or not it is appropriate to single out special localities (and, if so, by what means of selection) or design area-specific initiatives are questions we shall consider in later chapters.

General definition and broad typology of inner areas

We define 'inner areas' as those residential zones contiguous to major industrial developments whose form began to take shape some 100 to 150 years ago and which (due to technological obsolescence, economic and social change, and the accompanying selective migration of people and firms) have remained starved of the resources necessary to maintain a level of reinvestment in the built environment and neighbourhood services commensurate with generally rising public expectations and aspirations.

8

The general outcome of the process of change to which these areas have been subjected has been progressive decay of the physical fabric, rising economic insecurity (manifested principally in terms of discontinuity of local industrial employment) and a tendency towards greater social instability and breakdown of the structure of community life.

Within this broad category of 'inner areas' two basic sub-types can be distinguished:

· *Areas of primary deprivation* (roughly equivalent to 'slums') which have always, since their inception, tended to house those citizens able to exercise least choice in terms of their jobs, homes and personal consumption. A great number of these areas have been subjected to policies of clearance and comprehensive redevelopment. Those that remain contain the characteristic mixture of industrial plant, warehouses, railway yards and canal heads, interspersed with high-density small terraces and/or tenements built for the manual labour who worked in the factories and yards. Many, scheduled for future redevelopment, lie in varying stages of dereliction and blight.

· *Areas of secondary deprivation* (roughly equivalent to what have variously been called 'zones of transition', 'twilight zones', etc) whose original housing functions have been gradually superseded and into which have increasingly come to be funnelled, by the effects of public policy as well as market forces, groups whose relative position in society is similar to that of those for whom the housing in areas of primary deprivation was constructed. This process began as a result of the pressures of over-crowding and attendant problems in areas of primary deprivation and in some cases was accelerated by displacement through war damage. In recent years it has frequently been aided by the spillover effects of (neighbouring) redevelopment and new patterns of immigration. The physical character of such areas may vary considerably, depending on the functions and fortunes of their particular urban setting at different points in time, but will tend to comprise medium-sized and/or large (now subdivided) terraced housing, built either for the skilled artisan and lower-status white-collar worker or for the more affluent middle classes. They may or may not contain pockets of commercial and light industrial activity, public open space, or major space-consuming traffic arteries. They are much less likely to be scheduled for comprehensive redevelopment but may be threatened with selective clearance, in some cases for major road construction, and thus be affected by blight.

This general definition and typology are not intended to be precise. They do not, for example, permit a clear distinction to be made between those exceptions to the typology (such as a small 'infill' council estate or an 'oasis' of gentrification/vestigial middle-class settlement) which might nevertheless be ignored, like individual houses or blocks, as relatively insignificant deviations and those which should properly be regarded as separate areas even though completely surrounded by zones which obviously meet the criteria of the typology. However, we believe they afford a reasonable guide to the environments which are the concern of our study. They are clear enough to explain why we shall exclude from our policy considerations (at least, directly) areas which have already been comprehensively redeveloped, more recent council estates on the edge of towns or cities, and areas like substantial parts of Edgbaston and Moseley in Birmingham which – while they may lie close to the city centre, contain much old housing and have undergone important changes in their functions – continue to cater for higher-status social groups. We do not deny that these areas, too, may pose serious policy issues, in some cases quite similar to individual issues we shall be identifying, but we would contest that the overall experience of life in such environments is qualitatively different enough to warrant quite different combinations of strategy.

The example of Small Heath

Towards the end of 1972, when preparatory work on the study was just beginning, Small Heath was fast becoming recognised as one of Birmingham's problem areas. The Member of Parliament for Small Heath constituency was pressing for a study area in his part of the city and councillors represented on the steering committee set up to guide the study identified Small Heath ward as one of a short-list of potential choices, together with Sparkbrook and Sparkhill also to the southeast. To help narrow the choice we conducted a brief comparative analysis using a classification of enumeration districts (EDs) made by the city statistician and the city medical officer from 1966 census results for the purpose of EPA (educational priority area) declaration. The classification designated as 'deprived' those EDs which scored above the city average on at least seven of the following eight indicators:

Proportion of resident population under 15 years of age
Proportion of population born in New Commonwealth
Proportion of households living at over 1.5 persons per room
Proportion of households sharing a dwelling
Proportion of households without exclusive use of a fixed bath
Proportion of households without a car
Proportion of economically active males in Class V (unskilled)
Proportion of economically active males unemployed in the previous year.

Five out of 16 EDs (31 per cent) in our eventual study area rated as deprived on this count, compared with 12 per cent in the city as a whole, 24 per cent in what the city then described as its 'middle ring' and 34 per cent in what the structure plan reports of survey classed as 'inner wards'. The particular groupings of wards referred to here and intermittently through the text are illustrated in Figure 1.

While we could have chosen a study area with a higher concentration of deprived EDs (eg, Balsall Heath/Sparkbrook West, Aston/Lozells), Small Heath[1] had a number of other advantages. It was thought to be about the right size (falling in a preferred population range of 30,000 to 40,000); had sharply defined physical boundaries which, as subsequent research confirmed, coincided closely with people's 'mental maps' of their district; presented a fairly good mix of land uses (Figure 3),

1. Throughout the text we use the name Small Heath to refer to the whole study area which in fact includes that part of Sparkbrook ward north of the Birmingham–Oxford railway line and a small corner of Deritend. Where Small Heath ward, Small Heath constituency, Small Heath employment exchange area or Small Heath planning district are referred to, this different usage is made clear. For the respective boundaries, see Figure 2.

**Figure 1
Birmingham:
Ward boundaries**

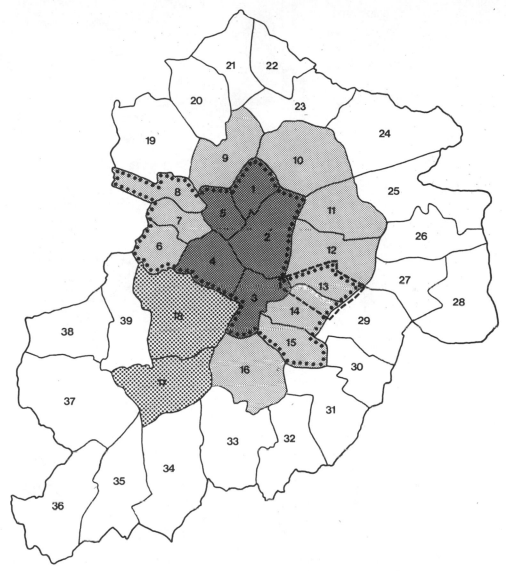

Inner core

Inner wards (BCC structure plan definition)

Inner ring (BIAS)

Wards which when added to 'inner ring' make up the middle ring (BCC)

0   1   2mls
0   1   2   3kms

List of wards:

 1 Aston
 2 Duddeston
 3 Deritend
 4 Ladywood
 5 Newtown
 6 Rotton Park
 7 All Saints
 8 Soho
 9 Handsworth
10 Gravelly Hill
11 Washwood Heath
12 Saltley
13 Small Heath
14 Sparkbrook
15 Sparkhill
16 Moseley
17 Selly Oak
18 Edgbaston
19 Sandwell

20 Perry Barr
21 Oscott
22 Kingstanding
23 Stockland Green
24 Erdington
25 Shard End
26 Stechford
27 Yardley
28 Sheldon
29 Acocks Green
30 Fox Hollies
31 Hall Green
32 Billesley
33 Brandwood
34 Kings Norton
35 Northfield
36 Longbridge
37 Weoley
38 Quinton
39 Harborne

11

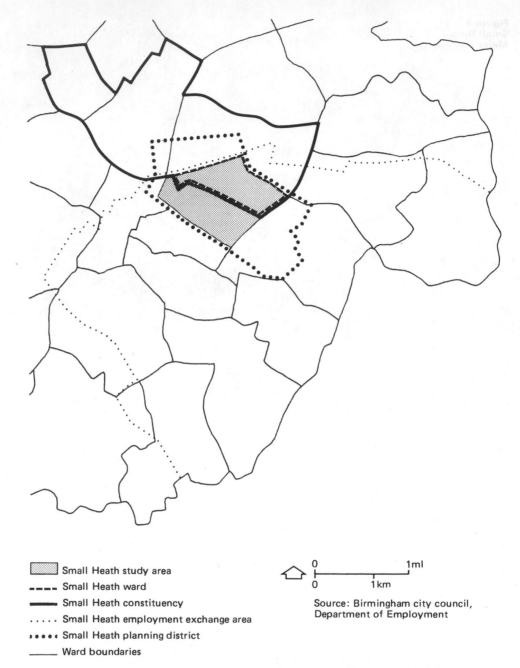

**Figure 2
Small Heath:
General location**

Small Heath study area
- - - Small Heath ward
───── Small Heath constituency
· · · · Small Heath employment exchange area
•••• Small Heath planning district
───── Ward boundaries

0 ────────────── 1ml
0 ────────────── 1km

Source: Birmingham city council,
Department of Employment

housing and environmental conditions, and tenure groups; was not scheduled for large-scale redevelopment beyond its western end; did not have an 'abnormally high' proportion of immigrants (such as to make it totally atypical in terms of social and racial mix); and had not been subject to major previous research.

Although our choice was based on 1966 data, the latest census results then available, use of information from the 1971 census would have made little difference. Despite significant shifts in the incidence of individual deprivations from district to district, largely as a consequence of clearance and redevelopment, deprived EDs remained

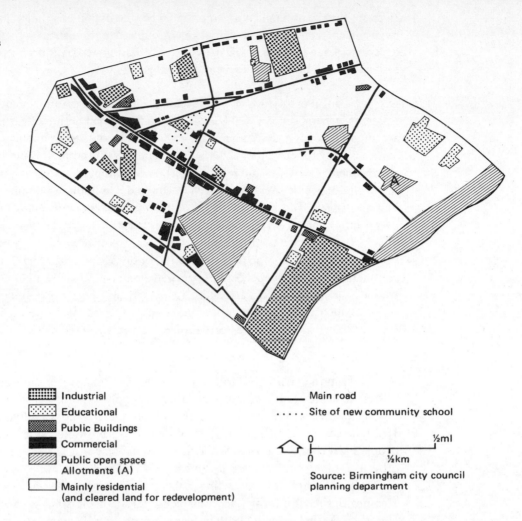

**Figure 3
Small Heath:
Major land uses**

Industrial

Educational

Public Buildings

Commercial

Public open space
Allotments (A)

Mainly residential
(and cleared land for redevelopment)

Main road

..... Site of new community school

0 ————————— ½ml
0 ————————— ½km

Source: Birmingham city council
planning department

clustered principally within a broad band of nineteenth and early twentieth century development encircling the city centre and redeveloped areas from northwest round to south. Small Heath's relative position in terms of the concentration of deprived EDs was much the same.

The hypothesis behind the use of a combination of census indicators in the selection of a study area was a simple one; that 'inner areas' of cities have certain economic, social and physical characteristics that may collectively be termed 'multiple deprivation' (Project Report, March1973). The hypothesis does not imply that the characteristics in question are necessarily interdependent or causally related, but it does emphasize their tendency towards concentration in specific urban environments. This, of course, is not quite the same thing as saying that individual persons or households who live in such environments will suffer from a similar combination of problems (ie the sense in which 'multiple deprivation' is most commonly used). For example a high incidence of male unemployment and a high incidence of overcrowding does not mean that unemployed men therefore live in overcrowded conditions. There may be any number of different combinations.

13

Even so, there is an implicit assumption within the hypothesis that a 'multi-deprived' environment somehow has a depressing or unpleasant influence on the life experiences of all people who live there, exacerbating whatever problems might be associated with their individual circumstances.

Our subsequent experience in Small Heath has furnished ample evidence that residents' general state of well-being is certainly affected both by their immediate surroundings (living conditions in their own home) and by the quality of the physical and social environment they share with others. What is more, it is the social environment – activities and relationships – which appears to be every bit as important in people's minds as the character and condition of buildings, streetscape and open space. This holds true even of those people in extreme hardship whose over-riding concern is with making their income stretch to provide minimal standards of subsistence for themselves and their children. In other words there seems to be a very distinct locational focus of satisfaction or dissatisfaction which is to a considerable extent independent of personal circumstances. Even more important, people's satisfaction or dissatisfaction is strongly influenced by the changes they see to be taking place over time. Indeed in the case of Small Heath we found that a sense of the area's decline was perhaps the most strongly felt aspect of deprivation of all.

We shall return in Chapter 2 to a more detailed examination of these aspects of 'collective deprivation'. At this point we wish simply to point out their significance, especially when looked at over time. In trying to understand what living in Small Heath means it is essential to grasp that there is a deep-rooted ambivalence in people's attitudes to the area. While there is obviously still a fair degree of attachment few people, especially long-established residents, are pleased with the direction of change. It is interesting in this respect to compare evidence from Small Heath with similar information available for the Lambeth study area and for the country as a whole. Small Heath residents appear simultaneously to have a greater attachment to their area and (perhaps because of that) to regret more strongly what is happening to it than their counterparts in Lambeth.

Table 1 General attitudes to home district

	Small Heath %	Stockwell (Lambeth) %	General population %
Nothing to like	17	30	14
Nothing to dislike	38	35	41
Has improved in recent years	10	23	30
Neither better nor worse	16	22	27
Has gone downhill in recent years	61	43	36
Don't know/not applicable	13	12	7
Base (all adults)	1,744	2,023	5,315

Sources: Small Heath Birmingham: A Social Survey; SCPR 1974:
People, Housing and District; Lambeth IAS 1974:
Road Traffic and the Environment; SCPR 1972.

14

Census indicators give some hint of collective deprivation by picking out the concentration of certain problems of poor housing, low incomes (via indirect indices), unemployment, social need etc in small areas. But the picture they present is far from complete. They overlook entirely what is truly common: the attractiveness of the place, the adequacy of its facilities and services, the extent of social interaction and community life, the degree of harmony or conflict, the general state of morale and confidence. They tell us nothing of residents' priorities, interests and concerns. They offer very little understanding of the processes of change which are at work, the forces that shape individual and collective experience. Even with the benefit of intercensal comparisons (adjusted for boundary changes) the picture that emerges is still rather static. It gives us a record of the distribution and coincidence of some problems *in* the city. That is not the same thing as an account of the problems *of* the city.

The programme of research by means of structured questionnaires and depth interviews which we initiated during the main phase of the study went a long way towards filling the gap. It certainly brought us closer to appreciating residents' own perceptions of their circumstances. But to arrive at a more dynamic explanation of Small Heath's development – how it has become what it is today, how it may change in future – we had also to explore the way its major functions as industrial location, source of employment and provider of housing to various social groups have evolved over time, from its inception to the present day, within the context of the city as a whole.

Growth: The period to World War I

Small Heath developed comparatively late in the nineteenth century. Early expansion east of the city was blocked by the marshy valley of the Rea at Deritend. Even in 1860 Small Heath was little more than a scattered hamlet linked to Birmingham by three of four 'omnibus' journeys a day. The first major impetus to development came in 1861 when BSA set up their factory on land adjoining the Warwick Canal and the Birmingham–Oxford railway. Small Heath station opened close by two years later.

The second half of the nineteenth century marked an important turning-point in the history of Birmingham, with large factory sites spreading out along major rail and water transportations links (see Figure 4). Until that time industry had been concentrated mainly in small workshops, dependent on skilled craftsmanship. Now, the rapid growth of new technologies using large resources of cheap labour led to the hurried construction of lodging houses and back-to-back in every available space close to the factories and yards. Towards the centre of the city conditions very swiftly deteriorated. The environment became notoriously noisy, crowded and squalid.

Settlement in Small Heath clustered first around the junctions of the Coventry Road with Green Lane and Grange Road (Figure 5). About the mid-century a number of substantial suburban villas were built in this vicinity. Before very long, however, they were engulfed by new working class housing which mushroomed

Figure 4
Birmingham:
Historical
development of
industry

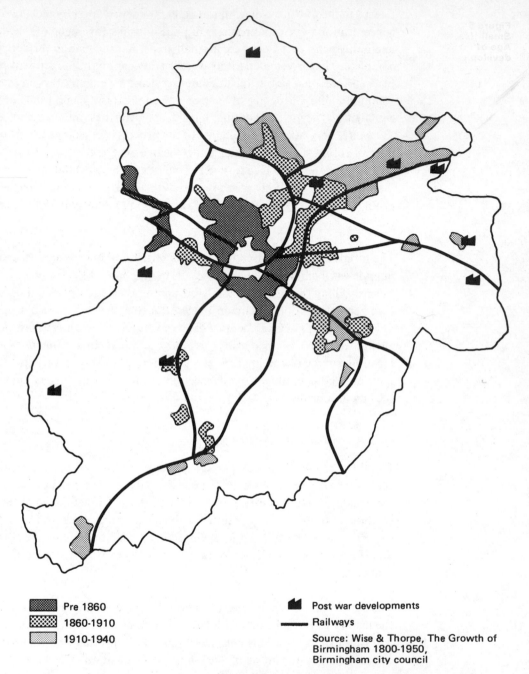

Pre 1860

1860-1910

1910-1940

Post war developments

Railways

Source: Wise & Thorpe, The Growth of
Birmingham 1800-1950,
Birmingham city council

during the 1860s and 1870s, overflowing from Bordesley and spilling up across the
railway from the long ribbon of factory and warehouse development which now
linked Digbeth/Deritend with the old, formerly waterpowered industrial centre of
Hay Mills. Part of this growth was due simply to industrial and population expansion.
Part too resulted from displacement of workers from the congested centre by
street improvements. Growth was further aided, however, by the enactment of a
bye-law in 1876 that put an end to the construction of the insanitary back-to-backs

16

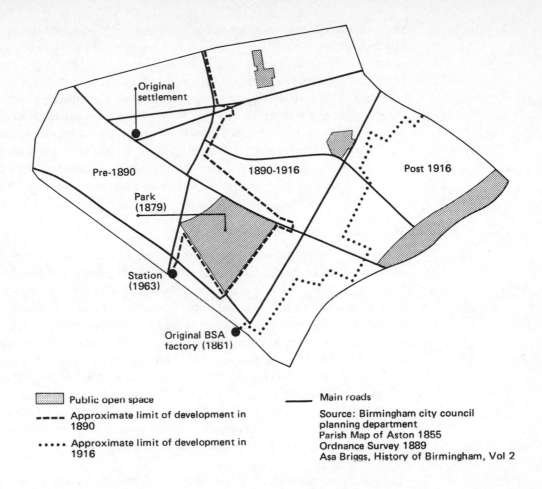

Figure 5
Small Heath:
Age of major
development

Original
settlement

Pre-1890

1890-1916

Post 1916

Park
(1879)

Station
(1963)

Original BSA
factory (1861)

Public open space

Main roads

- - - Approximate limit of development in
1890

..... Approximate limit of development in
1916

Source: Birmingham city council
planning department
Parish Map of Aston 1855
Ordnance Survey 1889
Asa Briggs, History of Birmingham, Vol 2

which were then such a feature of Birmingham's working class quarters and which
in 1914 still housed 200,000 people or over 1 in 5 of the city's population. The now
familiar rows of street-facing '2-up, 2-downs' and back terraces took shape
throughout most of the western part of the study area. By the late 1880s when the
tramways came into operation along the Coventry Road, Small Heath had increased
to the size of a town as big, to borrow a comparison from Asa Briggs, as the Oxford
or Worcester of its day.

The original suburban villas in the west of the area were abandoned and demolished.
As the city's prosperity continued to rise, however, the eastern part of Small Heath
became a favoured settlement for the more affluent skilled craftsman and for the
lower middle-classes. Victoria (now Small Heath) Park was opened by private
donation in 1879. Around it, first on the west side, sprang up what are today the
area's largest houses. These were first occupied by families wealthy enough to have
servants. They form a distinct enclave. Most of the new houses built between 1890
and the first world war were small to medium-sized terraces, with short front and
long back gardens, set out along fairly wide streets, frequently lined with trees. By
1916 practically the whole study area had been developed, with the exception of the
Heybarnes inter-war council estate.

Small Heath residents relied for employment originally on large local factories like BSA and on the proliferation of smaller factories and workshops interspersed among the dwellings. Then, as the area expanded and the bicycle and more efficient public transport came into their own, dependence on local industry diminished. That part of the district laid out after 1890 was almost exclusively residential. People began to travel farther to work. Small Heath residents might find employment anywhere in the central city or in the zones of diverse industrial and commercial activity thrusting out in long tongues to the northeast and southeast. Likewise, people who worked in Small Heath might live elsewhere, in neighbouring wards or in the fast growing outer suburbs such as Acocks Green and Yardley.

Maturity: The inter-war years

Between the two world wars there occurred a massive shift of Birmingham's population and industrial investment. In 1919 the city contained about 194,000 dwellings housing 910,000 people. By 1939 over 100,000 new dwellings had been built, almost half by the local authority (Figure 6). Most of this represented a clear increase in stock, since only 6,000 dwellings or so had been demolished under the new slum clearance programme which began in 1931. Yet the city population rose during this period by less than 150,000. In all, the net housing gain was something like 700 units per 10,000 people. Between 400,000 and 500,000 people had moved into the new homes. The population of the central wards (already long in decline) fell by well over a fifth and that of the 'middle ring' (which included Small Heath and Sparkbrook wards) by a quarter, mainly due to falling household densities, while the number of residents in outer suburbs nearly doubled.

The pattern of manufacturing development was broadly similar. Although the older industries continued to operate primarily in their established centres, the new generation of Birmingham industries which entered into their heyday after the first world war (notably motor vehicles and components, electrical engineering) tended to set up their factories on the periphery where large tracts of undeveloped land were available at comparatively low cost. The chief locations were along the Tame Valley to Perry Barr in the north and Bromford/Castle Bromwich in the northeast, along the Bristol railway in the extreme southwest and in Hay Mills/Tyseley/Acocks Green to the southeast.

The Heybarnes estate in Small Heath was laid out in conformity with a town planning scheme for East Birmingham approved as early as 1913. It and similar 'garden' estates of the period tended to cater for the better-paid worker who could afford the higher rents and, in many cases, higher travel costs to and from work. In 1938 over a third of workers living on municipal estates had jobs in the central districts, corresponding roughly to the present five 'inner core' wards. Poorer workers and households like elderly couples and single persons who were not provided for on the new family estates either moved into older terraced houses vacated by the more fortunate or remained in the slums; for, despite, the large amount of new house construction, only 24,000 people were rehoused under the pre-war slum clearance programmes, some of them near where they previously lived in municipal flats and maisonettes. The first flats built under the post-war

18

Figure 6
Birmingham:
Historical
development of
housing

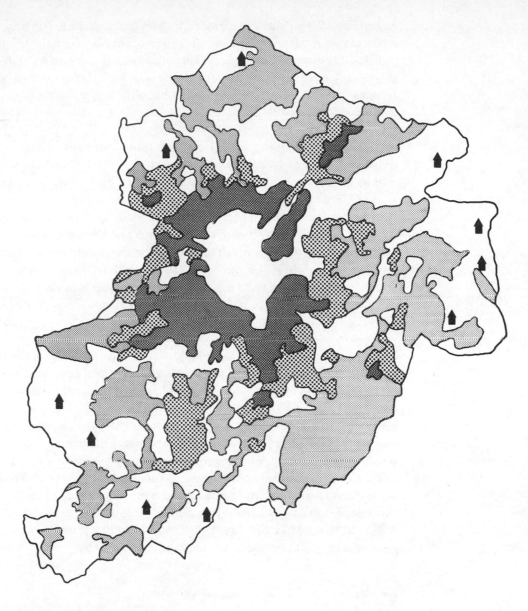

Figure 6 Birmingham: Historical development of housing

■ Pre-1890 (before redevelopment)
▧ 1890-1916
▨ 1917-1947
⬆ Major post-war housing developments
(excluding redevelopment)

N.B. Parts of the map left blank
represent areas of predominantly non-
residential uses

Source: Wise & Thorpe, The Growth of
Birmingham 1800-1950.
Birmingham city council.

Housing Acts were in fact erected in Garrison Lane, just outside Small Heath,
in 1925.

Even at this early stage Small Heath had begun to be affected by a 'filtering' process
as more prosperous households and their children relocated to new suburbs or to
rural areas within commuting distance, a movement aided by the increase in car
ownership. Already by 1938 the number of private cars registered in Birmingham

19

had risen to 50,000 – half as many as 20 years later and a quarter their 1973 level. As wealthier residents moved out, their places came in time to be taken increasingly by relatively lower income groups. Part of the process no doubt involved short local moves on the part of 'respectable' working class households from the smaller terraces in the west, now 50 years or so old, to the bigger, better houses in the centre and towards the east.

As a location for industry Small Heath was quite fortunately placed by lying close to the Cole Valley where a considerable acreage of land adjoining the old Hay Mills industrial centre remained undeveloped. BSA first built a factory on the west bank of the Cole during the first world war to step up its armaments efforts. At the end of the war this familiar multi-tiered factory switched to car production and was sold to Singer in the late 20s. It is now a spare parts distribution centre for Chrysler. The rest of the west bank site, which lies just within the eastern boundary of our study area, was developed in the inter-war years. Again BSA was prominent, acquiring its Waverley works which became the centre of its bicycle manufacture in 1925. The original factory across the railway line (later NVT) now concentrated on motor cycles.

Additional employment was also provided fairly near-at-hand on the eastern side of the Cole. But if these convenient sources of employment continued to grow so too, it must be remembered, did the residential areas in the southeastern suburbs of the city. The wards of Yardley, Fox Hollies and Hall Green all saw their biggest expansion between the wars. Another factor that affected employment opportunities was the major change in manufacturing methods, with increased mechanisation, standardisation and the introduction of the mass production line. Openings for many of the old skills declined; jobs began to polarise more between unskilled and semi-skilled factory work on the one hand, and a growing range of administrative and supervisory work on the other. Incommuters tended to occupy the latter posts; Small Heath residents were becoming increasingly likely, on the whole, to be employed in the former capacity.

Obsolescence and decline: The post-war years

At the end of the second world war the city faced up to the task of consciously planning its future. Despite the very substantial gain achieved between the wars, a huge housing problem persisted. In 1946 the Public Works Committee estimated 103,000 houses would need to be built over 10 years, largely to replace unfit dwellings and tackle overcrowding. Many factory premises too were inadequate, especially in the central area where less than 40 per cent of industrial acreage was considered to be 'good'.[1]

The broad strategy adopted was to contain the growth of the city, thus reversing the pre-war expansionist trends. Housing deficiencies were to be dealt with by

1. This finding, quoted in the city's 1952 development plan, is taken from a survey of 439 acres of industrial land within one mile of the cathedral. Nearly a quarter of this acreage was declared as 'bad', 35 per cent as moderate. By contrast, 72 per cent of 2,003 acres surveyed in the 'outer district' was declared to be 'good', less than 8 per cent 'bad'.

Gordon King

My husband had a job near, and we got the house, well the one next door, off the gaffer. We needed somewhere quick, we was getting married. We came from Balsall Heath. Small Heath seemed a posh area then compared to that; but now . . .

Circumstances of Families

comprehensive redevelopment and by overspill arrangements. Industrial land was to be provided to allow for 'natural expansion' and for relocation of businesses affected by redevelopment; but new industry was not to be encouraged within the city. When the overspill programme began in earnest in the mid 1950s, under pressure from an unexpectedly high rate of household formation and a decline in average household size, the city actually made strenuous efforts to persuade industry to move out, so as to reduce the risk of unemployment in overspill areas.

**Figure 7
Birmingham;
New
Commonwealth
population**

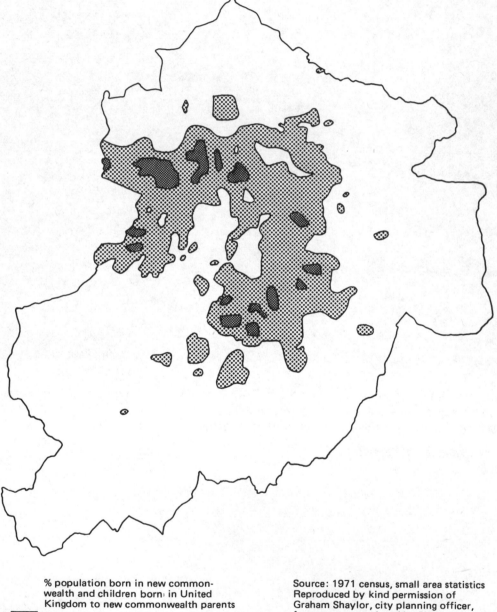

% population born in new commonwealth and children born in United
Kingdom to new commonwealth parents

☐ under 8%
▨ 8% to 40%
■ over 40%

Source: 1971 census, small area statistics
Reproduced by kind permission of
Graham Shaylor, city planning officer,
from symaps produced by National
Computing Centre

Since 1946 over 120,000 new dwelling units have been added to the city's stock, about two-thirds as a result of council building. This has been double the number of demolitions. Additionally, 15,000 dwellings have been built by the local authority outside the city boundary and over 10,000 through overspill arrangements. There has been a net migration out of the city of over 250,000 people, many to the surrounding 'commuter belt', and a further massive shift of population within the city away from the centre to the periphery. Allowing for boundary changes, the population in the central wards has fallen since the war by about two-thirds and that of the 'middle ring' by a fifth, while the number of residents in outer suburbs has grown by almost a fifth. During this same period the immigrant population in the older parts of the city has been steadily rising. The city's coloured population increased roughly 10-fold between the mid 50s and the early 70s, by which time 85 per cent were concentrated in the central wards and 'middle ring', where they constituted respectively 18 per cent and 20 per cent of all residents, as opposed to only 2 per cent in the outer suburbs.[1] The distribution of New Commonwealth immigrants is shown in Figure 7.

Most of the industrial investment in Birmingham since the second world war has taken place in the outer zones. Large firms already located there have undertaken major work on factory extensions and modernisations. Other firms have moved there, sometimes rationalising on one site production formerly carried out in several premises scattered about the city or conurbation. For instance, in 1947 Fisher & Ludlow moved the operations of 16 different works to a single new location at Erdington. The general pattern of movement has been for firms in the central districts to make short radial moves further out and for firms further out to relocate to other parts of the periphery or to overspill areas fairly close to the conurbation. In accordance with city policy, very few firms indeed have moved into the city.

New manufacturing investment in Birmingham was probably at its highest in the early post-war years. Although some of the new investment replaced labour with capital, the general rise in output was also reflected in employment growth until 1960. Since that time manufacturing employment has progressively fallen. While rising employment in services compensated for this fall until the mid-60s, over the past 10 years or so total employment has also been falling, faster than the economically active population. At the same time net commuting from outside the city has been steadily increasing[2].

Just after the war Small Heath housed about 50,000 people. Sixty per cent or so lived in the western (pre-1890) part, at densities $1\frac{1}{2}$ times higher than the eastern part. Very few households in the western part had separate amenities. A number (no less

1. In Ladywood and Newtown wards, where over two-thirds of residents lived in new redeveloped estates, the coloured population was significantly lower than in the rest of the central district (11 per cent compared with 22 per cent).
2. Between 1966 and 1971 total employment in Birmingham employment exchange areas fell by 13.4 per cent, the numbers of the economically active declined by 8.8 per cent and net commuting went up by 4.2 per cent. Since 1971, despite a short-lived upturn in the regional economy in 1973/74, total employment has continued to go down. Whereas, for example, numbers in work rose by 35,000 (+1.6 per cent) between mid 1971 and mid 1973 in the West Midlands, in Birmingham they fell by 29,000 (−4.8 per cent).

than 10 per cent) still lived in back-to-backs, even though this type of housing was far less prevalent in Small Heath than in the inner core wards where they generally accounted for nearer half the stock. During the 1950s dwellings classed as unfit started to be voided and demolished as part of the city's slum clearance programme; then in 1957 roughly half the western area was declared for comprehensive redevelopment. By 1961 the total population had dropped by over 8,000, over 80 per cent of the fall coming in the western part. Population then became more stable for a time until, in the late 60s, large-scale demolition began. A further clearance area (St. Aidans) was designated in 1973. Although part of the new redeveloped St. Andrews estate has now been completed, Small Heath today probably houses under 32,000 people. The proportions in the western and eastern parts have, in the space of 25 years, been almost exactly reversed.

One of the consequences of slum clearance and redevelopment has been that, in those areas affected, large numbers of cheap dwellings have been removed from the private market. In the western part of Small Heath, between 1961 and 1971, the number of private dwellings (most of them controlled-rent unfurnished lettings) fell by over 2,000 or more than a third. Many of the poorer households who lived in this housing were found alternative accommodation in the new peripheral council estates and some may have obtained relets on older estates, even though the available stock declined at the end of the period through sale for owner occupation. Others, however, made short moves into neighbouring areas, as houses there were vacated by workers who could afford to move out. It was especially into these 'buffer zones' between redevelopment areas and what had previously been the outer suburbs that also flocked new immigrants to the city, excluded (by compulsion or choice) both from council accommodation and the dwindling stock of older private housing in the central districts. Coloured residents currently make up roughly 30 per cent of the Small Heath population.

Data on socio-economic groups give a clear indication that the skill levels (and, by implication, income levels) of residents are declining. Between 1961 and 1971 the proportion of male skilled workers fell from 50 per cent to 41 per cent while that of the semi-skilled and unskilled rose from 35 per cent to 46 per cent. The SCPR survey broadly confirmed the pattern: 45 per cent of household heads resident less than 10 years were semi-skilled or unskilled, compared with 37 per cent of those resident over 10 years. This mainly has to do with the rising proportion of immigrants who generally are forced to take lower-skilled jobs. However, even white newcomers are marginally more likely to be lower-skilled.

In recent years there has been a very noticeable decline in the fortunes of large industry in the Small Heath area. In the 15 years or so after the late 50s about 40 per cent of Small Heath jobs seem to have disappeared. The largest single decline was due to the closure of BSA Waverley cycle works after sale to Raleigh and rationalisation of production in Nottingham: 1,600 jobs were lost. Although 300 new jobs were created on the site by BSA Sintered Components, this itself was a local move from across the railway in Montgomery Street, Sparkbrook. More recently the collapse of NVT has led to further large-scale redundancies (about 1,200) and transfer of the remaining components and spare parts production to Montgomery Street.

24

Heavy redundancy has also hit the Chrysler plant on the Coventry Road.[1] Since 1967, in the wider Small Heath employment exchange area, which includes the whole of the Hay Mills/Tyseley/Acocks Green development, perhaps a quarter of all jobs (nearly 30,000 in all) had been lost even before the NVT and Chrysler crises. This was much larger than the population change in the corresponding labour catchment area.

The fortunes of small firms have varied. Up to about the mid 60s there appears to have been a fair amount of movement into Small Heath, predominantly by businesses 'zoned out' of neighbouring CDAs. Since Small Heath itself became subject to large-scale clearance and rebuilding, however, the pattern has been reversed. The number of manufacturing units recorded in the redevelopment part of Small Heath fell from 60 in 1967/68 to 43 in 1973/74 and service units (mainly shops and merchants) from 401 to 232. In contrast, manufacturing units outside the redevelopment part increased from 62 to 68 and service units from 583 to 656. As well as closures and moves out and in, there was also a considerable amount of movement within the area. Sites and premises falling vacant were often quickly reoccupied by firms looking for new premises or others starting up. No matter how resilient the small firm, it should nevertheless be remembered they employ quite a small proportion of the total labour force.

In pure numbers the decline in local employment opportunities has been partially offset by an increase in office and other service jobs only a short bus-ride away in the city centre. However, except for some young people still living with their parents and women doing part-time cleaning work, any such trend scarcely stands to benefit Small Heath residents whose work experience has largely been gained in the yard or on the factory floor. In view of all this it is hardly surprising that since the early 60s unemployment in Small Heath has been steadily rising relative to that of Birmingham as a whole. In 1961 according to the census Small Heath's unemployment rate was 1.16 times that of the city as a whole. By 1966 the difference had increased to 1.35 times and by 1971 to 1.53 times. The concentration of male unemployment in the older parts of the city at the last-mentioned date is illustrated in Figure 8. Department of Employment data (see also Chapter 2) suggest that by mid 1976 male unemployment in Small Heath might well have stood at fully twice the city rate. It is likely, too, that workers forced to look for new jobs and newcomers to the area have to travel further across the city or out to the periphery in order to find employment.

Small Heath's role today

The history we have sketched in the preceding pages is no more than an outline; but it illustrates how our study area has come over time to play an increasingly residual role in the economic and social life of the city. As its locational advantages

1. The job losses fall with particular severity on the semi-skilled and unskilled who tend to be more local (and less mobile). In 1974 only about 22 per cent of works jobs in the Small Heath area were skilled; 58 per cent were semi-skilled and 20 per cent unskilled. Nearly 40 per cent of workers in these jobs worked at nights, permanently or in rotation. For a fuller review of the Small Heath employment situation, see Barbara Smith's Employment Opportunities in the Inner Area Study Part of Small Heath, Birmingham, in 1974, which is the source of most evidence cited in these pages.

**Figure 8
Birmingham:
Male
unemployment**

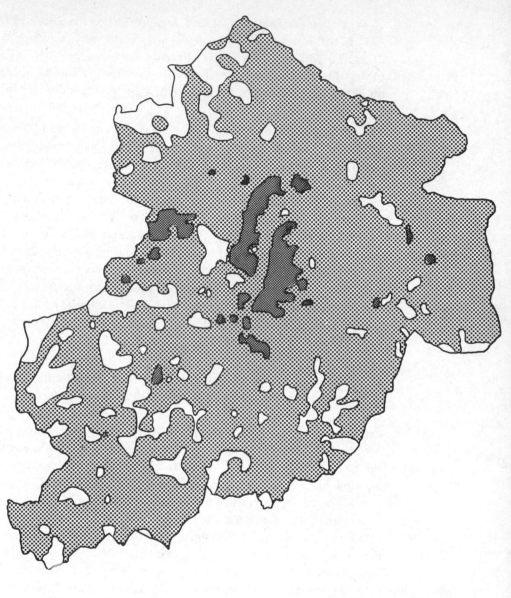

% of economically active males
seeking work

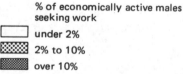
under 2%

2% to 10%

over 10%

Source: 1971 census, small area statistics
Reproduced by kind permission of
Graham Shaylor, city planning officer,
from symaps produced by National
Computing Centre

for housing and industry have decreased, so capital has progressively deserted it.
Because it is no longer attractive to capital, the industrial activities which remain
tend on the whole to be marginal or more-than-usually vulnerable to the forces of
market change and competition. Most people who live there now do so largely
because they have little real alternative choice. Residents tend therefore increasingly
to be those who, because of low personal attainment, discrimination or other
disadvantage, live on low incomes, perform those tasks demanding least skills, are
most vulnerable to economic recession and are least equipped to exercise control or

exert influence over the decisions which govern their lives. As we shall see later, to those whose choices are limited the area does still offer positive advantages of cheap accommodation, good access by public transport to city centre and industrial zones, and a fair range of local shopping opportunities. But many people are in severe personal hardship; and all are, to a greater or lesser extent, affected by the worsening state of the physical environment brought about by the fall in investment and, even more importantly, by the general atmosphere of neglect and decline.

Redevelopment (as well as being an open public acknowledgement of decline) marked a bold attempt to reverse the processes at work by the injection of massive public capital and increased social control. We shall in the course of this report have something to say about how far we think redevelopment has been successful. But it is with those areas which still await the 'solution' to their problems that we are most concerned.

Small Heath seems to us, on the basis of both the current and historical evidence, to exemplify the kinds of issues which are now becoming so well documented in urban research and so familiar in the practice of urban planning. There should, we maintain, be no great controversy over what constitutes an 'inner area'. Even though the particular combination of symptoms may vary, both qualitatively and in intensity, from one area to another, in part reflecting the stage on the cycle of decline they each have reached, there are, we believe, crucial and fundamental resemblances which clearly emerge through all their differences. We have attempted to summarise briefly the essential features of what these areas have in common, from the perspective of their evolution over time, in our general definition and broad typology.

In the next three chapters we shall examine in greater detail the range of problems with which urban policy-making is faced today, analyse more fully the causes of these problems and consider the prospects, under present circumstances, of effective action to alleviate them. Again we shall draw our examples from the specific context of Small Heath. Our contention is, however, that although different combinations of symptoms will call for strategy combinations flexible enough to respect the diversity of circumstances between and indeed within areas of the size and complexity of Small Heath, the basic condition of urban deprivation, its causes and the prospects of successful treatment form a sufficiently discrete focus of concern for our diagnosis, prognosis and prescriptions to be of more general relevance.

Gordon King

I'm ashamed of this area. It looks filthy and depressing. The houses themselves are not too bad but we have no bathroom or inside toilet, and no privacy. There are five of us children all in one bedroom. It's too small a house to improve and it's falling down. We don't want to go too far away from Small Heath, but I just want to move to a clean area. I just don't know what we'll do.

SCPR Exploratory Study

2 Examining the symptoms

We have already made a distinction between those aspects of deprivation or
disadvantage which relate to the shared environment and those more directly
attributable to the particular circumstances of individual persons and households.
The former we called 'collective deprivations'; the latter we shall term 'personal
deprivations'. The two are obviously related in a number of ways and the borderline
between them is somewhat arbitrary. For instance, households with sufficient
income to run a car will be less restricted in their leisure opportunities than their
poorer neighbours who must rely primarily on the choices the local environment
has to offer. Again, lack of housing opportunities of the right kind at 'reasonable'
cost may be regarded as a collective deprivation, and a concentration of poor
housing clearly affects the quality of the shared environment; but living in poor
housing (without amenities, overcrowded, in a bad state of repair) we shall consider
as a personal deprivation. The higher the incidence of personal deprivations, the
greater certain (but not necessarily all) collective deprivations are likely to be.
We shall explore some of the inter-relationships later. For the present it is convenient
to examine deprivations associated with personal circumstances and those to do with
the collective environment separately.

Deprivation and personal circumstances

Personal deprivations are chiefly a matter of low spending power – the inadequacy
of available financial resources (earned or unearned) for meeting the rudimentary
(though culturally conditioned) needs of the individual household. The cost of these
needs is affected by the size of household, by the ages of people within the household,
by special requirements arising from ill health, disability, dietary and other observances of different ethnic and religious cultures and by differential access to certain
goods (particularly housing).

Incomes, expenditure and poverty

Household incomes in Small Heath are low, the mean being only about two-thirds
that of the West Midlands. In early 1974 only 14 per cent of Small Heath households
had gross incomes over £60 per week; and in 94 per cent of cases this was due to
the household having more than one wage-earner. The median gross income for
households with only one wage-earner was under £35 per week. Yet Small Heath
households tend to be large, over 25 per cent containing more than 5 persons
in 1971 compared with 16 per cent in the West Midlands. According to the census
the average number of persons per household in Small Heath was 3.35, against
2.97 in Birmingham as a whole. The ratio of dependent children to working
adults was roughly $1\frac{1}{2}$ times that of the city. The SCPR survey suggests average
household size may have risen still further by 1974, to 3.42 persons (27 per cent of

households over 5 persons). Less money, therefore, has generally farther to go. It should also be borne in mind that Small Heath households are further disadvantaged by the fact that very few have any significant reserves of wealth they can draw on in adversity.

In early 1974 possibly one quarter of households in Small Heath were in poverty (in the sense that their income, net of housing expenditure, did not exceed 140 per cent of their theoretical supplementary benefit entitlement). In more than 4 out of every 10 cases identified the primary cause of poverty was retirement and dependence on a pension. Unemployment was the primary cause in 14 per cent of cases. Another 12 per cent were in poverty because the household was a single parent family. Although nearly one in 5 cases identified were households with 4 or more children – and indeed, about a third of households of this type were in poverty – the main cause of poverty was usually not size of family per se. In most instances there was only one parent, or the head of household was unemployed, or the household incurred high housing costs. High housing costs were defined as mortgage repayments of £10 or more per week and rents of £6 and over. Roughly 30 per cent of all households paying these sums were in poverty.

It is worth noting that, despite the generally low level of incomes in Small Heath, fathers in large families usually earned enough (if in work) to put their household above the poverty line. However, this was frequently as a result of doing substantial overtime and/or shiftwork, which through its effect on family life may also count as a form of deprivation. Ninety-two per cent of individuals earning over £30 per week worked more than a 40-hour week. Thirty-five per cent of these higher earners did shift work, as opposed to 16 per cent of all other workers. Irish and Asians were especially likely to work overtime, Asians and West Indians to work shifts.

The proportion of households below the 'poverty line' in Small Heath does not seem to have been especially high compared with the national average in early 1974. In fact, data quoted in Poverty Report 1976[1] while not perhaps strictly comparable, suggest that the incidence of families living below a more restrictive criterion of 120 per cent of supplementary benefit entitlements in Small Heath, at 17 per cent, may have been a percentage point or two lower than the national figure, some 7 per cent lower than in Stockwell (Lambeth IAS area) in late 1973, and as much as 14 per cent below a figure obtained from a smaller sample in Bethnal Green earlier in 1973. Early 1974 was, however, a time of fairly low unemployment when Small Heath's comparatively young population should have put the area at an advantage. Conversely, with very high unemployment, as at present, we must expect the number of families in poverty to be up substantially, both absolutely and relatively. In terms of individuals in poverty Small Heath would be disproportionately affected too in the current situation by its large average household size.

Further analysis of households in poverty showed that multiple deprivations fell most heavily on the unemployed, the chronically sick or disabled and single parent

---

1. *Sharing Inflation? Poverty Report 1976:* a report by the Institute of Community Studies (edited by Peter Willmott), Temple Smith 1976.

families. Grouping these types of household together, two-thirds of those identified as in poverty suffered a combination of two or more forms of deprivation: housing, health, social (see Table 2.) The retired poor were almost identically prone to experience ill health or social deprivation but much less likely to be deficient in housing space or standard amenities. Nearly half the retired, however, lived in houses affected by damp, in turn a hazard to their health. Of those who lived alone half were chronically sick.

Table 2 Poverty and multiple deprivation*

Households in poverty suffering from other forms of deprivation	Retired (No.=65)	Large families/ Low pay/ High housing costs/ (No.=45)	Unemployed/ Sick/ Single parent/ (No.=46)	All (No.=156)
	%	%	%	%
Housing	22	24	43	29
Health	52	20	52	43
Social	77	47	80	70
Housing and health	5	2	7	5
Housing and social	5	13	20	12
Health and social	23	7	28	20
All three	9	0	11	7
One only	43	47	32	40
None	15	31	2	16

Criteria of deprivation:

Housing (if 3 out of these 5 criteria are met):
1. Household living at more than 1 person per room
2. Household without exclusive use of 3 basic amenities
3. Household forced to move from previous accommodation
4. Household intends or would like to move from present accommodation
5. Accommodation needs treatment for damp

Health:
If anyone in household suffering from long-standing illness or disability

Social:
If household possesses neither a car nor telephone and belongs to no organisation other than a trade union or welfare association.

*Too much reliance should not be placed on small differences in the figures since the sample numbers are small and differences lie well within the range of a standard error in some cases. This applies to other evidence in this report based on sample survey data.

Source: SCPR Household Survey 1974; hand analysis.

Interestingly, in view of its smaller proportion of households in poverty, Small Heath had a higher incidence than Stockwell of multi-deprived households, taking multiple deprivation as being deprived on at least 3 out of 6 variables: income, housing space, housing amenities, possession of car/telephone, disability, job instability. Part of the reason for this is that in Stockwell, much of which has been rebuilt for council lettings, the link between income and housing deprivation has been partially broken. In Small Heath the link is still strong. The proportions in the two areas multi-deprived and deprived on each of the six variables are shown in Table 3.

Table 3 Total incidence of household deprivations

Households deprived in terms of	Small Heath (No. = 854) %	Stockwell (No. = 1,161) %
Income	15	17
Housing space	22	15
Housing amenities	26	18
Possession of car/telephone	55	42
Disability	21	29
Job instability	7	10
Multi-deprived (3 or more out of 6)	17	14

Note: Small Heath data are for early 1974, Stockwell data for late 1973. For the criteria of deprivation used, see original source.

Source: Lambeth IAS, Second Report on Multiple Deprivation, Department of the Environment, 1977.

Our Circumstances of Families survey, a series of depth interviews with a number of the poorer households in Small Heath recorded in late 1975, gives some idea of what it means to live on very low incomes and of how, in such a situation, worry over money can come to dominate people's lives. Most households drawing social security benefits found it extremely difficult to make ends meet. While the position of families with earned income, especially if there were several dependent children, was often little better financially and sometimes perhaps no better at all, unemployment brought additional stresses, including loss of self-esteem and tensions with family and neighbours as well as economic hardship and insecurity. We found no evidence of people actually preferring to live on benefits, even when they had by force of necessity or habit become resigned to it.

Money problems centred largely around such basics as heating, food and clothing. Heating bills were sometimes inflated because houses were damp or leaky and fires had to be lit (even in summer) to dry out bedding or prevent possessions going mouldy. Food, which invariably had to be very carefully budgeted for and, even more so, clothing were a particular cause of concern to mothers. Mothers often ate very little themselves, for the sake of feeding their children. Households had to adjust to a cheap, monotonous and nutritionally poor diet, consisting heavily of cereals, bread and potatoes. Most people ate meat at least once a week, because they had been brought up to feel it important to do so, though there was a noticeable lack of fresh fruit and vegetables. Likewise, mothers (though not Asians) would frequently wear second-hand clothes or give up entirely the fight to keep up their own appearances in order to save enough or meet the credit payments to keep their children adequately dressed. Shoes caused the biggest headache because they wore out quickly and could not be passed down by older children; parents could sometimes only afford to buy 'pumps'. In general people felt their poverty most acutely through their children, especially young teenagers who demanded fashion clothes as much as teenagers anywhere. In September, when we interviewed them, some parents were already worrying, with a sense of dread, about how they could afford presents for their children at Christmas.

Few lower-income households had use of a car or telephone. Out of those whose gross income fell short of £30 per week in early 1974 – 35 per cent of all Small Heath households – only 1 in 10 had use of a car or van and 1 in 5 use of a phone. Absence of a phone was not usually considered a hardship, even by the elderly who seemed to think it more important their children should have one. Old people had a similar attitude to a car. It was not a practical proposition; in any case, they had free bus passes which were almost universally recognised as a great boon. Only a few families with several children felt the lack of a car as a serious inconvenience.

The large majority of people we interviewed were extremely modest in their expectations, feeling a little extra would make a big difference. To be rich was to be able to pay your bills. People with large families tended to name small amounts like £4 or £5 per week as being all they needed to be really comfortable. Pensioners were reluctant to speculate, or mentioned tiny sums.

Although there were occasionally signs of poor budgeting, most women interviewed, including pensioners, seemed very price-conscious, 'shopped around', and did not pay over the odds unless they could not reach a supermarket or had too little money at any given time to buy in bulk. Pensioners generally preferred to go without rather than fall into debt. But young mothers with large families, whether or not supported, often lived in perpetual debt, arrears and consequent anxiety. People's budgeting was weakest, in fact, with regard to credit – the tally-man, the catalogue, the loan finance shop. Loans were easy to get, but very often people simply did not understand how expensive they were in terms of annual rates of interest. Paying the equivalent of 300 per cent annual interest on short-term loans was quite usual. Such arrangements were resorted to out of necessity. The clothing clubs played a large role in the life of people on benefits. The one main 'extravagance' people permitted themselves was normally a colour TV, though living in the squalor, hardship and stress that many did this had become more of an 'essential', as a distraction, the 'one bit of pleasure in life'.

People and their housing

Very few of the low-income households we interviewed rated housing as their major problem. This may appear surprising, for two reasons: first because housing has been given such a high priority in recent government initiatives to combat deprivation, second because housing conditions in Small Heath are in very many cases below what are taken by government to be reasonable standards and in some cases nothing short of appalling. People who did express great concern tended to be council tenants living in acquired properties, often scheduled for demolition, which were sometimes in a dreadful state of disrepair.

These findings echo the results of the SCPR survey. Half of all residents declared themselves to be 'very satisfied' with their accommodation; another third were 'fairly satisfied'. Nearly three-quarters of heads of households resident less than 10 years found their present house or flat better than their previous accommodation and only 15 per cent found it worse.[1] Against this, very nearly half of those in council-acquired property considered their present accommodation worse. Over half of heads of household and housewives in this type of property were dissatisfied with its state of repair (compared with 30 per cent of private tenants). Again, about half had been in dispute with the housing department, usually over repairs, in the past two years, whereas only a fifth of private tenants had had disputes with their landlords. This may of course reflect high standards expected of the council and the fact that private tenants might feel more intimidated. Even so, opinions about the condition of accommodation and empirical observation give weight to the proposition that council-acquired housing, in which over 10 per cent of households lived in early 1974, is generally the worst in the area. It should be pointed out too that households in council-acquired property were also quite likely to be overcrowded and lack amenities. For instance, 40 per cent or so lacked a bath or shower, almost as many did not have a hot water supply, and over a fifth lived at a nominal density of over 1 person per room. The reality of overcrowding was in all probability appreciably worse, since not all rooms in this type of accommodation were habitable on account of their condition, 60 per cent of houses being affected by damp.

Yet, even when we exclude households in council-acquired accommodation, there remains a fairly high incidence of what are normally taken to be housing deprivations. At the time of the 1971 census Small Heath rated considerably worse off than Birmingham as a whole and rather worse off than the average of 11 inner wards (the city's 'middle ring' minus Edgbaston and Selly Oak) on indicators of overcrowding, sharing and lack of amenities (Table 4), although, as Figures 9 to 11 show, their distribution is only partially correlated. All sharing and nearly three-quarters of overcrowding and (as an example of amenity) lack of a bath or shower were found in the private sector.[2] Similarly, of the third or so of all dwellings considered to be in need of damp-proofing and repointing, respectively two-thirds and 70 per cent were in the private sector. It is significant that people were generally

Table 4 Indicators of housing deprivation

Households	Birmingham %	Inner ring %	Small Heath %
Living at > 1.5 persons per room	3	6	7
Living at > 1.0 person per room	10	15	18
Sharing a dwelling	4	8	8
Without exclusive use of all 3 basic amenities (hot water, bath, inside wc)	22	40	49

Source: 1971 Census.

1. Less than 40 per cent, however, found the district better, even though a very high proportion were making only local moves or moves from very similar areas, often affected by clearance.

2. The cross-tabulations are in fact from the SCPR survey which showed some improvement over the 1971 figures, due primarily to clearance and redevelopment (14 per cent living at over 1 person per room, 41 per cent without exclusive use of amenities).

**Figure 9
Birmingham:
Overcrowding**

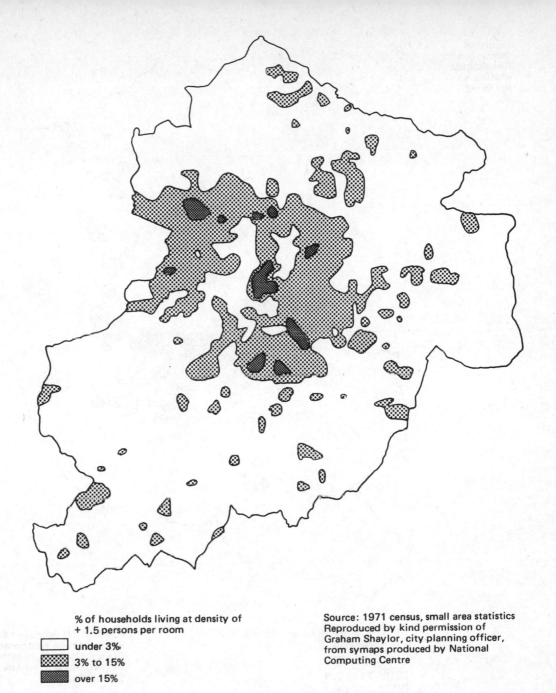

% of households living at density of
+ 1.5 persons per room

☐ under 3%

▨ 3% to 15%

■ over 15%

Source: 1971 census, small area statistics
Reproduced by kind permission of
Graham Shaylor, city planning officer,
from symaps produced by National
Computing Centre

more concerned over the condition of their housing than over possession of
amenities. In some cases they did not want 'improvements' because conversion
would mean loss of space or because they made a conscious trade-off between
amenity and expenditure, other things having a higher spending priority.

But if people are generally more satisfied with their accommodation than might be
expected, it is also apparent that in many cases they are making the best of a fairly

**Figure 10
Birmingham:
Households
sharing a
dwelling**

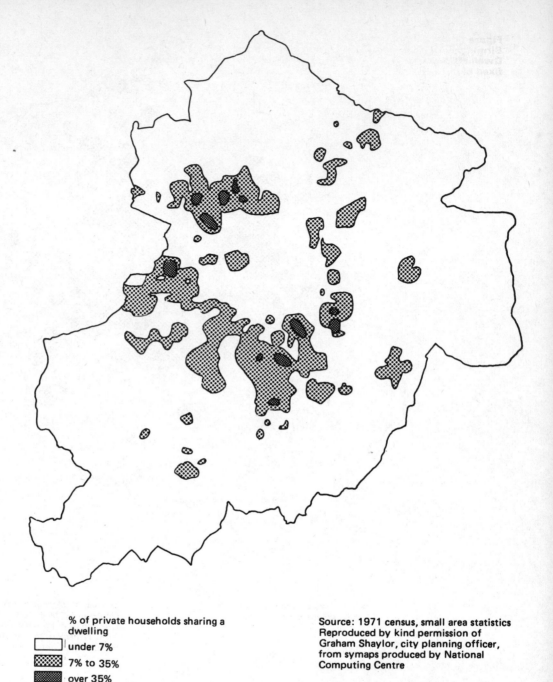

% of private households sharing a
dwelling

☐ under 7%

▨ 7% to 35%

▩ over 35%

Source: 1971 census, small area statistics
Reproduced by kind permission of
Graham Shaylor, city planning officer,
from symaps produced by National
Computing Centre

bad job. Only 27 per cent of households moving to their present address in the 10
years up to 1974 were positively attracted by their new house or flat. Most either
had to move or wanted badly to get away from their previous accommodation.
Two types of cases were particularly common: council tenants forced to move
because of redevelopment (54 per cent gave demolition of their previous home as a
reason); and immigrants seeking to escape from crowded and otherwise unsatisfactory
lodgings (54 per cent gave the desire for better living conditions as a reason).

36

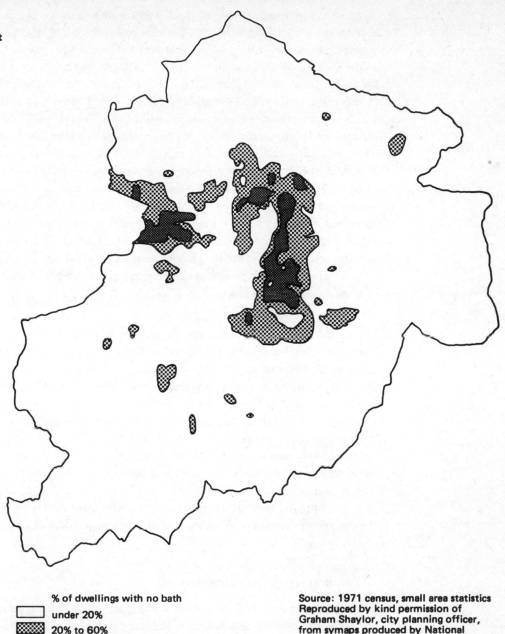

**Figure 11
Birmingham:
Dwellings without
fixed bath**

% of dwellings with no bath

under 20%

20% to 60%

over 60%

Source: 1971 census, small area statistics
Reproduced by kind permission of
Graham Shaylor, city planning officer,
from symaps produced by National
Computing Centre

Immigrants were the group most positively motivated to move. The average density
of all immigrant movers in their previous accommodation seems likely to have been
marginally above the 1.5 ppr indicator of severe overcrowding. Often the new
accommodation offered simultaneously the chance of home ownership to a resident
landlord and more space for his tenant. However it is unfortunately impossible
to draw from the evidence a clear distinction between a 'lodging' situation and an
'extended family' one.

As further confirmation of general satisfaction with housing, even if that satisfaction reflects low expectations, about 80 per cent of household heads had no definite intention to move – a figure only 5 per cent below the national average, according to the General Household Survey (1973). Of these 80 per cent, less than 1 in 3 said they would move even if they had the chance. In the case of immigrants, intention to move was lower still, fewer than 10 per cent being firmly committed and less than 1 in 5 of the remainder who would have liked to move, given the chance. Potential movers tended, naturally enough, to be tenants rather than owner-occupiers. The (rather obvious) point should be also made that people in the redevelopment zone and in short-life property were much more likely – over twice as likely in fact – to be seriously thinking of moving than people elsewhere. Excepting those whose impending move was due to circumstances outside their control, like a CPO, there was a clear tendency for lower-skilled workers to be less likely to move than those in skilled or non-manual occupations. So, although desire to move may overall be somewhat above the national norm, housing in Small Heath is for one reason or another – ownership status, space, cheapness, nearness to friends or relations – seen by many as a real asset.

We seem to have a situation where the number of potential out-movers may be declining, both because further opportunities are blocked to those (eg, long-established, white owner occupiers) who might otherwise like to move and because the area (or, more accurately, the central and eastern parts of it) has become for certain groups of disadvantaged citizens one of the major remaining outlets for the type of accommodation they are compelled to seek. It is perhaps somewhat beside the point to speculate on the degree to which Small Heath's relative position in the city's housing market may have fallen in the process of affording a 'step-up' to those who might formerly have occupied worse housing in areas now being cleared. The challenge (which we shall return to in Chapter 5) is how physical conditions may be improved without undermining the preferences of residents themselves and the discretion in terms of spending and life style which depends on these preferences.

Employment security and unemployment

Low spending power and the household budgeting problems it entails have quite a lot to do with employment histories. Relevant here are not only the rising level of unemployment and the generally low incomes currently earned by Small Heath residents but also the regularity of past employment and the effect that interruption of earnings may have on opportunities to save. For example, nearly 3 in every 10 employed men in Small Heath lost pay during the 3-day week in early 1974 (West Indians appearing to be particularly vulnerable). Only a third of these claimed benefit; three-quarters lost over £5 income in the week prior to interview. Fifteen per cent of all men and women seeking employment had experienced at least one period of unemployment during the previous year. Young persons aged 16–24 and West Indians had the highest rates, 20 per cent in each case. West Indians also figured prominently among those 18 per cent or so who gave redundancy or dismissal as the reason for leaving their last job, and tended to be unemployed longer than did people from other ethnic groups.

38

At the time of the last census 9 per cent of economically active males in Small Heath were unemployed, in early 1974 8 per cent. Given the socio-economic structure of the working population, these rates were not particularly high. Indeed, in 1971 the unemployment rate in Small Heath ward for semi-skilled workers was just 80 per cent of the national average and for classified unskilled workers only 70 per cent, in contrast to the general tendency for inner wards in provincial cities to have proportionately higher skill-specific rates than nationally. It is the fall in socio-economic status of the Small Heath population, especially males (see Table 5), which largely accounts for its rising unemployment rate in relation to the city as a whole. The reason why its skill-specific rates have been relatively low by national standards is largely explained by, first, the comparative prosperity – until recently – of the West Midlands and Birmingham and, second, Small Heath's high proportion of Asian working males, among whom unemployment in lower-skilled work in both 1971 and 1974 was generally lower than among the rest of the population.[1]

Table 5 Socio-economic status of economically active males

	Professional and managerial (SEGs 1–4, 13)	Junior and intermediate non-manual (SEGs 5 & 6)	Skilled manual (SEGs 8, 9, 12, 14)	Semi-skilled and unskilled manual (SEGs 7, 10, 11, 15–17)
	%	%	%	%
Small Heath				
1951 (est)	7	— 60 —		33
1961	5	10	50	35
1966	4	10	45	41
1971	4	9	41	46
Birmingham				
1951	14	— 59 —		27
1961	10	14	47	29
1966	10	15	45	30
1971	11	14	43	32

Note: For 1951 the threefold classification was: Social Classes I & II; Social Class III; Social Classes IV & V. Data for this year are therefore not strictly comparable, but they do illustrate the broad direction of change.

Source: Census.

Since 1974 the situation has changed dramatically. From nearly 3,300 in June 1974 the numbers of wholly unemployed adult males registered in the Small Heath employment exchange area had risen by June 1976 to almost 7,700 – an increase of 134 per cent. Extracting records on a 1-in-4 sample basis for Birmingham 10, which corresponds quite closely to our study area (Figure 12), we found that almost 1 in 6 males aged 18 to 64 were registered as unemployed at the end of July 1976. Adjusting for those who do not register, total adult male unemployment must have been close on 20 per cent. We calculate that this was roughly twice the average for the whole of the Birmingham labour market zone, including the neighbouring exchanges of Sutton Coldfield (now part of the metropolitan district),

1. This is deduced from census data and from evidence presented by David J Smith, *The Facts of Racial Disadvantage*, PEP, February 1976.

Figure 12
Small Heath:
Postal districts

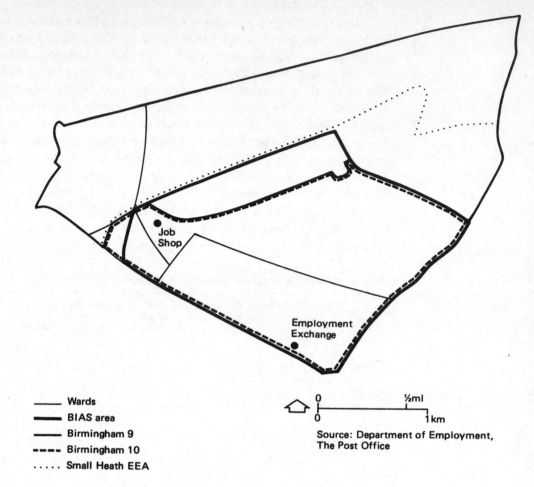

Wards
BIAS area
Birmingham 9
Birmingham 10
Small Heath EEA

Source: Department of Employment,
The Post Office

Chelmsley Wood and Solihull. Unlike at earlier periods the level of registered
unemployment in Birmingham in mid 1976 was above the national average, by some
1½ per cent.

One feature of recent unemployment has been its increased duration, especially for
younger age-groups who in times of comparatively low overall unemployment
tend to find new jobs quickly. Hence, in the Small Heath exchange area only 26 per
cent of 18 and 19 year old males registered as unemployed in July 1974 had been
out of work more than 3 months; by July 1976 the proportion had risen to 57 per
cent. Their actual numbers had gone up by 670 per cent and their ratio to all adult
males unemployed over 3 months from 2½ per cent to 7 per cent. At July 1976
more than 56 per cent of all men registered as unemployed had been without a job
for over 6 months, compared with less than 42 per cent 2 years earlier.

Another feature has been the way unemployment has disproportionately affected
immigrants. The general pattern appears to be that, as total unemployment increases,
so too does the proportion of immigrants among the workless (Table 6). More than
28 per cent of men registered as unemployed at the Small Heath exchange in May
1976 were immigrants. That is well over twice what one would expect pro rata to

the representation of immigrants in the labour force in the south-east quadrant of the city. Likewise, 47 per cent of immigrants among men out of work from Birmingham 9 and 10 is more than one and a half times their relative strength in the local male working population. At 41 per cent of the total, Asians were even more over-represented. These figures suggest that, allowing for non-registration, about 1 in 4 immigrant men may have been without jobs in the Small Heath area, fractionally more in the case of Asians. They suggest too that Asians' skill-specific unemployment rates were considerably above those of white workers at this point in time and somewhat higher than West Indians.

Table 6 Male immigrant unemployment

	Birmingham EEAs		Small Heath EEA	
	Total adult male unemployed (excluding temporarily stopped)	Immigrants as % of total	Total adult male unemployed (excluding temporarily stopped)	Immigrants as % of total
1972	21,622	12.5	5,550	23.8
1973	14,113	10.7	3,405	20.1
1974	13,388	9.3	3,280	17.8
1975	23,496	11.7	5,173	23.0
1976	33,380	15.1	7,677	28.3

Note: The figures of total male unemployment are for June, those of immigrants for May. Birmingham employment exchange areas include Sutton Coldfield, Chelmsley Wood and Solihull.

Source: Department of Employment.

Female unemployment in Small Heath, 6 per cent at the time of the last census and 4 per cent in early 1974, has also almost certainly worsened relative to the city as a while. Recession will have hit hardest at immigrant women whose rates of unemployment tended to be significantly higher than those of white women (as well as of minority ethnic group men) even when labour demand was comparatively high in 1974. Particularly affected would be younger age groups, in their teens and early twenties. These are the sections of the Small Heath Asian female community, predominantly Muslim and with very low overall activity rates (only 10 per cent in 1974), most likely to be seeking work. Youth unemployment has recently risen to unprecedented levels, for both sexes. In July 1976 three-quarters of Birmingham school-leavers were reputed to be on the careers service register; four registrants were chasing every vacancy. In July 1973 unfilled vacancies on the lists of careers offices outnumbered registrants 12 to 1. The problem is not strictly a Small Heath or inner area one; but Small Heath is disproportionately affected, not only by a higher rate of refusals but also due to the additional economic burden placed on low-income households.[1]

Educational attainment

Job prospects are obviously linked (though not, as we shall see in Chapter 3, as closely as one might imagine) with educational attainment. Only 1 in 10 of Small

1. See in this connection the Young Volunteer Force Foundation report on *Youth Unemployment in Birmingham* 1975/76 which draws on case histories in Handsworth and Small Heath.

But people with young children. I mean what's going to happen to them? They just don't get enough from social security, it's not enough to live on. It's just enough to exist on, and that's about it.

Circumstances of Families

Heath residents over 16 years old in early 1974 had remained at school longer than the current minimum school-leaving age and only 17 per cent possessed any sort of qualification. Both length of schooling and achievement correlated strongly with age. Practically no-one over the age of 45 had passed any school exam; 8 per cent of men between 45 and 64 and 5 per cent of those 65 and over had, however, obtained a full industrial apprenticeship. By contrast, less than 5 per cent of men between 25 and 44 and only 1 per cent of men under 25 had an apprenticeship; but 11 per cent and 35 per cent of all adults in these age-groups possessed other credentials. A not insignificant proportion (5 per cent of 25 to 44-year olds and 8 per cent of under-25s) had obtained some 'higher' qualification: at least the equivalent of 'A' levels or a nursing, teaching or other professional diploma.

The educational attainment of the Small Heath workforce is lower than one would predict simply on the basis of its social class composition. As Table 7 demonstrates, the disparity is especially wide in the higher skilled groups. The pattern is broadly confirmed by the 1971 census which showed, for example, that in Birmingham as a whole 14 per cent of intermediate and junior non-manual workers possessed ONC or 'A' levels, while in Small Heath and Sparkbrook wards the proportions were respectively 11 per cent and 7 per cent. The explanation for this is probably not so much that (a comparatively small number of) Small Heath residents compete successfully for higher skilled jobs despite poorer than average qualifications but that they tend to occupy relatively less important and lower paid posts within each skill band. It should be noted that no significant change in the general pattern emerges if the data are disaggregated by sex or ethnic group.

Table 7 Workers without educational qualifications

SEG	Small Heath (No. =1,162) %		GB (No. =13,961) %	
Professional and managerial	47	(4)	34	(13)
Intermediate and junior non-manual	60	(18)	43	(31)
Skilled manual	76	(34)	65	(28)
Semi-skilled manual	87	(33)	85	(21)
Unskilled manual	96	(10)	93	(7)
All economically active	78	(100)	60	(100)

Note: Figures in parentheses refer to the proportion of the workforce (male and female) in each SEG.
Source: SCPR 1974; General Household Survey 1972.

Small Heath residents with the highest qualifications tend to be grown-up children still living with their parents or newly-formed young families perhaps getting their first home together. Both groups are likely soon to leave the area. We know, for example, that only about 1 in 10 of children who have left their parents' home to form their own households have actually remained in Small Heath; the socio-economic status of the out-movers is, on average, significantly higher than either the stayers' or newcomers' (see also Chapter 3).

Conclusion

The personal deprivations we have been considering are by no means confined to inner areas. If, for the sake of argument, we took the worst 15 per cent out of urban EDs according to the 1971 census on each indicator as representing inner areas, then these would still account for only 45 per cent of economically active and retired males in SEG 11 or 21 per cent of households without a car (as proxies for low income); only 36 per cent of male unemployment; and only 61 per cent of severe overcrowding or 64 per cent of households in dwellings without a fixed bath (as proxies for housing deprivations). Furthermore, the degree of overlap between the worst 15 per cent on each variable would be very far from complete. In the case of male unemployment and severe overcrowding, for example, the overlap in 1971 was 44 per cent; that is, less than 7 per cent of urban EDs came in the worst 15 per cent on both indicators. Adding a third variable (lack of exclusive use of all three basic amenities), the overlap dropped to little more than 18 per cent. Hence the incidence of other personal deprivations covered by the worst 15 per cent of urban EDs on any one criterion is really quite low.[1]

In our view, however, personal deprivations may be properly regarded as part of the 'inner area syndrome' if within inner areas the following criteria are met: the degree of concentration of any one individual deprivation is high; there is a significant association between various (but not necessarily all) types of deprivation; the concentration and association are not accidental but can be shown to result, at least in part, from the interplay of distinct societal forces; these forces and their effects on the collective environment create an additional dimension of disadvantage which intensifies the overall experience of deprivation.

Taken as a whole Small Heath is not one of the most severely deprived areas in the country. Yet, as Table 8 shows, it contains a well-above-average proportion of households and individuals suffering from various forms of personal deprivation or disadvantage – poor housing conditions, low social status, employment insecurity, presence of special needs groups. In certain cases, lack of housing amenities and numbers of New Commonwealth born for example, the mean value is particularly high in relation to national norms. Parts of the area, of course, would exhibit even higher concentrations and associations. To give just a swift indication: 44 per cent of Small Heath EDs (33 out of 75) came within the worst 15 per cent of urban EDs in Great Britain on at least 8 out of 16 common indicators of deprivation, according to the 1971 census; 32 per cent fell within the worst 5 per cent on at least 4 indicators; and almost 10 per cent came within the worst 1 per cent on at least 3 indicators.

The first two criteria stipulated above are therefore met. To consider the validity of the other criteria we shall examine in greater depth the state of the collective environment in Small Heath, the way people view the circumstances in which they live and the relationships between present circumstances and past change.

---

1. The examples given are taken from Sally Holtermann, 'Areas of Urban Deprivation in Great Britain: An Analysis of 1971 Census Data', in *Social Trends*, *Vol. 6* (CSO) HMSO 1975.

Table 8 Performance on selected indicators of deprivation

Indicator	National mean (all areas)	National mean (urban areas)	National mean plus 1 standard deviation (urban areas)	Small Heath mean
	%	%	%	%
Households without exclusive use of all 3 basic amenities	17.2	20.2	43.8	48.7
Households living at a density of > 1.5 persons per room	1.9	2.3	6.8	6.7
Households sharing a dwelling	3.4	4.7	16.5	8.3
Males seeking work or sick	5.4	5.8	10.7	9.5
Males unskilled (SEG 11)	7.4	8.3	18.3	14.9
Households with no car	48.7	53.9	74.0	74.0
Population aged 0–14	24.3	23.0	30.4	30.5
Population born in New Commonwealth	1.8	3.6*	11.0*	18.1

*Includes also children born in this country to immigrant parents.
Sources: 1971 Census; Sally Holtermann (*op. cit.*).

Deprivation and the collective environment

Collective deprivations may be understood as a gap or shortfall between the quality and quantity of the opportunities an environment provides – for home life, work, education, recreation, shopping, movement, social interaction – in relation to the needs of the people who share that environment. Collective need is a relative concept, even more difficult to describe in objective terms than the basic needs of the individual household; it depends as much on the expectations and aspirations of the various groups who make up the local community as on norms and values prevalent in society as a whole and on the standards adopted by makers of public policy. In assessing the nature of opportunity in Small Heath we shall therefore not only make use of data indicative of actual levels of provision but also give considerable weight to residents' own perceptions of their adequacy, in the belief that our understanding of collective deprivations must take into account the comparisons people make (only in part consciously) between the environment they experience and the kind of environment they have come to regard as reasonable to demand.

We have already made the point in Chapter 1 that, however attached residents may appear to be to Small Heath today, with 8 in 10 able to name 'likes' about the area and only 6 in 10 prepared to cite particular dislikes, there is a general feeling that it is fast deteriorating. Less than 3 in 10 interviewed in early 1974 could think of any improvements, despite the fact that construction of a new council estate was in progress, whereas 9 out of 10 could find at least one example of how it had gone downhill. Among longer established residents comparisons were even more unfavourable, over 80 per cent of those living in the area more than 20 years seeing it as having got worse in recent years, compared with 50 per cent in the rest of the population.

**Figure 13
Attitudes to
Small Heath as a
place to live**

1 Improved or gone downhill

2 Attractive in appearance

3 Interesting and full of variety

4 Dirty

5 Noisy

6 Depressing

7 Dangerous to go out at night

8 Good for children to grow up in

9 Good community spirit

10 Hate to leave

11 Recommended to live in

12 Good public transport

13 Central for work

14 Good for cheap accommodation

15 No point looking after homes

16 Satisfied with present house/flat

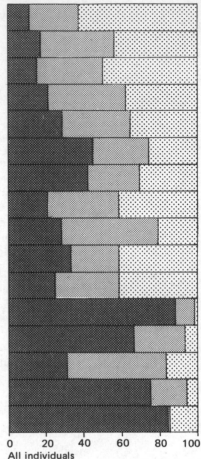

0   20   40   60   80   100
All individuals
(No. 1744)

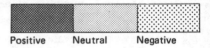

Positive   Neutral   Negative

Notes:
Line 1   'Improved a lot' and 'improved a little' are counted together as a positive response, 'gone downhill a little' and 'gone downhill a lot' as a negative response. 'Neither better nor worse' and 'don't know' are counted as neutral.

Lines 2-15   'Very true' or 'not at all true' are counted as positive, depending on whether the attribute in question is positive or negative. The antithesis is counted as negative. 'Partly true' and 'don't know' are classed together as neutral.

Line 16   'Very satisfied' and 'fairly satisfied' are counted together as positive, 'fairly dissatisfied' and 'very dissatisfied' as negative. 'Don't know' is counted as neutral.

Source: SCPR individual questionnaire Qs 4a, 5, 8a

Figures 13 and 14 give general profiles of resident attitudes to various aspects of life in Small Heath and to services and facilities provided. They help to explain the ambivalence we have noted and we shall go into them more deeply later in the chapter. First, however, we would make one further point by way of introduction. People's perceptions are formed not only by their personal experience of the environment in which they live; they are conditioned too by the 'public image' – the stereotype or

46

Figure 14
Attitudes to
services and
facilities in
Small Heath

1   Street cleaning

2   Rubbish collection

3   Car parking facilities

4   Community facilities (e.g. halls)

5   Shopping facilities

6   Doctors

7   Public transport

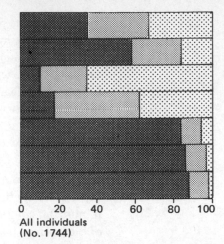

All individuals
(No. 1744)

8   Child welfare services

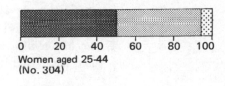

Women aged 25-44
(No. 304)

9   Nursery facilities

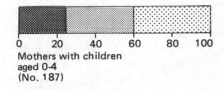

Mothers with children
aged 0-4
(No. 187)

10 Safe places for children to play

11 Good schools

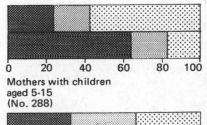

Mothers with children
aged 5-15
(No. 288)

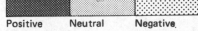

Positive   Neutral   Negative

Notes:

Line 7   Taken from figure 13, line 12

All other lines 'Very well off' and 'quite well off' are counted together as positive response, 'quite poorly off' and 'very poorly off' as a negative response. 'Average', 'don't know' and 'no answer' are classed together as neutral.

Source: SCPR individual questionnaire, Qs 7, 4a.

simplified set of associations which has become attached to the name(s) of the place and which is diffused through various communications media to the public at large, whether or not they have any direct experience of the area in question, its people and their circumstances. Because the public image has a very real influence on the attitudes and behaviour of residents, users and other agencies alike (and indeed had a major part to play in the choice of Small Heath as a study area), we start here.

According to its public image Small Heath is a 'problem suburb' or 'twilight area' made infamous by the reputation of Bolton Road 'the worst street in Brum', where people live in slums in conditions of 'mediaeval squalor' and are plagued by vandals and 'night-time terrors'.[1] The reality, of course, is very different. Although conditions for some people in some parts of the area are every bit as bad as the image makes out, the picture received is certainly not true of most of the area. Yet for anybody who does not know the area well it is the popular stereotype which sticks, based as it is on 'newsworthy' human interest stories. In turn, the portrayal of Small Heath as a deprived or slum area conjures up a variety of images about the area's residents who are thus seen as slum inhabitants with all the negative connotations that label often has. As a result people from Small Heath – any part of Small Heath – may find it more difficult to get a job or a mortgage than would be expected on the basis of their personal qualifications and economic circumstances. They themselves, even schoolchildren, are consciously aware of this. The labelling process and the reactions it provokes on the part of government, absentee landlords and other agencies in housing allocation policies, maintenance and the provision of services may also reinforce whatever tendencies towards deviant behaviour there might already have been. That is, the stereotype threatens to become a self-fulfilling prophecy.

The public image is derived from facts. But it distorts the facts and further undermines confidence in the area's future, especially on the part of those residents who have looked to it as a source of opportunity and identified with it as a symbol of their own status in the past. The association between image of the place and self-image is an important factor which clearly influences what people say both about Small Heath and about their neighbours. It will come through frequently in the following pages where we review the main features of the collective environment, physical, social, educational, economic.

The physical environment

An assessment of environmental quality[2] we carried out in spring 1975 recorded (if the completed part of the new council estate is excluded) a clear overall improvement in scores from west to east. Moving through 5 housing zones from St. Andrews CDA in the west to Heybarnes in the east (Figure 15) the proportions of streets surveyed that scored above the average for the area as a whole were respectively nil, 20 per cent, 50 per cent, 75 per cent, 100 per cent. A similar progression was found on all three sets of variables – character, condition, potential land use conflict – though the improvement was not as smooth. The average combined score for the area as a whole was just over 40 per cent the theoretical maximum. The 'best' street scored 73 per cent, the 'worst' 17 per cent.

1. The terminology is from the Birmingham Press. See John Lloyd, *The labelling of Small Heath*, BIAS, April, 1975, which examines in particular the role of the press in creating the image of a deprived or slum area. The author presents his findings in the wider framework of a discussion of labelling theory and the sociology of deviancy.

2. *Environment Quality Assessment*, BIAS, September 1975.

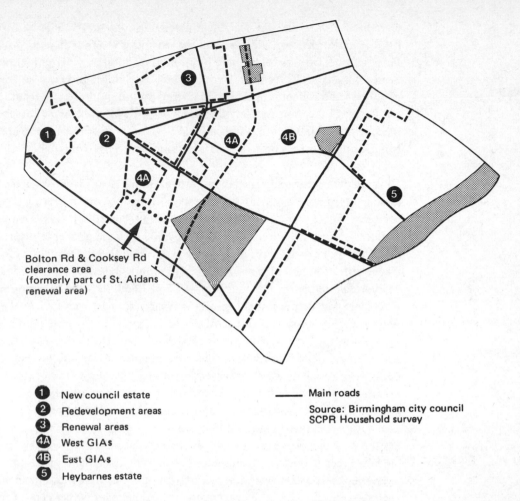

Figure 15
Small Heath:
Housing zones

Bolton Rd & Cooksey Rd
clearance area
(formerly part of St. Aidans
renewal area)

1 New council estate
2 Redevelopment areas
3 Renewal areas
4A West GIAs
4B East GIAs
5 Heybarnes estate

— Main roads

Source: Birmingham city council
SCPR Household survey

The kind of technique used is not truly objective since the choice of variables that form the basis of the assessment and the methods by which they are measured and ranked imply a number of value judgements; but it affords a reasonable degree of consistency for comparative purposes. All other things being equal, we should expect residents' perceptions to reflect the scores fairly closely. And indeed the pattern, according to the SCPR survey, was broadly similar. Positive opinions rose steadily from west to east. If we add together responses that it is 'very true' or 'partly true' the district is 'attractive in appearance', we get the following progression: 24 per cent, 33 per cent, 51 per cent, 62 per cent, 71 per cent. However the general response still tended to be rather negative, even on the Heybarnes estate where more people found it 'not at all true' than 'very true' that the district was 'attractive in appearance'. Since by any criterion Heybarnes is a well-kept, spacious, pleasant enough garden estate, this is a clear indication that dissatisfaction with what people regard as their area – the area generally known as Small Heath – colours their appreciation of their more immediate neighbourhood. Conversely, it is hard to imagine that anyone living among the rubble of the redevelopment zone could find the area even remotely attractive. Yet some did. Small Heath obviously meant more to them than their local collection of streets and buildings.

Complaints about the physical environment accounted for about half of all stated dislikes about the area and over half the reasons given for it having gone downhill. Particular concerns were the deterioration of housing in general (mentioned by nearly 4 in 10 adults resident over 20 years), dereliction and rubbish-strewn sites, dirt, litter and rodent infestation. Industrial pollution, noise and traffic problems got far fewer mentions, mainly because what little large-scale manufacturing takes place within Small Heath is basically non-pollutive. Just outside the area, in Hay Mills, both industrial noise and lead pollution are very real issues.

Housing deterioration in the better parts of Small Heath is most visible in terms of structural soundness and condition, especially at the rear, reflecting the age of property. This goes some of the way towards explaining why concern over deterioration was almost as high outside zones blighted by slum clearance or proposals for a new Coventry expressway (since shelved) as inside them, despite the fact fully 40 per cent of households resident over 12 months had had the outside of their house repainted in the previous year and 8 in 10 adults strongly disagreed with the view there was no point looking after one's house in an area such as theirs. But it is not a complete answer. Significantly, only 44 per cent of people even in the redevelopment zone were in full or partial agreement with the sentiment it was not worth looking after their homes. The general pattern seems to be that longer-established residents were concerned about blight, whether or not their own house or street was directly affected, liked to believe they themselves were doing everything possible to keep up appearances, and blamed the decline they saw on others, associating it in their minds with a 'poorer class of people' coming into the area – a point we shall shortly return to. Newcomers, who in fact were every bit as likely to have had recent work done on their houses, were less able to make comparisons. Even they, however, when they ventured an opinion, were more inclined to be negative than positive in their reactions to change, over 60 per cent of reasons given for decline being concerned with the physical environment, 25 per cent with the deterioration of housing.

Work with schoolchildren[1] confirmed the negative picture of the physical environment. It was noticeable that opinions tended to get worse as children grew older. Not only had secondary school children been around longer, they were also able to make wider comparison with other parts of the city. Small Heath often rated unfavourably even against similarly labelled 'problem areas' like Saltley and Handsworth. Overall, only Handsworth scored worse, Small Heath being preferred on a 'paired comparisons' test by 56 per cent of children. As with adults, there was a marked tendency for children in the east of the area to be somewhat less negative in their reactions, but negative none the less.

Attitudes to public services which affect the physical environment were divided. People were on the whole quite satisfied with the standard of rubbish collection, nearly 60 per cent giving a positive response (ie, finding the area 'very well' or 'quite well' provided), though residents in renewal areas, over which there was at

1. See David Spencer and John Lloyd, *A Child's Eye View of Small Heath*, CURS, August 1974, and John Lloyd, *The Labelling of Small Heath*, *op. cit.*

the time great planning uncertainty, were less pleased and Asians gave a rather lower rating for this service than might have been anticipated – an interesting point in view of the conflict with neighbours that has been observed over the disposal of offal from home-slaughtered poultry, etc. Opinions about street cleaning were generally less favourable (35 per cent of responses positive), only Heybarnes residents appearing reasonably satisfied. Car parking facilities were criticised heavily everywhere except on the new council estate.

The social environment

When we move from the area's physical appearance to what might loosely be termed the social environment neighbourhood variations become far less important and on certain issues virtually disappear. Residents in the east of the area were neither more nor less likely to find the place 'interesting and full of variety' than residents in the west. 49 per cent of all residents considered these attributes to be 'not at all true'. Residents of Heybarnes were every bit as negative in their opinions (54 per cent finding the attributes 'not at all true') as those in the redevelopment zone (53 per cent). In fact, in terms of 'community spirit', people in the redevelopment zone were more prone to give a favourable judgement than those on Heybarnes, respectively 68 per cent and 53 per cent finding it 'very true' or 'partly true' that community spirit in Small Heath was good.

Opinions divided much more strongly along ethnic lines, West Indians and especially Asians being much more positive in their responses than the Irish or UK born. It may of course be argued that immigrants, as relative newcomers to the area, are less able to make unfavourable comparisons with the past, are less ready to criticise and in any case bring with them a vastly different experience of modern urban living (nearly 70 per cent of Asians, for instance, originating from villages or small towns). The divergence in opinions is so great, however, we believe it also reflects genuine differences in patterns of social interaction and cultural life within the area's sub-communities. Eighty-one per cent of Asians, for example, found it 'very true' that Small Heath is 'interesting and full of variety', compared with only 36 per cent of UK born. They were also considerably more likely to think people in Small Heath have a good community spirit, to speak positively of social life and to give friends and relations as a reason for moving into the area.

Asians, 85 per cent of whom are Muslim, keep very much to themselves. Very few, at least in early 1974, seemed aware of any conflict or tensions within the wider community. The relatively 'closed' nature of their social life provides important mutual support and protection for its members. It does on the other hand make it that much harder to promote inter-racial contact and co-operation, especially where there are language barriers. Children of Asian parents, particularly girls, also frequently have great difficulty – and experience considerable stress – in adjusting mentally to new values and life-styles first encountered at school; they are forced, as it were, to live between two cultures, belonging fully neither to one nor the other.

Whereas nearly 70 per cent of residents (60 per cent even in the case of the UK born) considered people generally get on well together and a quarter spontaneously mentioned social relationships as something they particularly liked about the area, quite a number, especially those who had lived in Small Heath for over 20 years, complained of what they saw to be a decline in community life and neighbourliness. The SCPR survey indicated that the major blame for this was attributed to the arrival of new immigrants, rough neighbours and 'problem families' rather than to friends, neighbours or relatives moving away. For example, 27 per cent of long-term residents – a higher proportion still in the central parts of the area where minority communities are concentrated – mentioned immigrants specially as a reason for the area having gone downhill. 'Problem families' and rough neighbours seemed a particular concern among elderly people on Heybarnes. However, over half the complaints named by those 30 per cent of residents who confessed to there being problems between different groups in the area were very general in nature – people just don't socialise, you have difficulty getting on with them – rather than to do with particular cultural observances or habits, hygiene, or care of property.

Our more recent depth interviews suggest that people in the host community are generally coming to feel more isolated. This is probably as much a reflection of more mobile modern living, the breakdown of kinship and family life, the dispersal of old communities of work and leisure[1], and possibly too (as in the case of new estate tenants) strange environments without established patterns of socialising, as it is of the arrival of immigrants and other newcomers per se. People interviewed often gave as an explanation for changes in neighbours' attitudes such reasons as 'more money', 'more cars', 'television', or (apparently associated in their minds with more money) 'they don't want to know you now'. There simply seems to be less contact, and it is the elderly and mothers of large families, those most tied to their homes, who suffer most. The presence as neighbours of immigrants, whose womenfolk – in the case of Asians – usually speak no English, observe different customs and are frequently confined indoors often exacerbates this situation.

The lack of social and community facilities, especially for the elderly and for youngsters, was almost universally deplored. (In fact, outside the churches, Small Heath has virtually no provision for youth.) Only 18 per cent thought the area was at all well off for community facilities, younger age groups and West Indians being especially critical, and not many more (24 per cent in all) considered it at all well provided with children's play facilities. Where facilities were particularly poor, such as around the Talfourd Street estate, or sited very close to people's windows, like the adventure playground on the new Saint Andrews estate, older people, shiftworkers or other adults at home during the day were liable to complain of children as a nuisance. Only on Heybarnes was there reasonable satisfaction with opportunities for children. Heybarnes recreation ground – an extensive linear park alongside the River Cole, easily accessible from the estate – had recently been regraded and grassed when our first interviews were carried out.

Small Heath Park, though it occupies close on 50 acres and provides for a fairly wide range of activities, tends to have an extremely local or only casual use. It is

1. A count of the number of times names in the electoral register changed against Small Heath addresses (excluding houses not since demolished) showed that for these houses the turnover of occupancy has been half as high again in the 70s as in the 50s.

popular with Asians and West Indians living in the vicinity but most older residents interviewed would not set foot in it and quite a few mothers said they forbade their children to play there, considering it unsafe. According to SCPR, a great number of elderly people, especially those living alone, found Small Heath in general too dangerous a place to go out in at night. But, on the whole, more people found this view 'not at all true' (42 per cent) than 'very true' (31 per cent). Again, loneliness, suspicion and rumour play their part, isolated cases of mugging and violence reported in the press or passed on by word of mouth tending to get blown up out of proportion. Vandalism and burglary do, however, appear to be on the increase, possibly associated with high unemployment, particularly among youths. Kerb-crawling is a common source of annoyance to women in streets adjacent to the park.

Social life locally, such as it is, centres mainly around the pubs and the social clubs which in early 1974 claimed nearly 1 in 5 adults as members. Social clubs have long waiting lists; they attract members and visitors from quite far afield; they also function sometimes as informal labour exchanges where news of vacancies is put about among workers. Commercial cinemas have now all closed. Bingo is fairly popular among women but was found too expensive by some older people we interviewed. In fact, very few people in our Circumstances of Families survey went out at all regularly: the reasons they gave were that they were too tired after a long day's work; they had young children to look after and/or could not get (afford) baby-sitters; there was nowhere to go they liked, or they just did not have the money. While the city centre is not far away and public transport is held by practically everyone to be very good, the cost of entertainment there puts it beyond the purse of most residents with households to support, except as a very occasional treat.

Schoolchildren's attitudes again followed adults' quite closely, though juniors, whose social activity is very localised and confined closely to their home and the homes of friends/relatives, were much more likely than seniors to rate the area as 'interesting' or 'friendly'. Seniors came out strongly against the lack of facilities and entertainments. They were, however, very divided in their opinions about people. In written essays some children claimed that Small Heath people were warm, kind and 'stuck together'; others were very conscious about deviant groups and about immigrants whom, like their parents, they associated with the area's (increasingly) bad reputation. Despite the presence of Asian and West Indian classmates there was obviously quite a lot of racial prejudice, although a few children showed sympathy for the immigrants' situation and even some understanding of the reasons for their immigration.

Educational environment

It is not in any real sense possible to distinguish clearly children's (or, for that matter, adults') educational environment from the rest of the environmental circumstances in which they live. There is now ample research evidence to show that educational attainment – even judged by conventional criteria – has much more to do with home and family background and, to a lesser extent, with neighbourhood and community background than it has formal schooling. But, whatever the outcome in exams passed, undeniably the experience of school is or can be an important influence in its own right. This experience is affected in part by the type and condition of buildings and the facilities/equipment provided, and in part by what goes on within the physical environment of the school: the nature of school organisation, the quality and style of teaching, the size of classes, the nature of curriculum, the range of extra-curricular activities and so forth.

Professor Wiseman, cited in Plowden, argues on the basis of research in Manchester that 'home' variables have twice the weight of 'neighbourhood' and 'school' variables together when correlated with educational attainment. 'Home' variables include such things as parental attitudes, their linguistic habits, the interest they show in their children and the nature of their own relationships, as well as more tangible factors like incomes, occupations, size of family, housing conditions, etc. Wiseman claims that parental attitudes are more important than social status or background. Jencks' work too[1] attributes most influence to 'more elusive non-economic differences'. It is worth recalling that Small Heath has almost twice the national average incidence of divorced and separated persons, to say nothing of the many homes 'broken' in other ways perhaps even more injurious for the child.

Small Heath schools are, for the most part, old. In 1972, when our study began, 11 out of 13 primary schools (85 per cent) and 8 out of 9 secondary schools (89 per cent) serving the area were housed mainly in pre-1914 buildings, though some had more modern extensions. This compared with respectively 31 per cent and 27 per cent of schools in the city as a whole. Since 1972 the picture has changed somewhat for the better. Two new primary buildings have been opened in the redevelopment zone, allowing the phasing-out and closure of two older schools, and one new secondary building – a combined comprehensive school and community leisure centre – is under construction, scheduled ultimately to replace three older schools though initially, due to public expenditure cutbacks, two of these will have to be partially retained as annexes. Because of the delayed opening of the new comprehensive, children from the third school, whose previous premises have been transferred to the Catholic schools authorities, are being bussed daily three miles to Sheldon.

Problems of obsolete premises, often in poor physical condition and ill-equipped, have been aggravated by the fact that a number of schools were also too small to accommodate adequately the children enrolled. Consequently, annexes (sometimes on different sites) have had to be utilised and it is not uncommon to see school halls, offices and even cloakrooms pressed into service as teaching spaces. In practically all cases children have to travel considerable distances to sportsfields. Even the two new primary schools have not been able to be provided with adjacent playing fields.

Crowding in certain schools and the makeshift arrangements to cope with it have resulted in part from the inability to estimate accurately the effects on school population of the redevelopment programme and of in-migration patterns, the latter tending to raise the proportion of young children, the former to reduce child

1. Christopher Jencks, *Inequality*, Peregrine Books 1975. See also Chapter 3.

54

numbers generally – though not as quickly as first anticipated. There are signs that this situation too is now being relieved, at least temporarily, with the primary school population at last falling off and the number of secondary pupils appearing to hold steady over the past year or two. As a consequence of stabilising pupil numbers and a slight increase in staff, though spread unevenly between different schools, pupil: teacher ratios have recently declined and at the beginning of the 1975/76 year stood in most schools, both primary and secondary, at or even a little below city averages, themselves fractionally lower than national figures.[1] The average size of class in 1975, at just over 31 for primary schools and 27 for secondary schools, was virtually identical with the city norm.

Simple comparisons, however, mask the special needs generated by schools in which many children, quite apart from their other disadvantages, have severe language difficulties and some start with no English at all. Up to a quarter of pupils in Small Heath schools may have language difficulties, even at the secondary level. Overall, more than 1 in 3 on the register come from 'wholly non-European' homes, fully twice the average for the city as a whole. In some schools the proportion rises to between a half and two-thirds. The majority are of Asian origin, with little previous exposure to the values or customs of an Anglo-Saxon culture.

It has been recognised for some time that 'schools of exceptional difficulty' merit special assistance. Yet only two schools serving Small Heath figured in the 50 confirmed by the DES from Birmingham's nomination list of 191 in 1968. Subsequently the programme of positive discrimination was widened, raising the coverage from 1 in 10 to roughly 1 in 3 of the city's schools; the result was that as of mid 1975 all but 1 primary and 2 secondary schools in the Small Heath area were designated 'social priority schools', thus entitling them to increased capitation allowances and their teachers to a salary premium. Schools also receive additional staff support in the way of peripatetic language teachers and remedial and home-school liaison specialists. However, the numbers still remain well below what Plowden considered necessary – about half the recommended ratio for primary schools in mid 1975.

Although organisation and curriculum appear as a rule to be fairly orthodox, with attempts to deal with special circumstances improvised by the individual teacher rather than reflecting a consistent theory and practice of education for the multi-racial urban school, our evidence is rather too piecemeal to permit confident generalisations about the extent to which poor performance (as indicated by past records of 11-plus pass rates, sample reading assessment levels, proportions of pupils staying on beyond minimum leaving age and occupational classifications of school leavers by the youth employment service) may be attributed to the form, content and quality of teaching.

1. There is considerable difficulty here in comparing like with like. Including head teachers and counting part-time staff at full-time equivalent, average ratios in Small Heath primary and secondary schools in September 1975 were respectively 24.0 : 1 and 16.2 : 1. National figures for January 1975 were quoted in *Hansard* (5 March 1976, columns 771 & 772) as 24.2 : 1 and 17.2 : 1. The national statistics include fully-qualified peripatetic and supply staff, those for Small Heath do not. At a rough estimate inclusion of these omitted categories of staff would have reduced the Small Heath primary schools ratio to 23.5 : 1.

Despite the many difficulties of teaching in Small Heath, staff turnover in recent years has certainly not been as high as work in other older urban areas – or a reading of Plowden – might have led us to expect. In primary schools the proportion of staff leaving at the end of the 1974 and 1975 summer terms was respectively 8 per cent and 4 per cent; for secondary schools the corresponding figures were 11 per cent and 8 per cent.

Residents seem on the whole to hold fairly favourable views about the schools. According to SCPR, almost two-thirds of mothers with children under 16 considered the area to be 'very well off' or 'quite well off' for good schools. Mothers or guardians of children still at school were generally either 'very satisfied' (46 per cent) or 'fairly satisfied' (39 per cent) with the education they were getting. In most cases children were felt to be receiving a better education than their parents. Yet there was quite a strong opinion among parents of secondary school children that they should learn things which would be more useful in their future jobs. Immigrants seemed especially prone to hold this view. It is possible that doubts about the relevance of schooling to later life are associated with disappointment over the actual benefits Small Heath children generally appear to derive in employment or earnings experience from their time in school. Other complaints were that classes were too big and children did not get enough individual attention – rather stock replies – though a fair proportion (15 per cent) of UK born and Irish mothers were worried about the presence of Asian or West Indian classmates holding back their own children. Children themselves were most critical of the old buildings and poor facilities. However, in essays, poems and taped discussions they may understandably have been hesitant to make other, more radical kinds of criticism about their school experience.

Plowden and other work on educational priorities have stressed the importance of pre-school provision in helping to compensate for the disadvantages of children from deprived backgrounds. In early 1974 the number of nursery, daycare and playgroup places open to Small Heath children was estimated at less than half the city average. With all places taken up only 13 per cent of children aged 3 to 5 would have been able to attend, compared with the Plowden recommended minimum provision of 20 per cent. Most centres and playgroups had long waiting lists. Not surprisingly 40 per cent of mothers with children under school age felt the area to be either 'very poorly off' or 'quite poorly off' for nursery facilities, against only 25 per cent giving positive responses. Sixteen per cent of Small Heath mothers with children under school age used pre-school facilities either regularly or intermittently, some farther afield. Nearly 60 per cent of the remainder said they would like to use them, but they could not get a place, or the places were too far away.

When we turn to adult education it seems to be not only a matter of lack of provision (and publicity) as lack of interest, though this in turn is very much connected with the type of activities offered, which have very limited appeal or relevance to local residents.[1] There is one local centre in Small Heath, giving non-vocational classes three nights per week at old premises in Oldknow School. Its

1. Rex Bird, *Adult Education in Small Heath*, BIAS, September 1975.

Bob Marshall

There's jobs in abundance around here, but they're all £18 per week. The better jobs – and you've got to go for them with the cost of living today – are the ones that are scarce.

SCPR Exploratory Study

They're sending twelve blokes after one job now. So where can you get a job – nowhere can you?

Circumstances of Families

register of students has declined steadily from over 700 in the mid-60s to less than 200 per week, compared with rising enrolments in the city as a whole. The centre is not well known, even by those who live very close to it. A survey in 1970/71 showed that only a third of 450 residents living in the immediate vicinity of the centre knew at all what type of activities were offered at Oldknow. Only 40 per cent of students questioned in late 1974 were from Small Heath itself, though some of the remainder previously lived in the area.

The economic environment

Traditionally one of the major advantages of Small Heath, especially for the manual worker, was its employment environment: the wide range of job opportunities available within easy reach, on foot, on bicycle, or by public transport. These jobs, largely in the manufacturing sector, created a strong demand for labour and paid relatively good wages. And the general prosperity of industry was such that, if one plant closed or moved production elsewhere, the employment loss was quickly taken up by new firms or divisions moving in or starting up. Quick reoccupation of empty industrial premises in fact continued, often involving new conversions and extensions, long after Small Heath had ceased to be a location for important new site development. Small Heath's labour pool and its reasonably good location for industrial linkages and general communications remained attractions to employers. Commercial investment too was encouraged: Small Heath continued to function as one of the busiest shopping centres in the city.

As we saw in the previous chapter, however, this situation has been changing rapidly since the early 60s and particularly during the present recession. Local job opportunities have fallen faster than the population seeking work. Unemployment has risen, and activity rates (especially among women) have fallen in virtually all age-groups. Investment in new building appears to have dried up. Factory premises and shops lie idle, bearing witness to the area's economic stagnation. In Chapter 3 we shall explore to what extent stagnation appears to be a result of short term fluctuations in the national/regional economies and of changes in the fortunes of particular industries or to what extent other longer term processes may be at work. For the present, in describing the problems which Small Heath faces today, we shall simply spell out some of the more specific features within the general situation which give rise to concern.

At the time of the SCPR survey (a time of comparatively low general unemployment) very few people seriously thinking of moving or who said they would like to move if they had the chance gave the desire to be nearer work as a reason. Convenience for work got only about 3 per cent of mentions. Nearly a quarter of men (17 per cent overall) mentioned convenience for work as something they particularly liked about the area. As many as 65 per cent of all respondents found it 'very true' that the area was central for work. Significantly, however, the 16–24 age group (only 54 per cent of whom found it 'very true') and West Indians (56 per cent) were somewhat less enthusiastic. Even then there was perhaps a tendency for new entrants to the workforce, especially school-leavers, and some minority groups, specifically young

58

blacks, to encounter the kinds of problems getting suitable work which have escalated dramatically in the past two years.

A survey in 1974 of firms providing between them over 26,000 jobs in Small Heath itself or within a mile or so of its boundaries revealed less than 300 openings for school leavers, male or female, with or without training. The area covered served as the job supply market for roughly 40 per cent of Small Heath's working population which we estimate to have been between 14,500 and 15,000. Based on the ratio of school leavers to the total working population, over twice the number of openings would have been expected. There were few apprenticeships, since firms relied on poaching their skilled labour. Those which were available were not all taken up, presumably because rates of pay (in the short term) offered insufficient inducement. Furthermore the situation, already tight, was bound to get worse, unless there were a sudden leap in the general level of labour demand, because there was a pronounced bulge in the numbers of children reaching or approaching working age. 1971 figures showed that the number of children in Birmingham aged 10–14 exceeded the number aged 15–19 by 5 per cent. In Small Heath and Sparkbrook wards the increments were respectively 21.8 per cent and 6.5 per cent, the extraordinarily high figure for Small Heath ward probably due to the settlement pattern of large Asian families in houses recently purchased from smaller white households moving to other parts of the city or elsewhere.

Immigrants held 11 per cent of jobs in the establishments surveyed. Their relative position in the Small Heath working population was well over twice that proportion. Even so, they were just as likely as whites to be employed in the labour catchment area concerned, for two reasons: first, there was a strong bias among works jobs towards lower skilled manual labour, and immigrants tend to be employed in that capacity; second, white workers were faced with stiffer competition from residents of neighbouring wards and further afield for white collar and skilled manual jobs. The concern over immigrants is their greater vulnerability in the labour market. Fifteen out of 21 firms surveyed who gave an answer did not employ non-English-speaking immigrants unless their labour shortage became desperate. We suspect in fact that immigrants as a whole, especially Asians, are used as a 'buffer' group in the labour force, moved in or out of employment as production demand rises and falls. Judging from our recent depth interviews this is certainly the view of many Asians themselves. Such a view is consistent with the lower unemployment rate among Asian men in Small Heath at the time of the SCPR survey (4.7 per cent against 7.8 per cent in the case of UK and Irish born) and the higher unemployment rate prevalent today. If only because of the 'last in, first out' principle immigrant workers will have suffered particularly badly from redundancies and labour rundowns in Small Heath over the past three years.

To some extent the vulnerability of immigrant workers reflects the vulnerability of Small Heath workers in general, with their heavy dependence on manual jobs in manufacturing and particularly in the vehicles sector. Allowing for linkages (such as the production of parts and accessories) roughly 3 in 10 Small Heath workers were dependent on the fortunes of the vehicles industry in early 1974, a good one-and-a-half times the ratio for the city as a whole and high even for the eastern part of the city. In the case of Asians and West Indians the figure may well have topped 40 per cent.

Nearly three-quarters of immigrants were employed in manufacturing. Though the proportion of white workers with manufacturing jobs was considerably lower (at 47 per cent) and indeed 3 percentage points or so beneath the city average, this was still far above the national figure of about 37 per cent. As we pointed out in the previous chapter, it is manufacturing jobs which have been steadily declining in the city, both in absolute numbers and relative to service employment. Again, the major growth in service employment has been in the so-called 'quaternary' sector: the 'knowledge industries' which demand qualifications that few Small Heath residents possess.

Between 1951 and 1971 services increased their share of Birmingham employment from 32 per cent to 39 per cent, since when it will have risen further. The share of financial and professional services rose from 8 per cent to 17 per cent and must now be close on 20 per cent. In early 1974 only 6 per cent of Small Heath workers were employed in the latter sectors; and most of these were women doing junior clerical or cleaning work. Very local employment is biased towards distribution and other service jobs, affording wider (though lowly-paid) opportunities for women than for men. Hence women are about twice as likely to work in Small Heath itself than men. In the past it seems that constraints on activity rates (eg, lack of childminding facilities) have been more important in keeping women out of work than a shortage of available jobs. Although childminding provision remains well below demand, it is now almost certainly a job shortage which is the major constraint.

Both within and outside the manufacturing industries Small Heath residents tend to hold the lower-skilled jobs. While this was especially pronounced in the case of immigrants, nearly 60 per cent of whom held semi-skilled or unskilled jobs, it was also true of white workers, with over 40 per cent employed in these capacities. Generally it is the lower-skilled who experience most unemployment, especially in times of low labour demand, so the job prospects of Small Heath residents will have suffered disproportionately as a result of general trends, quite apart from local job losses. At the time of the 1971 census the unemployment rates for all occupational groups (including those off sick) in Birmingham, Small Heath ward and Sparkbrook ward were respectively 6.2 per cent, 8.9 per cent and 9.7 per cent. For unskilled workers they were 24.9 per cent, 27.6 per cent and 22.4 per cent. It is perhaps at first sight surprising that both on the day of the census and at the time of the SCPR survey semi-skilled workers tended to fare rather better than skilled workers. The census showed 4.2 per cent and 6.4 per cent of semi-skilled workers in Small Heath and Sparkbrook wards out of work as opposed to 6.3 per cent and 7.1 per cent of skilled workers. SCPR showed 3.9 per cent of semi-skilled males out of work, against 4.5 per cent of the skilled (7.7 per cent unskilled), excluding long-term sick. A possible explanation is that skilled workers, because of their greater specialisation, once out of work may have relatively more difficulty finding a suitable new job. When we take the case of workers who had experienced at least one spell of unemployment in the twelve months prior to the SCPR survey we find that the progression follows more closely the skill pattern. The rate for skilled workers was 7.9 per cent, for the semi-skilled 10.6 per cent and for the unskilled 14.1 per cent.

But if job and earnings opportunities are declining for Small Heath residents within comparatively easy reach of their homes, how about their access to centres of potential employment growth? Most of Birmingham's new jobs lie along the Tame Valley to the north-east (Gravelly Hill, Erdington wards) or towards the NEC site (Stechford, Sheldon wards). Both of those locations are close to major post-war housing developments and are also conveniently placed for travel from the Sutton Coldfield–Meriden–Solihull commuter belt. While the new centres are theoretically fairly accessible from Small Heath, the situation must be seen not only against the particular skill composition of the jobs provided or the skill/competence ratings of Small Heath residents but also against rising transport costs and the growing differential in car ownership rates between inner wards and the suburban/exurban residential areas. Between 1966 and 1971 car ownership in Small Heath fell from 27 per cent to 26 per cent of households. In the 'outer wards' of the city it increased from 47 per cent to 50 per cent. In places like Solihull and Sutton Coldfield both the absolute levels and the rate of increase were even higher, especially when second cars are taken into account. Although a quarter of Small Heath workers travelled by car to their jobs in early 1974, this is believed to have involved a significant amount of sharing. A worker falling out of work, whose need of a car to seek a new job further afield possibly increases, may no longer be able to take advantage of sharing arrangements.

But the economic environment of an area is not to be understood exclusively in terms of job opportunities and investment attractiveness. Important too (though related) is the value for money it presents residents in expenditure opportunities. Two aspects in particular concern us here: the range and quality of shopping; and the cost of housing.

Shopping came out high on the list of particular likes residents had about the area. It was mentioned by 32 per cent of all adults, 46 per cent in the case of housewives. Questioned more specifically, 59 per cent of all adults and 63 per cent of housewives rated the area 'very well off' in this respect. However, both long term residents (in the area over 20 years) and younger people (aged 16–24) tended to be somewhat less enthusiastic: 53 per cent of long term residents found Small Heath very well off for shopping facilities, compared with 63 per cent of more recent residents. Only 15 per cent of younger people gave shopping as a particular like about the area, compared with 36 per cent of all other age-groups.

It seems that once again most criticism was to be found among those remembering Small Heath as it used to be a generation or so ago and those growing up with higher expectations. In both cases the criticism appears to be associated with shops closing down, especially in the western part of the area, and with others changing ownership to become specialist food or clothing stores for immigrant groups. The latter change is, of course, extremely welcome to Asians and West Indians themselves, three-quarters of whom rated Small Heath 'very well off' for shopping.

We have been in this part of Small Heath about fifteen years. It's not too bad, on the whole, but . . . it seems to have deteriorated, since the coloureds have come in. Somehow they don't seem to speak to you or they don't communicate with you . . . The atmosphere is gone.

Circumstances of Families

Another reason why people dislike Small Heath is all the coloured people. The people have to live somewhere, don't they?

A Child's Eye View of Small Heath

Although Small Heath's relative position as a shopping centre is evidently on the wane[1] it has come to perform a very valuable function for cultural minorities whose special needs are largely uncatered for by city centre shops. As far as the gradually dwindling 'host' population is concerned, there has almost certainly been a real loss of amenity in terms of the range and variety of goods offered, particularly perhaps in clothing and certain household goods. Convenience shopping, however, is provided in new self-service stores developed in the 60s by multiple chains. The value for money offered by these stores explains why the passing of the 'corner shop' evokes, even among older residents, only mild nostalgia.

Housing costs in Small Heath, as measured by outgoings per week on mortgages or rents, are low by regional or national standards. To begin with, 25 per cent of all households in early 1974 owned their homes outright or lived rent free, which was slightly higher than either the national or West Midlands figure. Very nearly half the remainder paid under £3 per week, only 5 per cent paying £10 or more. About a third of mortgagors paid under £3 per week, over twice the national proportion. Comparable bases for rents are difficult to establish. What evidence we have suggests that council rents were perhaps 15 per cent below average for the region, largely on account of the relatively high incidence of inter-war and council-acquired property; that registered rents for privately owned terraced houses were close on 20 per cent lower than those for similar properties in the rest of Birmingham taken as a whole; and that other private rents were substantially lower still, principally because of the number of (unimproved) controlled tenancies and the small unit size of furnished lettings, the large majority of which were not self-contained.[2]

In view of the age and condition of much of the housing stock and the general quality of the environment it is not surprising that, in absolute terms, housing is cheap. The market value of property is also depressed by planning uncertainty and the limited length of most leases, usually under 25 years. Small Heath has this in common with many other areas of older housing in Birmingham, notably Sparkhill, Saltley, Handsworth, Soho. In late 1974 the range of asking prices for old 2 to 3 bedroom terraced properties coming onto the market in these areas tended to begin at £2,000 to £3,000. £3,000 was also the usual valuation placed on houses in good condition and with bathroom installed in the Little Green housing action area. The data we have are not sufficient, however, to determine whether there are consistent differentials between one area and another on the basis of location alone.

Residents tended on the whole to agree that Small Heath was 'good for cheap accommodation', 44 per cent of those who had an opinion finding the statement 'very true' against 24 per cent 'not at all true'. In groups which had a high

1. The number of shops in the Small Heath Planning District fell by 37 per cent between 1960 and 1973. A Public Works Survey in 1972 revealed almost a fifth of shops in the Coventry Road district centre to be vacant — the highest vacancy rate in the whole city. Coventry Road was still, however, the joint largest district centre in terms of occupied shops, though a poor third in gross floorspace.

2. Most of the comparative data are derived from the Family Expenditure Survey, supplemented in the case of rents by a 10 per cent sample of exclusive rents registered by October/November 1974 for houses within Birmingham. See also the BIAS report Housing Policies for the Inner City, Chapter 1.

representation of owner occupiers and private renters the agreement was even higher. Only tenants on the new council estate substantially disagreed. Asians, almost exclusively owner occupiers or private renters, were practically unanimous: 77 per cent of those who had an opinion found the statement 'very true', only 8 per cent 'not at all true'. This is especially significant since Asians were strongly represented among that group of owner occupiers who had recently moved to their address and tended to pay the highest housing costs. For instance 61 per cent of mortgagors resident less than 5 years paid over £6, compared with only 20 per cent of those resident over 5 years; 55 per cent of mortgagors paying over £6 were immigrant, predominantly Asian.

The question therefore arises: in what sense precisely is accommodation in Small Heath 'cheap'? Possibly we should make a distinction between cheapness in the sense of 'value for money', ie, cost related to amenity; cheapness in the sense of 'minimum available cost', ie, cost related to the cost of other housing, of whatever kind, in whatever location; and cheapness in the sense of 'bearable cost', ie, cost related to income. In the first case the focus is on the acquisition of a certain desired quality of housing. The occupant may be prepared to pay a comparatively high price for it. In the second case the focus is on the acquisition of 'shelter'. The price must be the lowest or near the lowest known to be available, irrespective of quality. In the third case the focus is on a trade-off between value for money and minimum cost, made in the interest of maximising total spending power.

Small Heath, we would argue, certainly provides a supply of accommodation, both for rent and for sale, at the bottom end of the market. Good value for money, however, is only available to those who have occupied their homes for some considerable time or to those more recent arrivals on higher incomes who can afford to meet the current high cost of financing the purchase of the better terraced houses towards the east of the area. There is in fact some slight evidence from the SCPR survey to suggest that house-buyers moving to their address between 5 and 10 years previously were more likely consciously to choose Small Heath for the cheapness of its housing than recent movers. Asian furnished tenants who appear to share owner occupiers' opinions about the cheapness of accommodation may be basing their views on their own experience as renters (most clearly feel themselves to be better off than before) or on their awareness of house-buying opportunities. In many cases the distinction between owner-occupier and tenant is blurred by the nature of the sharing arrangement. It should also be borne in mind that the receipt of rent by a resident landlord reduces the mortgage burden.

At the lower end of the income scale housing costs tend to be high in relation to incomes. For instance, we estimate that those mortgagors living on a household income of under £30 per week in early 1974 paid out a substantially larger share of their income in housing costs than was the rule nationally, whereas those on incomes of £30 to £40 paid out a similar share and those who cleared £40 spent a smaller share. In the case of people recently forced onto the housing market because of family break-up, discharge from an institution, eviction or other reasons, costs (normally in the form of rent) may be out of all proportion to the size or quality of accommodation offered. Again, evidence is sketchy; but in early 1974 the rents of furnished tenants identified as 'in poverty' ranged from £3 to £7 per week, usually for just one or two rooms. While many households may have been eligible for rent allowances, very few claimed them: only 7 per cent of private tenants in fact, though this excludes claimants whose rent was paid by DHSS.

Inter-relationships

The relationship between personal and collective deprivations is extremely complex. Small Heath has been shown to contain a relatively large number of households whose personal circumstances might lead them to be designated as deprived. There are also a number of obvious deficiencies in the shared environment that add to the disadvantages of deprived households and adversely affect the quality of life of all; not least the general sense of the area's decline. The experience of both personal and collective deprivations (and indeed what is perceived as such) is, of course, strongly influenced by the expectations, aspirations and previous experience of different social groups and even individuals. The border line between 'problem' and 'opportunity', as we have seen in looking at Small Heath's function as a source of low-cost (if relatively low-quality) housing and as a settlement area for cultural minorities, is not always clear. The various aspects of collective deprivation are also far from perfectly correlated, like the several forms of personal deprivation. However, evidence on the spatial distribution of a number of symptoms does suggest a broad pattern of association between the incidence of personal and collective deprivations. In particular, there is a marked tendency for the highest and lowest concentrations of personal deprivations to occur in those parts of the area where physical conditions of housing and the built environment are respectively worst and best.

Environmental condition and personal deprivation

To examine the relationship between condition of the physical environment and the incidence of personal deprivations we first grouped census EDs into sextiles (12 EDs in each) graded according to street scores recorded in our environmental quality assessment. The location of the sextiles is shown in Figure 16. Sextile 1 contains the EDs generally performing worst in terms of environmental condition, sextile 6 those doing best. The average of the mean ED scores on a range of indicators from the 1971 census was then taken for each sextile. These are given in Table 9. The results of the exercise must be treated with a certain amount of caution because census data are swiftly out-dated, especially where areas are subject to clearance and redevelopment, and because of technical limitations in the method used for classification, chief among which was the necessity to rate whole EDs based on measurements taken in only a sample number of streets.[1] Nevertheless, we believe some significant patterns emerge.

1. These difficulties were partly overcome by direct observation and comparison with evidence from SCPR and other BIAS projects. It should be noted that the parts of the area (in sextiles 1 & 2) affected by demolition were precisely those designated as the worst on housing and environmental grounds prior to voiding and clearance. EDs corresponding to the new council estate in early 1975 were excluded from the analysis.

Figure 16
Small Heath:
Environmental
condition and
personal
deprivation

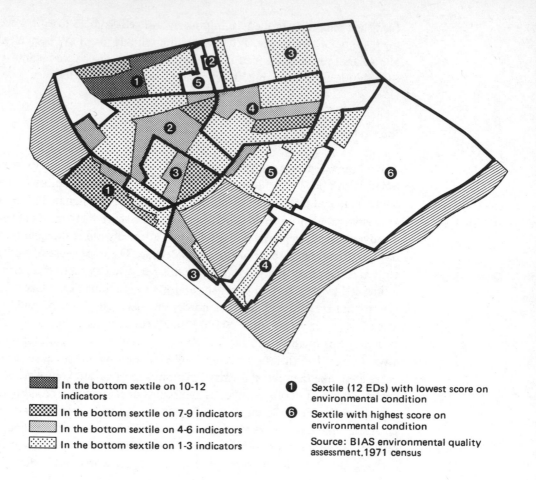

In the bottom sextile on 10-12 indicators

In the bottom sextile on 7-9 indicators

In the bottom sextile on 4-6 indicators

In the bottom sextile on 1-3 indicators

❶ Sextile (12 EDs) with lowest score on environmental condition

❻ Sextile with highest score on environmental condition

Source: BIAS environmental quality assessment,1971 census

The most striking feature of the comparison is that the 'worst' sextile scores consistently badly on a wide range of variables indicative of deprivation while the 'best' scores consistently well. For instance, sextile 1 has the highest rates of male and female unemployment, the lowest proportion of married women economically active, the smallest number of white collar workers, the largest proportion of no-car households, the biggest dependent child population, the greatest number of single parent families, most people per household or room, the highest incidence of overcrowding and dwellings without a fixed bath. Sextile 6 is at or close to the opposite end of the spectrum on all of these, though it does have a larger proportion of pensioner households than all other sextiles. Sextile 2 is clearly the second worst overall on key indicators of deprivation and conforms fairly closely in type to sextile 1. Between the two extremes (in sextiles 3, 4 and 5) the scores are much more jumbled. These parts of the area comprise a transitional zone and typify what we referred to in Chapter 1 as 'areas of secondary deprivation'.

The indicator with the highest degree of association with the classifying variable (ie, environmental condition) is, not surprisingly, dwellings without a fixed bath. Among indicators with poor associations the most significant are households sharing a dwelling and New Commonwealth population (which in the table includes

Table 9 Performance of sextiles ranked by environmental condition on 18 census indicators

Indicators	Sextiles					
	1 %	2 %	3 %	4 %	5 %	6 %
1 Male unemployment	13.1	10.8	5.7	6.2	6.8	5.3
2 Female unemployment	7.7	6.0	4.9	6.1	4.8	4.1
3 Married women economically active	32.8	39.8	41.5	39.3	45.5	46.0
4 Male white collar workers (SEGs1–6,13)*	7.6	10.0	13.3	13.1	15.7	17.2
5 Male unskilled manual workers (SEG11)*	16.1	11.0	14.3	16.5	13.7	5.4
6 Households without a car	81.8	77.7	72.3	71.2	72.1	69.3
7 Population 0–14	35.9	32.6	27.3	30.1	28.0	27.9
8 Children 0–4 per 100 females 15–44	88.7	81.6	67.5	70.8	60.9	43.5
9 Single parent families*	12.8	12.6	7.5	4.2	10.8	3.3
10 New Commonwealth population	25.1	20.1	25.7	40.1	29.8	8.4
11 Average persons per household	3.67	3.34	3.14	3.54	3.41	3.22
12 Average persons per room	0.78	0.70	0.64	0.68	0.70	0.63
13 Overcrowding (> 1.5 ppr)	11.0	8.4	5.8	7.8	7.7	2.7
14 Households sharing a dwelling	4.8	4.5	10.7	11.3	18.7	1.5
15 Dwellings with no fixed bath	71.2	57.0	22.3	14.8	6.3	4.9
16 Pensioner households	19.9	23.6	26.5	21.8	17.0	27.6
17 5-year movers*	29.2	31.4	28.2	33.8	29.5	25.0
18 Employed in manufacturing*	58.1	48.5	54.6	58.8	57.4	53.9

Source: Census 1971 (10% tables if marked*)

children born in Britain to New Commonwealth parents). The highest scores on both of these are found, like the highest incidence of registered multi-occupied properties, not in the physically worst parts of the area but in the transitional zone where, as Figure 17 shows, owner-occupied and private rented accommodation are concentrated. It helps to explain why New Commonwealth households, who in early 1974 accounted for roughly three-quarters of those sharing dwellings, commonly regard Small Heath as a 'respectable' or 'high class' district.

It is interesting that, despite the general association between immigrants and low socio-economic status and between low socio-economic status and unemployment, the sextiles with the largest immigrant population were not, at least at the time of the census, those with the highest male unemployment. If we compare male unemployment in EDs containing a low proportion of immigrants and their children (less than 25 per cent) against that in EDs with a high proportion (35 per cent and over) we find that in the western part of the area (29 EDs), which included all but two EDs in the bottom two sextiles on physical condition, the rate was 13.5 per cent in those EDs with comparatively few immigrants and 10.9 per cent in those with many; in the eastern part (46 EDs) which included all EDs but one in the top three sextiles, the rates were respectively 5.3 per cent and 7.2 per cent. What this seems to indicate is that where the physical condition of the environment was very bad there was likely to be found an especially high incidence of unemployment and other personal deprivations among white residents, but in comparatively 'good' parts of the area the incidence of personal deprivations tended to be greater

Figure 17
Small Heath:
Household tenure

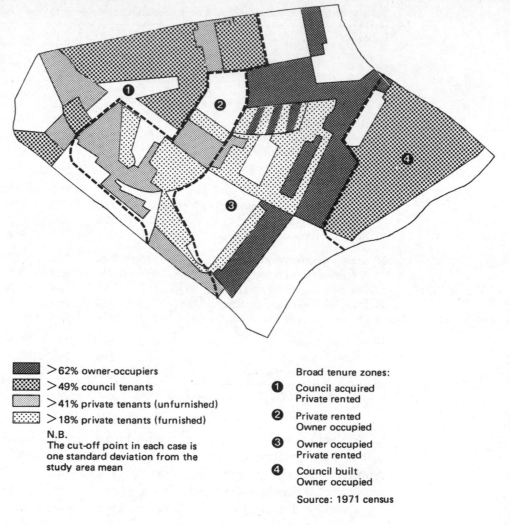

>62% owner-occupiers
>49% council tenants
>41% private tenants (unfurnished)
>18% private tenants (furnished)
N.B.
The cut-off point in each case is
one standard deviation from the
study area mean

Broad tenure zones:

❶ Council acquired
   Private rented

❷ Private rented
   Owner occupied

❸ Owner occupied
   Private rented

❹ Council built
   Owner occupied

Source: 1971 census

among immigrants. The explanation is mainly to be sought in the much greater
variation in personal circumstances within the white population. In the physically
better EDs where there were the highest concentrations of low-skilled immigrants
the white population tended to be more skilled, longer-established, home-owning,
and relatively secure economically. In the poorer EDs with fewer immigrants the
white population was more likely to be physically or mentally sick, jobless (whatever
their former skill level), newcomers or transients, or in difficult family circumstances.
This hypothesis, borne out broadly by SCPR data for different housing zones, is
given further support by the fact that schools with the highest populations of
pupils taking free meals are clustered in the physically poorer parts of the area but
are not generally those with the largest numbers of children from immigrant homes
on their registers.

The condition of the physical environment is, as we have suggested earlier, a poor
guide to a neighbourhood's social environment. Relatively stable and homogeneous
communities may, even in very poor physical environments, exhibit strong

compensating mechanisms of social interaction and mutual support. Older people and longer-term residents claim such mechanisms did formerly exist in the western part of Small Heath, among the back terraces and long rows of houses fronting directly on to the street. We do not believe the strength of these sentiments, encountered so frequently in interviews and in the course of our day-to-day experience in Small Heath, can be simply dismissed as a hankering after the 'good old days'. Conversely, social conflict, tension and individual isolation may be prevalent in neighbourhoods which are physically quite attractive and economically more secure. In Small Heath today, particularly in the central parts (sextiles 3, 4 & 5 in Figure 16), it is the immigrant sub-communities which on the whole appear to show the strongest social cohesion. Yet, because they have settled in zones of private housing where the host population tends to be longer-established and economically more secure (by Small Heath standards), their presence and different life-styles are liable to be perceived as a greater threat both to the environment and image of the neighbourhood and to residents' self-image than if they had located in physically poorer parts of the area.

The spatial concentration of various forms of personal deprivation

Grouping EDs into broad sextiles under a single classifying variable masks the considerable variations that occur within sextiles on other variables. The variations in average ED performances within sextiles in the comparison recorded in Table 9 were in practically every instance greater than the variation between the mean of any one sextile and another. To explore the spatial concentration and association of different forms of personal deprivation further we therefore conducted a second exercise with census data by determining the bottom sextile on each individual indicator, then ranking EDs according to their frequency of occurrence within these bottom sextiles. The results of the exercise are mapped in Figure 16, omitting this time the original classifying variable (environmental condition) and indicators 16 to 18.

No ED appeared all fifteen times. The highest number of appearances (twelve and eleven, respectively) were by two EDs in the redevelopment zone bordering on Little Green. Both have subsequently been cleared. The 'worst' EDs still inhabited when the main phase of BIAS got underway tended to cluster around Bolton Road (in the south-west of the area), in the vicinity of Grange Road and Muntz Street and west of Digby Park (in the centre of the area), and around Small Heath Park. EDs in these localities mainly came within the bottom sextile on between four and nine indicators. It is striking that only 21 EDs in all (29 per cent of those included in the exercise) figured in the bottom sextile on four or more out of fifteen indicators, while 28 EDs (39 per cent), predominantly in the east of the area, did not appear in any bottom sextile at all. Once again the evidence supports the view that, although there is a quite substantial spatial bunching of combinations of personal deprivations and the bunching is most pronounced in neighbourhoods which are the most deprived in terms of their collective environment, the combinations are by no means uniform and the degree of concentration varies considerably from one indicator of deprivation to another.

If we look now at the set of 17 EDs (24 per cent) which came in the bottom sextile on at least one third of the indicators, we find that the features most concentrated among them were persons per room (all twelve EDs in the bottom sextile on this indicator coming within the set), overcrowding (eleven EDs within the set), female unemployment and dwellings without a fixed bath (ten in each case). The features least concentrated were unskilled workers and single parent families (only five EDs from the bottom sextiles), economically active married women and New Commonwealth population (six). On the remaining seven indicators between seven and nine EDs from the bottom sextile fell within the set. If performance had been completely random, only three EDs from each bottom sextile would have occurred.

Two main series of associations between variables emerged. On the one hand, a large proportion of dwellings with no fixed bath clustered together with a high average number of persons per room, a large child population, a high fertility rate, male unemployment, low car ownership, low married female activity rate, and (to a lesser extent) female unemployment, all being most pronounced at the 'bad' end of the environmental spectrum. Sharing, on the other hand, was associated with a high proportion of immigrants and unskilled workers. Overcrowding and (to a lesser degree) large households overlapped with both the sharing and lack of amenities syndromes. Significantly, all seven EDs from sextiles 3, 4 and 5 in our original classification which figured in the 'worst' set of 17 EDs in the second exercise appeared in the bottom sextile on sharing, six in the bottom on overcrowding, and five in the one with the largest immigrant population; none appeared in the bottom sextile on housing amenities, none in the worst on male unemployment, and none in the sextile with the highest ratio of infants to women of child-bearing age.

Deprivation and investment flows

We do not believe that the concentration of personal deprivations and the existence of widespread collective deprivations in areas like Small Heath, in spite of variations in the degree of association, can be regarded as accidental. They are inextricably linked; what is more, they are linked causally in a mutually reinforcing fashion. Collective deprivations reduce still further individual households' level of well-being. In turn, the concentration of people suffering various personal deprivations is bound to have some impact on the collective environment – physical, social, educational, economic.

A key link between personal and collective deprivations is the flow of investment into and out of an area over time and the influence on this flow of the changing socio-economic circumstances of residents. Declining socio-economic status produces a relative fall in spending power. A fall in spending power is likely to result in a lower level of personal investment in housing maintenance and improvement, whether the costs are measured in capital outlays by owners or increased rents payable by tenants. Quite apart from escalating unit costs of repairs and improvements themselves (rising faster than retail prices in general), householders have to contend with the fact that the cost of maintaining old physical structures rises in real terms as the fabric approaches the end of its useful economic life. Investment by those individuals best able to afford it may not be considered worthwhile if it adds little to the marketable value of property – which in an area of relatively depressed prices and slack demand from all but lower income groups is liable to be the case. Others may prefer to withhold investment for the purposes of saving, either for repatriation or reunion with families in the case of immigrants or, more especially in the case of economically active whites, for moving out of the area.

A falling-off in personal investment, growing obsolescence of the housing stock, a run-down of the general physical environment, a worsening social environment and public image, and a drop in collective spending power (exacerbated by an overall decrease in population) will all tend to discourage private business investment in shopping, entertainment and other facilities, even though individual traders and entrepreneurs, from second-hand dealers to providers of specialist goods and services to cultural minorities, will find particular opportunities within the general pattern of decline. Industrialists, especially the smaller operator, may also be discouraged from reinvesting in noise or pollution control and in the maintenance of sites, particularly if they feel property is likely to be vandalised. Firms may also be deterred from reoccupying sites and premises vacated as a result of technological obsolescence and business cycle forces – themes we shall return to in the next chapter.

Lower socio-economic status, erosion of the area's economic base, an increase in the number of households in need and an intensification of environmental problems in turn place additional burdens on the public sector, whether in rebates and allowances, personal social services, community support, environmental care or renewal programmes, at a time when real income from rates will almost certainly be in decline. In a situation of generally rising expectations and competing demands on scarce resources the public sector will be hard-pressed to maintain an adequate level of provision, even if there is formal commitment to positive discrimination and redistribution on the basis of need. Any reduction (actual or perceived) in public facilities and services, compounding the effects of private sector investment decisions, must in its turn affect residents' morale, further diminishing their own propensity to invest money, time and effort in the area's future. And so a downward spiral is set in motion.

In assessing the effects of investment flows, however, it is important not to consider one area or small collection of neighbourhoods in isolation. Investment in the improvement of the housing, physical environment, facilities and services of one area may, if it raises the costs of living there or moving there, simply shift the problem of accommodating deprived households into other areas. Similarly, the withholding of maintenance and improvement investment may bring the relative costs of moving into and living in an area (such as the central and eastern parts of Small Heath) within the purchasing power of households who otherwise could not have afforded it. As long as large numbers of people remain in economic hardship and are forced to fend for themselves in the market for housing and other social goods, then they have to live somewhere. Usually that is in those areas which have always been or have become undesirable to people with greater power of choice. For many residents Small Heath today is a 'problem area'; for many others it is an area of opportunity, albeit limited opportunity by the standards of society as a whole.

A brief prognosis

There are fairly clear pointers in the patterns and trends we have been examining in the past two chapters as to what might happen to Small Heath in the near future unless there are further new initiatives to consolidate the positive effects of recent intervention, compensate for its negative aspects, and extend the scope of inner area strategy across the whole field of policy.

In the first place, the single class structure of the population will be perpetuated and is in fact likely to intensify, though there will be a locational shift within the area of the very worst off groups as a result of the redevelopment process. Per capital incomes and spending power will most probably decline further in real terms; aggregate spending in the west of the area will, however, rise as construction of the new council estate approaches completion.

The local supply of jobs in manufacturing will continue to fall in relation to the number of job seekers, so that economically active residents will be forced to look further afield for suitable employment. Unemployment among the low skilled and those with particular types of skill (eg, metal working) is almost certain to remain at high levels, even if there is an investment-led recovery in the West Midlands and Birmingham economies generally.

Once the current phase of redevelopment is complete there will be a fairly sharp polarisation of housing: a larger public sector, supplemented by a small but growing quasi-public sector in the hands of housing associations etc; and a diminishing sector of private housing, almost all of it for owner-occupation (though with some rented accommodation provided by resident landlords), which will cater especially for immigrant households and other lower income groups who by compulsion of choice are excluded from council accommodation. If competition for the diminishing stock of cheaper private housing increases – as is quite likely – then prices may be forced up as far as the market will bear, thus reducing its value-for-money to new purchasers and tenants. Overcrowding and sharing too may rise in the zones of private housing.

Pressure on housing stock will also tend to increase as a consequence of the present age-structure and household composition of the population, given the high proportion of present residents in the main child-bearing years, the already large number of very young children (who will not be leaving their parental homes for another 10 to 20 years), the reunion of immigrant families,[1] and the tendency for newcomers to consist of young persons and families with children. Any such pressure will be aggravated by public policies and programmes designed to reduce occupancy rates and enforce minimum housing standards. The present deep economic recession will have compounded the underlying trend towards a gradual blocking of opportunities for outward migration to those lower income white households who might otherwise have chosen to move.

---

1. Roughly 40 per cent of married Asian men were still separated from their wives in early 1974. Over half of Asians had definite plans to bring over further members of their families, though subsequent rises in unemployment may have compelled many to change their plans.

The proportion of ethnic and cultural minorities will continue to rise in neighbourhoods which consist predominantly of private housing. In the western part, redeveloped almost exclusively as council housing, their overall numbers will fall compared with the situation before clearance, though their representation among council tenants will go up. In the short term, increased concentration must enhance the risk of social tensions and conflict, particularly if competition becomes more acute over jobs and homes and minority groups are subject (or feel themselves subject) to greater discrimination over access to scarce opportunities. The persistence of tensions and conflict into the longer term will depend to a great extent on the speed of assimilation of minority groups – especially the second generation – and on the scale and scope of community relations initiatives. The formation of virtually exclusive immigrant communities, which appears close to realisation in small pockets of Small Heath, would tend to shift the focus of tensions from within to between neighbourhoods.

Public capital investment in new housing and environmental improvements must clearly lead to more attractive surroundings in parts of the area affected. Furthermore, people's perceptions of the general environment of Small Heath as a place to live may be positively influenced by the completion of current redevelopment and an end to massive blight and dereliction. Such improvements are unlikely, however, by themselves to have any great effect on voluntary house improvement and maintenance or on selective migration. If they did, this might well prove to the disadvantage of poorer residents who could end up competing for an ever-decreasing share of urban space.

Completion of redevelopment and the consolidation of minority sub-communities, now establishing themselves with the support of a range of specialist commercial undertakings and cultural facilities, will combine to slow down the overall rate of outward migration. The resultant stabilisation of population movement, if there were jobs within reasonable transport access, could lead to greater community stability and thus increased potential for community organisation and development; on the other hand, ethnic and housing tenure polarization, particularly in a situation of economic insecurity, are potentially divisive in threatening a fragmentation of neighbourhood identities and interests.

*

In later chapters we shall be presenting our views on the kind of strategy approaches that would improve the chances of tackling the problems of areas like Small Heath while conserving their positive functions and building on what opportunities they do already afford to particular groups of people. Before doing so, however, we shall enlarge upon our understanding of the present situation in inner areas, first by examining more fully the underlying forces which have produced that situation, then by looking at the potential inherent in agencies of urban government (including the communities of inner areas themselves) for effecting the kind of intervention we hold to be necessary.

It's a very bad place to get jobs. All the factories are closing. It's nearly all factory work and they're all closing down.

Of course there's always been a certain amount of unemployment, but it's got worse recently because there was so many of the old buildings pulled down and the old small firms and that packed in.

Circumstances of Families

3 Analysing the causes

In the last chapter we discussed the symptoms of inner area problems in terms of interactions between, on the one hand, spatial concentrations of households and individuals with various personal deprivations and, on the other, collective deprivations experienced to a greater or lesser extent by all residents. We now turn to their causes, which are just as complex. At the root of them, however, is the unequal distribution of society's resources between different social groups, between individuals within those groups and between different geographical areas.

The distribution of resources and the opportunities they provide is not fixed by conscious political choice. Indeed, the degree of inequality is widely held to be unacceptable. It persists in spite of political choice, despite a long history of welfare, tax and planning legislation, public investment programmes, social ownership initiatives and other attempts to deal with it. Hence the institution of Educational Priority Areas, Community Development Projects, Inner Area Studies, Comprehensive Community Programmes and so forth in a search for new approaches.

Other mechanisms limit such political will as may exist: the (much modified) 'laws' of the market place and their spatial expression in urban structure and change; cultural and technological forces; the nature of decision-making processes; the state of public consciousness; the conflict of interests between different groups in society; the differential access of groups to power and influence. Access in turn is in part determined by the resources – money, physical assets, skills, information – which different groups already possess. The question should also be posed whether the political will itself is sufficient, in the face of competing priorities, pressures and constraints.

This study is particularly concerned with the environment of inner areas. But since the nature of that environment is associated with the social characteristics of the population who live there, something must be said too about the origins of those social characteristics. We must try to assess the validity of possible explanations in terms of low personal achievement, deficiencies in collective opportunities and patterns of inward and outward migration. Without such an assessment we shall not be able to distinguish between 'solutions' which are marginal in effect and those which are more radical in that they get to the root of the problems.

Personal achievement

Personal achievement as measured by earned income or occupational status is partly the product of individual ability, effort and character; but it can be constrained by lack of available opportunities, by poor access to those opportunities, and by other disadvantages with which the individual may start life. To provide a background to our discussion we briefly mention below some research findings on different aspects of personal development and achievement.

Background, education and economic success

The National Children's Bureau report *Born to Fail*[1] defined children at age 11 as 'socially disadvantaged' if they came from a low-income, single parent or large family and lived in housing without a hot water supply or at a density of over 1.5 ppr. These children were found to be more likely than other children of the same age to have been born prematurely or be under normal weight, to be physically under-developed, to be subject to prolonged bed-wetting, to have been taken into care, to be frequently absent from school on account of sickness or accidents, to have a hearing impediment or speech defect, to be 'educationally subnormal', or to be from a home background with a history of mental health or crime/delinquency problems.

We have already pointed to the importance of home and neighbourhood backgrounds as determinants of educational attainment. It should also be stressed that educational attainment is only moderately associated with intelligence as measured by standard test scores. Moreover, neither IQ nor educational attainment are in themselves very reliable pointers to economic success. The work of Jencks and others referred to previously – mostly based, it is true, on American data – shows for example that just staying on at school predicts occupational status much better than test scores do and predicts incomes at least as well. They conclude that pupils who stay on exhibit attitudes and personality traits which make them more attractive to employers.

The General Household Survey (GHS), 1973, seems to confirm Jencks' assertion that socio-economic origins influence the amount of schooling; certainly, children from homes of manual workers were much less likely to stay on beyond the minimum school leaving age. The difference could not be due simply to different levels of intelligence or genetic endowment. It is worth recalling that the Robbins report on Higher Education (1963) showed that 34 per cent of middle-class children with test scores of between 115 and 129 entered full-time higher education compared with only 15 per cent of those from manual working-class backgrounds. Even so, Jencks' results indicate that family background, test scores and educational attainment together account for only about half the variation in men's occupational statuses and still less of the variation in their incomes. Although people with high IQ scores and high educational attainment generally earn more, the inequalities in income among high scorers or attainers are not so very different from inequalities among the working population as a whole.

We would contend that Small Heath residents, if they are black or have the 'wrong' accent or simply because they come from Small Heath, will have unequal chances in their quest for jobs and earnings even though their IQ or even their educational

1. Wedge & Prosser, Arrow Books, 1973.

credentials may be as good as their white, middle class or suburban competitors'. The one main exception would seem to be holders of industrial apprenticeships. SCPR evidence suggests that men with industrial apprenticeships earned substantially more than other male full-time workers and significantly more than skilled workers without such qualifications.

Even if the educational attainment of large numbers of disadvantaged citizens could somehow be raised immediately, there is nothing to suggest this would have any great effect on the degree of inequality in economic rewards. It might help to ensure that disadvantages were less concentrated in certain areas and within vulnerable groups strongly represented in those areas. But, unless substantial changes also took place in the scope of opportunities available and the distribution of rewards, we should still be left with the basic problems of low pay, unemployment, job insecurity and (for very many) poor conditions of work: X would simply have taken the place of Y in the queue. Indeed, the general tendency appears to be for entrance qualifications to rise for what are essentially the same jobs.

Family life cycle and the cycle of deprivation

The structure of economic inequality is such that for many households the price of anything better than the environment of inner areas is simply beyond their means. The effects of economic inequality fall most heavily on households at particular stages of the 'family life cycle': with young children, in retirement, or more exceptionally as a result of divorce, separation or early widowhood.

The SCPR survey demonstrates that in early 1974 per capita incomes were lowest in pensioner households and in large families with children. Counting the head of household as 1.0 consumer unit, each other adult as 0.7 units and each child as 0.5 units, the average per capita gross household income of large families with children was about £11 per week and that of pensioner households about £14 per week. For small families the corresponding figure was over £15 and for large adult families around £18. Adult singles and couples below pensionable age enjoyed the highest per capita incomes, between £26 and £27, although their comparative advantage would have been less after tax. Not only did large families with children have more mouths to feed, the housewife was also less likely to be able to work than in other families: only 27 per cent in fact did, compared with 31 per cent in large adult families, 49 per cent in small families and 64 per cent in two-person non-pensioner households.

The family life cycle offers only a partial explanation of economic hardship. We have already seen, in Chapter 2, how few households appeared to be in poverty primarily because of the size of their family. It was usually some other circumstance – unemployment, loss of the principal wage-earner, low pay – which tipped the balance. Similarly, the evidence indicates that the retired poor were as a rule in that position because of their previous employment history which had given them little opportunity to save or acquire private pension rights, so that they became dependent in retirement on state benefits alone. The tax and benefits systems are designed to compensate for the effects of the family life cycle within groups who are already economically disadvantaged. And to some extent, of course, they do. But they leave largely untouched the roots of that disadvantage which lie essentially in the low rewards accorded to those who fulfill the lowest status occupations. Although all societies exhibit in practice their particular forms of stratification and differential reward, we would argue (on the evidence of Small Heath alone, which is by no means among the worst deprived areas in the country) that the quality of life experienced by those on the lowest incomes must be considered intolerable by the standards of society as a whole.

Let us now look at changes over time. It would be incorrect to imply that the degree of structural disadvantage in British society necessarily creates a 'cycle of deprivation' that perpetuates inequalities in the distribution of incomes, wealth, political power and other social goods from generation to generation within the same families. Indeed, the surprising fact is perhaps that so many disadvantaged individuals do succeed in breaking the cycle. For example, 1 in 7 of the disadvantaged group of children surveyed in the NCB report cited earlier performed better on a reading test than half the ordinary group, even though on average the disadvantaged group were found to be $3\frac{1}{2}$ years behind ordinary children on their reading scores. Likewise, although GHS data show that persons aged 16–49 whose father was a professional, employer or manager were twice as likely to be students at the time of the survey (1973) than those whose father was a manual worker, over $8\frac{1}{2}$ per cent of the latter were nevertheless full-time or part-time students. Again, although 70 per cent of men in full-time employment with a degree or equivalent earned over £2,500 pa compared with only 10 per cent of those with no qualifications, this still means that 1 in 10 without any form of educational credentials earned more than 30 per cent of graduates.

These national figures are borne out by our own findings. In the SCPR survey residents were asked about the occupations of children who had left home. A comparison of the social class of children who moved with the social class of the parents indicates considerable upward mobility (Table 10), though it must be borne in mind that the SEG of parents is usually determined by the father's occupation and men are much less likely than women to be employed in (low grade) non-manual jobs. More detailed analysis shows that this upward mobility among children is spread among all groups of manual workers. An understanding of the problems of

Table 10 Socio-economic group of children who have left home compared with that of their parents

	SEG of children (No.=201) %	SEG of parents (No.=201) %
Professional/managerial	11	2
Non-manual	34	11
Skilled manual	38	46
Semi-skilled	15	31
Unskilled	1	9
	100	100

Source: SCPR Survey, 1974.

inner areas has therefore to include the realisation that there is a fair amount of social mobility, but that upward mobility is being balanced by the appearance of new economically or otherwise disadvantaged households.

National evidence suggests that the relative scale of disadvantage overall does not appear to be diminishing by very much. For instance, Trinder[1] shows that between 1949/50 and 1969/70 the top 40 per cent slightly increased their share of total pre-tax income vis-a-vis the bottom 30 per cent. Department of Employment statistics demonstrate that the earnings of the lowest decile of male manual workers also declined significantly between the early 60s and 1973 relative to average earnings and in fact were slightly lower at the latter date proportionately than when statistics were first collected in 1886. Since 1973 there has been some relative improvement in the wages of the lower-paid generally but at a time when prices too have been rapidly rising and the real standard of living of many has actually fallen. It seems that in British society coloured immigrants have filled many of the jobs vacated by 'socially mobile' working class whites. However, the ranks of the disadvantaged have scarcely dwindled overall, what redistribution there has been occurring mainly between the top and the middle. Given the social mobility that undoubtedly does exist, one must therefore seek explanations for the concentrations of disadvantaged households in inner areas in the pattern of inward and outward migration.

Inward and outward migration

Migration into and out of Small Heath has taken place on a scale sufficient to influence the social characteristics of the area significantly. Some 18 per cent of households in Small Heath have been at their present address for less than 2 years compared with 15 per cent for Great Britain, and 56 per cent of these recent arrivals have moved into as distinct from within Small Heath. Given Small Heath's social class composition, a figure lower than the national average would have been expected, since lower socio-economic groups normally move less frequently than higher ones. The level of mobility is not explained simply by the greater proportion of rented furnished property in Small Heath, but is associated in other ways with housing factors: people seriously thinking of moving quote housing and environmental reasons (rather than personal and work reasons) to a greater extent than is the case nationally.

In-migration

Heads of households resident in Small Heath less than two years are much younger than is the case nationally. As Table 11 shows, hardly any recently moved heads of households in Small Heath were over 65 and few were over 45. This young age

1. Chris Trinder: *The Personal Distribution of Income and Wealth*, University of Essex, 1974, quoted also in *Inequality*, Transport & General Workers Union, Spokesman Books, 1976, which presents evidence of a similar pattern in post-tax incomes. Data on 'final incomes' (ie, adjusted for all taxes and benefits) given in *Report No. 1 of the Royal Commission on the Distribution of Income and Wealth* show only a very marginal improvement in the position of the bottom 30 per cent compared with the top 40 per cent between 1961–63 and 1971–73.

Table 11 Age of heads of households

| | At present address less than 2 years | | All households | |
	Small Heath (No. =161) %	Great Britain (No. =1,634) %	Small Heath (No. =854) %	Great Britain (No. =11,558) %
Up to 24	21	21	6	4
25 – 44	62	49	38	34
45 – 64	15	20	36	37
65+	2	10	20	25
	100	100	100	100

Source: SCPR Survey, 1974, and GHS, 1973.

pattern is reflected in the types of household moving into Small Heath: those resident at their present address less than two years are predominantly newly marrieds and small or large families with children, with pensioner households and large adult families almost absent (Table 12).

Table 12 Household type by length of residence

	Less than 2 years (No. =161) %	2 – 5 years (No. =161) %	5 – 10 years (No. =130) %	10 years or more (No. =391) %
Single people and couples under 60	41	23	14	20
Single people and couples over 60	3	8	8	30
Small families	24	29	24	22
Large families with children	27	25	37	12
Large adult families	5	14	18	17
	100	100	100	100

Source: SCPR Survey, 1974.

If we look at those resident between 2 and 5 years and then between 5 and 10 years, we see the younger single people and couples decreasing and adult families increasing in numbers.

Household incomes supporting the family commitments of new arrivals are no higher than among longer-established residents, if we exclude pensioner

Table 13 Non-pensioner households by socio-economic group of household head and length of residence

	Less than 10 years (No. =424) %	More than 10 years (No. =240) %
Non-manual	7	18
Skilled manual	42	47
Semi-skilled and unskilled	51	35
	100	100

Source: SCPR Survey, 1974.

households. Indeed, the level of skills and socio-economic groupings are significantly lower among recent arrivals (Table 13). The educational attainment of recent in-movers is also lower than one would expect from their young age distribution. The pattern of in-movement to Small Heath has, then, contributed to the concentration of disadvantaged households by adding to the numbers of households with family commitments (especially large families) and people with poor educational attainment and low socio-economic status.

Out-movement

The pattern of moves out of Small Heath is harder to analyse since we only have data on moving intentions as distinct from actual moves and we cannot distinguish between probable moves within them. However the SCPR survey shows that large families are less likely to be seriously thinking of moving than small families. There is some evidence that those large families seriously thinking of moving are more likely to find difficulty in leaving Small Heath than small families. In the first place, fewer large families had actually found a place to move to (6 per cent as against 22 per cent of small families) and in the second, while large families moving within Small Heath outnumber small families, small families seriously thinking of moving outnumber large families. There is also some evidence that people choosing to leave Small Heath are likely to be higher income groups. Among those seriously thinking of moving 40 per cent of the households with incomes over £40 a week gave wanting to live in a better area as their reason, compared with only 21 per cent of the under £15 group who were more likely to be forced to move as a result of redevelopment. Again more of the higher income group seriously thinking of moving had actually found somewhere than was the case with the lower income group.

Another aspect of the selective nature of out-movement is what happens to children from Small Heath when they leave home. We have already pointed to the upward social mobility of children leaving home, and can now consider whether children have a high propensity to move out of Small Heath, or whether, among children moving out, the higher social classes are disproportionately represented. In fact, children seem not only to have upward social mobility but outward geographical mobility. Of 454 children for whom we have SCPR survey data only 10 per cent moved from their parents' home to another address in Small Heath. This appears to be a long established pattern: few people have relatives living near, and there is only a small correlation between having relatives living near and length of residence in the area. Had more children remained to live in Small Heath, the area's social class composition would now be more balanced. There appears to be very little tendency for those who have stayed behind to be less skilled workers. But if we look instead at the numbers remaining in Birmingham, rather than Small Heath alone, a more pronounced pattern of selective mobility is clear. Sixty-two per cent of children moving away who were economically active had remained in Birmingham. In the case of manual workers the proportions were 69 per cent and 70 per cent for skilled and less skilled respectively. For junior and intermediate non-manual workers the figure was 57 per cent and for professional and managerial workers as low as 35 per cent.

Gordon King

I was in rooms in Balsall Heath and I was moved out of there by the landlord. The council told me because I had six children in six years I had to take this house, so I had to take it.

I tried to sell my house some time ago. The agent had to fill in the form whether the property would depreciate in value or rise and he had to fill in depreciate.

SCPR Exploratory Study

These figures do not therefore demonstrate a selective migration (in terms of social class) of children out of Small Heath. There is a tendency for children to move out in general. What the evidence does point to is selective migration out of Birmingham and, it can be suspected, within Birmingham a selective migration out of the inner and middle ring of housing.

The settlement of New Commonwealth immigrants

To sum up the argument so far, the pattern of inward and outward migration has contributed to concentrations of relatively worse off households in Small Heath through the inward movement of large families with young heads and of low income households, and an outward movement of children leaving home and higher income households. We must now look at how immigrants into the United Kingdom fit into this picture. According to SCPR nearly one quarter of the adult population of Small Heath was born in the New Commonwealth. They comprised 65 per cent of all adults born outside the UK. Even though the arrival of New Commonwealth immigrants is a key factor in the process by which relatively worse off households have come to be concentrated in Small Heath, it (and indeed immigration in general) is not the only factor. In early 1974 New Commonwealth immigrants accounted for only 38 per cent of households moving to their present address over the previous 10 years and little more (42 per cent) of those who had moved in the previous 2 years. Even when we take all adults moving into Small Heath (whether to their present or previous address) during the previous 10 years, the proportion of those born in the New Commonwealth does not rise above 46 per cent. As many as 41 per cent (virtually all white) were born in the UK.

In respect of large families with children, young single people and young couples the numbers of New Commonwealth and white households moving into Small Heath appear to have been similar. The higher total number of white households moving in (about 4 in 5 of whose heads were UK born) is accounted for by small families. The concentration of New Commonwealth immigrant households has in fact come about as much by the pattern of out-movement as that of in-movement. Once in Small Heath, New Commonwealth households appear rather more likely to make their next move within Small Heath than white households. They accounted for 43 per cent of all households who had moved to their present address from within Small Heath over the 10 years to early 1974. Since fewer than one New Commonwealth household could be found for every 7 white households seriously thinking of moving, they are clearly much less likely to move out of Small Heath.

Collective opportunities

We have shown how many of the present social characteristics of Small Heath have come about by a process of selective inward and outward movement of households and individuals rather than by a cycle of deprivation within families. We have not explained, though, the underlying causes of the migration patterns that we have identified, nor have we considered the causes of the collective deprivations experienced to a greater or lesser extent by all residents. These two subjects are related: while there is no simple chain of cause and effect, the collective opportunities available in an area clearly influence the inward and outward movements of people.

The first obvious thing to be said about inner areas is that they are old. But not only old; they were constructed in response to the particular requirements of nineteenth and early twentieth century industrial expansion. Consequently they reflect the technology, economic constraints and social values of those times. As technology, economic criteria and social values have changed, they have become increasingly obsolete, the burden of reinvestment falling progressively upon the public sector. We have described these areas as playing increasingly 'residual' functions in the economic and social life of the city and argued that they tend to house those disadvantaged groups for whom there is little, if any, real alternative choice.

Now we shall look at what we hold to be key technological, economic and social forces that have combined to help shape the inner area environment of today.

Technological change and the economics of industrial location

Technological development has affected the functions of inner areas as an industrial base in two principal ways. First, changes in modes of communications have greatly reduced the traditional advantages to industry and bulk distribution of inner city locations. Second, changes in industrial processes and product life-cycles have hit at the viability of firms already in the inner city. The combination of both types of change with other economic considerations has deterred potential new investors from moving in to replace firms moving out or closing.

As we noted in Chapter 1, nineteenth century factories and warehouses were sited close to rail and canal links. It was the development of these technologies of mass transportation plus the telegraph (for communication of messages) which made possible the concentration of production and materials handling in the new urban centres that grew rapidly from about the third decade. At that time movement within the city continued to be by horse-power or on foot. Workers, who did not have access to carriages, had to be accommodated close to their work-place. The result of rapid industrial expansion was therefore extreme crowding of workshops, small factories, warehouses and dwellings on every available building space. Only when new production technologies, such as the substitution of steel for iron in metal-working, necessitated heavy capital outlays and larger plants and sites did industrial concerns (like BSA, Small Heath) start to move further out from central districts along major transport routes. New residential clusters then sprang up around the new factories. It was not until the advent of the tramway and the bicycle in the final decade of the century that the close association of home and work-place began to be broken.

In more recent years there has been a progressive shift to road haulage in the movement of goods, so that access to motorways rather than to rail or canal is now the most important communication factor in location decisions. Recent developments in rail transport, such as long-distance freightliner services, are also geared to feeder haulage by road. In parallel, journey to work patterns have also changed with the private car steadily gaining ground over travel on foot and by public transport, so that industrial location choices are less dependent on accessibility to residential areas and the provision of regular bus or commuter rail services. Finally, electronic transmission has increasingly replaced personal delivery and visits for conveying information, so that this factor is no longer a constraint on siting.

Changes in production technology have been even more important than changes in modes of communications which, all other things being equal, would widen the choice of locations rather than encourage the abandonment of inner area sites. There has been a growing tendency since inner area industrial sites were first developed for plant to replace labour in manufacturing. In most cases further mechanisation and automation have called for additional space which on the older sites, developed to the space requirements and plot densities of earlier technologies, has not normally been available. Consequently the newest and growth industries have tended to locate nearer the periphery of the city or on 'greenfields' sites. Those industries which remain in inner areas are relatively older, their products often in the advanced stages of their life-cycle. Premises tend to be old fashioned in layout and design, difficult or costly to adapt or convert, often without adequate car parking for workers or sufficient turning space for efficient loading and unloading of heavy goods vehicles. Examples of older generation premises in the Small Heath area are the multi-tiered factories occupied by Chrysler, Butlers and (until recently) NVT; in their time they employed the latest building and design techniques, the NVT plant being one of the first examples of a factory building using an exposed frame of reinforced concrete. Significantly, too, the three plants mentioned are all dependent on the fortunes of the motor vehicles industry, the longer-term viability of which in this country is now in serious doubt.

Not only is there selective siting by industry but also selective migration of industrial firms. Efficient firms, firms with ample capital resources and firms with good market prospects are the most likely to move out of inner area premises to new locations where they can modernise, innovate and expand; whereas less efficient units and those short of capital or confidence will tend to remain and eventually close or transfer production elsewhere as part of a corporate rationalisation programme, perhaps after a merger or acquisition. But whether a firm is able to increase productivity and output on site or is forced to cut back production through lack of demand, the effect is likely to be a loss of local jobs. Only an increase in productive industrial land-use or a change in plant occupancy to higher density uses would bring about a reversal of this trend. And where jobs are lost or production is curtailed it is the lower-skilled manual worker (who is more highly represented among local residents than managers, white-collar staff or supervisors) who gets laid off first or put on short-time.

Following closedowns or transfers of production, premises either remain unoccupied (and become derelict) or are taken over, after an interval, by new occupants. In the latter case they may be used more or less as they are (which is extremely unlikely), be converted, or the site may be redeveloped. Although it is possible to cite one or two instances from the recent past in Small Heath where a change of ownership has led eventually to increased employment, even in such cases there is usually a temporary loss of jobs and the new jobs provided may not be open to those previously employed there, either because they require different skills or because the new firm (which is perhaps making only a short radial move) brings much of its labour with it. Moreover, our own evidence and studies by Saltley CPD[1] indicate that, when premises or sites are reoccupied, the general trend is towards lower density manufacturing or warehousing uses, employing fewer workers and (in the case of warehousing) paying lower wages.

Inner area sites have become increasingly less desirable to large manufacturers making location decisions. Land plots are generally small, rarely big enough for efficient modern plants. Yet prices of land have been higher and are still about as high as those further out, even though they no longer reflect location value. Because of obsolete premises – uncomfortable to work in as well as technologically unsuitable – site redevelopment may be costly and take time, thus extending the period of dual site occupation in the case of firms relocating. Because of conflicting neighbouring uses, the costs of effluent disposal, noise and pollution control may be higher. The neighbourhood may have a poor physical environment and thus be unattractive to commuting workers, especially executive, administrative and secretarial staff. Employers may be deterred by the neighbourhood's image and fear vandalism, theft and even violence to personnel. It is also commonly assumed that labour productivity in older urban areas is low, that labour and staff turnovers are high (thus involving increased recruitment costs), and that more manhours are lost through sickness and other absence than in more salubrious locations. Certainly labour turnover in Small Heath is high: 23 per cent of adults had been in their job less than a year according to the SCPR survey, compared with 15 per cent nationally. The main reasons given for leaving their last job (redundancy, job finished, wanted better wages or better conditions) were all ones, however, which could be associated with the characteristics of firms rather than social factors.

But if the trend is for larger manufacturing concerns to leave inner areas voluntarily, at the same time many small firms are being forced to move or close down against their wishes, as a direct result of local planning policy. Small firms do not need large plots of land; they can operate virtually anywhere. What they seek first and foremost are low rent – albeit old – premises which they can use intensively. They have preferred inner area locations also because of an established local labour supply (particularly men with the more traditional metalworking and engineering skills) and because of supply and especially demand linkages. Small firms not only provide jobs; for some residents they provide a qualitatively different and preferred working experience, even though the premises may be uncomfortable and wages sometimes lower than, say, on large factory production lines. It is also often argued (eg, in the Bolton Committee report[2]) that small firms contribute to industrial innovation and diversity, as well as being more efficient than large concerns in certain sectors. Yet planning action to remove 'non-conforming uses' from residential areas, road building proposals and extensive redevelopment have combined to create

1. *Workers on the Scrap Heap*, 1975.
2. Cmnd. 4811, November 1971.

a climate of uncertainty and a set of financial circumstances (the costs of business disruption, moving, equipment replacement, bridging finance, higher rents) with which many small firms are unable to cope.

Regional economic influences

We may conclude then that, irrespective of the state of regional industrial prosperity, areas like Small Heath will be disproportionately worse off in terms of the distribution of output, profits and jobs. If the regional economy thrives, voluntary relocation may increase. If the regional economy is depressed, much of the more vulnerable inner area industry will be hard put to survive. Inner areas benefit neither from the underlying centrifugal forces which drive large manufacturers to seek extensive, relatively low cost space at or beyond the urban periphery nor from the underlying centripetal forces which lead to increased specialisation of the central districts in office and 'prestige' service sector activities. The general prosperity of the region does, however, have an impact on the employment experience of inner area residents. For the greater the overall provision of jobs, the greater will be their chances of competing for new jobs, even if that does mean longer journeys to work. The greater, too, will be the opportunities for promotion and upgrading within firms and, if there is a structural surplus of jobs at any particular skill level, for training and retraining. It is because of all this that the recent decline of the West Midlands within a national situation which itself gives rise to serious anxiety is of particular concern.

Government regional policy, by giving positive incentives to industry to invest in development and intermediate areas and in new towns, has probably had some negative effect on the number of industrial development applications in Birmingham and the West Midlands in general. Some potential employment growth within Birmingham has no doubt also been diverted as a result of the local authority's own policy, subsequently revoked, of discouraging the occupation of new industrial premises by firms new to the city. These policies could have discriminated in particular against new forms of manufacturing which are much needed to maintain a vigorous and diverse economic base. Together they are likely to have had a greater impact than IDC controls alone which between the mid 60s and their relaxation in 1972 appear, through refusals of applications, to have 'lost' the city fewer than 2,000 jobs (under 3 per cent of the total decrease in manufacturing employment), though this figure admittedly takes no account of firms deterred from making applications in the first place. Job 'loss' through IDC refusals in the West Midlands county as a whole over the same period was proportionately only two to three times higher.

Yet, whatever influence regional incentives and IDC or other planning controls have had on the performance of the Birmingham and West Midlands economies, several factors seem clear. Both public and private investments have been lagging behind those in most other regions; the region's industrial structure has become increasingly dependent on manufacturing sectors such as vehicles and metal goods which are no longer growth industries; large firms within these sectors achieve poor productivity and value-added ratios and find the return on their overseas

John Peverley

My children have already decided for themselves. Not one of them wants to live in Small Heath. When I told my daughter that when I go she can have my house, she said she wouldn't want it. My son has bought a house out of Small Heath. He wouldn't live in Small Heath, neither would they tell people they meet that they live in Small Heath.

SCPR Exploratory Study

investments more attractive. As a result of all these factors, new building has failed to keep pace with the rate of obsolescence.[1]

Changes in regional prosperity are closely bound up with change in the fortunes of the particular technologies, industries and firms found in the region. Decline in the West Midlands means that areas like Small Heath, formerly less disadvantaged than their counterparts in other parts of the country such as Merseyside and Clydeside whose major industries suffered earlier reversals, now face the prospect of unaccustomed economic hardship. Not only are Small Heath residents more likely to be employed directly in the vehicles industry (26 per cent of employed males in 1974) than Birmingham or West Midlands residents in general; they are also (or were, before recent closures and cutbacks) more likely to be employed in especially vulnerable sectors of that industry (cycles, motor cycles) and in especially vulnerable plants, eg, old first-generation car production factories whose output is being progressively transferred to newer, large sites elsewhere in the West Midlands or in other regions which may now be undergoing a phase of comparative recovery.

The problems, however, cannot be put down simply to the aggregate effects of various product life-cycles or vicissitudes in regional prosperity. Economic activity in inner areas is extremely vulnerable, though it may vary from region to region or within regions. It is the natural by-product of an economy whose survival is dependent on investment in more efficient and internationally competitive production. The pursuit of such an end produces differentials between areas in employment opportunities. The government has acknowledged this for many years; it has been compelled to intervene in the economy to an increasing extent to preserve and create jobs, secure provision of training, improve conditions of work, encourage investment, redress regional imbalances, stimulate changes in the mix of products and services, reduce environmental pollution, control the marketing of dangerous substances, and so forth. Significantly three West Midlands firms (British Leyland, NVT, Chrysler) receiving substantial government assistance under section 8 of the Industry Act 1972 or through the NEB have factories in Small Heath or within two miles of it. Increasingly the maintenance of employment in inner areas seems to involve diversion of industrial investment from alternatives that the 'market', the way it currently operates, finds more profitable.

Housing policy and social values

While deteriorating employment opportunities are an important part of our overall understanding of inner area problems, they do not offer an adequate account of the selective patterns of inward and outward migration. It is in fact housing opportunities rather than employment opportunities that explain much of the recent movement in and out of Small Heath. In the nineteenth century housing and industrial development in Birmingham were more closely interrelated than they are today, and it is relevant to consider how the present housing market has developed from that situation.

1. For details of trends see WMCC's *A Time for Action*, September 1974 and *A Time for Action: Policy Proposals*, 1975.

89

During the second half of the nineteenth century rapid industrial and population growth close to urban centres led to appalling conditions of squalor and overcrowding in which all kinds of pollution, disease and (at least in some quarters) criminality and vice were rife. As early as October 1875, Birmingham's Medical Officer of Health could report to the council that parts of the city contained dwellings in such a dilapidated state and so deprived of light and ventilation that they were 'unfit for human habitation' while other houses, left abandoned, had become 'receptacles for rubbish and filth' and constituted a 'danger of the gravest kind to the health and well-being of the whole town'. The same report quoted statistics to show that the death rate in St Mary's ward (at 26.82 per 100 habitants) was over twice that in Edgbaston[1] and referred also to the generally low condition of the population's health, 'indulgence in stimulants', 'debased morals', 'dirty habits', and the risk of epidemic.

The construction of courts and back-to-backs was a response to the 'economic' problem of housing people within walking distance of their work on high-value land but at rents they could afford. A Birmingham bye-law prevented building of this type after 1876, though 50 years later almost a fifth of the city's population still lived in these houses (by then in worse structural state) and it took a century to clear them. That state and municipal intervention were ultimately considered necessary could not, however, be put down solely to the rise of working-class organisations or the growth of liberal consciousness; it was due also to 'enlightened self-interest' on the part of employers (who needed a productive labour force) and the more affluent classes in general (who feared the spread of disease, criminality and dissent).

Suburban living, born of the desire to escape the industrial city's 'contagion', began with the wealthy. It became possible for middle income groups (including some skilled workers) to move out when advances in public transport and later the private motor car brought within reach what were formerly villages or small surrounding townships, and agricultural or unutilised land could be purchased cheaply and developed at low densities once the city, which between 1891 and 1911 annexed so much territory that it more than quintupled its acreage (see Figure 18), had carried out drainage and sewerage works. Thus the poorest citizens, who could not afford to move, continued to live in crowded conditions on the highest priced land at the heart of a fast-growing urban sprawl which was pushing the open fields further from their homes, while public spending indirectly subsidised the more spacious housing of the more affluent.

Although population in the central districts progressively fell and those workers whose wages permitted moved into new bye-law terraces or houses in older areas vacated by the socially mobile, vast numbers nevertheless remained trapped. Meanwhile, society's expectations continued to rise as the nation's wealth increased; technology made great leaps forward; basic schooling became universal and new norms and values were widely disseminated by the expanding mass media. By 1914

1. In 1973 the death rate in 5 central wards was 17.8 per 1,000, compared with 12.7 in 13 'middle ring' wards and 11.8 in the rest of the city. Over the 10–year period from 1964 the rate in central and middle wards taken together averaged over 40 per cent higher than in outer wards where the pensioner population was also significantly higher.

Figure 18
Birmingham:
Expansion
1836-1966

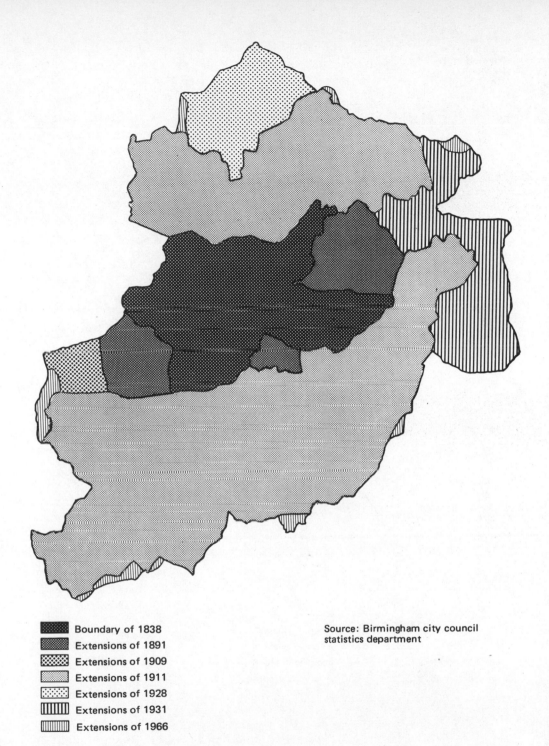

	Boundary of 1838
	Extensions of 1891
	Extensions of 1909
	Extensions of 1911
	Extensions of 1928
	Extensions of 1931
	Extensions of 1966

Source: Birmingham city council
statistics department

the Birmingham council was calling for plans for the ultimate reconstruction of the central built-up area. In 1920 road improvement lines were laid down and the task of assembling land as it came onto the market was begun. The same year saw the first municipal houses built on edge-of-town estates as the beginning of a drive to provide homes for new families, reduce overcrowding and build up a stock for rehousing slum dwellers. Nine years later a local act gave statutory authority to

Figure 19
Birmingham:
Redevelopment
and urban
renewal

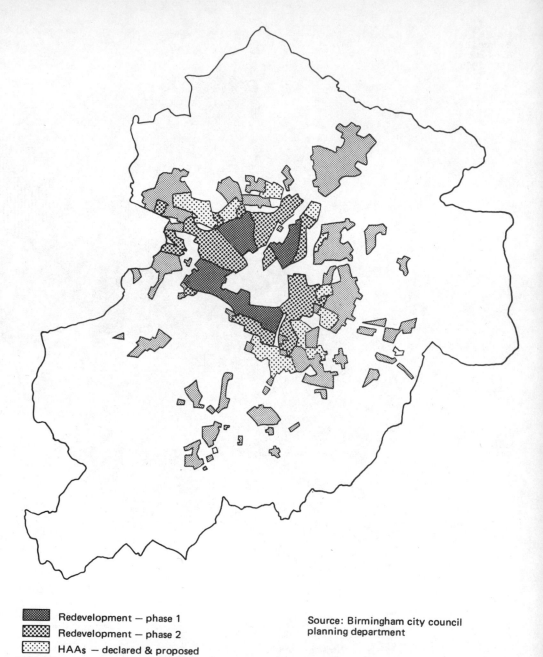

Redevelopment — phase 1
Redevelopment — phase 2
HAAs — declared & proposed
GIAs — declared & proposed

Source: Birmingham city council
planning department

detailed planning schemes for any area whether or not it was already substantially developed, thus anticipating the 1932 Town and Country Planning Act. The first slum clearance area was represented in 1931. Then in 1937 came the declaration of the city's first redevelopment area at Nechells Green.

But despite the large pre-war building programme and the commitment to raising housing standards for all citizens, 29,000 back-to-backs still remained at the end of of the war and getting on for 200,000 people lived in houses then considered unfit

92

for habitation. The city's response was to step up redevelopment. Using new powers under the 1944 Town and Country Planning Act to facilitate speedier slum-clearance in tandem with post-war reconstruction, 4 further comprehensive development areas were scheduled, bringing 32,000 houses into the programme. In the late 50s 15 new areas, including Saint Andrews, were designated, adding 30,000 more houses. The location of first and second phase redevelopment areas is shown in Figure 19, together with the coverage of Birmingham's subsequent urban renewal programme, discussed in later chapters.

By the beginning of 1974 nearly 60,000 houses had been demolished under the clearance programme and new homes provided by council building or overspill arrangements for almost 95,000 households. Between 1959 and 1971 the council waiting list fell from nearly 65,000 to just over 20,000, partly as a result of administrative pruning, though it has subsequently gone up again under pressure from increased applications and fewer relets. Some of the properties demolished were technically fit but the vast majority were not improvable to satisfactory standards, and considerations of social justice would have demanded their removal long before. The climate of the 50s and early 60s, with the rise of the welfare state and the 'affluent' consumer society, made further delay inconceivable. However, redevelopment came to present many problems. Progress was so slow that in the late 1940s the council was forced to switch the emphasis to repair work. The initial effect of delay, before clearance and also during clearance for those households still remaining, was a further decline in housing and environmental conditions as a result of blighting. Blighting, in turn, not only affected the physical environment but also produced uncertainty, insecurity and psychological stress. Time lags between clearance and (re)construction, in many cases unforeseeable, also tied up resources in idle land and buildings. Even when the programme did get into full swing, in the mid to late 60s, there were unfortunate side effects: disturbance of relationships between homes, schools and jobs, loss of leisure opportunities, and the disruption of social and commercial life which was felt as a real hardship by many individuals affected.

The effects of redevelopment on neighbouring areas

One of the serious side effects of redevelopment has been a blighting of adjoining areas. Expenditure on the repair and maintenance of houses has tended to be less in areas adjacent to the clearance zone. Table 14 shows how in Small Heath work on repairs has tended to increase progressively from the redevelopment area outwards. The difference between renewal areas, which constitute a kind of buffer zone, and GIAs becomes much more pronounced when respondents' opinions about the need for repairs are examined. For example, 45 per cent of household heads in renewal areas considered their house needed treatment for damp, 34 per cent that it required rewiring and 44 per cent that it could do with pointing. The corresponding proportions in west GIAs were 26 per cent, 24 per cent and 29 per cent.

To some extent the differences might have been explained by increasing owner occupation in the outer areas, although redevelopment appears to have had a blighting effect on sales of previously rented properties. Again, while the difference

Table 14 Repairs done in last 12 months

	Redevelopment area (No.=87)	Potential HAAs (renewal areas) (No.=116)	West GIAs (No.=188)	East GIAs (No.=332)
	%	%	%	%
Painting and decorating inside	39	57	62	69
Painting and decorating outside	12	40	40	44
Treatment for damp	1	5	3	4
Rewiring	4	6	8	9
Pointing	6	5	8	10

Source: SCPR Survey, 1974.

in repair and maintenance expenditure is associated with the ability of owners to pay for it, people's decisions on where to live are themselves influenced by their expectations as to how an area is going to change.

We are not out to question the end-product of slum clearance and redevelopment – the new environments of either the inner core or the urban fringe at places like Chelmsley Wood. Our concern is with the process itself, the means by which the end-product is arrived at. For redevelopment remains one of the strategic options for inner areas; and redevelopment has been an important factor in making Small Heath what it is today. By removing what was usually the cheapest available accommodation for sale or renting and by pre-empting many of the available council houses, rapid slum clearance increased housing demand in the worst remaining older areas. Those seeking accommodation in the worst remaining areas were those for whom council housing was either not available or unacceptable and included former residents of redevelopment areas, newly formed households and newcomers to the city.

The 'areas of secondary deprivation', as we termed them earlier, have become havens for successive waves of immigrants, especially of late from New Commonwealth countries. They initially came to Birmingham when the employment situation there was more attractive than in other cities such as Cardiff and Liverpool which had attracted earlier waves. But their location in Small Heath, the majority from overcrowded first stage settlement areas like Sparkbrook, was a consequence of the workings of the local housing market and the city's housing policies. During the early 60s roughly 4,500 New Commonwealth immigrants, mainly West Indian, were arriving in Birmingham each year. They had to seek accommodation in the low-priced sector of the private market. But that market was declining as housing in the older areas was compulsorily purchased and over 2,000 dwellings per year demolished.

In the late 60s about 3,500 New Commonwealth immigrants arrived annually, mainly Asians this time. Again they had to look for cheaper private housing, at the outset mainly to rent, later increasingly to buy. But not only was the net stock of lower-priced housing falling as a result of redevelopment, the effects of rent legislation

were leading to the progressive demise of the private rented sector – especially
unfurnished tenancies. Between 1961 and 1971 the stock of private rented dwellings,
more than half of which were located in 16 inner wards, fell by over 40 per cent or
roughly 25,000. Whilst the stock of owner-occupied dwellings rose by 20 per cent
or almost the same absolute number, most of this increase came in the 23 outer
wards which contained 70 per cent or so of the city's owner-occupied stock, usually
newer housing in the higher price ranges.

The influx of immigrants could not have been accommodated without a
corresponding exodus of other residents, particularly when account is taken of the
higher rate of new household formation. Net annual migration from the city, which
in the 50s averaged between 5,000 and 10,000, rose to over 15,000 in the early 60s
and to about 20,000 in the late 60s, a third or so going to overspill areas or new
council estates outside the city limits. Immigrant influx, at first permitted by this
out-migration, later tended also to reinforce it, as neighbourhoods which radically
changed their ethnic composition and became preferred locations for minority
cultural groups, because of the community support services and social organisation
that came gradually to be established, began to perform as specialised housing
markets with slack demand from the host population – which is the situation in parts
of Small Heath today. The changes for the 10 years to 1974 can be seen from
Table 15. Looking at those resident at their present address less than 10 years, white
heads of households account for less than half of new owner occupiers, but nearly
9 in 10 new council tenants. The effect of the virtual absence of New Commonwealth
immigrants on the large council estates means that their social impact on particular
neighbourhoods is much greater than their overall numbers would indicate
(Figure 20). The fact that the owner occupied sector is taking fewer UK born

Table 15 Tenure, length of residence and place of birth

	Base (=100%)	New Commonwealth born %	Born elsewhere (including UK) %
Owner occupied:			
less than 10 years at address	191	53	47
more than 10 years at address	215	13	87
Rented from council:			
less than 10 years at address	117	12	88
more than 10 years at address	79	—	100
Privately rented, unfurnished:			
less than 10 years at address	57	14	86
more than 10 years at address	81	1	99
Privately rented, furnished:			
less than 10 years at address	73	70	30
more than 10 years at address	12	33	67

Note: Percentages should be read horizontally.
Source: SCPR Survey, 1974.

Figure 20
Small Heath:
New
Commonwealth
born

% population born in new commonwealth:

Source: 1971 census

▓ 0 — 7.68% (> — 1.00 SD)

▓ 7.69% — 17.76% (< —1.00SD)

▓ 17.77% — 27.84% (< + 1.00SD)

▓ over 27.84%

in-movers helps to account for the falling proportion of skilled labour among UK born in-movers. The loss of skilled labour from Small Heath is not merely the result of an influx of less skilled immigrant workers, but also of the fact that UK born in-movers are less skilled than the existing labour force.

The influx of immigrants and other minority groups has been a further factor in the progressive break-up of old communities, already affected by changes in patterns of work, travel, leisure and family life. In most inner areas community ties have long since ceased to exert much countervailing influence on the tendency of the more economically successful and mobile people to gravitate towards the suburbs, exurbia or new towns. The consequence has been to intensify a single class structure while simultaneously dividing residents along ethnic and cultural lines.

*

The concentration of the worst off members of our society in collectively deprived areas such as Small Heath has, then, come about through selective inward and outward movement of people. The origin of collectively deprived areas lies in physical obsolescence and social and economic change, but selective migration adds to the downward spiral and produces further collective deprivations.

Collective employment opportunities have deteriorated not just because of the obsolescence of industrial premises and economic changes, but because the pattern of selective migration has made the labour force less attractive to employers. Housing has deteriorated not just because of age, but because selective in and out movements of people have reduced the capacity of residents to pay for the maintenance, let alone the improvement, of their homes. For those who could afford to spend more on their homes, an outward move offered better rewards in terms of improved social status and physical environment.

Central government and local authority intervention has progressively increased, and it is now difficult to discuss the nature and causes of inner area problems in isolation from housing, economic and other public policies. In the process inner area residents have become increasingly dependent on or affected by public service provision. We shall examine some of the problems arising from the relationship between people and government in turning now to a consideration of the potential for change inherent in existing agencies and in the present context of urban government. Later, in developing approaches to deal with the problems identified, we shall be concerned with assessing the effectiveness of policies followed in the past and present.

The tax people think you are out to diddle the country, Social Security thinks you are a layabout and Housing that you want cheap housing as your right . . . I hate going to those places. First time I went to the Social Security place I felt I was right at the bottom of the heap. People had said 'Don't answer back or they won't help you'. Mate, they are there to help people, or supposed to be.

Circumstances of Families

4 Assessing the potential for change

The failure of successive attempts at central and local government intervention to deal effectively with the problems of personal and collective deprivations which prevail in inner areas testifies to the fact that either the measures adopted have been inappropriate or the resources allocated in support of the measures have been inadequate. In the first case this would seem to point to a lack of understanding about the nature of the problems and therefore the ways in which they need to be tackled, in the second to an unwillingness (or inability) to make the solution or substantial alleviation of the problems a high enough political priority. It is our contention that both conclusions would be true. Moreover, the two are related. Insufficient political commitment inhibits better understanding, because it diverts attention and energies to other issues, both national and local. Lack of understanding inhibits greater commitment, because it leads many in government to believe that the problems of deprivation are marginal, affecting relatively small numbers of people in isolated pockets; or that, where the problems do exist, they are largely the fault of the deprived themselves; or that, however widespread the incidence of deprivations or blameless the victims, alleviation of the problems is entirely dependent on action taken to resolve other issues, like the stimulation and maintenance of economic growth.

Clearly, both lack of understanding and insufficient political commitment are substantial barriers to change. If therefore change is to be achieved, specific strategies must be designed to lower the barriers, to increase understanding and generate greater commitment. We shall return to this theme explicitly in Chapter 14. Meanwhile, much of what we shall propose in intervening chapters will derive from certain conclusions we draw, first, about how the process of urban government may obscure understanding of inner area problems and, second, about how the present context of urban government is simultaneously creating a situation of even greater urgency in inner areas and placing yet further constraints upon the necessary response to that situation. We regard obstacles to change inherent in the process and context of urban government as an integral part of the deprivation syndrome. In consequence it is pertinent to conclude this first part of our report and the response to objective one of our brief with a discussion of such issues. Our starting-point will be the relations between people and government in Small Heath. Next we shall attempt to crystallise some more general conclusions about the nature of urban government and how it works in practice, from the perspective of inner areas. Then we shall examine the economic and political background against which urban government is currently taking place and is likely to take place in the near future. Finally, in preparation for subsequent chapters, we shall concern ourselves with some basic principles of urban strategy, relating the exigencies of context to the need and scope for changes in process, as revealed by what we see to be major flaws in current approaches to intervention on behalf of inner areas and their residents.

People and government in Small Heath

Because of the ever increasing scale and scope of public intervention in its various forms the everyday lives of people in inner areas like Small Heath are more directly and powerfully influenced than most others by the impact of government decisions and actions. This is equally true whether we are talking about the state of their collective physical environment, the condition of their own homes, the care and education of their children, the security of their employment, or the money in their pockets. Over 9 in every 10 Small Heath households either rent from the local authority or, if they rent privately or own their home, live in an area which is subject to a council redevelopment or renewal programme. Home buyers are more likely than those in more affluent areas to be dependent on a council mortgage. Home owners seeking to improve their houses will require a government grant and possibly a council loan. Because earned incomes are generally low, unemployment high, jobs insecure (with lay-offs and short-time not uncommon), few will have acquired any substantial personal savings; very many will depend on a range of central government and local authority benefits, allowances and rebates. A high incidence of divorced and separated persons (especially women), unsupported mothers and single parent families, quite apart from the stresses and tensions of living in a poor environment and/or harsh economic circumstances, leads to a relatively large number of children in short or long term care or under supervision of the local authority and probation services. And, as a general rule: the tougher the circumstances, the greater the dependence. People in the appalling housing conditions of Bolton Road, living in great uncertainty, often without a source of earned income, may be reduced to virtual powerlessness in terms of the crucial decisions which govern their lives. Yet, despite its pervasive influence, government to most people remains remote; residents' relationships with its officers and representatives are usually uncomfortable and sometimes traumatic; and there is a great deal of suspicion, scepticism and even outright hostility among sizeable sections of the community towards the agencies on which people have come so heavily to depend.

The image of 'the council'

It is 'the council' which is generally perceived as the most immediate embodiment of government decisions and actions, particularly with regard to the unkeep of the collective environment. Even people who have 'paid their way', bought their own houses and pride themselves on their personal independence of government agencies may be very conscious of (and even quite obsessed about) the council's responsibility to 'do something' about the area. Attitudes towards the council, as a collective body rather than as represented by specific departments, officers or members, are therefore a good place to start our examination of relationships.

The SCPR survey showed that 46 per cent of residents found it 'very true' the council didn't tell people enough about what was going on in the district. This was $4\frac{1}{2}$ times the number who considered it 'not at all true'. On the Heybarnes estate the figure rose as high as 57 per cent. Although Heybarnes itself is not directly affected by present physical planning programmes, it is clear that residents are frustrated by their lack of information on the changes they see to be going on around them.

Even in the redevelopment and renewal areas, where residents had been exposed to notices, circulars, public meetings, local press coverage and suchlike, as many as 47 per cent (63 per cent if we include those finding the statement 'partly true') considered the information they had been given inadequate. Asians and newcomers too, amongst whom there was a large proportion of 'don't knows', tended to be negative in their responses when they were able to give an answer.

Nearly 6 in 10 heads of household claimed not to have heard of any plans affecting the district. Of those who did have some knowledge of plans 40 per cent lived in redevelopment or renewal areas. Nonetheless, 31 per cent of household heads in these areas still pleaded ignorance. In the redevelopment zone only 53 per cent knew of plans to demolish their own house; far fewer had any idea when they were likely to be rehoused. In renewal areas, despite the emphasis of policy on retention and improvement of properties, the over-riding impression of residents who claimed knowledge of plans was that houses were to be demolished. In Little Green (later declared an HAA) it subsequently took a great deal of intensive effort on the part of project team officers, councillors and the local residents association to overcome the confusion and restore a measure of confidence in the area's future. Some of the confusion which initially reigned and the antagonism to the council it provoked are reflected in the video film 'Time Decays' made by residents themselves with technical help from the Artist Placement Group project.

Heads of household who professed some knowledge of plans – and only a third of them seemed really confident of the accuracy of their information – tended generally to be pleased that something was being done. Those expressing themselves to be very or fairly happy with plans outnumbered those who were unhappy about them by almost 5 to 2. The ratio shrank in renewal areas to less than 3 to 2, most opposition being centred on the threat of demolition to respondents' own houses. It is interesting to note too that immigrants were considerably less happy than whites, with the numbers expressing satisfaction and dissatisfaction equally matched; 41 per cent of immigrants were unhappy about plans compared with only 19 per cent of whites. The attitude of immigrants, especially Asians, is doubtless conditioned not only by a negative reaction to the prospect of losing their own homes, often newly-acquired, but also by the fear of disruption to their close-knit communities. Their discontent was most marked in areas actually or rumoured to be subject to large-scale or selective clearance. In GIAs, where knowledge of plans was strongly associated with street improvements and the provision of rear access roads, reactions were generally much more positive.

It would obviously be wrong to imply that council plans were universally or even widely opposed. On the contrary, many people who had some knowledge of plans did apparently support them, even in the redevelopment zone which at the time of the survey was already very seriously blighted. However, the fact remains that, taking Small Heath as a whole, very few heads of household indeed (almost certainly less than 1 in 10 and possibly as low as 1 in 20) had heard about plans, were reasonably sure that what they had heard was correct and were firmly in favour of what they had heard. Yet this was in a situation where roughly 85 per cent of households lived in areas subject to some kind of area-specific redevelopment or improvement programme and 7 out of 10 lived in areas where programmes had already been initiated. A further point of significance is that only half the householders who had heard of plans seemed to have first acquired their knowledge directly from the council or one of its employees by visit, letter, notice or meeting. Over a quarter said they had picked up their information from friends and neighbours and a further 14 per cent cited newspapers as their source. The proportion claiming to have heard of plans through newspapers was roughly double this in renewal areas. It is quite possible that some respondents, in Little Green especially, were referring here to newsletters issued by the council's urban renewal project team. On the other hand, press coverage at the time had featured 'human interest' stories in the Little Green and St. Aidans areas. Although many residents had no doubt forgotten or simply ignored council communications, the evident implication is either that insufficient effort had been made to inform people adequately or that inappropriate media or channels of communication had been employed.

It is one thing to have a reasonably good idea what broad plans or intentions the council has for a particular district and even to approve of them; it is quite another to feel in touch with what is actually going on from day to day in committees and departments, to be aware of progress against plans and of important decisions which may change their timing or course, to feel confident that one's own case is being dealt with in the appropriate quarters. And it is only a short step from an awareness of not knowing enough about what is going on to the impression of being deliberately kept in the dark. The first may breed frustration, the second is more likely to give rise to deep feelings of resentment, indignation, bitterness.

Most conflict with the council that we have observed in Small Heath – and conflict which compels people to organise is just the tip of the iceberg of resentment – has had little to do with the declared objectives of plans themselves; concern has been rather with the manner of their execution (or non-execution), with the apparent inconsistency of certain decisions and actions with stated policy, and with the impact of decisions which were perceived to have been taken without due representation of community interests and without adequate warning to the parties affected. It was not because they opposed redevelopment that residents of the devastated Bolton Road/ Cooksey Road clearance area blockaded their street to gain publicity or marched on the Stratford Road Housing Centre to demand rehousing but because they felt forgotten, passed over, left to wait indefinitely on what seemed like a bureaucratic whim. Similar, if less dramatic, examples abound. Residents in Bordesley Green, Little Green and Victoria organise and agitate for faster action on urban renewal programmes. Parents, teachers and community workers protest about the proposal to bus Oakley School children three miles to Sheldon every day because the opening of the new community school has been delayed and their own premises are being transferred under an earlier agreement to the Roman Catholic school authorities. The Small Heath Community Federation campaigns for greater local involvement in the planning and management of the community school and calls for a reconsideration of form entry cuts which will mean the continued use of old inadequate buildings, sometimes a fair distance away, as annexes. The Federation attempts also to take up the concern of its affiliated organisations over the reduction of certain local services, including withdrawal of financial support for a number of BIAS initiatives, due to the council's particular interpretation of the exigencies of public expenditure control . . .

Closely related to the council's communication of information is its receptivity to information flowing in the opposite direction – feedback from community organisations, interest groups and individuals on their needs and aspirations and on the perceived outcome of council decisions and actions. Nearly half of all residents interviewed by SCPR had insufficient awareness of the workings of the council as a body or contact with its individual members and officers to be able to express an opinion as to whether the council listened to people's views or not. In the case of Asians the proportion of 'don't knows' rose to 70 per cent. Significantly, in those parts of Small Heath where contact is likely to have been most frequent – in the redevelopment zone and renewal areas – the negative response was highest: 26 per cent and 29 per cent respectively considered it 'not at all true' that the council was receptive compared with only 10 per cent in each instance who found it 'very true'. Even here 'don't knows' still accounted for 46 per cent and 43 per cent of answers. On the Heybarnes estate, where almost two-thirds of households were council tenants, the proportion of 'don't knows' fell to 37 per cent but negative responses outweighed positive replies 22 per cent to 16 per cent, the remainder being neutral 'partly true' answers.

Contacts with councillors and individual departments

Less than 30 per cent of all household heads (1 in 10 in the case of immigrants) knew where to contact their local councillor, though all councillors held or shared regular surgeries. We do not know how many of these had actually been in contact, nor how satisfied they were with the outcome of such contact. On the other hand, our Circumstances of Families interviews, though a much smaller and less representative sample, did give quite a strong impression that people in acute need were more at ease in approaching their local councillor or MP than they were in approaching officers of departments or 'organisations'. Residents who appealed as individuals directly to their elected representatives were generally pleased with the courtesy and consideration their request or enquiry received. We did, however, encounter some scepticism, especially among those living in the worst conditions, as to whether councillors carried enough weight or influence to help them, however much they might care.

It cannot be denied that from time to time quite serious friction has arisen between local councillors and either the Federation or its affiliated residents associations over opposition by the latter to various council acts (or failures to act) which they saw as detrimental to people in Small Heath. But it is probably more accurate to attribute the root of such friction to what councillors seemed to take as a challenge to their legitimate authority as elected representatives, or as an unreasonable attitude in face of real constraints, than to councillors' unwillingness to listen, failure to understand residents' perspectives or lack of sympathy with their priorities. In dealing with local organisations councillors are faced with conflicts of roles, which is not a problem with individual casework. This is an important point we shall come back to in the second part of the chapter.

To most people in Small Heath personal contact with the council means contact with officials appointed by particular departments. Even those who do come in touch with councillors are likely to have more frequent dealings with officers, whether they are acting in an individual capacity or in concert with others. Thus, three-quarters of household heads surveyed by SCPR knew how to contact the housing department. The proportion remained above half even in the case of immigrants, despite the fact that very few were or ever had been council tenants. Six in ten householders knew where to go for social services, more than half for the local health centre. As many as three-quarters of immigrant household heads knew the whereabouts of the social services department office. There may have been some confusion in the minds of certain respondents between social services and social security, which with the housing department was the agency most commonly resorted to among households in our Circumstances of Families sample, but it is likely that a substantial proportion of families have had dealings with at least one branch of social services at one time or another. In contrast, very few residents have had reason to come into contact with the planning department. Less than a quarter of householders claimed to know where it was.

Part of the reason for the high awareness of the housing department is to be attributed to the 'latent' demand for council housing. Apart from the 49 per cent of private tenants and 7 per cent of owner-occupiers either on the council waiting list or actively considering an application, there were a considerable number of other respondents in the private sector who had not applied because they felt they had no chance of obtaining a council house or flat rather than because they didn't want one; quite a few would probably have made enquiries. In addition, many house owners and private tenants may have contacted the housing department for advice on council mortgages, improvement grants, rent allowances, rate rebates or on other 'housing' matters, whether or not they are in fact the department's responsibility.

It is significant that Asians, especially those in private rented accommodation, have recently begun to join the waiting list in larger numbers. The SCPR survey showed that 11 per cent of immigrant household heads were on the waiting list in early 1974, with a further 16 per cent seriously considering an application. In the case of white household heads the proportions were respectively 30 per cent and 2 per cent, but most of these were council tenants already, awaiting rehousing from clearance areas or transfers to more suitable accommodation. The PEP national survey referred to earlier, carried out in mid to late 1974, indicated that both West Indian and Asian private tenants are now more likely to be on the council lists than white private tenants, though Pakistanis and Bangladeshis are still less likely to apply than other Asian groups. No doubt this reflects growing familiarity with the British housing market and a gradual change in attitudes due to the process of cultural assimilation, but it may also point to a real shrinkage in opportunities to buy. Whatever the reasons, more and more residents are coming in one way or another to depend on state housing provision and to come in contact with government housing officers.

Apart from rent collection, relations with Housing Department officers are mostly to do with rehousing or with requests for repairs or redecoration. Rehousing is a concern particularly among former private tenants and owner-occupiers living in redevelopment/clearance areas and among households allocated (because of rent arrears, behavioural problems, homelessness or some emergency) to short-life or other old council-acquired properties. The need for repairs, as our Circumstances of Families interviews and experience on the FSU 435 Centre project have shown, is a virtually permanent obsession with households in short-life housing maintained even officially only on a minimal 'patch and mend' basis; but evidence from SCPR and the Talfourd Street improvement project suggests that requests for, and disputes over, repairs are also rather more frequent on older purpose-built estates than they are in the private rented sector. According to SCPR, a third of Heybarnes council tenants had had disputes with their landlord (Housing Department), mostly over repairs or redecoration, in the two years prior to the SCPR interviews, compared with a fifth of private tenants.

Very few people seem to have positive attitudes towards the housing department. Furthermore, the greater the degree of a household's dependence, the more discontent, even embittered, its members appear to be. Among households interviewed in our Circumstances of Families survey the feeling was widespread that officers did not understand or even try to understand the predicament they were in. The housing department was frequently seen as an organisation where the right hand did not know what the left was doing. Respondents rarely felt that complaining or protesting would do them any good. Complaints were put aside or explained away, leading many to believe it was a waste of time even to open their mouths. Others were frightened to complain because of the immense power the department had to determine the conditions in which they lived, when they might be moved, and where to. Coupled with these feelings there was a strong sense of the arbitrariness and unfairness of bureaucratic decisions, which provoked not only resentment about the household's own treatment but jealousies between households on the grounds of queue-jumping or discrimination and tended therefore to undermine the potential for mutual support and collective action with the community.

Plainly, many council tenants suffer intense frustration over getting repairs done. People we interviewed in short-life properties had more often than not given up hope of succeeding, even though their houses might have very serious (and sometimes dangerous) structural defects. Elsewhere we found the problem to be not so much whether or not the work was ultimately done but the time that elapsed before it was done – a time which tenants claimed could run to months, years even. True, council tenants expected repairs to be carried out because they held them to be the council's responsibility, while private tenants had rather lower expectations of their landlords and would frequently do their own repairs or make their own alterations. Council tenants were therefore more likely to show impatience or anger when jobs were left undone. However, the fact remains that the nature of tenancy agreements and the operation of the public housing sector generally encourage such attitudes of dependency. Besides, vulnerable householders like pensioners living alone and unsupported mothers who would usually be unable to do their own repair work suffered as much frustration having to wait (even if they did not have to wait as long) as other tenants. Whether the demands made of the housing department are 'reasonable' or not, they are for a substantial number of tenants apparently not being met, even in cases where there may be overall satisfaction with the nature of the accommodation itself. What is more, our experience suggests that the department's rather poor image as a landlord is by no means confined to council tenants; the opinion is quite liable to be shared by owner-occupiers and, more especially, private tenants who may be already on the council waiting list and thus in a sense predisposed in their attitudes.

As a final slant on the issue of repairs and redecoration it is instructive to compare the attitudes of council tenants with those of owner-occupiers in our Circumstances of Families sample who, though they might have considerable difficulty 'making ends meet', tended to take pride in the fact they owned or were acquiring an asset of value and, rather than worry about the need for repairs and redecoration, frequently derived a good deal of positive satisfaction from carrying out work on their homes. It seemed that repairs, improvements and redecoration enhanced not so much the value of the house but the value (in terms of achievement and independence) they were able to place in themselves as persons.

Negative attitudes to the housing department (or other public agencies with similar power to shape everyday life experience) are bound to colour the way people feel about the council and even about government in general. They are likely to feed on the popular media image of government, especially local government, associated with waste, inefficiency, incompetence and misuse of public money. But more important still perhaps is the way people's relations with government bodies may make them feel about themselves. It is probably legitimate to conclude that any habit of passive acceptance, feeling of powerlessness, or loss of belief in the self as an agent of independent decision and choice must limit not only the individual's strength to face fresh challenges but also his sense of his own worth and even, by extension, of his 'fitness' to participate in political activity in pursuit of change. This is, of course, only one factor in the complex set of reasons why people in inner areas like Small Heath may appear to be politically apathetic. Nor does 'political' apathy (abstention from voting, joining a party or pressure group etc) necessarily exclude types of fairly spontaneous (and non-continuous) individual or collective action in pursuit of essentially 'personal' ends, as the Bolton Road blockade and march illustrate. These are issues we shall return to in the second part of the chapter, after consideration of some further evidence.

Dependence tends to mean stigma and stigma expresses itself in many subtle forms of humiliation. Those residents we interviewed who had no direct or regular dealings with government bodies were invariably glad they did not, regarding it as a matter of pride and self-congratulation. Unfortunately such feelings are not far from self-righteousness which, when projected outwards, so easily becomes disapproval of others who do not share their independence and who are liable to feel demeaned enough already in their own eyes. We do not mean by that to imply people are not helped by the agencies on which they depend. On the contrary, they may be both helped and grateful for that help, yet resent deeply the fact they need help and are forced by circumstances to seek it. This ambivalence is brought out most clearly in relations with social workers and especially with the social security system.

Gordon King

I rarely seem to get any satisfaction out of the system. You're only a person against a whole machine like . . . I never seem to get anywhere. They don't seem to understand.

Certainly they don't give much away, but we don't know if they *know* everything anyway. They could be in the dark, the whole of local governments, so I just take things as they come.

Circumstances of Families

Contact with social workers was not widespread among Circumstances of Families respondents but when it did occur it appeared, like that with probation officers for whom social workers might be mistaken by neighbours, to single people out as 'failures' or 'problems' and, whether or not the stigma was largely imagined, cut them off from the wider community, thus increasing still further their dependence. Social workers did not share quite the authoritarian image of probation workers, they were credited with meaning well, but they did not seem to enjoy their clients' confidence or provide them with the kind of support they wanted. Social services home helps, on the other hand, were very much appreciated, and not simply for their cleaning work. They seemed, however, to be provided only to people in the better (purpose-built) council housing. In contrast, attitudes to the community workers at the Family Service Unit 435 Centre were invariably positive. Practically everyone in the neighbourhood appeared to know the senior worker personally, often as a friend. The difference here was that the worker was available to all residents of the neighbourhood, without distinction; he could be turned to whenever needed, at residents' own initiative; he responded to their own concerns and aspirations, did not simply advise them what to do but was prepared to act vigorously on their behalf, as an advocate; he encouraged people to think about the concerns they had in common and tried (though with only limited success in this respect) to stimulate joint action; his independence of bureaucratic structures – not directly employed by the council – made him more easily accepted as 'one of us' rather than 'one of them'.

Experience of social security

Inevitably many people in Small Heath (unemployed, single parents, those on low incomes but with large families to keep, pensioners with no other source of income) are entitled to claim supplementary benefits. For most people we interviewed (other than pensioners) going to the 'social security' was an unpleasant, even degrading experience. Drawing benefits was like accepting charity. Some would resist claiming despite the fact they might be in extreme hardship. Unemployed men, in particular, were prone to suffer an acute sense of shame, feeling their role of supporting the family had been seriously undermined. Single parents, predominantly women, were less inhibited about claiming than unemployed men but frequently resented the form of questioning, sometimes of a very intimate nature, to which they were subjected. Even old people, though they might complain about the inadequacy of their pensions, to which they believed they were entitled by virtue of past 'contributions', would sometimes hesitate to apply for supplementary benefits out of pride because of some past rebuff.

While it is not possible to determine accurately the relative importance of the various reasons for failure to take up benefits, it was plainly not only lack of knowledge that deterred potential applicants. True, most people had only a limited sense of their entitlements, of how the system worked, or of the rationale behind individual decisions; but our evidence suggests that embarrassment, shame, fear of stigma and similar reasons were probably as much to blame for people not seeking further information as they were for them failing to apply when they knew or suspected they did qualify for payments. Attempts to clamp down on the much-publicised abuses of the social security system will almost certainly have the effect of deterring still more potential applicants.

Claimants' attitudes to social security personnel clearly depended to some extent on the particular officials they happened to see, though experience of different personalities led to a certain amount of confusion as to what were the best tactics for a claimant to employ. People seeking discretionary allowances seemed on the whole to believe you got more by being aggressive and persistent in your demands. It is a feature of the system, however, that claimants felt compelled to adopt particular strategies to avoid refusal. Another feature of the system of discretionary allowances – now granted to something like 40 per cent of claimants nationally – is that it leads both to feelings of unfairness, antagonisms and jealousies among claimants, and to resentment in the wider community. Quite a number of residents seemed to feel bitter that claimants could receive allowances for bedding, children's shoes and a host of other items, the range of which was no doubt enlarged by force of rumour, when they themselves put in a full week's work, tried to 'stand on their own two feet', and had very little more to show for it. Such feelings were divisive and, like the bickerings over rehousing decisions in the Bolton Road area, destructive of community spirit and morale.

The comparatively few Asians we interviewed who had had experience of the social security system expressed themselves to be well satisfied with their treatment, perhaps reflecting once again the general tendency of Asians to be rather more instrumental in their attitudes than other ethnic groups. The majority of Asians, however, seemed very conscious of criticism within the host population of immigrants taking advantage of welfare opportunities. They tended to view the claiming of benefits with distaste and to disapprove of those who did apply, fearing it would bring minority communities into disrepute. Whatever their wishes it appears certain nonetheless that high unemployment, job insecurity and the consequent difficulty of maintaining high mortgage interest and other financial commitments must currently be forcing many more to seek assistance.

The need for information and advice

Despite the limited state of knowledge about social security entitlements and other benefits, people as a rule did not feel in particular need of new or improved information services. Residents living near the 435 Centre knew they could get basic information on benefits if they wanted it. Fewer of our respondents had experience of Osbourne House, the local authority advice centre on Coventry Road, but those who did praised its services. Frequent mention was also made of the Citizens Advice Bureau, though the nearest branch is in the city centre. Even before local centres came into operation almost half of household heads, according to SCPR, considered they did not have any problems an advice centre could help them with. In the case of immigrants the proportion rose to nearly two-thirds. Our Circumstances of Families interviews confirmed that Asians tended to turn for advice to some respected or more experienced person within their own community. Single parents and young mothers with large families more frequently expressed the need to talk to someone in the same predicament as themselves, someone who really understood, rather than a professional advice giver. Old people living alone said they could do with more help and advice, though that reaction too may have sprung as much from a general feeling of loneliness and isolation as from a specific need for information.

Two-thirds of specific issues named by SCPR respondents who thought they would benefit from an advice centre concerned housing. A further 14 per cent of mentions were to do with planning matters, mainly urban renewal and redevelopment, again very much with a housing emphasis. Over 70 per cent of issues raised by council tenants, who professed most interest in advice services, regarded clearance schedules, rehousing or questions of house repairs and maintenance. Social security advice accounted for less than 10 per cent of all mentions, with little difference between the various sub-groups.

Records kept by both advice centres receiving BIAS grants show that in practice housing issues remain the chief single field of concern but that their predominance is less pronounced. In its first six months of full service operation[1] Osbourne House dealt with almost 1,700 inquiries (rising to close on 400 per month). Quite a number were of a general or casual nature, as might be expected with a centre which draws a substantial proportion of its users (roughly 40 per cent) from people who live outside Small Heath and happen to pass by while in the area for shopping and/or work; but of the 1,000 or so identified as requests for specific information or assistance 45 per cent were to do with housing and nearly a quarter with social security. At the 435 Centre, which served a particular small neighbourhood on a more intensive basis, 31 per cent of all 1,365 inquiries over a period of 21 months were specifically concerned with housing, 18 per cent with social security. In the last three months of that period (January to March 1976), during which the number of inquiries had risen to over 100 per month, many followed up by positive action, housing matters accounted for over half, social security for 12 per cent.

Even an average of 350 advice requests from local people handled each month by two small shop-front centres is in itself a not inconsiderable statistic, in an area of some 10,000 households. That figure, remember, is not counting requests put to councillors, MPs and direct to individual officers, or 'phoned in and put in writing to departments, or made at other advice bureaux in the city centre and nearer the place of work. If a substantial proportion of residents see no need of an advice centre, it is perhaps because they prefer alternative means of finding out what they want to know, through more informal channels, or because, having experienced frustration at the hands of one agency (in most cases, the housing department or DHSS), they are somewhat reluctant to take their problem to another, especially if it too represents formal authority. Again, it may be they believe information or advice will serve no great purpose: that the real problem lies in the intractability of the government agencies themselves, whose decisions the individual has little chance of influencing; or that government has neither the resources nor the power to do much more than it is doing already; or that their situation is beyond remedy. All

1. The period in question was October 1975 to March 1976, following the appointment of a full-time senior advice worker. For over a year prior to this the Small Heath Family Advice Centre (Social Services Department) had run a more restricted general advice service at Osbourne House in addition to its casework, community work and play-group activities.

this is not to deny that quite a large number of people in Small Heath do genuinely feel self-sufficient, in no need of help. In fact, our interviews tell us just how important such feelings are. We merely wish to point out there may be other reasons too for not appreciating the potential value of information and advice as instruments of change.

Participation in political and community activities

It is hard to escape the impression that, despite the immense influence which government decisions are coming to have on the everyday lives of more and more Small Heath residents, none but a very small minority see themselves as playing any active part in determining what those decisions shall be. The basic policy options that delimit their range of opportunity are taken to lie entirely outside their sphere of control or persuasion. What resident involvement there is in public programmes such as urban renewal, in which field Birmingham has probably gone further than most authorities in recent years to take account of residents' views, tends to be concerned primarily with means, that is, the way particular policy commitment is to be implemented. Energies are therefore diverted, as in the case of rehousing or social security applicants seeking advice and advocacy in their disputes over individual bureaucratic decisions, into getting the best deal available under existing policies. That is, of course, important and will help to reduce the level of individual hardship. But more fundamental change, of the kind that might materially affect the unequal distribution of social goods and opportunities between different groups and between different areas, is left to a political process in which very few participate. Government, in short, is by 'them'.

Membership of political parties in Small Heath is less than half the national average. The SCPR survey showed that only 3 per cent of adults belonged to a political party and two-thirds of these had not attended a party meeting in the previous twelve months.[1] Those who were members tended to be in the older age-groups (4 per cent of over 65s compared with 1 per cent of under 25s and 3 per cent in the middle age groups) indicating perhaps that even what membership there was had largely been left over from an earlier period when local parties were more active in inner areas.

Similarly, participation in municipal and parliamentary elections is low. In the past five municipal elections turnout in Small Heath and Sparkbrook wards has been consistently well below the city mean, which itself has only averaged about 33 per cent. Turnout figures, usually lower than in English county boroughs and cities generally, are no doubt depressed in Birmingham as a whole by the city elections office's policy of keeping as many names on the register as possible, a policy which will also tend to affect disproportionately turnout levels in areas of rapid population turnover. Even so, this could scarcely account for the fact that the poll in the two wards averaged under 30 per cent and in Small Heath in 1975 fell as low as 20 per

1. The comparable figures for Great Britain, though taken from an earlier survey, were 8 per cent party members and 4 per cent who had attended a meeting in the previous year (Jean Morton-Williams, *Attitudes towards Devolution*, SCPR 1971). In 1964 Butler and Stokes found 14 per cent of the electorate who subscribed to a local party and 25 per cent who were nominal party members, including through trade unions.

cent or only two-thirds the city mean. Exact comparisons cannot be established for national parliamentary elections, since constituencies are much larger, in the case of Sparkbrook reaching to the city edge; but polls in both Small Heath and Sparkbrook constituencies have tended to be about 10 per cent lower than the city mean in recent elections, allowing for boundary changes.

At the time of the SCPR survey, membership of formally constituted local interest groups was likewise well below the national average. Only 2 per cent of adults belonged to a parents' association, 3 per cent to a residents' or tenants' association, 1 per cent to any other community or pressure group, compared with national figures of 7 per cent, 6 per cent and 3 per cent respectively. In the past two and a half years this picture has, however, changed quite dramatically, due to the city's urban renewal programme, with its emphasis on resident involvement on an area-specific basis, and also (though to a much lesser extent) as a result of the availability of BIAS funding and support for local initiatives such as the Small Heath Community Federation and action projects in the fields of education and environmental care. Residents' associations and action groups have been most affected. Whereas in early 1974 membership of residents' associations in Small Heath was confined largely to one organisation (with a strong long-established Irish owner occupier influence) active in the north-east of the area, nine residents' associations or action groups now cover a territory containing between two-thirds and three-quarters of all households. Actual membership is more difficult to assess, since some associations demand subscriptions while others work on the principle of open membership, as of right, to all residents living in their area of activity, but on a basis comparable to that of the SCPR data it could scarcely be lower than 10 per cent of all adults and may even be considerably higher. One may have reservations about the relatively sectarian and parochial interests pursued by groups like residents' associations, or about the extent of their involvement in real city policy-making, or about the degree to which they represent the most vulnerable sections of the community, such as racial minorities, poor tenants and 'problem families'; on the other hand, it is hardly to be denied that a growth in local collective organisation on the scale taking place is at least a significant potential force for positive community development. This is a theme we shall return to in the next part of the chapter and again in Chapter 7.

Finally, mention must be made of what is undoubtedly the most prevalent form of organisation in areas like Small Heath, the trade union. SCPR data showed that 38 per cent of Small Heath adults belonged to a union, as compared with 25 per cent nationally. In the case of full-time employed men the proportion rose to 72 per cent and in that of full-time employed women to 46 per cent. Rates of membership were high in all ethnic groups. Among Asian full-time male workers it reached 83 per cent, despite the tendency of Asians (especially from rural Pakistan/Bangladesh) to cultural insularity and the difficulties many of them have with spoken English. In their national survey carried out at roughly the same time, PEP found that 59 per cent of Pakistani/Bangladeshi men working more than 10 hours per week belonged to a union, against 64 per cent of West Indians, 63 per cent of Indians, 51 per cent of African Asians and 47 per cent of white males. Membership amongst those with no English was 60 per cent, one of the very few instances where command of English did not materially affect access. True, Asians from Small Heath were probably more likely to work in 'closed shop' plants and their attendance at meetings was much lower than other groups', only 17 per cent of members having attended a meeting in the previous twelve months, compared with over 40 per cent of UK-born members and over half of West Indian members; yet the extend of their unionisation is striking none the less.

To date, trade unions have taken few initiatives in the field of race relations, nor have they concerned themselves in any concerted way with the interests of inner area residents as a whole, outside the employed worker's pay and conditions in the individual workplace. Indeed, SCPR and PEP evidence indicate quite strongly that a smaller proportion of members from inner areas (if Small Heath is typical in this respect) and racial minorities are likely to hold union office than their numbers would suggest, though the ratio of officers to active members is very much closer, possibly even higher than in the national sample for Small Heath workers born in the UK or Eire. In view of the very high overall union membership among immigrants and inner area residents in general it is open to question whether the movement could (or should) not play a more positive role as an agency for change in their situation.

The nature of urban government today

Urban government, like all forms of political choice, is about the generation and allocation of resources to meet particular sets of perceived needs. What and whose needs are perceived as important, the way they are defined, the nature of the decisions and actions taken in response to them, all depend on who participates in the process of government, the values and attitudes they bring with them, how they see their own interests and the interests of the collectivities they represent, the language and conventions they use, the limits of the functions and responsibilities imposed by the organisational relationships between them, and the power and influence that they and the collectivities they represent can exert.

Inner area residents, we shall argue, are politically disadvantaged because their social background, education and experience tend to isolate them not only from familiarity with the 'rules of the game' but also from the predominant orientation towards that game – the broad consensus about what the purpose and style of urban government should be. They are ill informed, or rather the information that they have, first-hand knowledge about what life in inner areas really means, is not in a form which is readily assimilated by those who control the flow of information through the appropriate channels. They possess few assets with which to bargain. They have little direct and then only irregular access to those in authority. Even when they do successfully organise (often at great cost to scarce free time) their dealings with elected government members and appointed officials are likely to be extremely frustrating, due to problems of communication and conflicting perceptions, goals and responsibilities. Nor do their localised and fragmented organisations, in the absence of common cause with national working class movements, carry much weight against highly-developed and powerful competing lobbies. Finally, their elected representatives are inhibited in exercising their

113

constituency role by the increasing scale and scope of government activity and by the organisational and operational arrangements adopted to cope with such activity.

In exploring the theme of political disadvantage we shall focus our attention around three crucial and interconnected issues: the extent to which the interests of inner area residents are represented through existing political structures; problems arising from the growth of bureaucracy; and the potential for reform of political structures through community organisation.

Voting behaviour, party membership and political representation

The chief way for the individual to participate formally in urban government is by use of the vote, in both parliamentary and municipal elections. Nearly three-quarters of the electorate apparently consider it more important to vote in general than in local elections, against 1 in 7 who hold the opposite view.[1] In view of this it is not surprising that only about half of those who vote in general elections vote in local ones. Furthermore, turnout has been tending to decline over the past twenty-five years, after an initial burst of post-war interest. From a peak of 51 per cent in 1949 the average Birmingham poll fell to just under 40 per cent in the 50s, to around 33 per cent in the 60s, and in the 70s it has dropped to fractionally below that. An examination of turnout by ward shows that the even lower polls experienced in Small Heath in recent years have been fairly typical of similar predominantly low income areas, in both municipal and parliamentary elections, even though there are individual exceptions to the general rule (Figures 21 and 22). In the 1975 and 1976 municipal elections, for example, the average poll in 16 inner wards (including the redeveloped central core) was 27.1 per cent and 33.6 per cent compared with 31.7 per cent and 37.6 per cent in 23 outer wards and 43.7 per cent and 51.1 per cent in middle class Sutton Coldfield. Similarly, the two wholly inner ward constituencies of Ladywood and Small Heath, comprising eight wards in all, have averaged the lowest polls in the last three parliamentary elections, approximately 90 per cent of the city mean.

The individual vote is a blunt instrument. It allows no more than the expression of general satisfaction or dissatisfaction with a party's performance, the endorsement or rejection of a broad political platform in face of an extremely limited choice of alternatives with which in any case, as many opinion polls and voting studies have conclusively demonstrated, the voter is likely to be largely unfamiliar. It is fairly clear that the greater urban public in general and lower income groups in inner areas in particular have little confidence in the value of voting as a political act, especially so in local elections. It may not be strictly true that confidence now is lower than ever before (the poll in contested wards in Birmingham pre-war was little higher than it is at present), but electoral behaviour certainly indicates that few traces are left of the surge of interest in local politics which took place after the war.

Lack of active participation is reflected too in big falls in individual party membership. Falls have affected both major parties to similar degrees, each losing about

1. *Attitudes towards Devolution*, SCPR, *op. cit.*

**Figure 21
Birmingham:
Poll in municipal
elections**

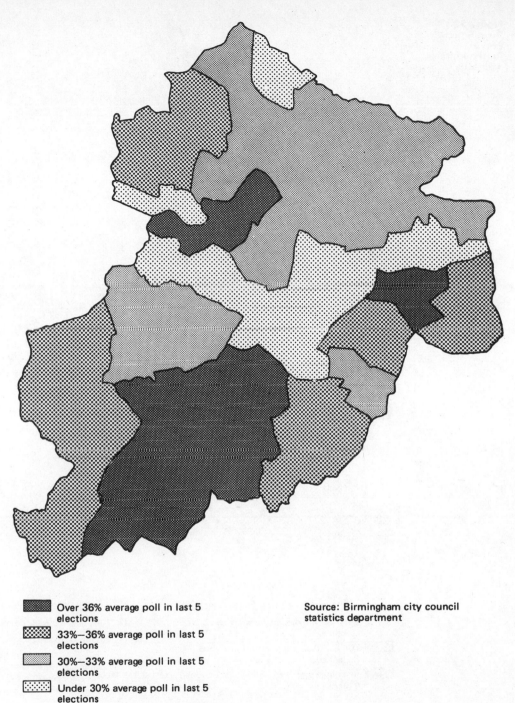

Over 36% average poll in last 5
elections

33%—36% average poll in last 5
elections

30%—33% average poll in last 5
elections

Under 30% average poll in last 5
elections

Source: Birmingham city council
statistics department

half their national membership in the 20 years since peak enrolment in the early
50s, despite short-term recoveries from time to time. Within this general pattern a
striking feature has been the relative poor performance of large cities. In the late
1960s the total membership of Birmingham's 13 constituency Labour parties
(CLPs) was just over 5,000, representing only about half the ratio of Labour members
to electors as in the country as a whole. The proportion of all provincial city CLPs

Figure 22
Birmingham:
Poll in
Parliamentary
elections

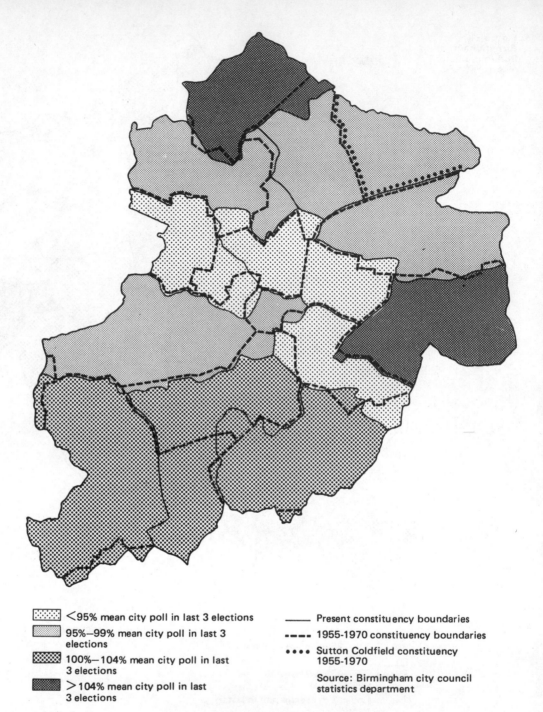

▦ <95% mean city poll in last 3 elections	—— Present constituency boundaries
▦ 95%–99% mean city poll in last 3 elections	‐‐‐‐ 1955-1970 constituency boundaries
▦ 100%–104% mean city poll in last 3 elections	•••• Sutton Coldfield constituency 1955-1970
▦ >104% mean city poll in last 3 elections	Source: Birmingham city council statistics department

in 1969 claiming the minimum affiliation number of 1,000 members was likewise half the proportion of CLPs nationwide. Significantly, in view of the fact that inner area constituencies and wards are predominantly Labour strongholds, the average membership of both Conservative and Labour parties nationally was substantially lower in 'safe' Labour seats than in Labour-held marginals.[1]

1. The principal sources of evidence quoted are Tom Forester, *The Labour Party and the Working Class*, Heinemann, 1976; Kenneth Newton, *Second City Politics*, Oxford, 1976; and Richard Rose, *The Problems of Party Government*, Macmillan, 1974.

Many reasons might be put forward to explain the present state of affairs. The surge of post-war interest (perhaps too frequently taken as a reference point) might be dismissed as a temporary aberration in the history of an otherwise 'allegiant' political culture in which people are content to leave the complicated business of government to the professional or committed few who understand it. Or the decline in activity since that period might be attributed to changes in life styles, with home-centred activities replacing the essentially 'social' activity that ward organisations formerly provided. Or again, it could be argued that changes in national electioneering, employing nationally networked media, and the lessening importance of local issues in local elections have reduced the functional role of constituency parties and ward organisations. Yet, whatever the precise combination of factors held to be responsible, the simple fact remains that people in inner areas do not participate because they see no advantage to themselves (or to the groups with whose interests they closely identify) by doing so. Our experience in Small Heath leads us to conclude that in the last analysis this is because the existing political structures of urban government serve inner area residents particularly poorly. We shall seek to support this contention by examining certain aspects of the present structures, beginning with the position of the elected representatives whose constitutional responsibility it is to advance their constituents' interests.

In one sense inner areas are comparatively well represented since inner city constituencies and wards, at least in Birmingham, tend to have smaller populations than outer ones. They also have a lower ratio of electors to total population but this is due to a proportionately large number of minors rather than to the presence of adults not qualifying for the vote, so in this respect too it would be wrong to talk of under-representation. However, in the case of especially disadvantaged though sizeable minorities (especially immigrant communities) it is clear that a 'first past the post' electoral system inhibits the return of an MP or councillor who will represent their specific interests, a problem which becomes most acute when, for the sake of administrative convenience, inner areas are incorporated within constituencies or wards whose dominant social composition and general environment are 'middle class'[1]. We believe there are in fact two distinct senses in which inner areas might be regarded as quantitatively under-represented: first, in relation to the magnitude and intensity of their needs which demand in turn a disproportionate input of resources, including human time and energy; second, in relation to their ethnic and cultural diversity and the more particular nature of the issues which urban government has to resolve. Much more important than any quantitative under-representation, however, is the qualitative under-representation of inner area interests within the urban government system. This hinges not so much on the personal competence of representatives (who may in fact be every bit as competent and, by the nature of the task which confronts them, even more energetic than their counterparts in other areas) as on the way candidates are recruited, the way roles in office are determined, and the way public decisions are made.

1. Part of the Bolton Road area of Small Heath is currently in Edgbaston constituency, as is Balsall Heath (the focus of Birmingham's EPA project) which prior to 1974 constituency boundary changes was part of the equally 'middle class' Selly Oak constituency. Anomalies are obviously fewer at the ward level; but ward boundaries frequently cut across what residents generally perceive to be distinct local neighbourhoods or communities.

It is clear that party activists who select candidates for parliamentary and municipal elections are tending to go increasingly for people with higher education credentials and a professional background. Over half the Labour MPs in the present parliament are graduates and less than 30 per cent were formerly in working class occupations, compared with 1 in 7 and three-quarters in the 1924 parliament.[1] New members, largely irrespective of constituency now that trade unions are less insistent on the sponsorship of working class candidates, and holders of high office are even more strongly biased towards a graduate and professional mould. These trends, though hardly surprising in themselves because of the increasing 'professionalism' of government, mean that the gap in experience between the party leadership and their electors in inner areas is growing wider. Similarly, the number of working class councillors is steadily getting smaller, though the somewhat sporadic evidence suggests that local council membership in large cities was strongly biased towards non-manual workers even pre-war. Roughly a quarter of the Labour-controlled 1974 Birmingham council followed or had followed working class occupations, compared with nearer a third 10 years earlier, at which time the socio-economic composition of the council was very similar to that of the sample of county boroughs drawn for the Maud Committee report.[2] One-third of 45 councillors representing inner wards (excluding Moseley with its substantial middle class vote) held manual jobs, virtually all skilled. Seven lived in their own ward, 10 in other inner wards, the remainder (62 per cent) in outer wards. In contrast, 54 per cent of councillors sitting for outer wards lived in their own wards and a further 43 per cent in other outer wards. Classifying wards into four broad groups – old working class, new working class, mixed, middle class (see Figure 23) – we find that 46 per cent of the city council lived in middle class wards and only 13 per cent in old working class wards, which correspond most closely to inner areas. Yet middle class wards return only 26 per cent of the council membership and old working class wards 31 per cent. In the present Conservative – controlled council the skew will be even more pronounced, though Conservatives hold only two inner ward seats.

The above findings corroborate evidence from other cities which show that in all types of ward Labour party activists and, even more so, officers tend to be drawn very disproportionately from the ranks of professionals and other white collar workers. It is hardly surprising their choice of candidates should reflect this pattern. Besides, white collar workers are more likely to be able to combine their job with the duties of a councillor or partyworker. Representation among councillors, prospective candidates, officials and activists of semi-skilled or unskilled workers is negligible, even in wards where they constitute a fair proportion of party members. It should be noted too that not only do councillors for inner wards tend to live in other areas; they are liable also to be members of ward parties in areas they do not represent.

1. These data are taken from Richard Rose (*op. cit.*). We concentrate on the Labour party because inner city constituencies tend to be 'safe' Labour seats.
2. Comparisons with earlier studies are complicated by the use of old social class groupings, with their large and heterogeneous class III. But adjustments have been made as far as available data permit.

**Figure 23
Birmingham:
Classification of
wards by social
class**

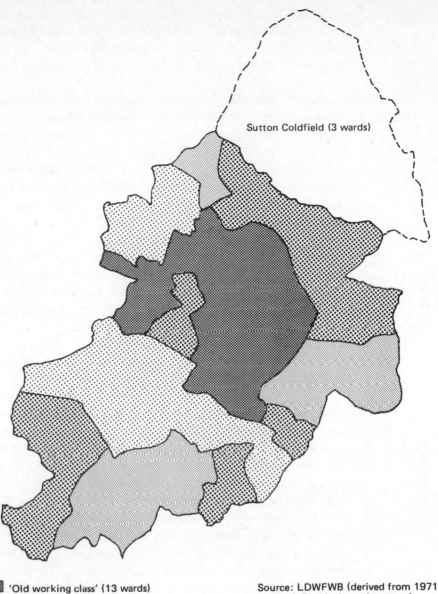

Sutton Coldfield (3 wards)

 'Old working class' (13 wards)

'New working class' (11 wards)

'Mixed' (7 wards)

'Middle class' (8 wards)

Source: LDWFWB (derived from 1971
census & Birmingham abstract of
statistics.)

While it is no doubt true that non-resident councillors, especially if they come from a
different social background, will have relatively greater difficulty in appreciating the
full range and subtlety of their constituents' needs and concerns and in maintaining
the frequency and style of contact on which local confidence may be built, we would
not like to place too great a stress on this aspect of the problem. After all, quite a
few live or will previously have lived in similar areas. Others will have working class
parents. Some will also gain insights into their constituents' circumstances through

119

experience at their place of work. Certainly councillors are not in the same position as full-time MPs spending most of their time on national business in Westminster. Rather more significant than residence, occupation or even social background are the roles which elected members come to play once in office.

Like MPs councillors do not merely represent individual constituencies, they serve on committees responsible for the city-wide provision of particular services, and they belong to a political party and/or political pressure group. As committee members they must develop a symbiotic working relationship with the officers who provide them with information and advice; they have to assimilate the professional 'specialism' in question and interpret and defend that specialism in deliberations of the full council and within their own political party caucus. As party members they are concerned with hard political realities of retaining or seizing majority control, with satisfying a wide cross section of the electorate, responding to the demands of powerful lobbies and interest groups; they are called upon to uphold the official party line on local and sometimes national issues. Finally, they are involved as individuals in the furtherance of their own political career. It is plain that interests and responsibilities that do not accord with the needs and demands of the communities or sub-communities they represent will obstruct the satisfaction of those needs and demands even when they are well understood, when the resources to satisfy them are potentially available, and when their non-satisfaction is recognised publicly as a 'problem'.

Evidence from Birmingham[1] suggests that Labour councillors tend on the whole to be more orientated than their Conservative counterparts towards policy issues as opposed to individual problems, and to be less likely to put ward responsibilities first. This is despite the much greater tendency of Labour representatives to hold regular and frequent surgeries. Holders of 'safe' seats appear especially prone to play down the 'delegate' aspect of their role. Furthermore, they look upon themselves virtually without exception as specialists in the work of just one or two committees rather than generalists who make it their business to concern themselves with all major fields of council policy. Councillors in both parties attach considerable importance to maintaining party unity in public. But there is some indication that Labour members have a greater propensity to vote with the group because of their stronger orientation towards policy and to see issues in policy terms. When they depart from the party line (a rare event) it seems it is more likely to be over a major issue of general policy than over a local issue.

This evidence and our experience in Small Heath supports the view that there is a considerable dichotomy between the orientation of elected members in inner areas towards policy-making for the city, county or (especially in the case of MPs) nation within a narrow range of policy fields and the concerns of residents about policy execution and its outcome in terms of personal experience across the whole range of inter-connected programme areas. Recent local government reorganisation, by cutting the number of representatives and encouraging their more exclusive concentration on policy formation, has tended if anything to exacerbate this situation.

1. Newton (*op. cit.*).

The vertical division of responsibilities, resulting both from the general structure of central and local government organisation and from the particularly specialised nature of large city operations,[1] means that where committee decisions do happen to be made that impinge directly upon the level of services in any particular ward or neighbourhood it is quite likely that no local councillor will be a member of the committee concerned. This was precisely the difficulty we encountered when BIAS action projects came before individual committees or sub-committees for approval or continued funding. Again, it is not that inner areas are quantitatively under-represented on committees, though representation will obviously vary according to party control and the actual year-by-year composition of the council. During the 1974/75 session, a time of Labour control, inner ward members as a bloc held respectively 50 per cent and 44 per cent of places on the key service committees of housing and social services and 34 per cent of places on principal service and resource committees overall, compared with their 31 per cent share of full council seats.

The fault lies rather in the nature of the committee system itself which is not geared to respond to complex situations in specific parts of the city and whose scarce time, when not devoted to the establishment of general policies and programmes or the control of aggregate performance, is concerned primarily with demands for individual service initiatives articulated with particular force by particular advocates at particular points in time. Inner area residents are especially disadvantaged by such a system because their preoccupations with detailed problems of implementation tend to be regarded as technical or administrative matters, to be dealt with by officers, and their common concerns rarely find expression in powerfully and clearly articulated demands.

Associated with the last point is the fact that the most common avenue for individuals and, especially, groups to employ in pressing demands is via appointed officials or administrative departments. SCPR found in their national survey on attitudes to devolution that, while over a quarter of individuals had at some time or another sought help through an appointed official, less than 1 in 5 had contacted a councillor and fewer than 1 in 10 their MP. Newton's investigation of 166 politically active voluntary organisations and community groups in Birmingham, in the study referred to earlier, showed that contacts through departments outnumbered those through council members and MPs by about 5 to 2 and 9 to 2 respectively. Organisations are also more likely than individuals to approach senior councillors or committee chairman, ie, elected members performing their service-oriented rather than con-stituency role. Significantly, the available evidence suggests that organisations are generally rather better pleased with the response they get than are individuals and that well-established organisations are most satisfied of all. We shall return later to the relatively greater difficulties faced by inner area residents in organising successfully for the satisfaction of their needs. At this juncture we wish simply to

1. In 1965 Birmingham had 31 committees and 82 sub-committees compared with a mean of 21 and 37 for all English and Welsh county boroughs. By reorganisation in 1974 the number of committees had been reduced to 20 (including 6 principal service committees and 3 resource committees). The largest service committee, Education, had 28 members excluding the Lord Mayor. The number of committee memberships per councillor ranged from one (34 per cent of cases) to six (in the case of the current and former council leaders). In interpreting these figures it should be recalled that Birmingham has the largest spending commitment of any second tier authority; 1974/75 total net committee spending £137 million.

stress the important role played by officers in controlling the flow of information about needs and demands and in preparing the agenda of government business.

The growth of bureaucracy

There are good grounds for arguing that the influence and effective power of public and civil servants have been steadily growing in line with the expansion of government activity and its greater complexity. This power is reinforced by the fact that those who hold it enjoy continuity of office, which is particularly significant at the local government level where the professional, long-term and full-time nature of their appointment contrasts with the amateur, short-term and part-time status of elected members – even though evidence from Birmingham indicates that quite a few council members (up to a third or so, depending on political control and the year-by-year composition of the council, with the tendency relatively more pronounced among representatives of outer wards) are able to devote virtually a full working week to council business, due to retirement, absence of other full-time occupation or special arrangement with the organisation with which they are employed.

The senior officers whose influence on political decisions is greatest as a rule have little in common with the people of inner areas. They are likely to be set apart by their place of residence, life-style, education and professional formation, if not also by their social origins. They work for the most part in central locations. The needs and demands of communities in parts of cities like Small Heath are translated for them into abstract statistics and technical reports. The theories, values, norms absorbed during their professional training frequently clash with the priorities and preferences held locally. Their functional responsibilities are usually towards nation, region, county or city as a whole. Because they are appointed, not elected, their loyalty may prove to be towards the organisation rather than to the people that the organisation serves. Within the organisational structure they tend to protect their own budgets and establishments, defend the interests of their own specialism and professional status and cultivate their own professional language and style.

The picture we have just drawn is, of course, a stereotype. There are clearly many exceptions. It is not to be taken as a reflection upon the intellectual capacity, skill or technical competence of officers, upon their integrity, endeavour, or even their personal desire to serve the public interest in general or provide particular assistance to groups in special need. It is intended merely to highlight some aspects of urban government which frustrate an effective response to the problems of inner areas. It helps too, we believe, to explain why senior officers' perceptions of urban deprivation diverge so widely and why their understanding of how their own departments' activities impact upon the problems of deprivation is often so hazy.[1]

We suspect the validity of the stereotype generally increases with the size of authority or department, with the length of the hierarchical chain of command and the degree to which administration and operations are centralised. Our own experience,

1. See, for example, the Institute of Local Government Studies report on *Local Government: Approaches to Urban Deprivation, Occasional Paper No.* 1 published by the Home Office Urban Deprivation Unit, 1976. Birmingham was one of two areas selected for this pertinent study of officers' attitudes.

particularly in observing the activities of local advice centre workers and urban renewal project teams, has convinced us that understanding grows and has more chance of filtering up through the organisation when officers work together from a local base in a mutually supportive team situation which brings them in touch with people in their own home and neighbourhood environment. The shorter the chain of command, the more senior officers will be open to the influence of such direct experience. The greater too the opportunities for middle echelon officers with experience of this kind to gain promotion to senior positions. The theme of decentralisation is one we shall return to in Chapter 6 and intermittently elsewhere.

The rise in the importance of bureaucracy, which has been accompanied not only by a disproportionate growth in the numbers of appointed officials in relation to elected representatives but also by a multiplication of the communications links between them has made the process of urban government more technical, more 'expert', and thus more and more unintelligible to the vast majority of the electorate, certainly to those whose needs are greatest and whose lives are the most dependent on government decisions. It has also made the process more secret, more remote. Public and civil servants, because they are not democratically elected, have very restricted formal power of decisions. To safeguard the integrity of political choice and to ensure public accountability they operate for the most part within fairly rigid structures of delegated responsibility, personal anonymity and collective inscrutability. The devices designed to guard against abuse of authority, misappropriation, wastefulness, behavioural unreliability – that is, hierarchies of command, closely defined roles, formal regulations, strict protocol, established routines – have tended to become self-justifying, ends rather than means. Indeed, they may well be regarded as counter-productive in that they inhibit the capacity of the urban government system to adapt swiftly and sensitively to the effects of technological, economic, social and cultural change. What is more, the scale and complexity of urban government today, which have led to the superimposition of alternative forms of working, make them extremely costly to maintain and of dubious efficacy as controls.

The potential for community organisation

The individual resident has very little opportunity of influencing the way policy decisions are made. The inner area resident least of all; for his social reality and perceptions of what government is about are farthest removed from those of the decision-makers. His contacts with officers and elected representatives are confined almost exclusively to the realm of immediate personal problems and have virtually no effect on policy formation. He can only participate actively in urban government by joining an organisation which will act on his behalf, lobbying for the resolution of issues of common concern and for changes in particular policies and programmes. Yet, despite the pressing nature of his needs, he is less likely than more privileged members of society to belong to such an organisation. And if he joins he is less likely to become deeply involved in running it. For example, quoting once again from the SCPR national survey, the proportion of managerial and professional workers 'very involved' in political and/or community affairs was (at 44 per cent) over twice as high as that of skilled manual workers (21 per cent), nearly three times greater than the proportion of semi-skilled workers (16 per cent) and roughly $4\frac{1}{2}$ times greater than among unskilled workers (10 per cent). For other non-manual workers the corresponding figure was 32 per cent. Four in ten unskilled workers, a third of semi-skilled workers and 26 per cent of skilled workers were 'not at all involved' compared with 14 per cent of professional and managerial workers and 16 per cent of other non-manual grades.[1] We have no reason to suppose, judging from our experience in Small Heath and findings in similar areas, that the degree of involvement among socio-economic groups would be materially different in areas where they are highly concentrated. If anything we would expect it to be lower, for there is some evidence to suggest that political and/or community activity among lower socio-economic groups may be higher in socially mixed areas where there are a greater number of middle class residents, especially professionals and students, to serve as potential activists.

In view of the fact higher socio-economic groups tend to be disproportionately active in political and/or community affairs it is not surprising that the organisations which represent their interests and the interests of the higher-income communities in which they tend to live usually have at their disposal relatively greater resources – finances, staff, contacts. This is in essence what Newton found in his investigation of over 4,000 voluntary organisations and community groups in Birmingham. Conversely, vulnerable minorities like the city's coloured communities, who at the time of the fieldwork in the late 60s were already approaching 10 per cent of the city population, had very few groups representing them and none that would be called a well-developed organisation.

The comparative lack of organisation among the most needy social groups and in inner areas is partly to do with possession of the appropriate social skills, partly with time and resources available and partly with belief in the potential efficacy of collective action. The latter is hampered by the extreme sense of powerlessness felt by the most vulnerable sectors of society, a sense which came through strongly in our own surveys and observation and which evidence from the SCPR national sample confirms to rise as socio-economic status falls. But some of the explanation lies too in the experience of groups which do succeed in organising. First, such groups, because of the very particular nature of their concerns, are faced with a very real dilemma. If they remain small, it will be hard for them to generate resources and gain sufficient political weight to function as an effective lobby. If they grow large, they stand to lose their unity, strength of purpose and broad agreement on means. In that case they will tend to break up, or power cliques will emerge in what then remain only nominally representative groups. Experience with the Community Federation and observation of other residents' organisations in Small Heath provide ample illustrations of this dilemma. Second, the language and style of community action, usually emotive and often hostile to 'authority', will be alien if not unintelligible to most officers and will frequently antagonise elected representatives who may resent what they see as a challenge to their constitutional position or criticism of policies and programmes for which they share responsibility. The generally favourable disposition of officers and members towards the voluntary sector, which in Birmingham takes annually the equivalent of perhaps £5 million in grants and aid to support services the local authority is unable to provide, is apt to dissipate when

1. Degree of involvement was assessed by SCPR on the basis of a composite index of various forms of political and community activity, including active membership of trade unions.

Bob Marshall

When I came I said to her 'There's no bathroom'. And she said 'We know there's no bathrooms in that house but you'll only be there eighteen months . . .' And of course I've been here six years this January. But they haven't offered us nothing at all.

I've had a rat in this front room, you know. We took the rat down to Bush House and he chucked it on the counter . . . 'Oh', she said, 'Move it!' He said 'No – you move us!'

Circumstances of Families

groups abandon the customary acquiescent and co-operative style, seeking only modest gains within the existing framework of policy, and vigorously question decisions and actions taken by formally elected government agencies. In such situations continued access is easily denied and pressure ignored or diverted into bureaucratic 'channels', leaving groups with a second dilemma: whether to moderate their demands or remain relatively powerless. In neither case are their members likely to be satisfied.

When people's concern about their predicament reaches the point of desperation and frustration is constantly met in trying to get the predicament dealt with through normal political processes, recourse may be had to direct action – rent strikes, demonstrations, sit-ins, squats, appropriation of unutilised private or public land, and so on. These conditions are most likely to arise if the situation or the threatened situation (loss of jobs or homes, the withdrawal of valued services or facilities) affects a large number of individuals. Clearance proposals, urban motorway schemes, factory closures and now perhaps cutbacks in public spending have created or are creating such situations in inner areas. Given sympathetic 'human interest' media coverage, which can usually be counted on if the action is carefully planned, direct action may offer the prospect of a more tangible outcome, or at least a more satisfying experience, than more orthodox methods of protest or appeal.

Are we to expect an increase in direct action – and, one might add, more anti-social ways of expressing dissatisfaction and frustration – or will the existing agencies of government and formal political structures be able to respond of their own accord more effectively to the needs of people in inner areas? Or is there a third alternative? It is here that the emergence of residents' associations and community groups as an integral part of urban renewal and local planning activity is significant as a new potential base for political revitalisation. The proviso is that, through participation in such activity, residents are given real choices to shape the future of their communities and neighbourhoods and are not just involved in a public relations exercise or in a superficial form of consultation. We shall explore this theme in subsequent chapters. At this juncture we wish to stress the opportunity afforded by specific programme-oriented community organisation in breaking through the vicious circle, namely, that people do not join organisations because they do not have the appropriate attitudes and skills, but that they will not acquire the attitudes and skills unless they join and become involved.

At present residents' and tenants' associations, neighbourhood groups and claimants' unions operate largely outside the party political structure of government. Their activity may often not be seen as political, or if it is, its legitimacy may be questioned. We believe that the stimulation of community organisations and their deep involvement along with representative bodies from the workplace in government decision-making at the local level may well be the key to bringing elected representatives and the parties to which they belong into closer touch with the grass roots. It also seems reasonable to envisage that greater resident involvement in forming political choices and their acquisition of organisational or negotiative skills may also promote a reawakened interest in the membership of political parties. If so, that can only be to the good of democratic practice.

126

The present context of urban government

The nature and scale of the problems which beset inner areas are such that no real or lasting 'solution 'is to be expected without a substantial change in the distribution of social goods and opportunities. Because problems of personal deprivation, irrespective of location, and of their concentration in collectively deprived areas are inextricably related, this will mean, first, initiatives to gain for disadvantaged groups greater influence over the political and economic forces that determine access to a variety of opportunities and, second, area-specific initiatives to compensate for an accumulated historical deficit in the geographical allocation of investment.

It is commonly argued that more vigorous redistributive measures must await the resumption of a moderate and sustained rate of aggregate economic growth; for to institute more progressive taxation and incomes policies and/or expand public expenditure on social services and programmes of positive discrimination in a period of recession would discourage the wealth-creating personal effort and productive investment on which the well-being of society as a whole depends. Yet it is precisely in a period of economic recession, especially when accompanied by endemic inflation, that those already at disadvantage will be rendered even more vulnerable to personal and collective deprivations. To postpone redistribution is to exacerbate the problems and increase still further the economic and social costs of dealing with them effectively.

The economic argument in favour of granting first priority to the pursuit of renewed growth may be influenced by the political consideration of gaining the 'floating vote.' It is unlikely that substantial redistribution could be achieved purely by even greater taxation of the very-rich whose standard of living the uncommitted voter might find unjustifiable. Its price must also certainly also be some reduction in the resources commanded by middle to higher income groups whose style of living he will tend to aspire to if not already actually enjoy. The vote of the inner area resident carries little political weight by comparison. And there is evidence that public opinion in general has swung against increased outlays on the social services. In late 1964 about three-quarters of the electorate appeared to be in favour of increased public spending on social services; within eighteen months or so, due probably to the action of the then Labour government in raising pensions and removing prescription charges, the proportion had fallen to just over a half.[1] Four and a half years later National Opinion Polls were showing that three-quarters of the electorate, almost as many Labour voters as Conservatives, thought there should actually be cuts in overall public spending, though attitudes to individual services varied. Opinions fluctuate and are clearly influenced both by the apparent degree of party consensus on key issues and by their treatment in the media. However, the current mood among uncommitted voters seems hardly to be propitious for redistribution, particularly if they are asked to meet a significant share of the costs by accepting sacrifices today or foregoing future reward.

1. This information is based on interview surveys reported by David Butler and Donald Stokes in *Political Change in Britain*, Macmillan, 1969.

One effect of current governmental policies to encourage productive investment and deal with the problems of the economy has been a cutback in real terms of categories of public spending which aid the most needy, despite the expressed intention that local authorities should safeguard services to high priority groups. A recent report by the British Association of Social Workers found that 41 out of 81 local authorities surveyed had pruned between them over £4 million from their personal social services budgets, the major savings coming from the closure of homes and day centres or from not opening newly-completed establishments. Grants to voluntary organisations and the provision of aids for the disabled had also been cut. Shelter has reported local authorities cutting back on assistance to the homeless at precisely the time when the numbers of homeless due to mortgage arrears are rising and a further increase in mortgage interest rates has threatened still more low-income house purchasers with foreclosures. The disabled, the mentally ill, the elderly, the homeless are all high priorities cases. When one comes down to 'lower priority' services the situation is much worse still, as we have experienced ourselves in Small Heath where valued services and financial help have been trimmed or terminated: for instance, the loss of community support in the clearance area through closure of the 435 Centre; the reduction of advice services at Osbourne House; and the reduction in grant-aid to a voluntary pre-school centre. Part of the problem is that local authorities are caught in a spiral of rising administrative costs which recent organisational reforms have tended to aggravate. Opportunities for increased productivity in labour-intensive operations (employees' costs account for well over half of Birmingham's total current expenditure) are limited. Meanwhile the unit cost of services provided continues to rise with inflation but faster than the standard index used for converting current to constant prices. As a result constraints on spending can be seen to bite hardest where services are most felt, at the point of contact or delivery.

Whatever the chances of swift economic recovery, the situation in inner areas generally is likely to get a lot worse under present policies before it gets any better. If and when private investment does pick up it can be expected to happen first in those industries and firms whose market prospects are strongest and on those locations where the potential return is greatest. In neither case, for the reasons given in Chapter 3, does this suggest much benefit to inner areas. Besides, the initial effect of new investment in a phase of industrial reconstruction is almost invariably the replacement of labour by machinery, which means redundancies. Recession, particularly when accompanied by a high rate of inflation, affects disproportionately the jobs, incomes and standard of living of the weakest sectors of the community, not least because they have few or no reserves to fall back on in adversity, and attempts to cut their living costs largely have to come through a reduction in basic necessities, often causing severe hardship. Growth alone will not make these sectors proportionately better off. One might be more optimistic if the record of redistribution and the diminution of deprivations had been more impressive in recent periods of growth. But, as we saw in Chapter 3, there has been little real improvement in the relative position of those at the bottom of the scale of incomes and wealth. We believe that while an aggregate increase in national product should facilitate redistribution, it is the commitment to redistributive policies rather than the fact of growth itself which is the determining factor.

128

This is perhaps not the place to enter into a detailed discussion of the complex arguments for or against widespread cuts in public spending. However, if cuts are to be made, we believe that at the very least finer distinctions should be drawn between different types of economic activity, productive and non-productive, with particular regard to their distributive effects and to their social costs and benefits. It is a question not of backing private enterprise at the expense of public sector activity but of reshaping the contributions which each in their different ways can make to social aims. A more productive use of even the present level of resources would release funds which ought, in principle, to be available for redistribution to disadvantaged groups and areas, and such is clearly central government's intention; but this will need rather more sensitive mechanisms of control than currently appear to operate.

*

Towards a framework for inner area strategy

Any strategy for inner areas must deal with crucial and interrelated issues of jobs, incomes and housing: the maintenance and ultimately the improvement of employment opportunities accessible to the disadvantaged groups who currently tend to be concentrated there; a marked increase in the real spending power of those groups relative to society as a whole; the provision for all inner area residents of a decent basic standard of housing of a type which reflects the needs of the particular household situation and at a price they can afford. Just to express the nature of the task in such terms (admittedly very broad) gives some idea of the large shift in resource allocation required, both spatially and more especially, because it is the circumstances of people rather than the fate of specific locations which is our prime concern – between social groups. However, it will be difficult for government to secure the degree of commitment within the electorate at large to undertake initiatives of the scale and scope appropriate to the size of the problem in the immediate future. The consequences for strategy are therefore, as we see it, threefold. First, whatever programmes are adopted in the present situation must be compatible with ultimate ends (ie a more equitable distribution of social goods and opportunities) and be capable of implementation in a flexible and incremental fashion, reflecting the pattern of future uncertainty. Second, programmes should be designed wherever possible to make more productive use of existing resources, in order to release savings which may potentially be deployed in positive discrimination. Third, programmes must include specific measures to unblock the constraints which currently inhibit more radical change. This last aspect is essential. Here we are concerned with fundamental issues of the distribution of power, access to opportunity and influence over the form of public decisions and the manner of their execution, with action in the fields of community organisation, government process, and education.

We contend that intervention must address simultaneously and cumulatively all major dimensions of disadvantage, which suggests a series of complementary (if initially comparatively small-scale) initiatives across the whole range of urban policy rather than, as has frequently happened in the past, separate programmes developed independently in response to a single manifestation of disadvantage, such as poor housing conditions, high unemployment or low educational attainment. Only then, we believe, will it be possible to respond sensitively to a variety of different situations at a very local level, avoid unforeseen impacts of narrowly-conceived programmes, maintain a balance between jobs, homes, schools, etc and prepare the ground for broad-based renewal, economic, physical, social and political. This is not to deny an 'absolute' order of priorities – clearly, a significant move towards reducing inequalities of personal incomes and wealth, earned and unearned, would do more than anything else to reduce both personal and collective deprivations and increase the choices open to those now in greatest need – but it acknowledges that in practice priorities will have to be 'relative': for example, immediate rehousing for tenants in the appalling conditions of Bolton Road, prompt council mortgages for low-income Asians seeking to buy old terraced houses in 'redlined' neighbour-hoods, the creation of new jobs for workers faced with redundancy in zones of aggregate employment decline. The strategies indicated in the following chapters are an attempt to devise a framework of action which is internally consistent and practical in the sense that both problems and the search for their solution are set within the context of 'real world' economic and political constraints.

PART TWO

The search for solutions: local perspectives

John Peverley

These back-alley houses look terrible and old and should be pulled down but from the inside they are completely different. They are clean and tidy and the inhabitants are happy there.

A Child's Eye View of Small Heath

There's only about three of us left and all these gardens were . . . kept beautiful they were; and it used to be really nice to walk up the road, you know. But now no-one seems to bother. They just let the places go.

Circumstances of Families

132

5 Improving the residential environment

The situation in Small Heath as already described reflects the impact of both national and local housing and environmental policies. Historically, these developed incrementally as Parliament added to the powers of government and local authorities. However, the multiplicity of powers has been built up to deal with fairly specific problems on the basis of often narrowly defined objectives. For example, powers to maintain standards of design, maintenance and management in the private sector have usually been formulated in isolation from powers to increase the provision of accommodation, either directly in the public sector or through encouragement in the private sector. This is often reflected in the way in which the administration of housing powers is divided among different local authority departments.

Quite apart from internal coordination problems, external constraints complicate the formation and execution of comprehensive local housing plans. There are government controls over local housing policies and finance and, when government policies and allocations of funds are erratic, there is little that local authorities can do to maintain a consistent strategy. Their room for manoeuvre is restricted in that virements between an allocation for one form of capital spending and that for another are generally not permitted.[1] The framework for national housing finance is itself in a state of flux – the provisions of the Housing Finance Act 1972 have been replaced by the Housing Rents and Subsidies Act 1975 which is only seen as a temporary measure awaiting the results of an ongoing review. Another external constraint is that a housing authority often does not administer an area within which its overall housing needs can be met – Birmingham provides a good example – and so the development of comprehensive policies requires cooperation with other authorities.

The constraints on the integration of environmental policies are no easier. Responsibilities are spread across several departments and authorities for a mixture of good and bad reasons. In the inner areas this has been a factor contributing to the situation in which the government subsidises capital investment in environmental improvements (grants for improvements in GIAs and HAAs) but urges local authorities to trim current expenditure on environmental maintenance and protection without having an overall reasoned strategy to justify this preference.

Housing and related environmental policies have thus been the sum of fragmented and changing local authority activities. This suggests looking at whether housing deprivation in Small Heath might not be alleviated by policies that are better integrated and more concerned with inner areas. This chapter therefore examines present policies with a view to changes that would give more priority to those in

---

1. This reflects the existing position, but some flexibility is being introduced from 1977/78 as a means of progressing towards overall housing investment plans, a reform which we support.

greatest need before summarising the financial implications and concluding whether
or not this approach is likely to be adequate or whether more fundamental changes
are necessary. Underlying our argument is the belief, substantiated in earlier
chapters, that apart from jobs, housing circumstances are central to the predicament
of the inner areas.

We nevertheless recognise residents do not always rank housing as one of their main
problems. While for most people in short life accommodation it undoubtedly is
the main problem, outside the clearance areas this is not necessarily so. A few
exceptions were encountered in the Circumstances of Families survey. There was an
elderly couple still disturbed by instructions from the environmental department as
to the improvements they should make to the house that they owned in a housing
action area ('Well we shall be broke; we don't have hardly anything as it is');
there was an old lady who found that continuing to live alone in a large and gloomy
house after her husband died was too much for her; and there was another who
was paying £6 a week rent out of her pension without help ('I don't get nothing –
just my pension; I've never asked for anything; will you ask for me?'). Among
slightly better-off owner occupying families, there was an immigrant family who
said that their greatest problem was to get their house up to standard, to
modernise it, and another immigrant family struggling under the burden of paying
£90 a month for housing loans out of one man's wages. A couple of other families
were concerned to find houses with more bedroom space for growing families.
These were, however, very much the exceptions. Thus, while we believe that housing
policy is one of the main keys to change in the inner areas, there lies behind our
proposals a wish to relate housing policies more closely to people's financial
circumstances and to their aspirations.

Quantity and size of dwellings

Although most housing policies affecting Small Heath concern the quality, cost,
or allocation of housing, they must all be seen in the context of the city's view of the
overall availability of accommodation of different sizes. In deciding investment
priorities a housing authority has to weigh up the physical deterioration of dwellings,
which besides reducing housing standards leads to the dereliction and loss of dwellings
against the overall shortage of dwellings. A balance has to be kept between investment in improvement, maintenance and new construction.

Birmingham has a building programme to the end of 1980 which it considers about
adequate to meet its perception of the dwelling shortage and to provide for the
formation of additional households and slum clearance. The declared objective of
the programme at the beginnning of 1976 was to build 21,000 new dwellings over
5 years and to provide an additional 2,100 dwellings by conversion of existing
council houses. Over the same 5 year period demolitions in redevelopment areas and
HAAs were expected to be less than 6,500, so there would be a net gain of 16,000
dwellings in addition to expected contributions of 3,200 dwellings from housing
associations, 6,650 from the private sector, and 4,000 (including relets) from overspill
agreements. This emphasis on construction was reflected in the 1975/76 capital

budget in which new construction accounted for £34 million as against only £6.15 million on council purchase and improvement of older dwellings and £3.25 million on renovation grants.

We do not dispute Birmingham's estimate of the number of dwellings required to meet the existing shortfall in dwellings and to provide for new household formation and slum clearance. According to these estimates, the building programme would reduce the excess of households and potential households over dwellings from 18,800 in 1975 to 4,600 at the end of 1980. However, the construction programme cannot meet all the requirements for dwellings of particular types and sizes – the familiar problem of matching dwelling sizes to household sizes – as recent demographic changes in the city make clear. Although the city's population was declining in the 1960s as a result of net out-migration, the number of households remained almost static. A decline in medium sized families (3 to 5 persons) was matched by an increase in small households (1 to 2 persons) over half of whom were pensioner households, producing a considerable mismatch between household sizes and dwelling sizes (see Table 16).

Table 16 Size of households and accommodation in Birmingham

Size of households	%	Size of accommodation	%
1–2 persons	50	1–3 rooms	16
3–5 persons	41	4–6 rooms	77
6+ persons	9	7+ rooms	7

Source: 1971 Census

The city attempted quite early to meet this situation by building more small dwellings, and to a lesser extent more large dwellings, notwithstanding the clearance programme's requirements for dwellings of all sizes. The mismatch developed despite the city's building programme. The shortfall of small dwellings is in fact so great that expecting to meet it by new building and conversion alone is unrealistic. Recommendations developed in this chapter start from a recognition of this predicament, and look beyond the existing city policies of increasing conversions and building more small dwellings (policies which we support) towards policies on sharing arrangements and the utilisation of the present dwelling stock generally.

The conclusion on mismatch is even clearer if we look at Small Heath: straight comparisons of households and accommodation sizes understate the numbers of large and small dwellings that would be required because:

Many of the large families do not occupy the available large accommodation (39 per cent of 3 and 4 room accommodation is occupied by large families, while 36 per cent of 5 and 6 room accommodation is occupied by single people or couples)

Hardly any of the available small accommodation is self-contained.

Occupancy rates (persons per room) are higher in Small Heath than in the rest of Birmingham, but at 0.83 person per room overall are not particularly high, drifting downwards as they have been with the decline in population in the city. In this situation continued new building in the hope of achieving one dwelling for every household is likely to result in very low occupancy rates overall and therefore poor utilisation of the dwelling stock.

It is, however, questions of finance in particular which can often make new construction a less attractive investment than rehabilitation or other possible alternatives. A 1975/76 budget of £34 million for one year's capital expenditure on new construction has serious financial implications. At the time the 1975/76 budget was adopted the average cost of a new house was £11,000 in Birmingham. The monthly debt charges at, say, 14 per cent per annum would have been £127, but the monthly income from a reasonable rent charged in the first year only £28, less rent rebate. However the nation's housing finance system is manipulated, there is no way in which monthly debt charges of £127 can be met from a household income of, say, £160 – more than the median for Small Heath in 1974 – without substantial subsidies whether found by raising rent on existing dwellings or by government grant. With inflation the rental income would eventually overtake the debt charges. Even so, it is bound to be difficult to effect rent increases large enough to balance future outlays (including management and maintenance costs) and future rental income when these are brought into current terms. This is particularly the case when interest rates and therefore discount rates are at historically very high levels.

Redevelopment could be speeded up by cutting the construction programme of peripheral development and by the switching of resources to the development of cleared sites in the inner city, which should be given high priority. In Small Heath itself, redevelopment will replace only about 750 of 3,000 houses cleared. Higher densities could increase this figure, but we feel that the proposed maximum of 60 habitable rooms per acre to be reasonable for the redevelopment bearing in mind that densities in adjoining HAAs and GIAs are likely to remain up to twice as high. Our main concern is not the form of rebuilding but the time it takes. At present 7.3 hectares of cleared land in the St. Andrews Redevelopment Area (much of which is in Small Heath) await housing development by the council, some of it cleared over seven years ago. Quick development of this land would:

Improve the visual environment

Reduce expenditure on temporary maintenance of undeveloped sites

Improve the chances of clearance area residents being rehoused locally

Provide at an earlier date a better mix of housing quality in the inner areas

Speed up rejuvenation of community facilities and shops hit by population loss

Bring land owned by the council into income earning use at an earlier date.

There is nothing new about recommending quicker development – we can only hope that reiterating the advantages will encourage efforts to overcome the obstacles already recognised by the government.[1] Although we attach great importance to the quick development of these cleared sites they do not account for much of the total building programme – of 16,700 dwellings for which the city had sites at December 1975, less than 9,000 were within the developed urban area of the city, the remainder being peripheral sites. Giving inner areas priority in housing and environmental

1. *Housing: Needs and Action, Circular 24/75*, DOE.

expenditure need not, as is often supposed, be at the expense of new towns and town expansion schemes (the city currently nominates tenants for overspill schemes in Daventry, Droitwich, Redditch and Tamworth). Cutting peripheral expansion in Birmingham is an alternative which we advocate.

An assessment of the construction programme would not be complete without some consideration of the scope for improving utilisation of the existing housing stock. Various approaches to improving utilisation have been exploited by Birmingham – conversions to self-contained units but to prevent those that were to less than full and exchanges. On conversions the city's strategy was until recently to promote conversions to self-contained units but to prevent those that were to less than full self-containment. The numbers have been disappointing and the city expects only a net gain of about 2,850 dwellings through conversions in the four years to 1980 (council 1850, housing associations 600, private 400). The potential for conversions to full self-containment in inner areas such as Small Heath is unfortunately limited. New council dwellings, dwellings less than 5 rooms in size or in clearance areas can all be ruled out; vacancies occur in less than 10 per cent of undivided houses each year; conversions for sale are restricted by the reluctance of building societies to lend in Small Heath, let alone on converted properties; private conversions for renting are unlikely when market conditions favour sale of the undivided house. Statistics on grant aided conversions in Birmingham (P21 and P22 returns) indicate that almost all are outside declared GIAs and HAAs.

In contrast to conversions to self-contained units, conversions to less than self-contained standards, so-called multiple occupation, have at times proceeded quite fast in the recent past, and particularly so in inner areas. Although conditions in many multi-occupied houses are reasonable, they are often associated with bad management and poor social and physical conditions. Until recently the city interpreted the trend to multi-occupation as a threat to housing standards to be dealt with by strict control over existing multi-occupied houses and by stopping further conversions. This policy was backed by a special local act and included refusal of all applications for special grants towards provision of standard amenities which had been introduced in the 1969 Housing Act.

DOE advice to local authorities on multi-occupation distinguishes between families and single people. For families, policies to control the level of multiple occupation and secure the provision of necessary facilities are recommended but with the objective of providing decent self-contained accommodation. But when multiple occupation is providing a pool of cheap rented accommodation to single people, the DOE advises recognising this function and taking steps to ensure a continued supply of accommodation suitable for single people.

The breakdown of households in Small Heath who occupy 'rooms' is in fact as follows:

Families	25%
Single persons and couples	
aged under 60	74%
aged over 60	1%

Probably about half the single people and couples are aged under 30. One way of fostering a continued supply of cheap accommodation for single people and couples in Small Heath would be to allow renovation grants for conversions by owner occupiers for sub-letting purposes (as is already possible under the present grant system, other than for sub-letting to relatives which we understand the DOE is considering).

The advantages of the resident landlord system in Small Heath are:

It is the one form of private renting that has not been in decline in Small Heath (26 per cent of all tenants in 1974)

It generally does not have the management problems associated with absentee landlords (most resident landlords have only one tenant)

It supplements the income of low income owner occupiers (66 per cent of resident landlords had household incomes of less than £40 a week in 1974)

It relieves the pressure of demand on absentee landlord multi-occupied properties

It does not involve the same loss of family dwellings that multi-occupied, absentee landlord arrangements do (67 per cent of resident landlords have families).

For the 25 per cent of households in 'rooms' who are families, however, self-contained accommodation must remain the only acceptable objective.

The resident landlord system is particularly important as a stepping stone to owner occupation among immigrants, who in Small Heath account for over 80 per cent of tenants with resident landlords. The following extract from a Circumstances of Families interview with a Punjabi immigrant illustrates this:

'When we came here we had only £700 with us. We lived for about nine months with somebody else. Then we bought this house and borrowed money from different people. Now we repay that loan back and meet our own expenses also.'

There are not now many student lodgers in Small Heath. One owner occupier blamed enforcement of regulations:

'This used to be a terrific student area, very convenient for Aston University. There isn't any now. We've had students for 15 years . . . If they changed the law a little bit so that people could still take them in . . . You take in a student and what do you get? First of all the health authorities get you straight away and they're not out the door when the fire authorities are after you. And it means that you have to spend a terrible lot of money.'

While the enforcement of health and fire regulations is important, enforcement should usually be coupled with offers of renovation and loans which have not been hitherto available in Birmingham.

Our proposals for helping families in overcrowded or unsatisfactory shared accommodation are related to those for reducing the numbers of vacant dwellings. Figures relating to the drawing of the sample for the SCPR survey suggest that vacancy levels in Small Heath in 1974 were not particularly high – 2 per cent on council estates, 5 per cent in the redevelopment area, and 4 per cent elsewhere.

However, since 1974, the expansion of the city's dwelling stock and deterioration in the economic situation may well have increased vacancy rates. Moreover, there is evidence from rating statistics[1] and from the 1971 census that in the private sector vacancy levels are higher among the older inner area properties than among the newer outer area ones. The measures which we propose later in the chapter with regard to low income purchasers and mortgages on older houses are therefore partly aimed at increasing effective demand for older inner area properties and thereby reducing vacancies. The best results in terms of occupancy will be achieved if the position of large families in the housing market is improved, for the figures we quoted earlier show just how far they are from occupying the available larger houses.

We have now reviewed the city's building programme and considered possible measures to improve the utilisation of the existing dwelling stock. We have identified several grounds for thinking that the city's present building programme might be too ambitious:

It cannot of itself put right the mismatch between dwelling sizes and household sizes and will produce a dwelling stock that is under-occupied

It is very difficult to finance in the current economic situation

There is scope for improving the utilisation of the present dwelling stock

Insofar as national cuts in house construction have to take place, it may be considered better to cut peripheral expansion rather than redevelopment, committed new towns or town expansion schemes

It may come near to eliminating one form of housing deprivation (sharing of dwellings) whereas other forms of housing deprivation may be of greater concern.

The case for a cut back in council construction must essentially be made in terms of there being other priorities for expenditure. This would involve among other things issues of slum clearance, which we discuss below.

Slum clearance

Birmingham's building programme assumes that slum clearance is cut back to very low levels. It is in fact difficult to see how slum clearance could be cut back any further than the levels now projected by the city. At the beginning of 1976 the city's plans were to demolish 5,000 dwellings in redevelopment areas and a further 2,400 in HAAs[2] by 1980. These figures would have been much higher but for decisions in 1975 to retain, after all, some 1,500 dwellings in redevelopment areas and to demolish fewer in HAAs. Although large scale clearance has now been rejected by government and local authority alike, and we certainly endorse the change in emphasis, small scale clearance will always be with us. Even if dwellings were to have an average life of 150 years, a city the size of Birmingham could expect to demolish 2,000–2,500 dwellings a year – slightly above the current figure in

1. J. Tate and N. Moreton, 'Too Many Empty Houses?' in *Housing Review*, July–August 1975, pp. 102 to 104.
2. Unless otherwise made clear, the term HAA is used in this chapter to cover both declared and proposed HAAs.

Birmingham. Thus our concern here is not so much with the issue of whether dwellings should or should not be demolished, or even deciding which dwellings, but with how to handle clearance.

Physical conditions and social circumstances

One of the main findings from studying clearance in Small Heath is that the dwellings in redevelopment areas reached their present appalling physical condition only within the last few years. In the SCPR survey 61 per cent of residents in the redevelopment area thought the area had gone downhill a lot in recent years – a not altogether surprising figure until it is realised that the redevelopment area was declared in 1957, and that 'recent years' means since the decision to redevelop was announced (61 per cent of residents of redevelopment areas have arrived since 1959). There also appears to be a period of accelerated but less rapid deterioration in the few years prior to declaration – in Chapter 3 we gave evidence of the lower incidence of maintenance and improvement work in areas adjoining redevelopment areas which had not been given the guarantee of GIA proposals. Home interviews in the Circumstances of Families survey confirmed our conclusions from the SCPR data and revealed the factors behind the rapid deterioration following the decision to redevelop:

Lack of maintenance by owners (whether owner occupier, private landlord, or the council) in recognition of the council's predicted clearance date, delays in clearance lengthening this period of little maintenance by up to eight years

Damage to houses or services in demolishing adjoining houses

Damage to houses while temporarily vacant between tenancies

Damage to common services or common structural elements as a result of delays in boarding up vacated adjacent houses

Vandalism to occupied houses (mainly broken windows).

Most residents interviewed had had some, if very restricted, choice in moving to their present house and had originally found it acceptable, bearing in mind their financial circumstances. As one council tenant (who had been told by the housing department she would only be there six months) put it:

'And of course I've been here six years this January. But as I say I liked it when I first moved up here. It was very nice and the rent suited me then . . . it was quite a good condition when we first moved in. But we've had problems with the slates keep coming off and it was leaking and that you know . . . We have to put buckets upstairs to collect the water coming through the ceiling.'

The rapid decay in the physical condition of houses has been accompanied by a deterioration in certain (but not all) aspects of the physical environment. Our evidence for this came from three separate surveys: the study of children's environmental perceptions carried out for us by the Centre for Urban and Regional Studies, our environmental quality assessment and the SCPR survey. In the survey of children's perceptions it was evident that pupils attending schools in the GIAs and proposed GIAs have markedly different perceptions of environmental conditions in Small Heath than those in the HAA and redevelopment zones. In general, classes in the redevelopment areas and HAAs saw the local area in less favourable terms; fewer of them saw it as free from pollution, interesting (only half as many), clean (only a quarter as many) or not old. In all aspects of the environment studied, negative views predominated in the redevelopment areas and HAAs, eg, the place was seen as dirty rather than clean, boring rather than interesting.

The SCPR survey provided information on the views of adults and some insight into which environmental defects were of most concern. Some 46 per cent of SCPR respondents in the redevelopment area mentioned dereliction, rubbish and pests, both percentages much higher than in the rest of Small Heath. On the other hand very few mentioned traffic noise, or unclean or unlit streets or pavements. The environmental quality assessment confirmed that the cleaning and lighting of streets in the redevelopment area was indeed as good as in the rest of Small Heath. In only one other respect – proximity to a park – did the street environments in those parts of the redevelopment area remaining in spring 1975 compare favourably with the rest of Small Heath. In most other respects street scores were worse – more fly-tipping, fewer trees, fewer front gardens, gardens in worse condition, almost all rear garden walls and fences damaged, more non-residential land uses and car parking. Taking the SCPR survey and environmental quality assessment together the key environmental problem is empty sites and buildings.

The deprivation of living in bad housing and environmental conditions exacerbate, and are exacerbated by, the social problems of residents. We argued in Chapter 3 that the social characteristics of Small Heath derive primarily from selective inward and outward movement. However, the concentration of people with social handicaps in redevelopment areas is sufficiently marked to require further comment – Table 17 compares the social characteristics of households in the redevelopment area with those in the rest of Small Heath. The council itself, through compulsory purchase and its allocation policies for short life housing, has been a primary agent in this

Table 17 Percentage of total households with various social characteristics by area of residence

Households with	Redevelopment area (No. = 87) %	Rest of Small Heath (No. = 767) %
No working adult	20	18
Head of household not working	10	9
Only full time worker female	9	4
Household income less than £30 a week	42	31
Illness keeping person in bed	6	4
Recent visits to doctor	36	31
Recent visits to hospital	22	17
Persons suffering disability	33	26
More than 2 moves in last 5 years	10	5
Previously resident in a redevelopment area	19	17
Previously resident outside Birmingham (but in UK)	14	7
Divorced/separated head of household	10	4
Female head of household	26	16
Head of household widowed	18	13

Source: SCPR survey, 1974

selective inward and outward movement: 41 per cent of households in the redevelopment area of Small Heath were council tenants in 1974, and the great majority of outward moves were arranged by the council.

However, in addition to selective inward and outward movement our home interviews showed that the environmental conditions caused or aggravated health, social and financial problems. Here are some of the many examples unearthed in the Circumstances of Families survey:

> 'There used to be a door there where I've got the curtains now and it fell off the hinges two or three times because the wood's really rotten inside . . . . We haven't got a door to keep the room warm.'

> 'The ceiling collapsed upstairs, the plaster came in, we had it papered and all that came down, the water came down, it destroyed the carpets and everything. We did all this (decorations) and we only just walked out the doors and the lot came down.'

> 'The children were having upset stomachs because of the mice getting at the food.'

> 'I've had a nervous breakdown, and I've been in the North Birmingham Hospital having ECT electric treatment, but it's only this house that's done it to me.'

> 'I had bronchitis when I lived down in Handsworth you know . . . every old house I go to and it's damp, and it just gets worse.'

> 'That is my missus' wedding ring. We are halfway through a separation because of this house – it's depressing her that much.'

Just as the bad physical conditions have come about because of the long time delays between declaration of clearance areas and the completion of demolition, so we believe that the social consequences are made more serious by the length of time for which the bad conditions are endured. This is especially so in some cases when previous residence in redevelopment areas is taken into account – 34 per cent of households in the redevelopment area had made 3 or more moves in the last 5 years, and 14 per cent had to move because their previous house was due for demolition.

We have not been able to pin down the causes for the delays to our satisfaction. Figures given later in this chapter show clearly that, had the council given redevelopment area residents the same proportion of available tenancies in the last two years that it had in previous years, clearance would have been much faster. But it does not follow that the explanation is simply a policy decision to give more priority to transfers and general waiting list applicants. The shrinking clearance programme produces relatively greater geographical concentrations of families placed in short-life property by the council than existed in the past. This has been exacerbated by an increase in the numbers of families for whom the council has to find temporary or emergency accommodation. It is not that the council is deliberately deferring demolition to preserve a supply of temporary accommodation, but simply that the task of finding new tenancies for all the residents in a particular clearance area becomes more complicated as the proportion of residents who are in temporary or emergency accommodation increases. This is so because the council has to accommodate a growing demand for temporary or emergency housing in a shrinking pool of clearance properties. There has been a reluctance on the part of the council to offer property which is felt to be too expensive for a particular prospective tenant, while redevelopment area residents are determined not to accept sub-standard property again.

Whatever the precise explanation, every local authority with a large amount of short-life property has a range of reasonable short and long term policy options:

Immediate	Allocate a higher proportion of available lettings
	Carry out emergency repairs
Short term (up to 2 years)	Improve management of short-life property (increase maintenance expenditure)
	Improve demolition procedures
	Improve environmental care and protection
	Increase social services support
Long term	Give guaranteed future life to doubtful areas (including postponement of clearance)
	Spend more on maintenance
	Increase new construction to increase tenancy supply.

Rather than attempt to define a single best approach to short life property and slum clearance that would be applicable everywhere, we shall now elaborate on some of these alternatives by reference to three of the BIAS supported action projects: the public open space project, the 435 Centre and Shape.

Some lessons from action projects

The public open space project was concerned with the experimental development of part of the St Andrews Redevelopment Area for recreational use. The project had as one of its main objectives the provision of recreational space in a clearance area before redevelopment is complete. It was felt that provision of open space at an early stage of the redevelopment process would:

Provide continuity within a rapidly changing area

Limit vandalism by offering alternative play opportunities

Reduce the amount of vacant land subjected to fly-tipping and other abuses

Raise the morale of both new and existing residents by the provision of a rapidly maturing park.

Given these objectives, difficult problems of design and implementation had to be faced. The design had to allow for:

The temporary use of adjacent sites not zoned for public open space

Future inclusion of sites zoned for public open space but not available until uncertain future dates

The changing use of surrounding areas

The bisection of the site by a street which could not be closed for another year

The high risk of vandalism

Rapid implementation and maturing

Difficult soil conditions.

A detailed description of how the design and implementation problems were overcome would be inappropriate here, except to say that the design was based on a changing series of discrete areas connected yet separated by buffer zones to allow for a mixture of quiet and noisy activities. In order to introduce changes of levels and separate area uses about 3,000 cm of fill material was imported as part of an agreement with local civil engineering contractors. The quality of the fill material ranged from semi-rubble to near top-soil quality. A special planting technique was used to avoid the expense of buying top-soil. Efforts were made to involve local residents both at the design stage and at the planting stage.

The project has established that it is practicable to create a new open space during the redevelopment process within a year, and without using expensive top-soil or other expensive techniques. The ease with which cheap fill was obtained indicated that a programme could be worked out with major contractors such that in return for being allowed to tip in approved sites they might undertake some levelling free. The experience with the normal competitive tendering procedure suggested to us that negotiated contracts would produce better results for unusual projects requiring special supervision. Vesting overall control of the project in one officer is also essential for achieving quick results. Open space projects such as this will not be possible or even appropriate in every slum clearance situation, but we have at least demonstrated the nature of the redevelopment process is not in itself an excuse for postponing open space projects.

Shape was originally conceived independently of BIAS in 1973 as a unified approach to the problems of homelessness, community disintegration and alienation of young people in the inner city, using the rehabilitation of short-life housing as a medium. Shape now operates as a housing association renovating and managing short-life properties. It has been able to do this at the rate of about one a month. One quarter of the 35 tenants so far accommodated by early 1976 were already living in temporary accommodation of one sort or another. Four were being harassed or threatened with eviction and several were either living rough or involved in a domestic dispute rendering them homeless. Nearly all were badly placed for getting a council house, mainly because they had not lived in Birmingham for the required five years. Those applicants who were shortly to become eligible for rehousing and who would have lost points by becoming a Shape tenant were advised to stay put. By agreement with the council, Shape tenants were not automatically eligible for a council house when the Shape house was required for clearance, but considered solely as waiting list applicants. Shape tenants matched fairly closely the characteristics of tenants of the council's own short-life property – a history of housing and social difficulties, often referred to Shape by welfare agencies.

But Shape tenants were noticeably enthusiastic about their homes, which they saw as a substantial improvement on their previous circumstances. For some it meant the

144

Alan Clawley

I don't believe in them flats at all, for the old people . . . I mean, they take 'em out of these back houses, I know they're old back houses but they was all friendly, and they put 'em in these flats and they've got nobody, have they? . . . They all shut the door, and that's it.

Circumstances of Families

opportunity to re-unite separated man and wife or children in care. What was most appreciated was the increased space, the sense of security, a reasonable state of repair and separate accommodation. These features can all equally well be achieved by local authority provision, but the essential ingredients missing at present are:

Adequate initial expenditure to bring the house into reasonable repair

Acceptable maintenance standards, achieved partly by the ability to deal quickly with urgent repairs and partly by additional expenditure.

We would not argue therefore that a local specialist housing association is the only way a local authority can handle short-life housing. At £4 a week, Shape tenants pay significantly more than the usual £2 to £3 a week in council short-life houses. We believe that some tenants of the council short-life property would be prepared to pay for better maintained houses:

'This is £2 a week and if they found me one at £3 to £5 well I should have a bathroom and hot water and better surroundings, so that would not bother me.'

Thus the cost of better maintenance could be partly recovered in higher rents, and would also prepare people for the higher rent of the average council house.

Shape has been less successful in redevelopment areas with its 'community care' objectives. These objectives were first 'to help combat the physical and psychological decay that occurs in conjunction with the redevelopment process by maintaining community involvement' and second 'to encourage tenants and local residents to establish desired support activities, ie, childminding, playcentres, old folks activities, credit, bulk purchases etc'. The original ideal that Shape should operate in one area a unified approach to the problems of homelessness, community disintegration and alienation of young people broke down because:

The short-life houses made available by the council were spread over several wards

Some of the funding agencies were only interested in one aspect of Shape's work

Shape tenants tended to be too much in need of support to take initiatives themselves

Shape was opposed by some residents and a local councillor because it was seen as prejudicing early rehousing.

Birmingham City Council was opposed to the community care activities of Shape and felt that it 'should restrict its spheres of activity and concentrate its efforts on the renovation of short-life properties utilising homeless, unemployed youths and including the provision of training in basic building skills and including the provision of a hostel for the workforce.'[1] Because of the council's attitude and the reasons given above, the original concept of Shape as an integrated approach to local concentrations of deprivation such as in redevelopment areas has not been tested. We therefore have little hard evidence for recommending it and, though we still think the concept worth testing, we must consider the provision of social services on a separate basis.

1. Letter of Chief Executive to Shape, 8 January 1976.

146

The 435 Centre project run by the Birmingham Family Service Unit (FSU) is of some help in this. The FSU is a national voluntary social service organisation dedicated to providing intensive supportive social work for families with severe problems in coping with their lives. It has been operating in various redevelopment areas in Birmingham for some 20 years, and by 1973 had begun to think of a 'group' or 'neighbourhood' work approach to the shared housing and environmental problems of clearance area residents as a logical extension to its traditional family casework approach. The eventual BIAS-supported project was a combined play centre/community work/advice centre project operating from a converted derelict off-licence in the redevelopment area.

The play centre provision, both in term time and school holidays, took several forms. At the daily open sessions, some for any children between the ages of 3 and 17 and some for restricted age groups, the attendance was up to 30 during term time and 70 or more during school holidays. There were also closed sessions for particular children and sessions away from the centre. At times the activities generated hostility from some local residents who saw it as catering for the most unruly and least deserving children in the neighbourhood. Most of the vandalism is, according to residents, committed by younger children rather than by those in their mid to late teens, but inevitably the play centre must make alternative activities available to all children. The cost of the play centre was very low, using as it did property which would otherwise have remained vacant until demolition, and employing only one paid play leader. Nevertheless the council decided against continuing the play centre; no criticisms were made, and we understand the reasons to be financial. Recognising that financial factors preclude sufficient play provision to meet demands in the city as a whole, there are nevertheless good reasons for priority provision in redevelopment areas:

The high level of vandalism by children

The high concentration of families with social problems

The temporary nature of the provision required

The low cost of provision given the ready availability of vacant property

The exceptional difficulties faced by residents in trying to make their own provision

The hazards of children playing on demolition sites and in condemned buildings.

Our argument on the 435 Centre's community work/advice services follows similar lines. Although the number of enquiries was in absolute terms not very large – something over a hundred a month – this reflected the specialist function of the centre in serving a redevelopment area with a population of less than a thousand. In the SCPR survey households were asked what sort of problems they thought an information and advice centre could help with, and the pattern of responses indicated a much greater need in the redevelopment area (see Table 18).

The evidence of the SCPR survey as to much greater demand in the redevelopment area has been borne out by the fact that the 435 Centre was in fact visited by more than half the families living in the area at the start of the project. But the centre did

Table 18 Possible functions for an advice centre by area

	Redevelopment area % of total households (No.=87)	Rest of Small Heath (No.=767)
Information on what is happening in the area	9	6
Whether house is subject to CPO/demolition	11	1
Advice on housing repairs/condition	11	8
Help in finding new accommodation/rehousing	21	5
Information/advice on improvement grants	2	5
Advice on housing in general/other housing matters	11	8
Help with environmental problems, rubbish tipping etc	6	3
Advice about central/local government services (not housing)	2	2
Social security, pensions, family income supplement, etc	5	4
Information centre not needed/no problems in the area	0	1
Household has no problems/could not be helped by advice centre	29	44
Other answers	1	6

Source: SCPR survey, 1974

more than merely wait for visits. All the residents received leaflets and newsletters dealing with entitlements to benefits and progress with redevelopment. The value of the centre to the residents depended also on the chances of a response. It is clear from the Circumstances of Families survey that the 435 community worker was well known and trusted as someone who could sometimes get action and not merely give advice.

The community worker was less successful in getting the residents to tackle their problems by collective effort. The rapid turnover in population, the preoccupation of residents with getting early rehousing and their own personal predicaments, social divisions such as between newcomers and longer standing residents, the council's always optimistic views on demolition dates all conspired against significant collective action. Even if he had been a little more successful, a local authority providing support in similar situations still has to consider its overall availability of social workers. For example, the area office of the social services department covering Small Heath has consistently had over 400 children in care during the study with an average of only about 14 qualified social workers. Given this situation, employing social workers for family casework will inevitably take precedence over employing community workers. This is not to say that there is not more scope for social workers to use group work techniques where clients are as geographically concentrated as they are in parts of Small Heath. But it is the information, advice giving and advocacy functions of the 435 Centre that have been most fully validated, not the community work directed at stimulating collective efforts by residents. As with the play centre, the council decided against continuing to support the information and advice centre up to the completion of clearance in the area.

Our criticism of the handling of clearance in Birmingham is that the city has successively postponed demolition without providing either property management or social support appropriate to the social and physical conditions which themselves largely result from the council's action or lack of action. In the financial summary of our proposals at the end of this chapter, we have assumed that the city sticks to its present clearance dates, spends more on maintenance (£140,000 per annum)[1] and sets up play centres and information/advice centres to serve all the clearance areas in the city (£30,000 per annum).[2]

Area based improvement programmes

Birmingham has an extensive urban renewal programme consisting of proposed and declared GIAs and HAAs covering some 81,000 houses. The GIA and HAA declarations were initially phased over the period 1970 to 1978, a huge programme for eight years. The city adopted a programme on this scale on the basis that it matched both the extent of physical obsolescence and the city's remarkable post-war slum clearance record. The objectives of the programme include the physical improvement of houses and the surrounding environment, the avoidance of disruption to existing communities and the promotion of maximum public involvement in the process of urban renewal. Despite the size and scope of the programme, capital expenditure has been relatively slight – a budget of less than £9.7 million for rehabilitation in 1975/76, much of which was destined to be spent outside the renewal programme areas.

Most of the HAAs and GIAs in Small Heath are much larger than the DOE guideline[3] of 200 to 300 dwellings as a general maximum. For this reason there are pockets of housing worthy of HAA treatment in GIAs and vice versa. In Small Heath the large areas chosen for HAAs contain about 20 per cent of the dwellings within the GIA/HAA programme. In broad terms they are the worst areas according to the DOE criteria for choosing HAAs yet they contain no more than 20 per cent of the households suffering overcrowding and no more than 30 per cent of the households lacking exclusive use of the three basic amenities.

If there were more but smaller HAAs the incidence of bad housing conditions within them would be much higher. Nevertheless no more than half of the deprived households would probably be caught. Analysis of 1971 census ED data showed that overcrowding, sharing and lack of amenities are far from wholly concentrated in a small proportion of EDs, and that these three aspects of housing deprivation are not well correlated with each other. Thus the shortcomings of large HAAs cannot be eliminated simply by redrawing boundaries, and greater individual assistance is needed to reach those in need not in GIAs and HAAs.

Present housing legislation also fails to direct expenditure on environmental works to the worst areas first. Environmental quality is worse in the HAAs than in the

1. We have arbitrarily assumed a doubling of existing expenditure levels; it is unfortunately not possible to make estimates based directly on Shape's expenditure records.
2. Assuming no existing provision and 5,000 dwellings in clearance areas outside HAAs (where other provision is recommended).
3. *Housing Act 1974: Parts IV, V, VI: Housing Action Areas, Priority Neighbourhoods and General Improvement Areas, Circular 14/75*, DOE.

GIAs. Yet in an HAA the limit on environmental expenditure eligible for government subsidy is £50 per house and the works may not be on council owned or leased land, while in a GIA it is an unrestricted £200 per house. Not only is there a greater initial need in an HAA, but following declaration selective clearance may further increase both the need and the scope for environmental works. It would, for example, be a waste of land for a potential playspace or car parking site to remain vacant (and probably become a rubbish tip) pending an intended subsequent declaration of a GIA and the availability then of a sizeable environmental grant. Moreover environmental improvement may be just as important a stimulant to house improvement in some HAAs as in GIAs. We therefore feel that government subsidies for environmental improvements should be on the same terms as for GIAs. In some HAAs environmental improvements will not be important, and this possibility is catered for by other proposals given below for changes in the system of government contributions.

The value of environmental improvements in stimulating interest in house improvement depends very much on timing. Quite apart from the postponement of improvement inherent in the £50 limit for HAAs, environmental improvements in Birmingham take an inordinate time to plan and execute. The early GIAs have experienced a time lag of at least $2\frac{1}{2}$ years between declaration and completion of environmental works. As a consequence, actual expenditure on environmental improvements has been very low in Birmingham – only £6,521 in GIAs in 1975. Even the budget for 1975/76, £294,000, would at £200 per dwelling have covered only 1,470 of the 81,000 houses in the city's renewal programme. The time lags seem unlikely to shorten: critical path networks prepared by the city for GIA activities give earliest start dates for works outside highways as being month 31 and for works inside highways as being month 39. These delays reduce the value of environmental improvements as a stimulus to private house improvement and also mean that by the time the benefits are realised the real cost per house of the administrative inputs will be increased by a factor dependent on the level of interest rates.[1]

In contrast to capital expenditure on works of environmental improvement, increasing current expenditure on maintenance and environmental protection services is easier and quicker to implement, more effective, and has a better ratio of labour to administrative and professional employment. Even assuming that the environmental quality of an inner area can be brought up to the average standard in outer residential areas by a programme of works, the maintenance and protection problems are likely to be greater because of:

> Greater use of common spaces due to higher residential densities (eg, 123 rooms per acre in Bordesley Green GIA in 1971) and a greater proportion of children in the population (30 per cent of Small Heath's 1971 population were aged 0–14 compared to 24 per cent in England and Wales)
>
> More industrial and commercial premises in residential areas
>
> More derelict sites and buildings, and older fabric generally.

---

1. Ways of reducing the time lags are suggested in the BIAS report, *The Management of Urban Renewal.*

The SCPR survey gives evidence about GIA residents' attitudes to environmental services and a general indication of the shortcomings in Small Heath. On the one hand residents were less dissatisfied with street cleaning and (in particular) rubbish collection than with some non-environmental services and amenities, on the other hand dirt, rubbish, pests, dereliction, demolition, street lighting and housing deterioration figured prominently in their explanations of how the area had gone downhill. This suggests that the problem may be one of gaps in terms of what services do rather than any faults in the types of service currently provided. The city's environmental services department has shown some sensitivity to this by providing some supplementary services in connection with the urban renewal programme. For example, open skip containers are placed at selected sites in the renewal programme areas for five days each month to give residents a chance to dispose of material that they cannot readily get rid of through normal channels.

One of our action projects, the area caretaker, was an experiment in a more comprehensive method of plugging gaps in services. The experiment involved appointing an area caretaker responsible for an area with about 500 houses in a GIA declared in 1973. The area caretaker's work covered both routine maintenance and special jobs on an ad hoc basis. His routine responsibilities included:

Sweeping pavements, entries and rights of way (in conjunction with the local street cleaning gang who removed rubbish gathered)

Litter clearance from waste ground

Emptying litter bins

Checking for and reporting matters requiring specialist attention, eg, street lamps, damage to street furniture, broken paving stones.

Ad hoc jobs carried out during the project included arranging (and helping with) clearance of rubbish from dump sites, installation of additional litter bins, organising an anti-litter march for local school children and work within private curtilages (clearing gardens of rubbish, mending fences, cutting hedges etc). The work inside private curtilages was only done in special circumstances – eg, where a council responsibility was involved, or to help an elderly person. Wherever possible the caretaker carried out repairs himself and maintained a stock of materials and tools. As a resident of the area, the caretaker was able to give encouragement and advice to other residents on looking after the appearance of their properties.

A full time caretaker for 500 houses might be seen as lavish provision which could only be justified as a temporary measure to help bring a newly declared GIA in a poor state of environmental maintenance up to scratch. But part-time appointments and appointments for a larger area are, we believe, possibilities. Also, the area caretaker may be a limited substitute for certain existing council maintenance services, with a consequent saving to offset the additional cost of the appointment.

We feel, however, that there is a place for environmental works. The trouble is that the limits of £200 and £50 per dwelling encourage local authorities to spend these amounts in each GIA and HAA (although they have the discretion to spend more or less), whereas a more equitable distribution in relation to environmental deficiencies would be achieved by spending more than the limits in some areas and less in others. The system may also encourage an emphasis on capital expenditure rather than improving maintenance and protection services. We suggest, therefore, that the limits be increased but the rate of government contribution be reduced. This would give local authorities more scope for spending above the present limits but give them greater incentive to spend below the limits when circumstances did not warrant much expenditure on works or pointed towards the area caretaker approach instead.

If the principle of giving priority to the worst houses first is accepted, then it would appear logical to give HAAs priority over GIAs and in particular potential HAA declarations over potential GIA declarations. In Birmingham we estimate that even if the level of staffing on GIAs is restricted to one thirteenth of that for HAAs, at least 30 per cent of staff resources available to the renewal programme over the next few years has been pre-empted by GIAs already declared. A backlog of potential (undeclared) HAAs with worse housing conditions than in declared GIAs is therefore likely to persist in the city. This is another argument in favour of keeping HAAs small and restricted to conditions which could not be tackled by GIA treatment.

Despite the weaknesses of the present GIA and HAA programme in Birmingham, we generally support the concept of area based programmes when backed by the necessary financial commitment and improved organisation. Deprivation does tend towards concentrations in small areas. An area based approach facilitates public involvement and the planning of action. The various changes we suggest in this chapter and the next would improve the effectiveness of GIAs and HAAs. But overcrowding, multi-occupation and bad physical housing conditions are not so geographically concentrated that the declaration of a number of small GIAs and HAAs could include the majority of households suffering from these problems. The analysis of census ED indicators by Sally Holtermann[1] shows that the worst 15 per cent of the EDs in the country would have to be given priority area treatment in order to bring within the net 64 per cent of households lacking a bath. If the worst 5 per cent of EDs were given priority treatment 30 per cent of households lacking a bath would be helped. At present less than 2 per cent of the dwellings in England and Wales are included in GIAs. A way is therefore required to couple area based programmes with greater individual assistance to those in greatest housing need irrespective of where they live. This theme we develop in the rest of this chapter.

House improvement – private sector

Birmingham's area based renewal programme at present largely depends for its success on the response of private owners. The main assistance to them has been improvement grants. Even so, in 1975 only 2,151 grants were approved in Birmingham, and furthermore they did not go to the worst houses intended for retention.

Most (81 per cent) of the grants went to owner occupiers whereas tenanted properties have the greatest deficiencies in standard amenities and repair.

1. Holtermann, *op. cit.*

152

Most (70 per cent) of the grants went to properties outside declared GIAs and HAAs and over a third to properties outside declared or proposed GIAs and HAAs. The 81,000 houses in declared or proposed HAAs and GIAs attracted only 1,309 grants.

The average size of improvement grant (£870) was low, indicating that grants went to the best houses. (In Little Green HAA the grant needed against the average improvement cost, at spring 1974 prices, was estimated to be £1,500, excluding VAT.)

The use of other types of renovation grant more applicable to the worst conditions was negligible: only 62 intermediate grants and no repairs grants or special grants.

The picture is similar for municipal loans towards improvement expenditure. The city made 270 loans in 1975 of which only 68 were in declared GIAs and HAAs.

This pattern of improvement not taking place in the worst houses has persisted for some years. Analysis of the 1971 census showed that 20 per cent of households in Small Heath gained exclusive use of basic amenities between 1966 and 1971 but that the rate of improvement was greater in those areas that already had a higher proportion of dwellings with basic amenities. The pattern persisted despite the £175 rateable value limit because there are substantial numbers of properties under the limit outside the 81,000 houses in the renewal programme areas and anyway some exceptions to the limit were allowed by the government.

The simplest explanation is that, even with grants, the worse the house the greater the cost of improvement to owners. In Little Green HAA, 40 per cent of houses inspected had rehabilitation costs exceeding £2,500 at April 1974 prices, excluding VAT. The average for owner occupied property was £2,000 and for tenanted property £2,300; stringent pruning of inessentials would have reduced costs by an average of only 20 per cent. These estimates assumed complete improvement to give a 30 year life. Using a housing quality assessment method developed jointly by the London Borough of Southwark and the DOE[1] we concluded that the average quality of the rehabilitated houses would in Little Green HAA be 80 per cent of a new house, and in a nearby GIA 90 per cent of a new house (in terms of generally accepted standards, not residents' judgements). Bearing in mind that when the cost estimates were made in 1974 an average house in a potential Birmingham HAA cost about £3,000 as against £10,000 for a new one, it can be seen that rehabilitation represented good value for money, and we must look instead at owners' and occupants' other circumstances for explanations of poor grant take up.

In the case of owner occupiers, the worse the property, the lower the income of the household tends to be, and therefore the less the ability to pay. Table 19 shows that even within Small Heath the proportion of owner occupiers without basic amenities is higher in the lower income groups than in the higher ones. We found that even with a 75 per cent improvement grant plus a council loan (at 11 per cent) to cover the remaining 25 per cent, the average owner occupier in the Little Green HAA would

1. *Organising Improvement in East Dulwich*, London Borough of Southwark, 1973.

Gordon King

There have been changes recently, over the last twelve months, you know. I think it's since they brought out the Improvement Area; they stopped knocking everything down, and started reconditioning what's up . . . There's been a considerable improvement recently, you know, if you look at the houses in this street.

Circumstances of Families

in 1974 have had to find £1.30 a week or 4 per cent of his household's income (at £31.50 somewhat lower than in Small Heath as a whole). Comparing Small Heath with other areas, ability to pay is also restricted by the numbers of dependants: 51 per cent of owner occupiers with mortgages in Small Heath have large families, compared with a figure of only 17 per cent for owner occupiers with mortgages in Great Britain as a whole.

Table 19 Owner occupiers without exclusive use of basic amenities, by income

Basic amenity	Weekly household income			
	up to £15 (No.=40) %	£15–£30 (No.=51) %	£30–£40 (No.=105) %	£40+ (No.=173) %
Inside flush toilet	40	29	18	12
Fixed bath or shower	20	18	16	10
Wash hand basin	30	20	17	12

Source: SCPR survey, 1974

Although these financial factors severely constrain grant applications from owner occupiers in Small Heath, there are also several non-financial factors at work. Some of these could become critical if the measures we suggest for dealing with the financial problems are adopted. One is the leasehold system – 60 per cent of owner occupiers in Small Heath are leaseholders. Renovation grants are not available to owners with less than 5 years to run on their lease – 7 per cent of leaseholders in the Little Green HAA. Council loans (usually with a 10 year term) have to be repaid 10 years before expiry of a lease yet 71 per cent of leaseholders in Little Green HAA have leases of less than 20 years to run.

Lack of knowledge about renovation grants is not common, but what that knowledge may be is another matter. The SCPR survey showed that 73 per cent of owner occupiers lacking exclusive use of at least one basic amenity knew about grants. The figure was much higher (94 per cent) in the HAAs and potential HAAs where the council had conducted considerable publicity, but much lower (63 per cent) among households with incomes below £15 a week, many of whom were elderly single people and couples. A surprisingly high proportion of owners are satisfied with their dwellings anyway; only 28 per cent thought major repairs were required. Some, particularly the elderly, not intending to apply said they did not want the bother. People thinking of moving (about 11 per cent of Small Heath owner occupiers) are also unlikely to apply, especially in view of the 5 year rule on sale of properties.

The elderly owner occupiers are perhaps the least likely to apply for grants. In Small Heath they tend to live in the worst houses, are less likely to know about grants, are unwilling to face the bother of improvement, often live in houses which are much too big in any case, and invariably had incomes in 1974 of less than £15 a week. (The low income is an imagined rather than a real constraint in that assistance is available in the form of maturity loans, supplementary benefits and special levels of grants in HAAs.) As one of our research projects, an occupational therapist was attached to one of the local urban renewal teams of the environmental department and given the task of checking on the circumstances of disabled and elderly residents in HAAs and GIAs. The project did reveal that there was more scope for adaptations, in the past arranged by the social services department, being carried out under a renovation grant, as provided for in the 1974 Housing Act. It was also clear that the social services department was applying financial criteria for the payment for aids and adaptations which are not applied in the case of renovation grants. Arrangements for a closer working between the social services department and the environmental department have since been made.

The financial constraints on private landlords are even greater than those on owner occupiers. Their houses need greater expenditure, and the financial rewards are less. Our calculations in Little Green HAA suggested a probable increase in rent income of £1.50 for the landlord and an average cost to the landlord of £625 (at January 1975 prices and assuming a 75 per cent grant), giving a return over 20 years of only 11 per cent gross. In HAAs landlords must continue to let their properties for seven years, so the present value of the chances of an eventual capital gain (taxable) is low. Also the rent increase would in fact have to be phased over two years. Surprisingly the landlords of one in three rented properties in Little Green HAA indicated willingness to improve their houses, and despite the economics some landlords do apply for grants. We have no evidence that the financial picture is any worse for landlords in the worst housing areas than in the better areas; but the proportion of private rented property increases as one moves from the better to the worst areas, and this is a major factor in explaining why grants are not in the main going to the worst houses and areas.

Both landlords and owner occupiers appear to be affected by problems associated with a lack of confidence in the future of some areas. There is no doubt that in those parts of Small Heath adjacent to clearance areas uncertainty about council proposals and the expectation of eventual clearance led to a loss of confidence among owners and a higher turnover of residents – 45 per cent of households resident less than 5 years as compared with only 34 per cent in the GIAs furthest from the clearance areas. Council acquisitions and the suspected allocation of some houses to 'problem families' reinforced uncertainties. Lack of confidence is cumulative: the continued pattern of improvement investment tending to go to the better areas feeds the fears that areas are deteriorating. Housing was the single most important reason given by the SCPR survey respondents for their thinking that their neighbourhood was going downhill. Nearly half of all owner occupiers seriously thinking of moving gave 'we want to live in a better area' as the main reason, or 58 per cent if those in houses due for demolition were excluded.

There are now several reasons for making changes in present policies in order to direct a larger proportion of public expenditure on grants towards the worst houses and areas:

The need to overcome the lack of confidence in the worst areas

The extent of the imbalance in expenditure between the worst and the not-so-bad houses

The need to tackle first those areas most at risk of becoming clearance areas

The principle that the distribution of public subsidies ought to bear some relationship to people's relative need

The need to make the renovation grant system work in support of area-based programmes.

Assuming that the total public expenditure on renovation grants cannot be greatly increased, any redistribution of expenditure will require either more refusals of applications by local authorities or the devising of new legal formulae by the government. At present there is no financial incentive for local authorities either to discourage or refuse low priority applications – they recover from the government 75 per cent of the cost and secure an additional rate income. The proportion of the cost met by the government ought therefore to be reduced to, say, 50 per cent in order to give local authorities the incentive of refusing low priority applications. We believe that the government should not have relaxed the rateable value limit without having provided some such financial incentive.

The relaxation of the rateable value limit is nevertheless one of several restrictions which should be discretionary for local authorities to exercise instead of mandatory once they are carrying more of the financial burden. The others are restrictions on re-sale of properties, payments for applicants' own labour and length of leasehold interest. These relaxations should give local authorities more scope for concentrating improvement investment in the worst houses and areas. Local authorities could be compensated for the partial loss of government contribution by an adjustment to the rate support grant.

To stimulate more applications in respect of the worst houses, adjustments to the amounts of grants will be required. The basic principle to be adopted is that improvement grants should be proportionately larger on houses requiring more work. Houses in HAAs already attract 75 per cent grants as against 60 per cent in GIAs and 50 per cent elsewhere, so the principle is already partly recognised. We suggest that the rate of grant should be 75 per cent everywhere, but that the first £400 (say) will be ineligible for grant. The effect of this can be seen from the following example:

Cost of improvement	Grant under present system		Grant under proposed system
	GIAs	Elsewhere	
£3,200	£1,920	£1,600	£2,100
£800	£480	£400	£300

This system would discriminate in favour of the worst houses, and would also make declarations of GIAs and HAAs aimed simply at raising the rates of grant available unnecessary. For those owners who still will not be able to afford improvement grants, we recommend greater promotion of intermediate grants (only 5 were approved in Birmingham HAAs and GIAs in 1975). In addition, provided that the percentage central government contribution to renovation grants is reduced as recommended above, local authorities should be empowered to offer 90 per cent hardship grants in GIAs as in HAAs. These measures will, we believe, go some way to securing a better distribution of public expenditure on private house improvement. They will not, however, by themselves lead to a dramatic increase in applications from the poorer owner occupiers with large families or from private landlords.

The low income problem can only be partly tackled by housing finance policy, but we make suggestions on this later in the chapter. In the case of the private landlord, we see a future only for the resident landlord whose position is analogous to that of an owner occupier insofar as rehabilitation is concerned. For the absentee landlord, acquisition by the council, housing associations or owner occupiers is the most practicable route to rehabilitation, and later in the chapter we make recommendations on how acquisition might be speeded up.

House improvement – public sector

The progress of house improvement by the council in the inner areas of Birmingham has been even slower than in the private sector. As in the private sector, much of the council improvement work has hitherto been outside the inner areas, as the following figures for improvements and modernisations carried out by the city show:

	1974	1975
To inter-war council houses	1,789	1,427
Flat conversions	49	175
Inner areas modernisations	320	315
Four bedroom conversions	15	9

It is now the city's policy to increase the inner areas' share of total expenditure on council improvements, but even so there are real practical and financial constraints.

Improvements to acquired houses not only cost more than those to council built houses but also involve the additional expenditure of acquisition. Even if it had theoretically been possible to allocate all the 1975/76 budget for council house improvements to acquired inner area properties, concentrating on HAAs, the accompanying budget for acquisitions of properties with vacant possession would have had to be around £10 million more than the £5 million budget for acquisition. But since the number of properties offered for sale with vacant possession in the city's inner areas each year is only around 2,500 and since the council could not have wished to pre-empt purchases of these by owner occupiers, additional council acquisition would have had to be with sitting tenants. We had difficulty in getting statistics on this type of purchase, but in the second half of 1975 only 4 tenanted properties were acquired in GIAs and HAAs over the whole city (P11 return), at an average cost of under £1,000. We believe that the cost of an expanded acquisitions programme would in fact be very low because it would mostly involve acquisitions of tenanted properties. In fact it could be that the acquisition cost is as low in proportion to the rehabilitation cost as the land cost in proportion to the construction cost in the case of new building. Thus a shift in public expenditure from new construction to council acquisition and rehabilitation need not involve any change in total expenditure on building work.

In advocating increased acquisition we are not primarily concerned with making judgements about alternative tenures but with taking the worst houses out of the hands of their present owners in order to save them from further deterioration. In any case the acquired houses could ultimately be resold to owner occupiers or housing associations or be transferred to cooperatives. Of greater urgency than arguments about alternative future tenures is the need to put right the present situation in which there is more public expenditure on private house improvement than council improvement of older properties, when by and large the expenditure is not on the worst of the properties intended for retention. So long as private improvement is applied mainly to the better of the properties intended for retention, then council improvement should get sufficient of the available public expenditure to ensure the future of the worst areas. The financial arguments for urgent steps to avoid having to redevelop the worst areas in the GIA/HAA programme are strong. We undertook a detailed analysis of the economics of redevelopment versus rehabilitation in Little Green HAA using a computer model based on work by Lionel Needleman.[1] This showed that rehabilitation was economic for virtually all houses in the HAA except those whose rehabilitation costs exceeded £7,250, even at very low real interest rates and high rent differentials (which favour redevelopment).

The pattern that we have seen in both the private and council sectors of improvement activity taking place mainly outside the worst areas intended for retention is repeated in the housing association sector. Although neither the Housing Corporation nor Birmingham City Council could give us any statistics on housing association activity in the city, we believe that most of it takes place outside the renewal programme areas. Although the council had by the end of 1975 advanced £5 million to housing associations for the purchase and improvement of older dwellings most of them appear to have been outside the renewal programme areas, and the associations were in fact more active in building new dwellings, again mostly outside the inner areas. Improvements and conversions by housing associations in Birmingham totalled only about 380 in 1975, so their role is only likely to be significant in renewal areas if there is a shift in emphasis from new building to improvement and from outer to inner areas. We therefore support current DOE policy to restrict housing association activities to GIAs and HAAs.

The quality of housing is a matter of maintenance as well as improvement. As noted in Chapter 2, we found that council tenants feel their homes are in a worse state of repair than do private tenants. Our evidence for this comes from the SCPR survey, our action projects and from the Circumstances of Families survey. It is true that council tenants probably rightly expect a higher standard of maintenance from their landlord than private tenants have been conditioned to expect. But the main justification for the extension of the local authority sector in areas of older housing,

1. Lionel Needleman, 'The Comparative Economics of Improvement and New Building', *Urban Studies, Vol. 6, 1969.*

whether by redevelopment or rehabilitation, is that it is the best means of ensuring an improvement in housing quality. It is therefore important that the change from the private sector to the municipal sector is viewed by the occupants and other residents in the area as an improvement.

Government directives on housing expenditure have identified housing maintenance as an area in which local authorities should economise so standards are likely to decline rather than improve. Maintenance has to be paid for and it may be that in the public sector space and other standards have to be sacrificed in order to pay for better maintenance. Present housing policy takes standards (ie, Parker Morris) as fixed and maintenance as variable, whereas in reality it is possible to spend more on the one at the cost of less on the other. There is a case for giving local authorities some freedom to choose the balance between the two.

Housing costs and choice

Slum clearance, rehabilitation and new construction programmes inevitably affect the housing costs and choices of inner area residents and vice versa, in that residents' family circumstances and disposable incomes influence their housing needs and preferences. The growing complexity of housing subsidies and price controls has, however, made it increasingly difficult to see how this inter-relationship works in practice. Our analysis of the financial circumstances of each tenure group in Small Heath suggests that certain improvements in the housing finance system could usefully be made, but also that there are limits to what tinkering with the present system can achieve.

Private accommodation

In Small Heath, the most obvious anomalies of the present housing finance system are to be found in the owner occupied sector. Our interviews in the Circumstances of Families survey gave the impression, not always, but consistently, that owner occupation was very much the preferred form of tenure. It was certainly the preference among people for whom it was a realistic option. Asian and West Indian immigrants placed a particularly high value on home ownership. This preference appears to be quite independent of the factors we mention below as having restricted the access of immigrants to council housing. Most Asian owner occupiers have moved out of rented accommodation, frequently when the landlord demanded a rent increase:

> 'We were living in Sparkbrook on rent. It was a large family. I was living with my mother. The room was not sufficient. I thought I pay about £6 a week as rent. Why not buy a house and pay for that £16 or £18 a month? So I purchased this house.'

Part of the explanation for the desire to own homes was a particular attitude toward debt and security, and to use home ownership as a means of accumulating assets. Asians liked to feel themselves secure from mischance and 'unforeseen circumstances' and to have sufficient resources to visit relatives in Asia or even in some cases to resettle there.

160

Although successive governments have accepted owner occupation as a form of tenure to encourage, they have not directed support to the low income purchaser. Tax relief on mortgage interest is a regressive subsidy: less subsidy to the low income purchaser than to the high income one. Moreover it gives less subsidy to the low income purchaser than he would get as a council tenant or private tenant. In Small Heath, an average large family (3 adults and 4 children) in an old terraced house (£4,000 in 1974) with an 80 per cent mortgage at 11 per cent interest would be given a subsidy of only £2.25 a week. The same family with an income of £35 a week in 1974 would receive £2.80 rent allowance on a £3.25 rent (net of rates) for an old terraced house, or £4.50 rent rebate on a £6.00 rent for a new council house which itself is subsidised. These facts may in themselves justify changes in the tax relief system on the grounds of equity, but there are other arguments in favour of change. First, low income owner occupiers cannot take advantage of the bigger subsidies under other tenures; the council sector is barred to them and anyway has too few large houses, and the private rented sector has little accommodation suitable for families. Second, improving the financial position of owner occupiers in inner areas would stimulate house improvement, because the poorer owner occupiers tend to live in the worst houses. Third, many large families who are owners or prospective owners cannot afford houses of a suitable size, so improving their financial position would contribute to a better utilisation of the dwelling stock. Modifications to the tax relief system involve nationwide considerations of overall housing finance which we cannot analyse here, so we are reluctant to be too specific or dogmatic in recommending changes. However, one approach would be a revised option mortgage scheme offering specially low interest rates on small loans where tax relief is not being claimed on any other loan, to be financed by modifications to the tax relief system.

There is also need to improve the availability of mortgage finance to inner area residents. It would seem from the SCPR survey that about 15 per cent of owners with mortgages have higher repayments than one would expect from house prices in Small Heath in 1974. The trouble is that building societies are extremely reluctant to lend in the inner areas, and the take up of council mortgages has been disappointing. For 1976/77 the city has earmarked 60 per cent of its home loans budget for older properties, but from the evidence of the SCPR survey the sum would only be sufficient to cover about half the purchases made each year by owner occupiers in Birmingham's inner areas. Several factors restrain the demand for council loans: lack of publicity, restrictions on short leases, repairs requirements and links between finance companies and local estate agents. In nearby Saltley, the CDP found that 62 per cent of mortgages were held by major banks, 15 per cent by fringe banks, 13 per cent by building societies and 10 per cent by the city; our interviews in the Circumstances of Families survey suggested the pattern is similar in Small Heath. As noted earlier, some 60 per cent of owner occupiers in Small Heath are leaseholders and a large proportion have leases with less than 20 years to run (in Little Green HAA, 70 per cent of leases). Owners of these leaseholds do not enjoy the capital gains that other owner occupiers do, and cannot have local authority mortgages since the Housing Acts require advances to be repaid 10 years before the expiration of leases.

Asians seem especially vulnerable to leasehold problems and high interest payments. Several instances of lack of knowledge of the mortgage system emerged in the Circumstances of Families survey. For example:

> 'I got the mortgage from the bank actually. Because when I came in this country I was not very well acquainted about these mortgages, you know. I came across the agent – his name is B***** – who is Indian but in my opinion he is a bloody rogue. As you know he fixed us up and I'm paying about 14½ per cent. I should have gone to the building society actually. They are paying only 10–11 per cent.'

The same East African Asian mentioned that a friend had a loan arranged by the same agent at 22 per cent with 'the Finance, a sort of bank like that, you know'. Another Asian we interviewed was paying £55 a month for a bank loan to purchase a 25 year lease. Fortunately many Asians are able to borrow from friends and relatives at no interest, at least to pay a deposit.

There are two main schemes, both of them developed by Birmingham, which can be applied to these problems. The first is the city's 'half and half' mortgage scheme. The objective of this scheme is 'to enable more couples to start on the ladder of home ownership'. In broad terms purchasers buy half the house and rent half. For example, at 1975/76 prices a purchaser of an £11,000 house would make the following monthly payments:

30 year mortgage on £5,500 @ 11%, after tax	£35.08
Half reasonable rent	£14.08
	————
	£49.16

The total monthly payments of £49.16 are much less than the £70.15 (after tax) with a normal mortgage. Even so, they would still be beyond the majority of Small Heath residents whose median household income was less than £160 a month in 1974. If the objective of the scheme really is to make home ownership available to more people, then it ought to be applied to cheaper old properties rather than new ones. We believe that council mortgages, whether half and half or normal ones, should in fact be restricted to pre-1919 property in Birmingham so that an adequate supply of mortgage finance for the inner areas can be assured.

The other scheme introduced by Birmingham is council sales of unimproved older houses in a package deal which includes improvement, renovation grant and mortgage. The principal disadvantage of the council improving houses before sale to owner occupiers is that it is doubtful whether any benefit equivalent to the improvement grant can be passed on to the purchaser. Under the city's scheme the house is sold on a long lease and the improvement grant processed so that it can be given to the purchaser immediately the house is conveyed to him. The point of leasehold sale is that it puts the council in a stronger position to enforce covenants regarding the carrying out of the improvement work. The mortgage is given to cover both the purchase of the leasehold and the purchaser's share of the improvement costs, and in certain circumstances the repayments need not start until the improvement work is completed. If the city can increase the numbers of houses offered under this scheme (as yet very small) it would serve to make prospective purchasers less dependent on more dubious offers involving short leaseholds or bank loans at high interest rates. While the council can and should take an active part in leasehold enfranchisement, a prerequisite is to ensure that leaseholds with short unexpired terms are not commanding an unreasonably high price in the market because of lack of alternatives.

The housing cost in the private rented sector is rather different from the owner occupied sector. It generally offers cheaper but poorer accommodation than other tenures. The average rent in Small Heath was only about £2.60 in 1974, but over 70 per cent of private tenants shared basic amenities and 56 per cent lived at densities of over 1½ persons per room. The private rented sector is particularly valuable in providing cheap, short term accommodation to newcomers or new households in anticipation of an opportunity to buy or to get a council house. It is a very active sector of the housing market – private tenants account for 28 per cent of households in Small Heath overall, but 47 per cent of recent movers into and within Small Heath and 38 per cent of households seriously thinking of moving. In particular the private rented sector meets the needs of people excluded from the rest of the housing market by:

  The cost and delays involved in buying

  The eligibility rules for council houses (waiting time, residence, work place, etc)

  The shortage of small accommodation in the owner occupied and council sectors.

The private rented sector has, however, been shrinking quite rapidly in Small Heath through slum clearance and sales to owner occupiers and to the council. This has created a situation in which rent levels could well rise.

Means tested rent allowances, intended to cushion the burden of the rent increases which accompanied de-control, have not proved a particularly effective means (in Birmingham at least) of support, particularly for furnished tenants. The problem lies with take-up rates (eg, in 1974 only some 20 per cent of eligible furnished tenants in Birmingham obtained allowances) and the reasons for low take-up are not entirely clear, but appear to be most closely linked with lack of knowledge about eligibility. As rents rise, eligibility for allowances will become more widespread, and their selectivity in favour of the poorer tenant will be reduced. If take-up is significantly improved and rents do rise, the cost of the scheme could easily become three or four times as great as the £1 million spent in Birmingham in 1975/76.

We are therefore against reliance on the rent allowance scheme as a means of preserving a pool of cheap accommodation in the face of rising rents. In the case of resident landlords, the trend to higher rents could be controlled by increasing the supply. We have already suggested allowing renovation grants for conversions to less than self-contained standards, and in addition the government should pay particular attention to improving the resident landlord's situation in its current review of the rent acts. In the case of the non-resident landlord, we believe that in the inner areas of Birmingham there is no practicable alternative to his gradually being bought out by the local authority, housing associations and owner occupiers.

It is important, though, that acquisition by local authorities and housing associations are handled in such a way as not to prejudice the supply of cheap accommodation to rent. We have already explained that stepping up council or housing association acquisitions from landlords (which we believe essential if dwellings are to be saved from further deterioration) can only be achieved by buying properties with sitting tenants. We do not favour immediate complete rehabilitation of these acquired dwellings because it would invariably require temporary or permanent rehousing of the tenants and involve earlier rent increases. Instead the local authority (or housing association) should only carry out those repairs essential to preserving the building, postponing complete renovation. When vacant possession is eventually obtained the dwelling can either be sold for owner occupation or further renovated for continued local authority or housing association management according to the overall housing situation at that time.

Council accommodation

In contrast to the owner occupied and private rented sectors, access to council housing depends on essentially non-financial factors. Whether the sector provides better housing depends broadly on whether applicants are allocated council built, improved acquired housing, or unimproved acquired housing, the last being generally in poor condition. Allocation, rent and rent rebate policies determine the choice of accommodation, as well as the access to council housing of different groups; they together have a major impact on the social characteristics of residents in different parts of the city. Tables 20 and 21 show that there are, for example, significant differences in the household type and ethnic origin of council tenants between the different housing areas of Small Heath. In particular large families with young children and a few immigrants who are council tenants are concentrated in the older acquired properties in redevelopment or improvement areas rather than in purpose built council houses on estates.

Table 20 Council tenants by area and household type

	HAAs* and redevelopment areas %	GIAs* %	Pre-war council estate %	New council estate %	All Small Heath %
Single people and couples under 60	15	2	7	17	10
Single people and couples over 60	20	25	30	29	26
Small families	17	16	13	20	16
Large families with young children	39	30	15	17	26
Large adult families	9	27	35	17	22
Base (=100%)	59	44	69	24	196

*Potential and (GIAs only) declared, as at January 1974
Source: SCPR survey 1974

164

Table 21 Council tenants by area and ethnic origin of head of household

	HAAs and redevelopment areas %	GIAs %	Pre-war council estate %	New council estate %	All Small Heath %
Born in New Commonwealth	7	23	1	8	7
Born elsewhere (including UK)	93	77	99	92	93
Base (=100%)	59	44	69	24	196

Source: SCPR survey 1974

When access to council housing is considered, a distinction has to be drawn between residents of clearance areas and other residents. Until recently, the main factor enabling access to council accommodation for study area residents has been living in a clearance area. Under the Land Compensation Act 1973, statutory eligibility for council rehousing extends to all inhabitants of clearance areas resident at the time of the Compulsory Purchase Order and therefore includes groups who otherwise would be excluded from or have low priority on the waiting list. Although the proportion of all council lettings going to residents of clearance areas has been declining in Birmingham in recent years (from 49 per cent in 1972 to 30 per cent in 1974), it is still large particularly in the context of a decline in the total number of lettings (from 6,850 to 6,000 excluding transfers over the same period). However the new emphasis on retention and improvement means that the demands of the clearance programme on available lettings will continue to lessen, so that rules governing eligibility for and priority on the waiting list will take on much greater significance.

Outside clearance areas, access to council housing is determined by eligibility to enter the waiting list and priority for rehousing once on it. The Cullingworth report[1] advised that, in principle, no one should be precluded from being considered for a council tenancy. This ideal has not been achieved in Birmingham since three groups do not qualify for registration:

People who have not been resident or worked in the city for 5 years

Owner occupiers

Single people under 30 years of age.

All these categories are well represented in Small Heath, and the qualifications for registration tend to discriminate against residents of inner areas and thereby contribute to their relative deprivation. Immigrants, in particular, tend to fall into one or more of the categories, and a significant proportion of those experiencing housing deprivation in Small Heath belong to these categories.

In line with the Cullingworth report, in Birmingham, priority for rehousing from the waiting list is based on an assessment of housing need using a points system. A household's total points are increased by 20 per cent for each year of waiting. While

1. *Council Housing Purposes, Procedures and Priorities*, Housing Management Sub-committee, Central Housing Advisory Committee, Ministry of Housing and Local Government, 1969.

some consideration of waiting time is justifiable and although waiting time is less critical than formerly, a weighting of this magnitude could still discriminate against inner area residents who often have high housing needs points but little waiting time, and we believe this weighting should be further reduced.

Households at the top of the waiting list (including transfer candidates) are offered 'suitable' accommodation. If 3 successive offers are refused, no further offers are made for 12 months. There are no longer any publicly acknowledged criteria for making offers to different households, although the spectrum of types and quality in municipal housing stock is still wide, particularly in the inner city. It includes pre-1919 acquired housing at the lower end (both a decreasing number of unfit, short-life properties and an increasing number of properties bought for rehabilitation) and inter-war, post-war and new housing (mostly on estates) at the upper end. There are only special policies for a few prospective tenants considered likely to cause serious damage or likely not to pay – despite rebates – the higher rent for new housing.

Not having general criteria for allocation seems to be intended partly to avoid concentrating problem families in particular areas. Under a previous allocation system, the choice open to applicants depended largely on a subjective assessment of their 'suitability' (especially in terms of their housekeeping standards) for acquired and old or new purpose built housing. An offer of housing appropriate to or below an applicant's grading could be made, but not above.

The main effect of this was that families with housekeeping problems were concentrated in poorer quality accommodation (ie, acquired housing) in inner areas, and that all incoming tenants to such housing were considered problem families. This was not true. People who had waited a long time but were not in particularly bad housing circumstances could afford to hold out for offers of more popular accommodation, since there were no limits on offers. However, those who were further down the waiting list but had greater need, were more inclined to accept the less popular acquired housing (even short life housing) in inner areas, which they were offered in deference to the previous priority system, because acceptance meant speedier rehousing. Thus not all tenants of such housing were problem families. Nevertheless in the inner areas the knowledge that the housing department was allocating property to households judged 'unsuitable' for modern accommodation appeared to undermine the confidence of private owners and their willingness to spend on improvement and also affected the morale of existing council tenants.

Although no criteria exist openly at present, the broad range of housing types and quality which need to be allocated may encourage ad hoc criteria. This development could have a more negative effect on the distribution of 'problem families' than the previous open policy and could lead to a generally inequitable allocation. We believe that while the problem will not be truly solved until housing allocation is more firmly based on housing need as opposed to registration criteria and waiting time, changes in the rent and rent rebate system might help. The setting up of 'reasonable' rent levels for the city's council housing is designed, quite correctly, to reflect the considerable variation in quality of council accommodation. To avoid a geographical concentration of low income applicants in areas of less desirable and therefore less

166

Roger Coward

You go all round here and you've got thousands of acres and there's no signs of building on them. And yet the corporation, in their wisdom, they're going to start building at Sutton Coldfield.

Instead of knocking the street down they could say 'Right, before we move anybody else out, we'll build that street up again' . . . What they are leaving it for we don't seem to get to know.

Circumstances of Families

expensive housing the effectiveness of the rent rebate system is thus of particular importance.

In principle, the rent rebate system is a more selective way of providing income support to poor council tenants than fixing low rent levels, but – as with all means tested benefits – those eligible do not necessarily claim them, and those in most need seem to be less likely to do so. However, as a report by the Centre for Urban and Regional Studies (CURS) on rent rebates and allowances in Birmingham[1] emphasises, the system is less selective and ensuring take-up more difficult if eligibility is widespread – as when rents are high. The CURS study estimated that in 1974, including recipients of supplementary benefits (whose rents may have been paid by supplementary benefits, but who were otherwise eligible for rebates), 60 per cent of council tenants in Birmingham were elibible for rent rebates and half the total number eligible actually claimed them. The result is an ineffective and inequitable distribution of benefits. This problem of widespread eligibility could be resolved in two main ways. Greater efforts might be made to ensure take-up. However, based on experience to date, a lot of effort would be required to achieve a small increase in take-up. Moreover this would benefit a broad range of households, not simply the poorest for whom the system was devised. The alternative approach would be to restore the selectivity of rent rebates.

It might be possible to take into account the likely effect on eligibility for rebates when rent levels are reviewed and to hold down rent increases to prevent widespread eligibility. However, the government subsidy under the Housing Rent and Subsidies Act 1975 does not encourage this. On the one hand, rent rebate payments resulting from high rents would receive a 75 per cent government subsidy and only 25 per cent would be contributed from the rate fund. On the other hand, any deficit on the housing revenue account resulting from low rents would have to be covered by rate fund contributions, without additional government subsidy.

We believe that authorities should strive to set rent levels so that eligibility for rent rebates is not widespread. Council tenants should be able to trade amenity for a lower rent, but modern accommodation should not be priced beyond the means of lower income tenants. A rent rebate system can help ensure this so long as a high rate of take-up occurs (which is unlikely if rent levels are set such that a large proportion of all tenants qualify for rebates, as was the case in Birmingham in 1974). In addition it is hoped that the Housing Finance Review might lead to changes that help local authorities to keep rents in balance with rebates. In the meantime the need to keep rents down must weigh in council decisions on new construction.

Our discussion of the three main tenure types has focused on questions of access and availability, as determined by costs, eligibility and allocation rules. The private rented sector has been shown to meet certain needs which the owner occupied and council sectors cannot meet at present. The changes in the mortgage, tax relief and council allocation systems suggested above can only partially mitigate this problem. It has been often suggested that housing associations and other newer forms of

1. *Birmingham Rent Rebate and Allowances Study; Research Memorandum No. 44*, CURS, April 1975.

tenure are well placed to fill the gap left by the private landlord, but no conclusive arguments on this can be constructed from our evidence in Small Heath. There are three problems with housing associations filling the gap:

Most housing association activity in Birmingham at present takes place outside the inner areas

Housing associations which grow into substantial landlords may tend to take on at least some of the characteristics of local authorities as landlords, eg, eligibility rules and points systems to determine priority, such that accessibility to houses could become little different from that to council houses

Any equity sharing arrangement, while distinguishing a scheme from council house tenure, must inevitably cost substantially more in the initial years of tenure and thus preclude the function of serving the short term low cost requirements of many present private tenants in Small Heath.

In assessing the relevance of new forms of tenure to inner area problems, financial arguments need to be distinguished from housing management arguments. Equity sharing arrangements, whether co-ownership or Birmingham's innovative 'half and half' mortgage system, are certainly valuable in the context of overall housing policy in that they widen the choice available to people, but the financial circumstances of many Small Heath residents would prevent them taking advantage of the theoretical choice. The management argument for new tenures is that with expansion of council ownership, local authority management has become remote, depersonalised and ineffective. Now while the quality of housing management is important, it is not at present as central to the relief of housing deprivation in Small Heath as the council house allocation system, the ability of the council to allocate a sufficient number of houses according to its perception of relative housing need, and the maintenance of a supply of low rent accommodation. Genuine housing co-operatives (ie, societies in which outgoing members receive nothing more than the value at par of their share-holdings) would undoubtedly be valuable in widening choice for the lowest income groups in Small Heath, but cannot in the short term make a major impact on the role and nature of council housing insofar as inner area residents are concerned.

Financial implications

Our various proposals for changes to present government and local authority housing policies would have a major impact on the pattern of housing expenditure in Birmingham. As most of our data and statistical analysis covered the years 1974 and 1975 our financial analysis relates to the financial year 1975 to 1976 and is in terms of the prices assumed by the city in their budget for that year. It is of course too late to influence actual expenditure in 1975/76 and 1976/77; the tables given below are intended as a rough comparison of the financial implications of the strategy adopted by the city in early 1975 (and still being followed) with those of our own recommendations. (Had we used the city's 1976/77 budget and plans, the differences in the two strategies would have been even greater, since the gap between expenditure on rehabilitation and expenditure on new construction has been growing.) Our alternative capital expenditure programme is anyway not one that the city could adopt in its entirety by immediate and unilateral action, since its practicality is partly dependent on the measures we recommended for central government.

The crucial problem in defining an overall strategy for housing in the inner areas is how to finance faster rehabilitation. Table 22 sets out rough estimates of what full implementation of Birmingham's rehabilitation programme would cost central and local government at 1975/76 prices – some £219 million in all. By contrast actual expenditure in 1975/76 within the renewal programme areas was probably under £3 million, because of the tendency for a significant portion of improvement expenditure to be outside the renewal programme areas. Financing a faster programme is partly a matter of switching expenditure from new construction, and partly one of improving the ability of owners to pay for rehabilitation by changes in grant rules and in the tax relief system on mortgages, and by increasing the availability of council loans. So far as the switch in capital expenditure is concerned, Table 23 compares the 1975/76 city budget with what the balance in expenditure ought possibly to have been, given the change in emphasis we advocate.

We believe that council construction could be cut by up to a half in order to release funds for higher priority uses. On the basis of the city's own figures[1] a halving of

Table 22 Estimated total capital expenditure on rehabilitation required as at April 1975 to implement Birmingham's urban renewal programme*

	Numbers of houses	Unit cost £	Total cost £ million
HAAs			
Demolitions	2,400	—	—
Already fully renovated	100	—	—
Renovation of properties already council owned	1,250	3,000	3.8
Renovation grants	4,750	2,400	11.4
Acquition and renovation	4,000	7,000	28.0
Associated administrative costs	} 12,500	472	5.9
Environmental improvements		50	0.6
Total HAAs			49.7
GIAs			
Already fully renovated	1,900	—	—
Renovation of properties already council owned	6,800	2,500	17.0
Renovation grants	51,300	1,500	76.9
Acquisition and renovation	8,500	7,000	59.5
Associated administrative costs	} 68,500	35	2.4
Environmental improvements		200	13.7
Total GIAs			169.5
Grand total			219.3

*The figures are at price levels assumed in the city's 1975/76 budget and include associated non-recurring expenditure on administration; most of the figures are our own crude estimates.

1. *Report of City Housing Officer on Five Year Housing Programme 1976–1980*, December 1975.

Table 23 Capital expenditure on housing

	Birmingham 1975/76 budget £ million	BIAS illustration £ million
Council construction	34.0	17.0
Improvement, conversion and modernisation of council built houses	6.4	6.5
Acquisition of dwellings	5.0	7.0
Council improvement of acquired dwellings	1.1	5.0
Renovation grants	3.2	4.5
Environmental improvements	0.3	2.0
Total	50.0	42.0

Note: These figures include expenditure outside the renewal programme areas. They should not be taken as precise, as it is difficult to make estimates for the city as a whole when much of our data relates to Small Heath only.

the programme is the maximum cutback that would still enable significant progress to be made over the next few years in three important respects:

Increasing the city's dwelling stock (a gain of 10,000 by 1980)

Reducing the excess of households over dwellings (down nearly 6,000 by 1980)

Rebuilding on all the cleared inner area sites.

The cutback in council construction could be partly offset by our proposals for measures to reduce vacancy levels and to improve the utilisation of the dwelling stock (both specified earlier in the chapter) and by offering some council-owned sites to private developers willing to tailor their schemes to the city's housing requirements.

A case for going for the maximum practicable cutback in council construction would rest not just on the scale of government and local authority expenditure required for rehabilitation, but on the need to switch some investment from housing to measures to increase local employment. The changes in housing policies and housing expenditure recommended in this chapter will not by themselves eliminate housing deprivation. For fundamental improvements, incomes need to be raised so that people can afford the higher rents and other outgoings in housing that are inherent in rehabilitation and reducing overcrowding and sharing. It is thus appropriate to think in terms of switching some of the present housing expenditure to forms of industrial investment that we discuss in Chapter 10 for improving the employment situation in Small Heath. We shall see in the next chapter that under the present economic climate in inner areas, progress with rehabilitation programmes requires substantial expenditure on staffing and administration by local authorities, an effort that would not need to be as great if the underlying economic conditions in the area could be improved.

We went to meetings but we still don't know what's happening. You hear this, and you hear that, but nobody has bothered to come along and get a group of people together . . . and ask what we need.

SCPR Exploratory Study

The council should . . . ask people what they want. It would give them a better idea. They don't get information from the particular areas, they don't find out what people think.

Circumstances of Families

6 Coordinating services

The third item of our brief instructed us to look at the advantages of better
coordination of local services, and at an early stage in the study we concluded that
this aspect of our work should not be confined to issues of management within the
local authority. We had also to consider the relationship between the local authority
as the provider of services and the community as recipient, examine policy formation
and execution, and finally review the role of local government vis-à-vis local service
delivery. This chapter therefore looks at improving local authority policy making
and procedures while Chapter 7 discusses the development of a more organised
and articulate community – essential to any strategy for making the relationship
between people and government in inner areas more productive.

Our approach to coordination

There is an implication in the instruction to look at the advantages of better
coordination of services that it may be one of the keys to solving inner area problems.
But however bad the coordination of services may be, there are limits to what
improvements can achieve. Better coordination will not secure a better balance in
public expenditure between inner and outer areas, nor will it improve the effectiveness
of services which are simply inappropriate to needs. Since the advantages to the
inner areas of improved coordination depend so much on the appropriateness of
services and on the resource allocation between areas, we have widened the
discussion in this chapter to consider elements of political process as well as questions
of organisation and management.

Since any service is designed with the objective of meeting a perceived need, the
way in which need is defined, and by whom, will directly influence the type and
operation of the service delivered in response. The norms and values on which
standards, policies and programmes are based may well be very different from those
of the communities or groups for whom they are designed, and what is seen as an
adequate or appropriate response to need by policy-makers or administrators may
be viewed in an entirely different light by the public they serve. Hence, measures to
increase the cost-effectiveness of service management by maximising the
(measurable) output for a given input of resources will only be truly effective in
meeting needs if the needs are well understood in the first place. In our view, better
coordination of services is achieved both through improved decision making and
efficient management. The two must go together if resources are to be used to the
best effect, and both must be concerned with the quality of output as a priority.
Our experience in Small Heath has left us in no doubt that there is much that can
and ought to be done to improve services to inner areas; the following discussion
is an exposition of what we see to be the key factors in achieving that improvement.

Public policy and perceived need

It is not difficult to demonstrate the inadequacy of present public and private services in meeting the needs of an area like Small Heath. For example, welfare agencies cannot give adequate support to many people suffering severe personal hardship; problems within the Asian community (eg, the social isolation of women) and between the Asian and white community cannot be adequately tackled by only one multilingual community relations fieldworker; the severe environmental problems associated with the redevelopment programme persist; the maintenance of public highways, back alleys and vacant sites throughout the area is insufficient to prevent many from remaining strewn with litter and waste material. These are just some of the problems faced by both residents and the local authority. The area also suffers from a notable lack of private investment in recreation and entertainment facilities – a problem over which the local authority has no direct control, but is nonetheless a cause of concern when coupled with the fact that there are few recreation facilities of any kind for teenagers and the elderly.

Though there are many inadequacies in local service provision in the area, by no means all services are rated as poor by residents. The degree of satisfaction varies considerably from service to service, some (like public transport, shopping, medical care) being generally judged very favourably. However, expressions of satisfaction are insufficient as a true measure of whether or not a real need is being met, and should therefore be treated with caution. People's reactions to a particular service or services are coloured by their expectations, which in turn are conditioned by past experience and the knowledge or understanding of what is or ought to be available. We have found that in terms of housing and income, for example, many people have such modest expectations that they are satisfied with a standard of living which would be quite unacceptable to, say, most middle-income white collar or skilled manual workers. Where people's expectations are low relative to those of other groups there is a very real danger that resource distribution will tend to favour those with the higher expectations (particularly if they are more vocal or powerful), thus perpetuating existing inequities of service provision in relation to need.

Our experience in Small Heath has led us to the conclusion that failure to respond sufficiently to needs is probably more a matter of how those needs are defined, priorities set, and the necessary commitment of resources obtained than of how these priorities are translated into action and the efficiency with which available resources are used. Part of the problem here (at least in Birmingham) is that relatively few closely stated objectives or standards of service are to be found and where they do appear (in corporate policy documents, for instance) they bear an insufficient relation to specific needs situations in particular local contexts – that is, at the level of street, neighbourhood, community, ward, or even combination of wards.

It is of course essential that basic policy and objectives for the city as a whole are made explicit, but the limitations of generalised statements as a basis for local action have to be recognised. For example, the city's Corporate Policy Review of January 1975 firmly stated that in 1975/76 priority would be given to expenditure on housing and to policies 'designed to aid the disadvantaged and to aid economic growth', and this statement was supported by a number of proposals, some generalised (such as increased training programmes), others specific (a new day nursery, for example). However, the true extent of resource commitment in accordance with these overall objectives depended upon the decisions of individual service committees, whose concerns are primarily to allocate resources on the basis of the varying needs of their particular client groups city-wide, in accordance with the objectives guiding their particular policy areas. Yet even these are often too generalised as a basis for action. The long-term housing policy objectives contained in both the city's structure plan and corporate policy review, for example, do not provide an adequate basis for setting priorities and integrating programmes in the short term (eg, new construction versus improvement), which further compounds the problem of meeting local needs in areas like Small Heath where considerable public intervention in the housing market is required.

The net result is that assessing the likely total impact of public policy on a small area basis is virtually impossible. Although corporate management fosters a greater awareness among departments of the interrelationships between their respective spheres of operation, if there are no explicit statements of needs and priorities at the local level then the appropriate 'mix' of policies and resource allocations cannot be achieved at that level. This problem is certainly recognised by a number of officers and councillors in Birmingham, notably those involved with the urban renewal programme, and has been acknowledged in the approach to the Small Heath and District Plan[1] currently (1976) in preparation. The study is being carried out on an interdepartmental basis (coordinated by the planning department) with the principal objective of assessing how far public policies, and particularly those of the city, can be made more responsive to needs in the area, bearing in mind competing demands from other areas. At the time of writing this report, the Small Heath Study has progressed as far as the definition of priority (policy) areas for detailed investigation, and how successful it will be in achieving its main objective cannot yet be anticipated.

On the question of standards and their function in service provision, there is a distinction to be made between units of measurement (unit costs, water/sewer pipe capacity, load-bearing capacity etc) and normative criteria (Parker-Morris standards, pupil/teacher ratios, health and welfare regulations etc). Intelligent, responsible use of the former is essential; failure in this respect may well become a source of controversy, but the standards are uncontroversial, being simply matters of fact. On the other hand normative criteria are themselves open to dispute, since they represent a value position on what is 'good' or 'desirable' which may not be shared by all those whom they affect. This is inevitable in a pluralist society where consensus must always be to some degree a product of compromise, and it does not in any way deny the need for standards or criteria aimed at safeguarding or improving the health, safety or general well-being of the population at large. What it does point to is the need to recognise that such differences exist both in setting and applying standards.

1. *Project Report for the Small Heath Study and Plan*, Birmingham City Planning Department, 1976.

Residents' attitudes towards house improvement, discussed in previous chapters, are a case in point. If the city is to maintain a housing stock adequate to future needs and aspirations it must seek to achieve the highest possible standards in rehabilitated dwellings; at the same time it has to face the very real problem that the burden of cost (and in some cases also disturbance) of improvement is more than the benefit in the view of many current owners and tenants on relatively low incomes. In this case both the standards themselves and the way they are applied create the difficulties – too much emphasis is placed on achieving the highest standard in every case, whereas a more flexible approach (permitted by legislation) would be appropriate in many cases.

Where there are few explicit objectives or standards there can be no real monitoring and evaluation either. Hence policy-makers are not made aware of the impact of their policies except through sporadic reactions from their constituencies and the public in general (via the press or pressure groups) or, in cases where individual policy initiatives have led to the designation of special geographic entities, like GIAs/HAAs, through the progress reports of local officers. Even so most committees and departments remain largely uninformed about the effectiveness of their work at the point of delivery. If needs, objectives and standards are defined primarily in relation to the whole city, then it follows that few politicians or administrators will have anything but a fragmented view of the outcome of policy at the local level. The local interrelationships between the impact of policies determined and administered by individual committees and associated departments will remain barely understood.

The redevelopment programme in Small Heath illustrates some of the difficulties involved. The process of clearance and rebuilding has been subject to progressive delays with the result that the Bolton Road/Cooksey Road clearance area has now suffered from increasingly severe social and environmental problems for the better part of 10 years. The direct consequences of this situation for residents in the clearance area are well known to local councillors and officers working in the area, but are apparently insufficiently understood at central department and committee level. It is not simply that these people require better housing but that for as long as they remain in their present situation they need much more advice, information and support than currently the council provides. The problem is not amenable to measurement solely against housing programme targets any more than the quality of education services can be directly ascertained from pupil/teacher ratios and building standards. But in the absence of more sensitive measures, these proxies for success or failure tend to assume an unjustified importance, and the impact of policy in areas like Small Heath accordingly is assessed largely by virtue of the area's position on the league tables of new dwelling units, teachers, social workers, etc and not in relation to known local priorities.

The complexities of urban renewal provide some important insights into the outcome of monitoring action programmes (ie, measuring performance over time) at the local level. Our experience in Little Green HAA has made us sceptical of an approach which seeks to establish agreed objectives and goals in a situation where a number of interdependent parties are involved – officers of different departments

176

and authorities, residents, councillors, civil servants – each with their own professional and political values and particular interests to defend. Even if objectives could be agreed, many would conflict and so the problem of how to rank them would remain; without such ranking, programme evaluation in terms of progress towards meeting objectives would be of only limited use. An approach which seeks simply to achieve general agreement on the action to be taken, based on separate, periodic reviews of progress by the various groups involved, is both more practical and likely to lead to faster action on the ground, which is the only measure of progress that satisfies residents. In this case, as in others, residents' interests cannot be adequately assessed by the use of statistical indicators, and we consider that the results of statistical monitoring exercises should be tested against residents' reactions.

Central government influence

Local authorities' problems in responding sensitively to a multiplicity of needs are compounded by the influence of central government policies and controls governing the allocation of resources at the local level. However, central government's concern to establish and maintain control over local spending is not matched by any evidence of equal concern to assess the local results, partially no doubt because local authorities are usually the agencies of implementation. But, through the Treasury and individual departments, central government constrains the freedom of local authorities to decide on their own priorities and on the amount of resources required to respond to the needs of their particular sets of circumstances. With the activities of local government becoming increasingly dependent on government grants and increasingly subject to cost yardsticks, government directives and guidelines, and to government permission, local accountability and flexibility are being seriously undermined.

Moreover, the operation of government controls can in itself be an expensive business as a result of the delays that they often cause. In Small Heath a year usually passes between a housing CPO declaration and public inquiry, and a further year before the draft CPO is confirmed, modified or rejected. Meanwhile the condition of the dwellings deteriorates further, and the occupants suffer two further years of uncertainty and inaction. We are not suggesting that there is no need to protect owners' rights by an appeal procedure but simply that the process currently takes an inordinate time. Even when government approvals only take two months, as with GIA and HAA declarations, they can still be costly in that if a declaration is refused the local authority has already sunk considerable administrative effort into a proposal by the time it is forwarded to the DOE – probably £13,000 worth of officer time in the case of the average GIA in Birmingham. This indicates the need both for close, informal contact between local authorities and central government departments in the early stages of any proposal requiring ratification, and for local authorities to have maximum possible discretion in determining their own priorities.

Central government policy controls are notoriously 'uncoordinated' anyway because of the structure and traditions of the civil service and because of the nature of political process which is constantly adapting to changing pressures.[1] Local government therefore operates within a situation of great future uncertainty, both in respect of the directions of policies and the resources available to carry out programmes. The problem here, as effects filter through to the neighbourhood level, is not so much lack of 'coordination' as lack of consistency or reliability. The government exerts considerable controls over local authority policies and if the direction of government policies or, more specifically, the allocation of funds is erratic, then there is little that the local authority can do to carry out a consistent strategy. As the scope of government and local authority intervention in inner areas grows, it is increasingly difficult to pursue at the same time a national policy and an integrated comprehensive approach in every local authority.

The operation of housing and urban renewal policies in Birmingham demonstrates the effects of these problems. The government's stated first priority is to increase the supply of dwelling units, but for many local authorities the improvement of older housing is more important. In Birmingham, restrictions on council acquisitions, imposed in 1975, and renewed in 1976, will postpone improvement of some of the dwellings most in need of improvement (rented properties and the worst owner occupied properties), while expenditure on improving lower priority dwellings (the better of the owner occupied properties eligible for grants) will continue. These controls are particularly inappropriate in the city's potential HAAs where conditions in rented properties are much worse than in declared GIAs, yet acquisitions are automatically approved only in the latter.

The operation of loan sanction controls also has far-reaching effects on the city's ability to pursue consistent housing and urban renewal strategies. Sudden cuts in allocations, however necessary and justified in the light of the national economic situation, have adverse effects either on the programming of work (eg, improvement work to council houses) or on the allocation policies of the authority (eg, advances for house purchase). In Birmingham, the sudden (temporary) halt to advances for house purchase in 1975 necessitated by government restrictions was inconsistent with the objective of stimulating private investment in housing in renewal programme areas, yet the council had no option. In an area like Small Heath, where the halving of the intake to the new community school (as a result of government restrictions on capital expenditure in education) had already resulted in considerable local dissatisfaction and controversy, this additional apparent inconsistency on the part of the local authority is likely to further undermine the relationship between residents and the council. Yet in this case the fault clearly lies with central government.

The adverse consequences of cut-backs in loan sanctions could be mitigated by replacing the sytem of individual loan sanctions for specific projects or purposes by a system of block loan sanction. Such a system would operate by the local authority submitting annual expenditure plans for housing, education and social services to the DOE, DES and DHSS respectively. It would be the responsibility of each ministry

1. In Chapter 13 we propose that the Urban Affairs Ministerial Committee set up in September 1976 be developed into a permanent government body responsible for the coordination of public and private resource planning for inner areas.

178

to satisfy itself that the authority was giving sufficient priority to inner areas in accordance with government policy. If such a system were adopted, there would have to be improvements in the communication of government policies to local authorities. At present the ministerial circular and ministerial speeches are the main source of policy statements by the government to local authorities. Their principal weakness is that they usually only deal with one particular aspect of policy, while comprehensive policy statements are given only at irregular intervals. In the case of housing in particular this reflects the incremental nature of housing legislation and failure to recognise the interdependency of housing and economic policies. The need is for regular annual statements of national policies, plans and expenditure allocations as a guide to local authorities.

In formulating overall policies for housing, education and social services, the government would benefit from speedier information on the progress of local programmes. The system of statistical returns is particularly antiquated. In examining various housing returns made by Birmingham, we observed:

Long delays in the completion of returns

Returns often completed by relatively junior officers, who too often misunderstood what figures were required, failed to spot errors or did not know how to rectify them

Returns sometimes sent to the DOE incomplete because suitable procedures for obtaining the necessary information had not been established.

We would recommend efforts by the DOE and DHSS in particular to speed up the publication of analyses of local authority statistical returns. This could be done by a computerised system, perhaps with the returns re-designed as input documents. Local authorities and ministry divisions could be supplied with photocopies of the tables as printed out on a computer line printer rather than waiting for the more expensive properly printed tables. We believe that earlier publication of statistical analyses and greater use of them by the government would encourage local authorities to take more trouble over the returns in the first place, and to use their own returns as internal management information.

The need for change

Uniform national policies and uniform regional or city policies are clearly inappropriate where needs at a lower level in the spatial hierarchy are not uniform. The key to better policies is therefore greater sensitivity at central, regional and city government level to specific local circumstances and the circumstances of special needs groups. Obstacles to the achievement of such sensitivity include: the often quite different perspectives of policy-makers from those of residents; misleading concepts of social accounting which tend to transfer onto inner area residents costs generated by users and other agencies; and competing demands for limited resources from other interest groups who may be more articulate and exert greater bargaining power.

Bob Marshall

The council is going to change all of Small Heath, but I couldn't say how they will help really. Probably they would help if you went to them, if you know which way to go about it, but I wouldn't know where to go, or who to see. I've had my problems but I've never gone to anyone for help.

SCPR Exploratory Study

We need someone for emergencies, somewhere we can turn to and say, 'Right, you fight this case for us, you fight Bush House, tell them we can't go without a bedroom for eight months, so what are we going to do?'

Circumstances of Families

The relationship between central government's national policies and priorities and those of individual local authorities must be made more flexible if in turn the local authority is to respond sensitively and effectively to needs within its own area, and the central issue here is expenditure control as an instrument of policy. Chapters 12 and 13 explore this issue at greater length in relation to the problem of generating extra resources for inner areas; the relevant point here is that local authorities should have greater freedom to determine expenditure priorities within broadly defined limits, with consultation between local and central government concerning the resource requirements for special programmes to meet pressing local needs.

A more flexible approach to the control of local expenditure priorities will only produce additional benefits for inner areas and their residents – or any other areas/ groups in need – if the local authority has, or develops, an awareness of their specific needs and problems and the will to tackle them. In Chapter 4 we discussed at some length the very real differences in perspective between residents of Small Heath and councillors and officials whose task it is to provide them with the services they need, and the extent to which these differences constitute an obstacle to positive change in the area.

During our work in Small Heath we have found some striking differences in attitudes and understanding between officers working at the local level and those who are centrally based. As with local councillors, the former, by virtue of their close contact with the community often develop a high degree of sensitivity to its needs and to the perspectives and attitudes of residents. Obviously the development of a similar degree of understanding is much more difficult for officers whose brief is to consider problems city-wide and whose direct contacts with local areas are limited. For many, the consideration of problems either in terms of a relatively small area like Small Heath or in terms of, say, the subjective reality of the process of redevelopment requires a fairly fundamental change of approach. The extent of some officers' remoteness from the realities of a local situation is quite well illustrated by an officer who remarked (during a discussion of policy issues in Small Heath) that the area was experiencing only 'temporary' difficulties for 20 years or so, and that once redevelopment was complete, many of its problems would be solved. So there was no particular reason to be especially concerned with residents' problems in this area, any more than in another. The significant point here is that the time-span mentioned was not seen (by the speaker) as almost a whole generation, during which time people had to live with the 'temporary' problem, but rather as a phase in the reconstruction of the city.

It would however be a gross oversimplification to suggest that insufficient sensitivity to the needs of inner areas is solely a reflection of councillors' or officers' difficulties in grasping the problems confronting them. For they are operating within a political framework which still tends to favour (tacitly or otherwise) the majority interest groups in society at the expense of vulnerable minorities. Strategic decision making, for instance, does not sufficiently take account of the relative costs and benefits to local communities or special needs groups of policies and proposals aimed at resolving problems affecting the wider community of which they are a part. Moreover, the assumptions about what constitutes the 'public interest' and how it is best served are heavily conditioned by generally accepted social norms and are therefore unlikely to be appropriate to circumstances which deviate significantly from these.

Hence we come up against the problem of misleading social accounting referred to earlier. Probably the best example of how this affects inner area residents is the urban motorway, which continues to be a source of heated controversy. In Small Heath there is as yet no urban motorway, but there are plans for the Coventry Expressway linking the New Coventry Road with the city centre via the southern part of our study area. The route, adjacent to the railway, was first delineated in 1959 but implementation of the proposal has been subjected to progressive delays and is not included in the county's current TPP (Transport Policies and Programmes). In view of changing assumptions about population and traffic generation, plus likely resource constraints, officers consider the probability of implementation within the next 10 years to be extremely low, and admit the possibility that the road may never be built at all. But this does not remove any of the costs already incurred by residents as a result of the blighting effect of delay, nor does it alter important basic questions about the proposal itself.

The principal direct benefits accruing to Small Heath residents would be a reduction of noise and congestion along and in the vicinity of the existing Coventry Road. An indirect but ultimately more important benefit could result if the construction of this part of the regional highway network were to increase significantly the attraction of Small Heath and neighbouring areas as a location for industry. Against this there has to be set the necessary demolition of 200 houses for the construction of a large interchange with the Middle Ring Road (Golden Hillock Road) and the increased noise levels affecting housing in Bolton Road which, even when redeveloped, will be within 50 metres of the expressway. Moreover, since car ownership in the area is low (26 per cent in 1971) and shows little sign of increasing, the use of the road by Small Heath residents, for any purpose, is likely to be very restricted.

The proposed expressway is designed primarily to link the outer suburbs with the city centre, with minimal access in between. The route, like all other major links, is intended to help maximise the total number of trips on the regional network. This means connecting zones of high car ownership with zones of maximum attraction, such as Solihull (67 per cent car ownership in 1971) and the city centre, via areas of low car ownership like Small Heath. Hence car owners from the outer areas are benefiting from the road in terms of time saved on peak-hour journeys to work because they will maximise travel on the network. However, though much of the route through Small Heath utilises vacant land, cost-benefit analyses have not adequately catered for environmental impacts (noise, vibration, pollution, etc), neither have they sufficiently taken account of the social costs of disruption to the residents of houses demolished as part of the interchange scheme, nor of the opportunity costs associated with the diminution of the scare resources of housing and land in the inner area. Furthermore, residents in the areas affected by the delayed proposal have had to bear the psychological costs of uncertainty as well as the financial costs of the inevitable reduction in the value of private property.

182

No such costs are borne by the principal users; indeed many of them stand to gain financially if (as is likely) property values in the outer suburbs are ultimately enhanced by improved road access to the city centre.

The history of the Coventry Expressway also touches on important issues of power and influence within the framework of decision-making. We have already considered (in Chapter 4) the adverse consequences for inner area residents of competing demands for scarce resources from more articulate, powerful groups. Here we see a different facet of the problem of power and influence, which is simply the extent to which the interests of residents can be ignored by policy-makers and administrators.

Aside from committee approval and publication of the route, there has been no consultation or communication with Small Heath residents concerning likely programming of compulsory acquisition or construction. What little information is available has been left to 'filter through' and has doubtless done so largely through legal searches on private property in the affected area. The county is simply keeping its options open by continuing to postpone rather than abandon the route but in order to do so is disregarding (even if it recognises) the continuing costs of indecision for local people. It is difficult to imagine a similar situation persisting unchallenged in the more affluent, articulate areas the route is intended to serve.

Attitudes are of course slowly changing, both within Small Heath (and similar areas) and within government – central and local. In Small Heath the growth of residents' associations and the community federation during the past three years has been one positive step towards a more articulate, confident community which simply will not be ignored. At the same time, among politicians and administrators there is a growing awareness and acknowledgment of the problems of inner areas and their residents. But there is still a very long way to go before the processes of policy formation and execution encompass a real understanding of and effective response to inner area needs.

Towards more sensitive policy formation

If the key to improved policies for inner areas is greater sensitivity to local needs, then it would be unrealistic to expect the kinds of obstacles identified above to be overcome primarily by administrative change within the existing framework of local government. The inadequacies of understanding and commitment are such that they point rather to the necessity for changes in the decision-making process, for decentralisation, neighbourhood organisation and community education. Of these interrelated themes, we are here concerned with making the local political system more sensitive to need and more able to respond; related themes are pursued in subsequent chapters.

The principal reason for advocating change in the process of government is to enable residents of inner areas to have a much greater influence on the policy decisions which affect their lives. In seeking ways to do this it must be remembered that policy decisions are essentially matters of political choice. The further away the real locus of decision-making moves from the arena of open debate into the caucus or the bureaucracy, the slimmer the chances of residents influencing the process, however well organised or well informed on issues they may be. In Birmingham, for example, INLOGOV (The Institute of Local Government Studies) have found that officers have developed an increasingly powerful influence over policy formation, partly as a result of the increased workload of individual committees arising from the reduction of the total number of committees and of councillors following local government reorganisation. Furthermore, the size of the city is such that while a largely centralised organisation can be maintained that organisation cannot always be sufficiently sensitive to local needs. In this situation, elected representatives carry a heavy responsibility for ensuring that their constituencies' needs are adequately represented in committee and council.

Councillors in inner areas carry a particularly heavy burden in the performance of their constituency role, because the incidence of severe economic, social and physical need is higher than in other areas and places proportionately greater claims on their limited time. Moreover, if they are to represent their constituents effectively they not only have to understand local needs and priorities, but also bargain successfully for the resources to meet them. However, the scale, scope and organisation of local government activities (in Birmingham, at least) inhibit inner area councillors' ability to cope adequately with the competing demands upon their time, and this situation reinforces the inherent political disadvantage of areas like Small Heath.

We suggest that this disadvantage ought to be countered, in part, by positive discrimination through the political system itself. That is, the heavy responsibilities of elected members in inner areas should be acknowledged and a means sought whereby the burdens are reduced and members enabled to exercise their constituency role more effectively. This could, for example, mean increased councillor representation in inner wards, or the funding of small support teams directly responsible to area committees composed of elected members for the wards concerned, and attended by officers of properly constituted and demonstrably representative neighbourhood organisations. (The extent to which any neighbourhood organisation is ever likely to be fully representative is discussed in Chapter 7.)

Of these two approaches, we strongly favour the second, primarily because it would provide a framework for a coordinated assessment of local issues as a basic input to central policy making. It would enable residents, officers and councillors to work more closely establishing local needs and priorities, presenting demands for resource allocations to major spending committees, and developing proposals for policy change. The support team's main function would be to assemble and coordinate information on needs, the impact of council policies and on the progress of plans and programmes, the latter an area where councillors at present often experience great difficulty in obtaining information. The team would also obtain basic information required by both councillors and residents to enable them to identify and take decisions on local policy issues, and to function as an effective lobby in the city-wide political process of government. This information could also form a major input to local community reviews which, as we discuss in Chapter 13, would be an integral part of ongoing local planning.

We would advocate the establishment of area committees within those towns and cities where size and a centralised administration together seriously inhibit or frustrate sensitivity to local needs. The precise nature of the relationship between central and local committees, and the consequences for decentralisation of officer activity, will undoubtedly vary according to local circumstances. Current DOE sponsored experiments in 'area management'[1] should ultimately point to the likely extent of such variations. In Birmingham, we recommend that, without changing the existing committee structure, 'informal' area committees are established each covering an area similar in size to Small Heath, say one or two wards. These committees would be 'informal' in the sense that they would not be responsible for the administration and control of major service budgets. They would comprise ward members and ex officio representatives of local community groups. Their main role would be to act as representative and advocate, within the local government structure, on behalf of the local community. Committees for parts of the city with serious problems of urban deprivation (say seven in all) would enjoy positive discrimination in the provision of special support teams and would have the additional function of acting as a channel for central government programmes of positive discrimination outside the major fields of housing, education and employment, with some discretionary use of funds. Allocation of special central government assistance between committees in areas of urban deprivation might be decided by a central sub-committee (of, say, Policy and Resources) composed of delegated members from the various area committees concerned.

In recommending area committees we are aiming at a devolution of political responsibility accompanied by the decentralisation of much existing local government officer activity to the area level. This, we believe, would promote better coordination between the various agencies and departments responsible for planning, provision and control of services in those areas. But we are certainly not advocating an extension of bureaucracy, which we would regard as wholly undesirable. The corollary of devolution of political responsibility and decentralisation of officer activity should be: smaller central service committees/sub-committees meeting less frequently and concerned primarily with the generation, allocation and control of resources in accordance with the needs and competing demands of different areas; greater delegation of responsibility for policy execution to officers working at the local level; and a big reduction in central staff whose main functions would then be to provide common service inputs (accounting, personnel management and training, operations research, data processing etc), integrate planning activity city-wide and deal with such basic strategic tasks as land assembly. We consider that the approach suggested here would achieve not only better policy formation but also, as we discuss later in this chapter, more effective execution or service delivery.

Approaches to improved policy execution

The scale and range of inner area problems make it inevitable that any local authority strategy for dealing with them will make complex organisational demands.

1. Stockport, Liverpool, Kirklees, Dudley, Haringey, Newcastle and, until recently, Birmingham, who have now withdrawn following a change in the political control of the council in May 1976.

In our analysis of coordination problems between and within departments we have tried to avoid getting embroiled in questions of local authority and departmental responsibilities, concentrating instead on the sort of difficulties likely to be encountered whatever the pattern of local authority and departmental responsibilities in a particular area. Local government has been subject to so much reorganisation in the last few years that there is little point in contemplating any further major structural changes in the immediate future. Although we do refer to certain aspects of the organisational structure of departments and departmental responsibilities, we have tried to concentrate on developing those approaches to improve coordination that would be applicable in a variety of organisational contexts that might be associated with different inner areas.

Problems in achieving the effective execution of policy are only partly to do with the compatibility of one programme with another (ie, maintaining a balance between population structure, housing provision, school places, community facilities, available jobs and communications networks) and with the cooperation of one agency or department with another. They also have to do with the clear and prompt communication of information and decisions within agencies and departments, with the accurate estimation of the financial and manpower implications of policy decisions, with the intrinsic timescale of routines and procedures, and with the ability of individuals in lower echelons to respond swiftly and appropriately to the everyday challenges of tactical decision-taking. Our own experience suggests that the obstacles arising from the organisation, methods and operational circumstances of the individual service agency are every bit as important as the obstacles arising from the relationships between different service agencies. Furthermore, as long as these obstacles persist (and they cannot, of course, ever be completely removed) they will tend to frustrate such benefits that might derive from attempts to improve inter-relationships by organisational means.

The importance of compatible programmes and services

The compatibility of programmes is nonetheless of great importance in inner areas where public services and action exercise a very considerable influence over people's lives. The most obvious case is compatibility between capital programme targets in redevelopment and renewal areas – houses, schools, facilities for a given population – but there is also the question of achieving the appropriate mix, or combination, of services required by a household, group or area, overprovision or underprovision of any one of which may either be wasteful or weaken the utility of the others. Imbalances are most likely to occur where responsibility for interdependent services is split between two or more departments.

A particularly difficult case is services for pre-school children. The education department provides nursery schools or classes, the use of buildings for playgroups and a mobile playbus; the social services department provides day care facilities, playgroups, registration of and liaison with voluntary playgroups and childminders, and also a playbus; the area health authority provides health visitors, clinics for under-fives, playgroups for handicapped children and care and assessment units in hospitals; the amenities and recreation department is responsible for recreation

186

facilities and holiday playschemes; and finally there are voluntary groups and workplace crèches. The outcome of poor coordination in situations such as this can be very varied provision from one area to another, in terms both of the choice available and of the total provision of all types.

Certainly the multiplicity of agencies concerned with pre-school children have not succeeded in meeting local needs in Small Heath – where in 1974 provision of nursery school/class and playgroup places, for example, was less than half the city's 1971 average – and as yet have provided little real understanding of the appropriate balance between various types of provision in the area, which is the first step towards more effective coordination and utilisation of existing and future resources. Where an individual household requires a combination of services – the classic social services problem addressed by the Seebohm Report – the consequences of inadequate coordination can be even more severe, resulting in wholly ineffective services.

In order to overcome, or more realistically, minimise the gaps and overlaps in service provision created by the division of responsibilities between individual departments, committees and agencies there has been increasing and welcome emphasis on inter-departmental liaison and corporate planning and management throughout local government. In the two years following local government reorganisation Birmingham joined with this general trend (though following the recent change of political control there have been organisational changes which indicate a return to the tradition of strong unitary departments). However, despite growing emphasis placed on corporate planning and management, and some decentralised officer activity (notably urban renewal), the essentially centralised nature of the city's organisation has largely inhibited formal regular coordination at the local level.

The main service departments have divisional structures on a functional rather than a geographical basis. When, for instance, an interdepartmental task has to be performed, it is usual to find that the main coordinating device is an ad hoc interdepartmental group of officers, each having functional responsibilities covering the whole city, rather than, say, regular meetings of area officers to deal with all interdepartmental matters arising in a particular area. The absence of local coordinating mechanisms (other than the informal irregular contacts between officers working locally) not only reduces the potential for a more effective combination of local services but also necessitates unnecessarily lengthy, and therefore costly, interdepartmental communication procedures on local matters.

The costs of coordination

The question of costs is fundamental to any consideration of approaches to coordination. It is important to make a distinction between those forms of coordination which realise cost savings through direct increases in productivity and those that add to costs and must therefore achieve a return that outweighs these incremental costs if real benefits are to result. Thus harmonisation of service boundaries (provided it does not interfere with economies of scale), rationalisation of information posts and welfare offices, and the integration of delivery schedules of environmental services like rubbish collection and street cleaning may all bring savings as well as increase the satisfaction of users or consumers. But measures designed to improve communications between different agencies or departments will only have a positive result if they lead to significantly better decisions.

It is all too easy to fall into the trap of adding to an existing system or structure without commensurate pruning elsewhere. The costs of organisation rise exponentially with every additional communications link; unless accompanied by changes in the technology of information processing (eg, on-line computer systems), additional communications links will also increase the delay in making policy decisions and carrying them out. This is the essential problem that corporate or 'inter-corporate' planning and management approaches must cope with. Increased consultation between agencies and departments should therefore proceed in parallel with the shortening of lines of command within these same agencies and departments and with other changes designed to streamline and improve administrative practice.

Birmingham's urban renewal programme is a major interdepartmental task which illustrates many of the points made so far in this section.[1] Each GIA and HAA in the programme requires significant professional inputs from eight different city departments over a period of at least four years. There are six area-based project teams responsible for the day-to-day running of improvement projects, from plan preparation through implementation, comprising about one-third of the staff working on urban renewal. Coordination arrangements for urban renewal work are not however carried out on an area basis, since the primacy of functional (rather than geographical) subdivisions constrains the choice of arrangements.

The main organisational device for coordinating the urban renewal programme is an interdepartmental group of mainly third tier officers (with some fourth and fifth tier officers also) with responsibility for the whole of the city's programme and departments are frequently represented by more than one officer. However, because urban renewal responsibilities tend to be concentrated in one division or section, coordination could be achieved through meetings of one second tier officer from each department involved. In fact a wide measure of coordination is also possible at third tier level without requiring more than one officer from each department to attend meetings. The inter-departmental group meets once a week (or more if necessary) to discuss progress. We checked on arrangements for urban renewal in 11 other large metropolitan districts and found that 9 had similar inter-departmental working parties at a senior level.

The inter-departmental group in Birmingham, the Multi-Disciplinary Team (MDT), performs both planning and control functions, dealing with day-to-day and long-term problems. There is also a chief officers group on urban renewal, although it does not appear to have any distinctly different role to that performed by the MDT. The city's corporate planning system could carry out some of the MDT's planning functions, but the team has not been integrated with the system.

1. Since the arrangements for both corporate planning and the management of the urban renewal programme in Birmingham have recently been substantially changed, the description that follows relates to the former situation.

If they built something properly, straightaway. Instead of wasting so much time thinking about it, do something straightaway. But they don't.

Having declared it as an improvement area, with, you know, a little bit of common sense they could have said 'well, there's the basic plan; there's three models; they're all approved, you can have that, that, or that' and then finished with it. As it was, we had to get plans drawn up, and have them inspected, and some they want in triplicate . . .

Circumstances of Families

Several aspects of these arrangements are unsatisfactory, notably the overlapping functions of the chief officers group and the MDT, and the separate operations of the MDT and the corporate planning system, which means that urban renewal is not adequately related to the city's overall housing policy or social priorities, and its policy and programmes do not always fit in with the annual corporate planning cycle. Both situations point to the possibility of excessive costs due to duplication or unnecessary incompatibility of tasks. With regard to the MDT itself, a major problem has been an excessive workload, mainly attributable to the size of the city's programme, and the very long timescale of both preparing and implementing GIA and HAA plans. Essentially we believe that these problems can be overcome by a better matching of programmes to the resources available, and by speeding up plan preparation and implementation in ways we discuss further below. Adoption of our proposals would mean that at any one time inter-departmental groups would have fewer plans or projects to consider, and would have greater assurance that the necessary resources were available.

The importance of financial appraisal

We have already shown in the previous chapter how wide the gap was between the city's declared urban renewal programme and actual financial commitment. We suggested that this gap could be closed by a combination of local authority and government measures. To achieve greater administrative efficiency the gap could equally well be closed by a drastic reduction in the size of the programme, although that would not be our recommended approach to dealing with inner area problems. The difficulty is at present that there is simply inadequate financial appraisal of major expenditure programmes such as urban renewal. The only forward financial plan approved by the city is the one year capital and revenue budget approved at the beginning of the financial year; there is no programme of capital or revenue expenditure to match the programme of GIA and HAA declarations. Furthermore, a review of urban renewal by Birmingham's Performance Review Committee 'to consider the reasonableness of the committed programme in relation to the available resources' had no analysis of staff requirements or annual expenditure.

Yet without the necessary basic financial data (much of which in the case of urban renewal could be readily assembled on the basis of project teams' work schedules and estimates) there is the danger that policy decisions will not always result in the optimum allocation of resources, and that administrative effort will be wasted in preparing programmes that cannot be implemented because of resource constraints. Moreover, financial appraisal not only helps to avoid, or at least minimise problems of this kind, it also reduces coordination problems of sequence (delays in any one task delaying everything), by enabling more realistic forecasts of task completion dates, and those of combination, by relating basic considerations of the merits of different types of service to practical considerations of available buildings, staff and money in any one area. The administrative costs of pursuing ambitious programmes on paper in defiance of the financial circumstances can be very heavy. For example, we estimated that under Birmingham's proposed staff allocations for GIAs and HAAs, the cost of staff time was, at end 1975 prices, around £472 per house in HAAs and £35 a house in GIAs. These figures exclude administrative costs incurred by the metropolitan county, the Department of the Environment and the water authority, and also some of the costs of handling additional applications for planning, renovation grant or building regulations approval. In this case we are not suggesting that the problem is gross overmanning, but that trying to get owners to improve their houses when, as now, many simply do not have the money, is a task likely to defeat even the best of administrators.

One unfortunate aspect of the high administrative costs of preparing and implementing plans is that at present the benefits to the community are not realised until some years after the initial administrative expenditure, thus worsening the ratio of discounted costs to discounted benefits. It is thus important to try to compress plan preparation and implementation into shorter periods for this reason as well as for the benefit of overall programme coordination. When reviewing network analyses, for instance, a hard look should be taken at activities on both critical and sub-critical paths with a view to identifying which, if any, activities might be carried out in tandem rather than in sequence. Referrals to committee are another area where time-saving might well be achieved; certainly they are a significant cause of delay in the preparation and implementation of urban renewal plans. For example, they account for 30 of the 100 weeks it takes to move from HAA declaration to action programme approval. We estimate that some 14 of the 30 weeks could be eliminated simply by altering the timing of reports without actually either reducing the information given to councillors or increasing delegation to officers. Reporting chains also need shortening; at present urban renewal teams are three tiers below chief officers in the administrative hierarchy, making them too remote from committees. If the timescale of project planning and implementation were shortened as we have been suggesting, there would at any one time be fewer items on the committee agenda and scope for project leaders attending committee meetings. Furthermore, shortening the timescale would reduce the effects of loss of continuity through annual changes in committee membership.

Where, as in urban renewal, the local authority is committed (by statute or its own good intentions) to securing widespread public involvement in the planning and execution of a particular programme, a difficult balance has to be struck between fulfilling this commitment and controlling administrative costs. In Birmingham, the council's efforts to inform and consult residents in HAAs and GIAs have been impressive in their scale, comprehensiveness and experimentation with new approaches. The objectives of the work have been as wide as the methods used. Apart from the value attached to consultation as an end in itself, the local urban renewal teams aim to revive aspirations to better living conditions, to change attitudes towards the council, to restore confidence in neighbourhoods, to improve the prospects of grant applications generally and to ascertain attitudes of owners. This breadth of objectives and methods is seen also in DOE circulars – eg, Circular 13/75[1] recommends 'using every possible channel of communication'. The costs incurred as a result are not inconsiderable, both in terms of actual staff time spent on public participation work and the added elapsed time taken to

1. *Housing Act 1974: Renewal Strategies, Circular 13/75*, DOE.

prepare plans, which means that it may take longer to reap the benefits of administrative expenditure.

Though it is difficult to assess the true proportion of staff time attributable to public participation, evidence from Little Green HAA suggested it could be in the region of 25 per cent of the total man months spent on plan preparation in HAAs. The added elapsed time, on the other hand, is readily ascertainable. In the case of HAAs in Birmingham only about 4 weeks are added, but in GIAs some 31 weeks are added. The main reason for this difference is that the participation work in HAAs is essentially intensive, street meetings taking place simultaneously with survey and technical work for plan preparation instead of in sequence. However, the added time in GIAs could probably be cut substantially, possibly by as much as 15 weeks, partly by analysing the critical path task networks and adjusting the sequence of activities. Not only would this reduce administrative expenditure but, by reducing delays in the programme, would be of direct benefit to residents, who naturally tend to become disillusioned when, as in Small Heath, programmes fall behind schedule. Indeed, by contributing to delays public involvement can serve simply to increase cynicism as to a council's real intentions; in Small Heath, if past moving trends were to continue (which is by no means certain), by the time the environmental improvements in a GIA actually materialised, about one-third of residents consulted would have moved. The careful use of a more discriminating approach to identification of objectives, methods and priority groups would improve the management of public involvement without reducing the commitment to thorough consultation.

Staff deployment and decentralisation

One of the principal difficulties in achieving more effective service delivery in inner areas is lack of flexibility in staff deployment, which is constrained by rigid establishments of permanent posts. Some pressing inner area needs are temporary – an information/advice centre and play provision during slum clearance, or a local office to prepare an HAA plan – and these temporary needs can be met in two alternative ways: either peripatetic officers can be appointed to permanent posts to work either individually or as a mobile task force, or officers can be temporarily seconded from permanent posts. On the basis of our experience, we consider that neither approach is used sufficiently in Birmingham (although there are some peripatetic officers in the housing and education departments) with the result that some temporary needs are either inadequately met or wholly neglected. To take a case in point, the process of GIA and HAA plan preparation could be considerably improved by more flexible staff deployment. At present local teams are built primarily around permanent appointments, supplemented by some seconded staff, with departmental representation at times appearing to be a concern more dominant than simply finding the appropriate mix of skills to do the job.

A more flexible approach, using wholly seconded staff, could be used to get projects started more quickly, by removing the need to seek an expansion of establishment and to compress plan preparation into a shorter timescale. The latter improvement would also remove one of the main objections by departments to temporary secondments – the length of time involved. Furthermore, if flexible staff deployment were used to shorten project timescales, the possibility of opening more temporary local offices (and hence improving contact with residents, some of whom are now over two miles from project teams' bases) would be increased. For instance, a temporary local office for an individual HAA is out of the question if 20 man months of local work is spread over 4 years (roughly the present situation) but would become practical if that same work, in terms of man months, could be done in a year. On the basis of our examination of, and involvement with, urban renewal in Birmingham, we recommend that all inter-departmental project teams consist of wholly seconded staff, reporting to a projects officer of chief officer status, not connected to any one department.

Quite apart from more flexible staff deployment to meet temporary local needs there is some scope for decentralisation of continuing routine services. A measure of decentralisation has been taking place in Birmingham since local government reorganisation, and in one or two departments is still continuing. All the main service providing departments (education, environmental services, housing, leisure services, planning and social services) have some form of decentralised area-based administration. There is, however, very little compatibility in the boundaries of the geographical subdivisions by which each department operates. One department, environmental services, even operates two completely different systems of local offices and areas – one for its urban renewal section and one for its public health section. The result of incompatible boundaries is that at the area level the number of opposite numbers in other departments with whom each area officer has to deal is perhaps doubled or trebled. While substantial rationalisation of boundaries could certainly be achieved, some major differences will have to remain – for example, the distribution of council houses constrains the housing department's freedom to change boundaries.

However it would be possible to get all departments to agree on common boundaries for certain planning purposes, preferably following ward boundaries while retaining variations essential to particular departments for day to day administration. It is not really practical, we feel, to establish entirely self-contained area budgets, incorporating all basic services. Quite apart from the very real problems of harmonising boundaries and apportioning the overhead and operating costs of shared depots etc, those services which are the responsibility of other agencies – the county, statutory undertakers or private concerns – would lie outside area control. There are also other advantages, as well as cost savings, in central accounting which can interpret rapidly (given good budgeting and feedback systems) the outcome for the city as a whole of the differential levels of service activity demanded by the various areas.

We should like to see moves towards greater decentralisation of officer activity accompanied by progress towards enabling area officers to exercise greater responsibility than currently they are allowed. This could produce quicker, more responsible and more cost effective tactical decisions, but there is of course the necessity of maintaining adequate public accountability. Here the area committee could play an important role at the local level by safeguarding broad accountability from officers to elected members (and from elected members to their constituents).

Public access to council services

It follows from our remarks about common administrative boundaries that shared local offices, or 'mini town halls', while ideally desirable are unlikely to be practical. Quite apart from the boundary question, the expense involved in building suitable premises, which would anyway be very inflexible, rules them out. What is both desirable and possible, however, is to make public access to council officers easier by allowing enquiries regarding all or at least more than one council service at existing local offices presently occupied by single departments.

We found that for very many people in Small Heath and particularly those most dependent on council services, the process of getting information, sorting out queries, applying for assistance and so on is confusing, time-consuming and often dispiriting. For instance, people living in short-life housing, anxious to know when they would be rehoused or needing urgent repairs to their houses, have either to contact the housing department's city centre office, or the area office in Sparkbrook. Phone calls are difficult for people dependent on frequently-vandalised call-boxes, and expensive when, as so often is the case, the enquirer is passed from person to person until the right one is found; personal visits too can be difficult (and if several are required, also expensive) for the elderly or mothers with young children, since both offices are a bus ride away – in fact a trip to the city centre office involves two buses. Moreover, both means of contact can be very time-consuming, which for people in work can result in a loss of wages. These difficulties are compounded by the lack of clarity and continuity in contacts with officers, which often makes it difficult to follow up queries:

> '. . . you go to the desk and they say 'Right, you see our Miss Jones' and when you see 'Our Miss Jones' she has had to go and see 'Our Mr Russell' and the 'Our Mr Russell' will see 'Our Mr So-and-So' and then they pass you back to 'Miss Smith' and so you are talking to Miss Smith with what you told Miss Jones in the first place, and it's a pat on the shoulder and 'Leave it with us'. Next time you phone, they've got no record of you talking to Miss Jones or Mr Russell; they don't know what you are on about.'
> (Circumstances of Families)

Where different departments, or different sections of the same departments, are involved in resolving a problem, all the difficulties discussed here are likely to be intensified.

Experience at both the FSU 435 Centre and the community advice centre (Osbourne House) showed how much people welcomed the availability of information, advice and practical assistance concerning their dealings with council departments, and the continuity of contact with people in a general atmosphere which many found less intimidating than large central council offices. This was particularly so in the case of the 435 Centre, where the worker often dealt directly with departments on behalf of local residents, very many of whom lacked either the confidence, knowledge of the system, or simply the time to pursue queries themselves. If basic information and advice on all council services were made available locally, there can be no doubt that this would improve services to the public. We recommend that this be achieved by establishing combined reception points for all local authority services where officers would try to sort out the query themselves, but where necessary provide all the information – forms, contacts, phone numbers – to enable people to pursue queries further, and advise them on how to use that information. The point would be provided by selecting those offices with the most suitable accommodation and location, irrespective of which is the occupying department. Sometimes it might be a social services area office, sometimes a housing department area office that is the best choice of premises. Alternatively, premises such as a large house or shop might be acquired at comparatively low cost from the private sector to serve as a reception point.

Finally, in addition to enabling easier access to council services, there is a need for more active 'marketing' of services by local authorities. We have seen, for example, just how far the actual distribution of rent allowances, rent rebates and renovation grants is from corresponding to priorities on which there is a wide consensus. The pattern of these three forms of assistance not going to the households who most need them has come about despite very considerable advertising and promotional effort. While there are undoubtedly improvements that can and should be made as regards advertising strategies, a further step towards a substantial improvement in the marketing of local government services is, we believe, the point of contact between officer and resident. The essential weakness at present is that the officer acts and behaves as a representative of his department rather than of the local authority and so tends to take a very restricted view of a particular problem. On introducing himself he says 'I'm from the social services department' rather than 'I'm from the council', or 'Oh you'll have to ask the housing department', which is both unhelpful and baffling to people who think in terms of 'the council' and do not understand departmental structures and responsibilities. The officer who has to deal with the public is constrained by nature of his professional training, by the professionalism of local government as a whole, and by the organisational structure of local government to maximise the cost efficiency of service delivery rather than client convenience or getting the right services to the right people. A small but useful improvement would be to give all newly appointed officers working in areas of multiple deprivation a common induction course covering the local authority's full range of services, criteria for provision and location of offices.

*

The foregoing discussion and proposals, though clearly not intended as a 'blueprint' for better co-ordination of services, do address what we see to be the basic problems of policy formation and execution as they affect inner areas. If changes are made on the lines we propose, we consider that in a situation of great future uncertainty local authorities will be better able to tackle the difficult task of planning and implementing an integrated series of initiatives across a wide policy field – which we see as the main function of inner area policy.

Nigel Holt

I honestly believe that Small Heath could be made a better place to live in if the people who did live in it tried to help both themselves and Small Heath. This could be done by them giving in their ideas on how an ideal Small Heath should be.

A Child's Eye View of Small Heath

You see, people don't seem to care any more for other people now . . . I'm just showing the general attitude, the atmosphere. There's no real concern for communication.

Circumstances of Families

7 Facilitating community organisation and development

So far in this report we have argued that the problems of inner areas will not be solved, or even significantly alleviated, without a very substantial change in the distribution of society's resources, and have acknowledged the political difficulties inherent in achieving the necessary commitment to change. Not least among these is the lack of influence of inner area residents in political process. Indeed it might be argued that perhaps the most fundamental aspect of deprivation or disadvantage is lack of power, both personal and collective. The measures we proposed in preceding chapters for changes in political and administrative organisation, and for enabling people in inner areas to gain greater access to opportunity, go some way towards remedying this lack of power, but unless residents become more organised it is unlikely that they will achieve a significantly greater voice. In this chapter therefore we look at means of helping the community to organise so that inner area residents may assume a much more active, influential role in relation to the distribution and use of resources to meet their needs.

The need for a catalyst

Despite the fact that in almost any disadvantaged community there are bound to be individuals, or even small groups, who perceive the general value of organisation as one means of securing an improvement in their circumstances and quality of life, their ability to stimulate the necessary interest and support among others is likely to be strictly limited. In areas where there is little or no resident organisation, and where many, if not most people are unaware of its potential value in relation to their own lives, it takes a fairly powerful catalyst both to engender interest and to secure active participation, particularly when personal circumstances often leave little time or energy for commitments beyond the daily round. The catalyst may take the form of an external agent, such as a CDP, or a particular issue which brings people together. In turn, an issue can be 'contrived' – for instance, the launching of an urban renewal programme with a genuine commitment to public participation – or it may arise spontaneously.

In Small Heath, the urban renewal programme has undoubtedly been the principal stimulus for community organisation, through the formation of residents' groups in renewal programme areas, which affect about two-thirds of all households locally. The Inner Area Study provided a further stimulus, notably by providing finance and other assistance for the formation of a federation of residents' groups (the Small Heath Community Federation) and through its environmental improvement activities on two council estates. In January 1974, when Birmingham's first urban renewal project team was set up in Small Heath, there was very little community organisation in the area, and the small number of groups that were in existence had no role in the city's decision-making process. Experience with preliminary plans in renewal areas throughout the city had led the council to favour a consultative approach to planning which would enable local communities to participate in the development of proposals; earlier approaches had invited reaction to proposals put forward by the council and for several reasons had proven unsatisfactory. The local project team was firmly committed to active resident involvement, and immediately embarked upon an intensive programme of newsletters, factsheets, public meetings and street meetings in Little Green, a renewal area (subsequently an HAA) of some 675 houses with a population of about 2,200. A planning committee supported and advised by the project team was formed from among 38 street representatives, and towards the end of the planning process the street representatives themselves started to initiate and organise activities, notably the production of a videotape on the process and dispiriting effects of physical deterioration in the area (with technical assistance from an artist/film-maker sponsored by BIAS) and the formation of a residents' association.

These latter developments occurred some 18 months after the project team's arrival, during which time their efforts had helped to build the confidence of a strong core of residents who were no longer content to leave the care and control of their environment solely in the hands of the council. The videotape had pointed to the unease created by the uncertainty in recent years over the council's plans for the Little Green area; there had been assurances that wholesale clearance was not contemplated, but the possibility of selective clearance was known to exist – although not where or when it would take place. The activities of the project team had done much to allay fears by involving residents in decisions on the future of properties in the area, but the street representatives saw the need to retain contact and control over the outcome of the planning process. They called a meeting, attended by 150 residents, at which they argued forcefully the benefits to be gained by being notified of planning applications, pressing for action to solve problems in the area – such as houses remaining void and derelict for long periods – and to carry out the proposals for improvement which the residents' planning committee had developed. The result was a unanimous vote for the formation of a residents' association, which has since flourished and considerably expanded its activities.

The influence of urban renewal activities was by no means confined to Little Green. The project team was concerned to promote residents' associations in each declared or proposed GIA/HAA in Small Heath and from early 1975 onwards residents' groups were formed throughout the area, primarily in response to the urban renewal programme, but with the added impetus of the development of the federation, which sought to represent the interests of residents throughout Small Heath, to act as a focus for liaison with the local authority concerning those interests, and to promote residents' associations and other organisations with the same general objective of improving residents' 'standard of life and living conditions'.

By mid-1976 there were nine residents' associations in Small Heath, eight of which together covered all local renewal programme areas, the ninth being on the new council estate; six of the nine were affiliated to the federation. Some associations were, of course, more active and cohesive than others, and on the council estate, where the initial impetus had been a relatively short-term programme of environmental improvement, it was proving difficult to sustain momentum in the face of the subsequent failure of another project. Nonetheless, the majority were apparently quite firmly established with interests and activities now extending beyond the initial (and still important) focus of urban renewal. The federation too was actively pursuing its objectives, despite the many difficulties inherent in setting up and running an 'umbrella' organisation.

The substantial growth of community organisation in Small Heath was stimulated by the initial efforts and commitment of a very small number of people – only three or four – genuinely concerned with involving people in plans and decisions which materially affect their lives. Though they worked closely with residents and community workers already active in the area, the number of people concerned still only constituted a handful in relation to the area's total population, yet the scale of response from residents was more than a well-deserved tribute to hard work; it reflected above all the extent to which the urban renewal programme was an issue of immediate local concern. This experience – a few people generating considerable local organisation on the basis of an issue understood as directly relevant to the well-being of a substantial proportion of the community – is by no means unique to Small Heath; it has been mirrored in countless other situations and is an important basic consideration for any strategy of community organisation.

The role of the local authority

If community organisation is to be seen as an essential part of the process of tackling inner area problems, and we contend that it must, then it cannot be left to chance. It must become an element of strategy in its own right for which the local authority takes responsibility not only by encouraging the formation of residents' groups as part of a particular programme such as urban renewal, but by giving practical and financial (grant-aid) support, and more importantly by the creation of a catalyst where apparently none exists. This we consider would best be achieved by the establishment of a small community development team (no more than three or four people for an area the size of Small Heath) whose task would be to stimulate community organisation by working with residents, councillors, other local officers, community workers, etc, taking a fairly clear local issue as their starting point. The team should have a combination of skills appropriate to the local situation – for instance, in Small Heath a knowledge of Asian language and culture, experience in working in a multi-racial community, and an understanding of housing issues would be among the key skills for such a team. Professional qualifications are not, however, an essential prerequisite for team members; it is far more important that they have the skills, attitudes and commitment necessary both to understand residents' needs and aspirations, and to enable them to establish a degree of self-sustaining organisation which will act as a lobby for residents' interests through direct dealings with the local authority.

The approach advocated here is more than a means of securing better 'public participation' in plan-making procedures and government programmes by developing better communication, in that it seeks to enable residents to participate more actively and effectively in political process, and thereby to exercise more positive, tangible influence upon policy-making and resource allocation in general. As such, it represents a challenge to both the political and administrative arms of local government, which are in general unaccustomed to a continuous working relationship with the public they serve, particularly in inner areas.

It is likely, therefore, that a strategy which seeks to promote the establishment of articulate community organisation will be viewed with unease, and even outright resistance, in some quarters. This is not to deny that politicians and officers alike will tend to welcome the potential advantages of community development – a community of people who are less passive in their attitudes and behaviour; who are mutually supportive; more inclined to improvise their own facilities and services; more willing to invest their time, energy and savings in house improvement or maintaining their gardens and fences; and more able to 'participate' constructively and creatively in local government plans and programmes. They may find it more difficult to accept or adjust to a situation where people claim greater influence over the full range of policy decisions which affect them, such as changes in the school building programme, the choice of urban renewal strategy, public spending cuts, etc. For this situation implies the need for a more open style of government and with it the prospect of more overt criticism and conflict, all of which can undoubtedly prove difficult to handle at times, and particularly in the early stages when there is likely to be uncertainty and misunderstanding on all sides. Nonetheless, if a serious attempt is to be made to reduce the gap between 'governors' and 'governed' in inner areas, these difficulties must be faced, and tackled constructively.

In this connection it is relevant to consider the question of conflict between the community and local authority in a little more detail, since this is almost certainly the most contentious aspect of a strategy of community organisation. For it may appear that such a strategy will simply lead to an increasing volume of protest, and to greater polarisation of views ('us'=the community, 'them'=the council) which will make the process of urban government yet more lengthy and costly, with perhaps little to show by way of better policies or services for inner areas. The possibility of such an unconstructive outcome has to be admitted, and if it should occur, it would point to a serious failure of the parties involved to communicate effectively with one another. Misinformation, lack of information, and misunderstanding are powerful inhibitors to a productive working relationship, and it behoves both the community and the local authority to try as far as possible to remove these obstacles to an informed debate on issues of common concern. In this, the onus (initially at least) falls particularly upon the local authority as the more powerful participant in the dialogue; the extent to which there is within the authority a genuine willingness to listen and to discuss issues frankly with the community and its representatives will in no small way influence the pattern of community involvement in decision-making processes.

The fact that conflicts will nonetheless arise must not be interpreted as a pointer to a general situation of conflict; conflicts are virtually inevitable when a community which previously has had negligible influence on its own future becomes aware of the potential for changing that situation. Initially, it is bound to demand more of the agencies on which its members have come to depend, generally through no particular fault of their own, yet the local authority may not consider all demands either justifiable or readily satisfied. Differences of this kind are not easily resolved, but it must be remembered that community and local authority will only work together more harmoniously once a much greater mutual awareness of each other's perspectives has been built up and good faith has been demonstrated, through a satisfactory resolution of conflict.

The experience of urban renewal project teams in Birmingham has shown that, while all conflicts are not necessarily resolved to the mutual satisfaction of residents and local authority, a constructive, creative working relationship can be developed by a frank exchange of information, ideas and opinion. Two of our action projects enabled us to observe this process in housing action areas: in Little Green where we were closely involved in the early information-gathering stages of the work, and maintained informal contact thereafter; and in Nechells (part of the inner ring outside the study area) where the Artist Placement Group explored the relationship between people and government by video-recording stages in plan preparation and approval – council committee meetings, officers' discussions, residents' meetings, officer/resident meetings and discussion.

In Little Green, it soon became apparent that the use of technical jargon and the lack of clear information about the purpose of the programme, its timing, organisation (including residents' role in its preparation and execution) and progress could lead to uncertainty, misunderstanding and hence conflict. In particular, local officers' inability always to answer queries frankly, largely because they themselves lacked either the necessary information or the authority to pass it on, became a source of frustration to residents, who resented officers' apparent evasiveness. However, serious efforts were made to overcome these sources of friction, and were largely successful in that team members and residents came to a sufficient understanding of each other's point of view to enable the production of a plan (approved by committee) which strongly reflected residents' wishes. Residents came to appreciate many of the difficulties faced by officers trying to organise a sizeable action programme, and in fact tended to draw a distinction between local team members and the council, blaming the latter (which was still seen as remote) for most of their grievances, including the 'evasiveness' which still rankled. Indeed, this continues to be a source of friction locally (though its causes are better understood), and there is no doubt that a lack of directness – even to the point of simply saying 'I don't know' and giving the reasons why – can considerably undermine relationships between the community and local authority.

In Nechells HAA we observed a direct clash between residents' and the council's interests which, had it not been satisfactorily resolved, would undoubtedly have made continued cooperation on the renewal programme extremely difficult if not almost impossible. The conflict arose over a reduction in the time to be allowed for residents to consider the proposed plan for their area, which was being drawn up by officers on the basis of ideas put forward in the residents' own proposals. A committee instruction concerning the submission of plans for approval during the forthcoming committee cycle effectively cut the time available for Nechells residents to consider their plan by almost two-thirds, leaving them with just two weeks in which to study the plan, discuss it and agree on any amendments. The reason for suddenly squeezing the Nechells programme was not given, but was clearly linked to the committee's desire to complete as much business as possible before the unavoidable disruption and delay to be caused by forthcoming local elections, especially as they were almost certain to produce a change of overall control in the council (as in fact they did). It is unlikely that the committee consciously chose a substantial reduction in the residents' consultation period as being an acceptable trade-off in the circumstances; more probably they were simply unaware of the practical implications of their instruction.

However, residents were very quick to react; they made an unfavourable comparison between their two weeks for consideration of the plan and the total of almost four months required by the council to obtain all relevant committee approvals and strongly resented being placed in a situation where they were being virtually asked to 'rubberstamp' proposals on which they had been promised full consultation. They duly informed the local project team that the revised timetable was wholly unacceptable, and enlisted the support of a local councillor in pressing for a change. Again, the team was not seen as the 'culprit' but they nonetheless were placed in the unenviable, and noticeably stressful position of intermediary between their employers and the people for whom they were providing a service, both having strong and legitimate claims upon them as public servants. However, with other officers they finally achieved an acceptable compromise by speeding up departmental procedures wherever possible, thereby releasing more time for residents' consultation within the same timetable.

Both in Little Green, Nechells and in other Birmingham urban renewal areas, the attitudes and performance of locally-based officer teams were key determinants of the success or otherwise of attempts to build a working relationship with the community. As is so often the case, the more they worked with residents and developed a better understanding of their problems and perspectives, the greater their tendency to become advocates on residents' behalf. At times this gave rise to considerable differences of opinion between local officers and more senior, centrally based officers, some of whom were anxious to ensure that their teams' involvement with residents did not extend to an actual or apparent association with open criticism of the council, and doubtless many councillors shared their concern. To those who were unfamiliar with the day-to-day realities of 'community participation' it may well have appeared eminently reasonable that teams should seek to 'placate' residents by impressing upon them the extent of council action on their behalf, leaving outstanding grievances to be expressed directly to elected representatives. What they did not appear to appreciate was that such an approach was quite incompatible with the teams' task of securing residents' interest and investment in the urban renewal programme by enabling them to exercise considerable influence over the content of local plans and programmes.

Our observation of project teams' experience, and that of other local officers engaged in community development work, has led to the firm conclusion that the leader of a community development team must enjoy considerable autonomy and be able, particularly in the early stages of the team's work, to adopt a strong advocacy role, or his position vis-à-vis the community will be seriously compromised. On the other hand, his position will be equally compromised if he is unable to show that organisation works, for it may be too much to expect initial momentum and enthusiasm to be maintained in the face of constant rebuffs or inaction by the local authority. For instance, one of the difficulties faced by Small Heath Community Federation has been the frustration caused by the realisation that despite their considerable achievements in improving communication between the community and local authority, in particular concerning the use and management of the new community school, the preparation of the Small Heath District Plan, and latterly, the slow progress of the renewal programme, this improvement has not had a commensurate influence on decision-making. In other cases, some local residents' associations have at times become demoralised and have almost disintegrated while waiting for long-overdue urban renewal action in their area. The lesson here is that, while both necessary and desirable, 'dialogue' and 'communication' are of themselves an insufficient response to community organisation; they must lead to action.

To promote local authority action through the influence of the community development team, the leader should ideally be part of the authority's decision-making machinery, that is, appointed and paid by the council and accorded fairly high paid job status (similar, say, to that of an urban renewal project team leader in Birmingham) but not unduly restricted by departmental hierarchies and practices. Where the social services department is engaged in or developing community work as well as casework, it would be appropriate that it assume overall responsibility for the team at chief officer level, though members might well be seconded from other departments if they possess appropriate skills. Otherwise, maximum flexibility is likely to be achieved by attaching the team to the chief executive's department for reporting and general control purposes. At the local level, where area committees are established, the team leader would also be directly accountable to that committee. Furthermore, since there is likely to be a degree of overlap in the work of the community development team and area committee support team, staffing levels and composition for both should be assessed jointly.

Divisions within the community

In outlining a basic approach to community organisation in inner areas we have so far referred only to 'the community' as a single entity, that is, the people who live within an identifiable and commonly recognised locality. But it would obviously be naïve in the extreme to base a strategy for organisation solely on this particular concept of 'community', since it would presuppose a degree of widespread homogeneity and communality of interest among residents which patently does not exist anywhere, and certainly not in Small Heath. For indeed a major obstacle to community development and organisation is the division of interests and the tensions and conflicts within the wider community. This problem is particularly difficult where there are strong sub-cultural divisions along ethnic, religious and linguistic lines. Strategy must therefore be two-fold: it must concentrate on uniting different groups on issues of common concern whilst simultaneously working within different groups on issues specific to those groups and on issues that are an identifiable source of intra-community conflict.

The presence in Small Heath of a substantial and increasing immigrant population demonstrates clearly the need for such an approach – and some of the difficulties involved. The majority of immigrants are rural people from the Indian subcontinent (Pakistan, Bangladesh, India) whose language, culture and expectations not only differ widely from those of the white 'host' community, but also in significant measure from those of the smaller numbers of East African Asians and West Indians living in the area. Moreover, in addition to differences between immigrant groups, there are those within each group, the most common being those between first generation migrants and their children born and/or raised in this country. With immigrants comprising almost a third of the area's population, and that proportion likely to grow in view of Small Heath's attractiveness to Asian families, there are a number of problems which must be tackled to enable the various sub-groups in the wider community to co-exist and, where necessary, work together on the basis of a better understanding of each others' perspectives and needs.

While it cannot be said that interracial strife is a feature of life in Small Heath, there is undoubtedly a degree of unease and tension in relations between whites and non-whites. People living in areas with increasing concentrations of immigrants, or more precisely, non-white residents, are often disturbed by the presence of people whose appearance, behaviour, and in most cases, language are alien to them. Whether feelings of unease develop into overt dislike and antagonism on a personal basis of course depends very much upon the personalities and circumstances of individuals. For instance, we found that elderly people often feel isolated, and as a result even rather fearful when unable to communicate with their Asian neighbours, but are not necessarily antagonistic towards them. Similarly, people who dislike the size and concentration of the immigrant population frequently assert that they have 'nothing against them as individuals'. On the other hand, Small Heath Park is regarded by many as 'unsafe' because it is frequented by groups of Asian and West Indian youths, and the Hal'al method of chicken slaughtering practised by some Asians in terrace backyards is a particular source of bad feeling among their white neighbours.

A widely held opinion among white residents of all shades of opinion is that Asians in particular should make much greater efforts to integrate with the wider society. Indeed, their apparent unwillingness to do so is much resented:

> 'I find when people are leaving it's mostly the Pakistanis or the Indians who are moving in, and as you know, they don't mix with us. I mean they speak; they are friendly. But they don't like – when we go abroad we act – well – when you are in Rome you do as the Romans do. They don't! I mean, next door, they are very pleasant, very friendly, but they live their life the way they like and they don't care, which is, I suppose, alright for some, but I think they should mix more. I think they should be made to integrate myself – because they have their own shops, their own banks, they have their own building societies now, their mortgage and estate agents buying and selling houses. I mean you name it, they have got it! They monopolise the shops – well, alright, good luck to

Gordon King

I am happy in this country . . . But it is a strange country. It is not strange for my children because they live here and go to school here. But for me it is an alien country. After twenty years even I feel myself a foreigner and I think if I live for another twenty years I shall feel the same.

Circumstances of Families

them, but they are not doing anything for our economy are they? There is nothing coming in, it's all spending their own way and they live their own lives and no one does anything about it, which I think is wrong! . . . I mean regardless of where you come from – if you are not prepared to fit in, well there's no point in going, is there? And I think this causes a lot of ill feeling between immigrants myself.' (Circumstances of Families)

Less was said to us about West Indians, simply because they are relatively a much smaller group, but it is clear that many people regard them as 'outsiders'; for instance, the proportion of West Indian families has recently increased on one small council estate, and this has caused open ill feeling among other tenants.

What people so often mean by 'integration' is 'adopting the values and behaviour patterns of the majority' without realising (or accepting) that in a multi-racial society there must be adjustments by all groups if each is to become an equal, participant member of that society while retaining much of its own particular culture and identity. But again, it is all too easy to ignore the very real problems that face the 'host' community, as well as immigrants, in making adjustments to strange faces and strange habits; both groups need advice and assistance to cope with the situation. Our Circumstances of Families interviews, and the experience of the local (BIAS sponsored) CRC fieldworker, other advice/community workers and teachers, support the view that race relations must be tackled more vigorously at the local level. It is very much a house-by-house, street-by-street problem, and while discriminatory practices in housing, employment, etc, may to a large extent be curbed by legislation, attitudes and relations between neighbours require a more direct and painstaking approach. From our observation, it would seem that the Community Relations Commission, for example, did not address sufficiently the need both for small-area based fieldworkers and for the dissemination of practical guidance to local authority and other workers in multi-racial areas, and it is to be hoped that this will become a key element in the work of the new Commission for Racial Equality.

In Small Heath at present there is very little mixing between the three main racial groups (Asians, West Indians and whites), nor apparently between, say, Sikhs and Muslims or Punjabis and Bengalis. Although attempts have been made to involve Asians in the community federation, these have so far proved largely unsuccessful, and both they and West Indians take virtually no part in activities outside their own groups. The only significant exception to this is some West Indians' contact with white members of their church. The main reasons for the continued lack of mixing between whites and non-whites vary between immigrant groups, and the variations are an important consideration for measures designed to improve interracial communication and contact.

Our evidence and experience from action projects and the Circumstances of Families survey echo many of the findings of research on race relations in this country[1], which indicates that both Asians and West Indians have come to this country

1. Recent sources are: David J. Smith, *The Facts of Racial Disadvantage*, PEP 1976; Patricia Jeffery, *Migrants and Refugees*, Oxford University Press 1976; Lorna Bell, *Underprivileged Underfives*, Ward Lock Educational 1976.

mainly to take advantage of employment opportunities that are non-existent in their home countries, and for both it is likely that this economic motive in part serves a desire to acquire status and social recognition as well as a purely material concern to acquire money. The essential differences between the two groups' relationship with the indigenous white population would seem to lie first in language and second in the extent to which they see life in this country as a means to an end.

West Indians tend to identify with British culture; the Asians to insulate themselves from it. Whereas West Indians tend to recoil from rebuffs under the protection of a surface indifference and a concentration on their own family life, most Asians tend not to notice rebuffs, because they are much more aware of the barriers to contact which they themselves have erected. East African Asians, who in general have a fair or good command of English, have received formal education (often to a high standard) and are much more familiar with British attitudes and culture than are the majority of Asians in the area, have become aware of the existence of antipathetic attitudes towards themselves and particularly towards the more isolated, generally uneducated non-English speaking Asians. However, East African Asians interviewed in the Circumstances of Families survey did not display the same sense of rebuff and rejection as did West Indians, partly, it seemed, because they had not expected or sought the same degree of acceptance; they seemed on the whole to be satisfied with their polite, but usually rather distant relations with neighbours.

Approaches to better integration of the immigrant and white community in Small Heath must necessarily focus on the situation of Asians. The principal and most obvious barrier to mutual understanding is language. From our evidence (cross-checked with evidence on other similar situations) it would seem that no more than about half the male Asians (excluding those from East Africa) in the area have a reasonable command of English, and very few women have any, even rudimentary knowledge of the language. The problems this creates are two-fold. First, there are the practical difficulties such as finding employment; coping with an unfamiliar and complex system of laws and regulations, and in particular the difficulties created by immigration regulations which are a source of considerable anxiety among Small Heath's Asians; understanding the school system; and so on. Then there is the problem we have touched on before – their lack of awareness of the attitudes of others. While this does in a sense act as a protection against hurt and indignity, it also means that Asians are more susceptible to discriminatory or exploitative practices. Moreover, where antipathetic attitudes arise among neighbours who are offended, say, by standards of property maintenance (rubbish in gardens for instance) or behaviour which is considered odd or unhygienic, there is no possibility of stating and discussing the problem in the hope of resolving it.

The cultural differences between Asians and the host community not only constitute a considerable barrier but also create problems and tensions within the Asian community itself; indeed, in Small Heath, Asians are by and large far more concerned about difficulties within their own community than their relations with whites or West Indians. The differences stem basically from Asians' religious belief and practice, and from their present and previous economic circumstances, both of which combine to exert a very strong influence on their attitudes to life in this country. Here we are again focusing attention on the majority of Asians – ie, those from a poor rural background in South Asia. Much of the following discussion applies also to East African Asians – but with the proviso that their background and education tend to make them somewhat more adaptable to western mores and their inability to return to East Africa now or in the foreseeable future further distinguishes them from the majority of Asians and hence gives them a somewhat different perspective on life here.

Since Asian immigration is the direct result of poverty and lack of opportunity at home, and since most immigrants arrive with few or no personal assets, it is not surprising that their energies and interests are concentrated on providing a home, a living and a secure future for themselves and their families. Indeed, for the poorer families interviewed in the Circumstances of Families survey, the efforts required to meet the needs of the extended family (here and in the home country) virtually excluded all other activities and interests. The claims on an Asian family man's income are often considerable – high mortgage repayments (often, though not always, reduced by having single Asian male lodgers); remittances to family members at home; saving to bring family members over here and/or to return home either for a visit to cope with family problems or, ultimately, for good. White residents in Small Heath are frequently surprised and not a little annoyed that some Asian families, having bought a house, are apparently uninterested in maintaining and improving it – or indeed even furnishing it beyond the bare essentials. What is usually not understood, is that far from indicating a general slovenliness or irresponsibility, this situation usually reflects straitened financial circumstances. The expenditure on buying the house provides a measure of security and standard of accommodation far beyond what is possible at home, but maintenance and improvement may not – for a while at least – be a priority.

Religious beliefs and cultural traditions are dominant influences in Asians' lives, and even where language and economic circumstances do not constitute a particular barrier to closer contact and mixing with non-Asians, these influences tend to set them apart. Rules of dietary practice, for instance, inhibit socialising between neighbours, but the most striking difference is the position of girls and women in society. Tradition dictates that they play a secondary role vis-à-vis male members of the family; observe strict rules of modesty; that they enter into arranged marriages; and that once married, their lives are devoted wholly to family needs, often with very little or even no contact with people (and particularly men) outside the family circle. The rigour with which these traditions are observed obviously varies from family to family. However, where strict observance is maintained, a married woman may become extremely isolated, if she is unable to leave the house, except occasionally accompanied by her husband, and lacks the support and companionship of other women family members which she would have enjoyed at home. Even where observance is less strict (which seems in general to be the case in Small Heath) the fact that most women speak little or no English, are largely illiterate in their own language, and (if from a rural background) do not normally take up employment outside the home, means the potential for loneliness and isolation remains, particularly if there are no friends or family living nearby, and there is little opportunity of mixing with non-Asian neighbours.

Asians in Small Heath are facing a very real problem with regard to the maintenance of their cultural traditions. They are concerned at the shortage of facilities for social and religious activities, particularly Islamic teaching, and this is doubtless reinforced by anxiety over the effect upon the community of western values and 'permissiveness', especially upon women and, even more so, children raised in this country. For example, while many husbands accepted the practical value of English language classes for Asian women, they were at times uneasy concerning the resultant potential for increased contact with non-Asians (and therefore a different value system). The problems with regard to children are much more acute, and are a cause of concern not only to the Asian community but also to teachers, community workers and other members of the local community.

Education as an instrument of self-improvement (ie, the passport to a good job) is highly valued by Asians, and they welcome the opportunities for educational advancement which in general here far exceed those of their home country. However, many are very disturbed by the mixing of girls and boys (especially after the onset of puberty), and indeed some whose girls cannot attend a single sex school send them back home to finish their education. As for the majority of children who are wholly raised here, they inevitably acquire many of the values and aspirations of their non-Asian peer groups. For instance, their respect for their parents no longer necessarily extends to accepting arranged marriages and, once married, girls are less likely to accept the absolute authority of their husbands. Both trends inevitably undermine the existing structure of family and community life and, as teachers often observe, can place enormous stresses upon young people and again particularly girls.

The employment situation of young Asians is also a deepening cause of concern. Encouraged by their family and education in most cases to aspire to better jobs than their fathers hold, many now find they cannot get a job at all. To what extent they themselves see this solely as the outcome of the deepening recession in the West Midlands, or as being influenced also by racial discrimination, we do not know, but it is likely that if this situation persists they, like young West Indians, will develop feelings of alienation and rejection. Certainly other Asians are already worried by the effects of unemployment, which some blame for increased crime (notably burglaries) and vandalism within their community.

The problems outlined above illustrate the pressing need for special attention to the circumstances of Asians in Small Heath. In particular there is a need for more people with Asian language skills, knowledge of immigration rules and familiarity with Asian culture among community workers, advice workers, teachers, etc, in the area. One indication of the need is the experience of the CRC fieldworker, who, during her one year appointment with BIAS, found it extremely difficult to make time for community work with Asians because she was in constant demand either for advice on immigration problems or as an interpreter or advisor for other workers. If, too, there is to be a greater mutual understanding and cooperation between Asians and the 'host' community, then efforts to promote this must extend to local schools and organisations.

The implications for other multi-racial areas of the lessons learned in Small Heath would seem clear enough. In the first place, problems within and between groups must be tackled on the basis of detailed local knowledge. Second, every effort should be made to respect the culture and traditions of individual groups, while building bridges of communication and understanding between groups. Third, special attention should be paid to the social and family problems of children from immigrant families. We consider that, irrespective of special initiatives and appointments to deal with race relations/immigrants' problems, community workers, social workers, teachers, and some health workers, such as health visitors, should all be given short preparatory courses on immigrants' culture, customs and particular problems, preferably by members of the specific cultural group/groups concerned. Furthermore, in order to meet more adequately the needs of multi-racial areas, central government should encourage more positively the take-up by local authorities of special resources (eg, grants under section 11 of the Local Government Act 1966) for projects in areas of high immigrant population. Again, in both cases, the Commission for Racial Equality could play a valuable role in advising and assisting central and local government.

The potential outcome of strategy

If a strategy of community organisation is successful, community development teams will become redundant, at least as far as their initial role is concerned. Such redundancy should be planned for. We are convinced that there is quite enough talent and energy in every community for it to produce its own leaders, once the impetus is given. Certainly the experience in Small Heath of residents' associations, the community federation, and the setting up and management by local people of a successful pre-school centre has demonstrated considerable qualities of leadership and responsible management.

As a community becomes more organised, so its capacity for meeting many local needs will grow. There is no reason why the community should not progressively take on responsibility for planning its own activities and managing its own facilities, whether they are advice centres, clubs for young people or the elderly, playgroups or childminding schemes, even small parks or playgrounds. For instance, the Little Green Residents Association has refurbished an old school annex, now a thriving local community centre; local mothers are now running playgroups in Small Heath; residents have actively participated in planning the use and layout of SARA park in the redevelopment area and the Millward Street playground in Little Green. It is not a question of simply relieving the local authority of some of its burdens or obligations, rather one of making it possible for the community to exercise greater choice and control over the type and style of activities and facilities. The local authority's role would be that of enabler and facilitator, through the provision of grants, materials, equipment, premises and, where appropriate, professional assistance, either directly or acting as a 'clearing house' for voluntary resource agencies.[1]

1. For example, Action Resource Centre, which makes industrial and business skills available to local agencies, organisations, community groups, on the basis of voluntary part-time or temporary full-time secondments from industry and commerce.

If such a transfer of responsibility were achieved within a policy framework of positive discrimination then savings in public resources could be redirected into programmes which only the local authority can effectively provide on the scale required: housing, basic environmental services, education and personal social services. However, even in these programmes, there is scope for much greater community involvement – such as self-build and cooperative improvement schemes for housing; the appointment of part-time (or spare time) caretakers from among residents on council estates, to ensure a basic standard of environmental maintenance – an approach we tested on the small Talfourd Street Estate; and the appointment of locally-recruited non-professional auxiliary workers/instructors provided with basic training where necessary, to broaden the scope and capabilities of community work, personal social services and education programmes.

We feel that this last point is particularly important. There is an unfortunate tendency among professionals to believe that they alone are qualified to deal with the problems which fall within the purview of their particular field or expertise. Community workers (tnemselves a relatively new professional 'genre') are seemingly the first to openly recognise that this is not so, and to take positive steps to 'de-professionalise' their field of activity. In Small Heath, the experience of the Community Education Development Officer pointed to the potential for using local skills in the running of adult education courses – one of his most successful ventures was a home improvement course, run under his general supervision, with the instruction provided by local residents with relevant trade skills. Nationally, the Adult Literacy Campaign has in fact depended for its success upon non-professional instructors providing individual tuition to students. Again, it is not merely a question of providing extra services at low cost, but also a different style of service, which is likely to be less formal in style and for that reason more acceptable to those people (and there are many) who are frequently intimidated by the style and approach of professional workers.

If the community is to plan and manage many of its own activities and facilities, then the need may well arise for a mechanism for distributing local resources between groups. For an 'organised' community does not imply a single organisation. As we have seen in Small Heath, the more 'organised' it becomes the greater is likely to be the multiplicity of separate organisations – residents' associations, street committees, tenants co-ops, youth clubs, sports clubs, crafts and theatre groups, minority cultural associations, and so on. These different organisations will tend to crystallise around limited sectarian interests, and they will be competing for scarce resources, such as grants and premises; some may, for instance, under-utilise buildings and equipment, while others will be short of the same resources.

There is an important role here for a community federation of local residents' groups and organisations, similar to that established in Small Heath, in that it could help to distribute resources more efficiently and to resolve conflicts of interest. Its concerns would be the interests and well-being of the neighbourhood/community as a whole, and it could not only help individual groups to co-operate in achieving the best use of individual resources, but it could also provide practical assistance such as, say, small seeding grants to individual associations to enable them to establish or develop their facilities and activities. But the federation's role could extend beyond this. Certainly it has in Small Heath, where the federation has successfully undertaken activities on a wider front than is possible for individual groups: organising a carnival, producing a community newspaper and – a notable achievement – obtaining the (Urban Aid) funds for and setting up a neighbourhood law centre. Moreover, it could act as a powerful lobby on issues of common concern, especially where a system of devolved political activity, such as area committees, enables the federation to participate directly in local decision-making.

Since an 'umbrella' organisation of this kind can act as a key link between local authority and community, as well as playing an important role in the development of the community itself, we would recommend that the local authority actively encourage its formation by providing grant-aid and other practical assistance. In areas where a community development team has been appointed, one of their functions would be to explore the potential for establishing a federation, assisting in setting it up (drawing up a constitution, establishing financial arrangements, etc) and finding people with the necessary skills to enable it to function effectively. But the provision of support, and in particular grant-aid, should not be allowed to place restrictions (however implicit) upon the federation's freedom to frankly and vigourously represent the interests of the community in its dealings with the local authority. Only if it can do this will such an organisation have any chance of commanding the trust and respect of both community and local authority, and so exert a positive influence in the development of the community it represents.

Assuming that a significant degree of community organisation is achieved, there will remain nonetheless people within the community whose interests are not adequately represented, if at all. For some, of course, it will be a matter of choice, but for others, notably the most disadvantaged and vulnerable, the very circumstances which point the need for collective organisation and action may inhibit or frustrate their achievement. It is frequently pointed out (at times as an excuse for not recognising the representative nature of any grassroots activity) that community organisations tend to attract the relatively better-off, more articulate and extrovert members of the community, while those most in need (the inarticulate, withdrawn, housebound, desperately poor) remain beyond the pale, and there is no denying the basic truth of this statement. Certainly the extent to which the most vulnerable can be brought together is debatable. In the Bolton Road clearance area, for example, residents' severe housing problems, and the personal stresses these created, were not in fact a solid basis for organisation and collective action. Indeed, with the exception of short-lived sporadic activities, often stimulated by the efforts of the local community worker, residents showed no lasting inclination to come together, either on issues of common concern, or even for social activities. People simply wanted to get out of the area as soon as possible which militated against developing any sense of 'community'. There was also evidence of considerable tension between neighbours arising both from the pressures of their living conditions and personal circumstances, and a strong sense of 'competition' for alternative council accommodation. In these circumstances, community support (advice, advocacy and play facilities for children) proved to be of far more importance to residents than organisation.

212

Approaches to community organisation and development must recognise this problem, and aim to ensure that the needs of vulnerable groups are not ignored because they are not articulated by the groups themselves. Local organisations can do a lot to mobilise more practical help from within the community and from the local authority. (Here again, a community federation, with its broader perspective on local needs, could play an important role not only in securing more help and support but also in seeking action to remove the causes of severe hardship). The type and range of assistance (counselling, advocacy, special aids/services, etc) depends upon the particular circumstances of individuals; sometimes all that is needed is simply more neighbourly help and concern. There is definitely a role here for the para-professional worker: the active pensioner to help the housebound elderly; the person with experience of severe personal difficulty (eg, long-term unemployment) to help with counselling, and so on.

*

While there clearly is no simple prescription for community organisation, and no guarantee of its likely outcome, we do believe that it is almost certainly a prerequisite for restoring confidence in areas in decline and where few people with any great individual power of choice would currently choose to live. Furthermore, the growth of community organisation in inner areas could conceivably lead to a genuine 'movement' with more than local political influence. If this were so, it would be yet another positive step towards achieving the redistribution of resources essential to the alleviation of inner area problems.

Gordon King

Just take a look at Edgbaston, Sheldon and places like that, there you would be happy knowing that you live in a clean environment . . . People don't seem to want anything to do with Small Heath and the people who live there, they probably think we are right rogues just because where we live.

A Child's Eye View of Small Heath

8 Compensating for disadvantage

Our analysis of the problems of inner areas and their causes has confirmed our belief that the roots of urban deprivation do not lie in personal inadequacy but in societal forces which create situations of such serious disadvantage and deprivation for many people that they may be properly termed 'victims'. It follows that the focus of inner area policy must be to effect basic changes in the way our society functions in order to achieve a more equitable distribution of resources, and indeed this is the main thrust of our argument. Nonetheless, we cannot pursue the goal of redistribution without recognising that there remains the urgent need, and responsibility, to compensate those who now suffer deprivation and disadvantage, and that this need will remain for as long as poverty and severe structural inequality persist.

The nature of inner area problems is such that compensatory measures must necessarily address both the personal (household-specific) and collective (area-specific) elements of deprivation. There is also a distinction between measures designed to alleviate existing conditions of deprivation and those which aim at reducing their incidence. Household-specific measures are discussed in Chapter 11, where we consider the crucial issue of raising earned and unearned incomes. In this chapter we are concerned with area or location specific approaches, based on the concept of positive discrimination – that is, unequally generous treatment in the distribution of resources to areas suffering severe or exceptional needs. We discuss some of the shortcomings of current approaches to positive discrimination, and suggest ways in which the concept might be more effectively applied to the problems of inner areas.

Before starting the discussion, however, we should make clear our basic reasons for considering area-based approaches as a legitimate and worthwhile element of an overall strategy to combat urban deprivation and disadvantage. The rationale for household-specific programmes is clear enough: single-parent families, large families, the chronically sick and unemployed, etc., experience certain problems and privations which are common among most or many people in similar circumstances and when identified can therefore be addressed on a group-by-group basis. This approach attempts to cope with the incidence of personal deprivation, irrespective of location. The rationale for area-specific programmes is, as we see it, that high concentrations of disadvantaged or deprived people living in a collectively deprived environment present problems which are unique in their nature and scale,[1] and cannot be alleviated simply by a more intensive application of household-specific measures.

1. Or, as R. J. Webber puts it: 'Area-based positive discrimination is justified by the fact that life experience is unequal even within social groups and depends strongly on the social characteristics of the areas as well as the households they live in.' Webber, *Liverpool Social Area Study, 1971 Data, Final Report; PRAG Technical Papers TP14*.

Positive discrimination and national programmes

The concept of positive discrimination was first advocated in the field of education. The Plowden Report, published in 1967, urged special help for special needs, and with regard to schools with exceptionally large numbers of socially handicapped children it asked for ' . . . "positive discrimination" in favour of such schools and the children in them, going well beyond an attempt to equalise resources.' This statement was of profound significance. Not only were the report's recommendations on positive discrimination immediately reflected in educational policy (through the designation of Educational Priority Areas and Schools of Exceptional Difficulty), they also had an impact on thinking across a wider spectrum of social policy. The principle of equal resource inputs to all areas had hitherto been a commonly (if not universally) accepted goal; post-Plowden there has been an increasing awareness that the achievement of this goal would not in fact solve the problems of the most deprived urban areas.

Hence we have seen the establishment of a number of further programmes aimed at channelling additional resources to deprived urban areas, starting with the Urban Programme in 1968, which has funded projects such as day nurseries, advice centres, hostels for the homeless and limited job creation programmes. There have been action research projects into the social and environmental problems of areas of multiple deprivation: the National Community Development Project and Inner Area Studies, set up in 1969 and 1972 respectively, the latter following the Shelter Neighbourhood Action Project (SNAP) in Liverpool. The Urban Guidelines Studies, also set up in 1972, looked briefly at means by which local authorities could develop a 'total approach' to the improvement of the urban environment. More recently, in 1974, Comprehensive Community Programmes were set up, on an experimental basis, to identify and develop policies and programmes to deal with urban deprivation and disadvantage throughout the whole local authority area.

The widespread problems of ageing and decaying residential areas were given special attention through the Housing Acts of 1969 and 1974, with the establishment of GIAs and HAAs. Section 11 of the 1966 Local Government Act empowers the grant of special aid to local authorities with large immigrant populations. Some deprived urban areas were also affected by special employment policies, though where these operate on a regional or sub-regional basis (eg development areas) the net effect may arguably even be detrimental to inner areas as in Liverpool, where special incentives have encouraged industry to locate on the periphery of the city.

Clearly there has been no shortage of initiatives towards positive discrimination during the past ten years. Yet the fact remains that this particular approach to compensating for disadvantage has so far largely failed to achieve any real (as opposed to expressed) priority nationally because the actual commitment of public resources has been very small indeed. In seven years the total sums paid out in Urban Aid (under the Urban Programme) have amounted to little over £40 million, which is equivalent to a mere twentieth of 1 per cent of resources committed to spending on social services alone. Extra resources channelled to EPAs in the period 1968/69 to 1970/71 comprised between 0.2 per cent and 0.4 per cent of the schools budget. By

216

1974, the additional salary allowance for priority schools still only amounted to approximately 0.1 per cent of the total salary bill, and only 4 per cent of primary school children were in the schools affected, not 10 per cent as recommended by Plowden.[1] Special housing programmes have not fared very much better, due to the confused state of housing policy and finance, and the problems of slow progress and inadequate resource commitment in Birmingham's renewal programme appear to be reflected nationally.

If positive discrimination is to be effective in tackling urban deprivation, there must be a more serious commitment of resources, since marginally more generous treatment will have very little effect where the disadvantages to be overcome are enormous. The extent of the gap between actual and necessary resource allocations is well illustrated by the following statement: 'To take educational deprivation seriously may mean spending double the average amount on at least 10 per cent of the school population.[2] But however much resource allocations for programmes of positive discrimination are increased, they will only be effective insofar as they focus on key elements of disadvantage, and are pursued as part of a consistent strategy (or series of strategies) to deal with the problems of the people they are intended to assist. Otherwise, much of what is spent will not only prove to be an ineffectual use of resources, but may ultimately prove counter-productive in that, since many or most of the problems apparently addressed by the programmes will persist, positive discrimination could be widely discredited as an approach to alleviating deprivation. This is particularly a hazard in times of national economic hardship when there is strong competition for limited government resources.

The responsibility for the effective deployment of special resources in deprived urban areas is shared by both central and local government. While central government must undoubtedly remain the main source of funds, local government can and does exercise considerable influence over the way in which those funds are used. In the remainder of this chapter we look at the operation of 'positive discrimination' at the local level, and at means by which additional funds could be channelled to areas most in need.

Positive discrimination at the local level

Our general experience with action projects, and in particular those concerned with education and pre-school provision, provided some useful insights into the application of the concept of positive discrimination at the local level. Overall it would seem that there is a good deal of confusion as to what the concept really means, and how it should be applied; on the other hand, opportunities for applying it more effectively are not difficult to discern.

---

1. Jack Barnes, 'A Solution to Whose Problem?' and Howard Glennerster, 'A Basic Philosophy for Resource Allocation,' in *Positive Discrimination and Inequality, Fabian Research Series 314*, (editors: Howard Glennerster and Stephen Hatch), March 1974.
2. Howard Glennerster, *op. cit.*

Misunderstanding and lack of commitment

Though our programme of action projects did not amount to a massive injection of resources into Small Heath, it did provide an opportunity for applying the principle of positive discrimination through the use of 'special resources for special needs'. In the course of our work we found considerable misunderstanding and lack of commitment among certain individuals, in central and local government and other agencies which at the outset we had not anticipated. In discussing this, however, we have to recognise that our own understanding of what we were trying to achieve through individual action projects was in some cases not as clear as (with hindsight) it could or should have been, and this doubtless had some influence on our relationship with those whose cooperation and commitment we sought. Furthermore, negative attitudes towards the entire inner area study as a vehicle for ultimately achieving more effective compensation for disadvantage would be likely to condition reactions to initiatives stemming from it. While we have no way of assessing the importance of this additional factor, it must be borne in mind.

Misunderstanding of the concept of positive discrimination seems to arise in two ways. First, demand tends to be confused with need, and second, there is at times the assumption that special needs, where they are defined, can be dealt with simply by the application of non-specific or standard measures. Where such misunderstandings occur, they can obscure, obstruct and even frustrate the purpose of one or a series of initiatives intended to compensate for a disadvantage. For example, we encountered considerable difficulty in trying to develop stronger home-school links in two primary schools (an approach advocated by Plowden and first tested in EPAs). Both projects became dominated by ad hoc demands generated from within the school, and the notion of positive outreach into the community, the prime intention behind the work, was largely submerged. In fact, in one case it was never seriously attempted at all, primarily because (odd as it may seem in view of the fairly explicit briefing for the post) the liaison teacher apparently did not perceive this to be an essential part of the work. In neither school did there appear to be any real encouragement for the liaison teachers to act as much more than an extra pair of hands to take on substitute teaching and relieve class teachers of non-teaching tasks. The objective of developing strong home-school links was apparently either rejected as impracticable or unnecessary by some staff members, or simply not seen as something requiring a special staff allocation. Indeed both teachers experienced not only misunderstanding but also some initial resentment among staff, though this did in fact diminish over time. That such a situation can arise in deprived urban primary schools almost ten years after the publication of the Plowden Report is perhaps surprising; it is also sobering.

Our experience in trying to improve approaches to pre-school in inner areas was likewise illuminating. Like most of our projects, those concerned with pre-school care and education were concerned both with a better understanding of needs and finding appropriate means of meeting those needs. The necessary extra resources to meet special needs might in some cases involve new or improved 'physical plant', in others the emphasis would be more on having people with appropriate skills and attitudes to provide services, advice or aid, and in some cases a mixture of both.

Or it might mean simply enabling people within the community to develop and run services which meet special needs that cannot be met by formal organisations, by providing grants, loans, access to premises and other forms of support, legal, advisory or technical. All are aspects of positive discrimination but are not always recognised as such.

One of our four pre-school projects came into the last category. The Self-Help Pre-School Centre was already in existence when we came to Small Heath, primarily as a playgroup but also providing some welfare and other advice for mothers and some social activity through a 'keep fit' class. The centre was started and run by a highly energetic local woman, using a small annex to an old primary school in Little Green. However, experience had shown that there was a pressing need locally for full day-care as well as playgroup facilities for pre-school children who either did not qualify for the very limited number of places in the day-care centre run by the social services department, or whose mothers for a variety of reasons were reluctant to approach Social Services. Moreover many of the mothers using the centre were in extremely difficult circumstances, and the centre provided for some of them much needed psychological or practical support.

A proposal for BIAS grant-aid for a low-cost conversion of the annex (to provide a kitchen, inside toilets, laundry facilities etc) and the employment of full-time staff was accepted in principle (by our steering committee), but thereafter we encountered considerable resistance on the question of standards from DHSS with whom we were liaising and whose general approval of the experiment was desired. The resistance basically stemmed from the fact that, in the first place, the project did not fit the department's concept of good child care, and, in the second, objections were raised concerning the general applicability of premises and equipment standards which were lower than those currently set by DHSS. The department's views (or at least those of its representatives) were that the centre would not be adequately provided with trained staff to give very young children the attention they needed while away from their mothers all day.

However, the point here was that the children needed day-care precisely because their mothers could not be with them or give them proper attention for all or a substantial part of each day. They were likely to be receiving far less adequate care outside the centre. The arguments over standards revolved around the fact that in a non-experimental situation loan sanction would not be granted for facilities that were 'below standard'; our attempt to test a low-cost approach was therefore inappropriate. The possibility that the standards themselves should and could perhaps be modified to allow for more flexible approaches did not seem to have been seriously considered. Ultimately all these difficulties were resolved but they did point to insufficient appreciation of the practicalities involved in meeting special needs which are widely acknowledged to exist, and also a lack of the very necessary flexibility that will help to optimise the use of limited resources.

Lack of commitment is, if anything, an even greater barrier to effective positive discrimination than misunderstanding, because it represents a refusal, conscious or unconscious, to face up to the problems of disadvantage. (Indeed, at times, apparent misunderstanding may well be lack of commitment.) It is manifested in resistance to attempting new or unusual approaches to meeting need, lack of interest in considering or applying the results of experiment, failure to identify or maintain essential mutually reinforcing links between services, and unwillingness to divert resources away from high demand areas or groups to those with greater need. We have seen all of this during our time in Small Heath, as well as much hard work, initiative and commitment, and it is largely because lack of commitment in one quarter can frustrate or negate positive efforts in another that we feel we must draw attention to it.

Almost half our action projects involved the sponsorship of experimental appointments within local authority departments, while the remainder covered a broad spectrum of organisational settings – residents' groups, voluntary or quasi-public organisations and community arts. As the study progressed we saw the extent to which some individuals and groups can begin to make an impact, even in a relatively short period, where they have attitudes, aptitudes and experience appropriate to the problems they are trying to tackle. But we also saw how difficult, lonely and even defeating it can be for even the most committed and competent people when they are regularly faced with indifference or resistance within their parent organisation or department.

We found that in several cases initiatives which had apparently been welcomed or accepted by local authority departments or other organisations at the time they were proposed were in practice regarded either as a nuisance because they fell outside normal procedures, or were largely ignored, the worker involved being left to get on with the job without any apparent interest from his or her seniors and controllers. This placed a great strain on some workers, who sometimes had to fight hard either to be allowed to do the job they had been given, or to obtain basic working premises and equipment which should have been provided from the outset. Professionals working within their own field, but with 'unusual' tasks to perform, at times came up against a surprising degree of suspicion and even hostility from fellow-professionals. Partly this could be due to the fact that being attached to BIAS, some were seen (at least at first) as outsiders whose freedom from many of the normal departmental or organisational constraints and routine pressures gave them a 'soft option'; the stresses attached to experimental work were much less readily appreciated. But in the few instances where strong negative attitudes persisted (and, regrettably, some of the strongest resistance was found in the field of education) it appeared that they were rooted in an overdeveloped, overprotective sense of 'professionalism'; new or unusual approaches were seen as a threat to established roles and practices, and even as a slur on the competence of individuals already working in the area. Fortunately, those who encountered most resistance were, by and large, among the toughest and most experienced workers.

'People networks' and the assessment of priorities

Our experience with action projects demonstrated the value of 'people networks' in approaches to positive discrimination. Most of the projects depended primarily on people, not additions of physical plant, partly by virtue of the limited resources available, but more importantly because the needs we identified would not be solved solely, or in some cases, at all, by capital investment. As projects developed, we observed the formation of some strong, mutually reinforcing links between the majority of people principally involved. For instance, the community relations fieldworker and the workers involved with pre-school and community education cooperated in involving Asian women and children in playgroups, language classes, etc; workers from Playvan helped the pre-school community worker to organise play events; the youthworker and community education officer together arranged training for unemployed school leavers; advice workers helped the community education development officer to set up and run local courses on housing and welfare rights. These are just a few examples of the kinds of link that grew up. On a day-to-day basis there was considerable contact and cooperation between many of the project personnel, and one of the refreshing aspects of this process was the way in which people with diverse personalities and backgrounds could and did work together productively. However, perhaps the most important aspect of this situation is that, taken individually, none of the initiatives could have or has had more than a very limited impact, no matter how 'successful' in progressing towards its stated objective; taken together they may still have had no huge impact on the area as a whole, but without the degree of linking and mutual support their total and individual impact would doubtless have been much less than it was.

Clearly there is an important lesson here in relation to the allocation of special resources to disadvantaged areas. Having identified the key elements of disadvantage, it is important to assess to what extent compensatory measures are interdependent if resources are not to be misdirected or wasted. Not only must such an assessment be part of any strategy to improve housing, education, employment or spending power, it also applies to small-scale local initiatives of the kind we have just described. To take perhaps the most obvious case from our own experience: the CRC fieldworker, being the only locally based community worker with a knowledge of several Asian languages, as well as having considerable experience working with Asian immigrants, was an essential link between the non English speaking members of the Asian community and other workers, particularly those involved with pre-school care and education. For instance, without the CRC worker, many (often isolated) Asian women would not have brought their children to playgroups or attended language classes. Moreover, the worker was able to advise others on cultural mores which could have a significant bearing on work with immigrant adults and children. Obviously in an area with a substantial Asian population, the presence or absence of a worker (or workers) with appropriate language and other skills will make a significant difference to the impact or influence of other workers, and so help to ensure that resources intended for disadvantaged groups or areas are not rendered largely inaccessible to many people in need by reason of cultural or language barriers.

When the time came for the city council to consider the future of most of the BIAS action initiatives in Small Heath, we again encountered some revealing attitudes towards the concept of positive discrimination. We had hoped that final decisions could await the full assessment of all projects; we were fully aware that some we would not recommend for continuation, for others we would in all probability recommend continuation with a modification to the original approach, while the remainder would be deemed to be working effectively under existing arrangements and should continue. However the imperative of reducing local authority expenditure in 1976/77 meant that early in 1976, before a full assessment could be made, decisions on future funding had to be taken by committees. After some consultation with BIAS a series of recommendations for continuing or discontinuing funding were put forward by officers for consideration by Policy and Resources Committee, which then referred individual projects to the relevant service committees for decision, without any direction concerning priorities, each committee being left to make its decision on the basis of competing demands city-wide. The result was a somewhat haphazard deletion of certain projects which had been initially recommended for continued funding during the period.

This process emphasised what we have observed in other situations during the course of the study. First there was apparently a feeling that because Small Heath had 'done well' in terms of additional resources during the three years of the Inner Area Study, it was time to switch resources to other equally needy areas. What did not seem to feature significantly, if at all, in the general deliberations were the facts that Small Heath's needs still far outstripped the resource inputs generated by BIAS and whatever had been achieved was only a small beginning in terms of tackling specific problems. Second, there did not seem to be any appreciation of the need at least to try to assess the priorities for the area before reaching a decision, nor of the essential futility of spreading marginal resources yet more thinly among disadvantaged areas (the logical extension of the idea of switching). We do not deny that in times of stringent economic management, hard decisions have to be made, but this is all the more reason for ensuring that the hardest decisions are made in respect of those most, not least, able to bear the consequences.

Wider application of the concept

So far we have argued that despite a variety of approaches to positive discrimination, on a number of different fronts, there remains the need for more vigorous, coordinated action locally and nationally. Otherwise the backlog of disadvantage in areas like Small Heath will never be reduced. But if the personal and collective deprivations associated with inadequate incomes, lack of jobs, poor housing, etc, are to be alleviated, there is no doubt that there are sizeable resource implications attached to compensatory or positive discrimination programmes which are to make any real impact. Even in times of relative economic prosperity it would almost certainly be unrealistic to expect the sums needed to come entirely from additional revenues; in a time of recession it is clearly impossible. This means that resources for 'unequally generous treatment' must come from redistribution. That is, those areas or groups enjoying a privileged level of provision must get proportionately less, though since 'less' refers only to incremental capital spending and to the renewal of already high current expenditure much of the inherited historical advantage will of course still persist. Furthermore, ways have to be found of directing resources to those people and areas most in need, both through the better use of the existing policy framework and by means of special selection.

Jon Stevens

If you go into town and tell people you're from Small Heath, they think you're living in a slum. If you've got a teenage daughter and she goes for an interview for a job, if she says she comes from Small Heath her chances of a job have gone downhill. It's a terrible thing to say, but my daughter says she's from South Yardley.

SCPR Exploratory Study

We advocate the extension of the compensatory approach across the whole field of policy-making, including the process of local political representation as proposed in Chapter 6. Central government's role is likely to remain closely geared to the allocation of extra funds, either in the form of increased block grants and specific grants to authorities faced with problems of urban deprivation, or in the form of special allocations within major policy fields such as housing and education. At the local level, the individual spending authority can develop a much more fine-grained approach appropriate to variations in local needs. This means that, irrespective of special aid from central government, the local authority should give priority to the allocation of extra resources to those areas (and sectors of the community) most in need of public services, both in terms of the severity of their problems and their inability to meet the costs of private provision. This is not to deny the good sense, for example, of making available to community groups disused school annexes at peppercorn rents for renovation and use as youth centres, pensioners' clubs, workshops or whatever. But it does mean that if, say, purpose-built centres and full time workers are to be provided, then the first claims on them should be allowed to those most deprived and in greatest need of resources.

Selection of priority areas for government aid

If central government's approaches to positive discrimination are to be made more effective in tackling inner area problems, then there must be a means of distributing special resources on a systematic basis of need which takes account of the interrelationships between the various elements of urban deprivation: in effect, a national 'urban deprivation programme' which would enable the particular problems of specific areas to be addressed in a concerted, coordinated manner appropriate to local circumstances. Resources might be made available in the form of funding for individual projects, modifications to national aid programmes which would qualify such localities (and their labour market zones) for special premiums, rates of grant, investment incentives and relaxation of controls, or adjustments to local government financial support mechanisms (by way, for example, of specific grants or changes in the rate support grant 'needs element' formula) dependent upon the total number and size of designated areas falling within a local authority's territory. Type and mix of programmes would vary with local circumstances, as would the size of area covered.

In a programme of this kind, the method of selecting areas is clearly of crucial importance. The prime objective of the selection process should be to direct resources to areas in greatest need while taking account of different combinations of circumstances both between and within towns, cities, conurbations. The following discussion is concerned with one possible approach which we put forward on the basis of general experience in Small Heath, using local data and available information for other cities and Great Britain as a whole[1] as a basis for conclusions on quantitative criteria. Though we have tried to anticipate some of the worst pitfalls in a selection process of this kind, the method has not been tested so we cannot claim to have either identified or dealt with all of them. Nonetheless we would hope the discussion will be of value in the further development of selection procedures.

1. R. J. Webber, *op. cit.:* and Sally Holtermann, *op. cit.*

Selection and confirmation

The basic process would be the same as for most other special aid programmes: initial selection of areas by the local authority and confirmation by central government (preferably DOE, whose role in urban resource planning we discuss further in Chapter 13). The initial selection of areas, at the local authority level, should be the result of a political process of choice, drawing heavily on the breadth and depth of local knowledge and experience, involving ward councillors, area-based officers and (most importantly) representatives of local communities. In submitting a case for priority treatment to central government, there is an obvious need for quantitative data for the purposes of comparison but such data should be seen as supporting evidence for the case and not the case itself.

The argument in favour of politicising the process of selection rather than treating it as a purely technical exercise rests principally on three premises. First, the rich and complex texture of an area's life can only be appreciated by those with direct experience of living and/or working within the communities concerned. Second, people living in deprived areas, where the pervasive influence of government decisions and actions is most acutely felt, have a right to be party to those decisions and actions. Third, the success of public programmes is in no small way dependent upon the active support and cooperation of the people most affected by them; such support and cooperation will not be achieved unless people are able to identify both with the programme itself (which is taken as relevant to their circumstances and beneficial in its prospective outcome) and with those who will bear the main responsibility for its execution. However, the chief problem with an approach that is political rather than purely technical is that those areas where the community is best organised and has acquired experience and skills in articulating its demands or aspirations and pressing for their satisfaction will tend to be pushed to the front of the queue, whether or not they are in fact the 'worst' areas – and they are highly unlikely to be the very worst. Such a tendency places an additional onus of responsibility on councillors, officers, community workers, pressure groups and others closely involved with the most deprived communities. It also stresses the need for community organisation and development initiatives, as discussed in Chapter 7.

Confirmation of areas at central government level should be based on explicit criteria and fairly strict rules of qualification. Local authorities should be given clear guidance on the programme's objectives, its intended scope, the type of area it is intended to assist, and the rules of qualification. The purpose of suggesting a fairly strict qualifying procedure is to ensure that the numbers of serious applications are kept within reasonable limits and the degree of arbitrariness in assessment minimised. Furthermore, this would have the advantage of biasing ministerial discretion (which would be applied in exceptional or disputed cases) in favour of inclusion rather than exclusion.

The process of confirmation should take into account all evidence presented in support of the case for selection but must inevitably be strongly guided by performance on a number of quantifiable and therefore comparable indicators based on the census. It is suggested that the yardstick (or reference point) for comparison be in terms of the standard deviation from the national urban mean or, failing that, from the national mean. The actual degree of deviation set as criterion (it might be less or greater than 1 SD) will depend upon the extent of the programme envisaged, which will in turn depend upon the resources available; the greater the deviation, the smaller the programme (because fewer areas would qualify) and vice versa. Central government (DOE) would provide local authorities with the appropriate values for the indicators used. The full case submitted for ratification should present as complete a picture of the area as possible, the potential range of detailed information covering: a general description of the area, including the key characteristics of the population; the incidence of deprivation, with information on housing, social status/incomes, vulnerable minorities, social malaise, physical environment, services and facilities; the rate of decline or improvement; changes in functions; the state of community morale, stability, organisation; and a review of plans and programmes for the area.

Since the prime objective of the process must be to ensure that resources are allocated to areas in greatest need, the criteria which determine qualification must operate highly selectively but be flexible enough to allow for different combinations of circumstances both between and within towns, cities and conurbations. If the combination of circumstances varies, the combination of strategies required will vary too. Criteria used in selecting and confirming areas must therefore be very carefully balanced, so that they do not automatically discriminate in favour of one particular set of circumstances rather than another, where different sets may constitute a situation of similar gravity with regard to their effects on people's quality of life and the demands they place on the resources of local authorities and other agencies. This suggests that in order to qualify areas must exhibit clear signs of deprivation in several 'key sectors' simultaneously but that the precise balance of deprivations within each key sector ought to be kept fairly flexible. For example, areas would have to possess some kind of extreme housing deficiency, but whether the deficiency manifested itself primarily in overcrowding, in sharing and its attendant problems or in lack of amenities could be left open; they would have to contain a high proportion of (say) three or more special needs groups, but there need be no hard and fast rule whether these were New Commonwealth immigrants, large families with children, single parents, unemployed males, or all-pensioner households; and so on. We would argue further that no attempt should be made to attribute different weights to different key sectors. In difficult cases, where for instance obviously severe housing deficiency and a high proportion of special needs groups were found but few signs of social malaise (a situation likely in fact to be rare), the final decision would have to be left to local political choice and the exercise of ministerial discretion, though clearly evidence of a deteriorating situation over time would lend support to the argument for inclusion.

Information required

From the description so far it might appear that we are advocating a process which would necessitate extensive special surveys or investigations for those elements of the local authority's submission other than the key census indicators. In fact, this is not so; we have based our approach on the potential for tapping information and experience which is already available to the local authority. Evidence on residents' preferences, interests and concerns is possibly the most difficult to assemble, particularly where there is little or no community organisation. Little is known unfortunately about the correlation that might be expected between particular sets of objective circumstances and subjective attitudes towards them, and (as our own evidence from the SCPR and Circumstances of Families surveys indicates) there are certainly no hard-and-fast correlations which are universally applicable. Therefore, in assessing the evidence which is readily to hand, a careful attempt should be made, first, to relate indicators of consumption or income to indicators of need and, second, to evaluate need according to the likely special requirements of population sub-groups. What is 'likely' must clearly depend on the general state of knowledge about the circumstances peculiar to particular age, ethnic or other sub-groups under broadly similar socio-economic conditions. Thus, in the first instance, it would be important to compare data on socio-economic groupings (as a proxy for income, where direct income data are unavailable) against information on household size and composition. In the second, the special needs and the special social problems created by a high concentration of Pakistanis, say, should be considered in the light of the known circumstances of their immigration, their length of residence, their position in the housing and employment markets, and so on. The aim is not so much scientific exactness as an interpretation of the story behind the figures and which the figures, paradoxically, may actually obscure if taken at face value.

The kind of information useful in building up a picture of the collective environment (whether on the provision of open space or the amount of pollution and noise, the distribution by age and size of industrial development or the general condition of streets and buildings, the membership of active residents' associations or the incidence of vandalism etc) need again not involve extensive special surveys. Much of it can be put together simply by making use of the great deal of information already available in individual local authority departments or from other public and private agencies, supplemented at little cost in time and effort by direct observation, photography and the straightforward testimony of people active in the local community. However, in considering the nature of the collective environment and the quality of life of people who are constantly exposed to it, it is not enough merely to obtain a 'snapshot' of circumstances at any particular point in time; it is essential too to have a dynamic picture of how circumstances are changing over time. Crucial, for example, to the state of community morale and confidence – themselves key factors in assessing the type of strategies which may have the greatest probabilities of success – is whether things seem on the whole to be getting better or going downhill. This requires not only an awareness of the different needs of different population sub-groups and of the extent to which these needs are currently being met but also an understanding of what functions the area previously performed and to what extent people who were formerly well served by such functions may now be finding themselves at a growing disadvantage.

Previous census data may be used to help trace the evolution of the area's functions and fortunes over time. They will also give some indication of what may have been happening since the last census, which is often quickly outdated. On their own, however, they are unlikely to present a clear enough picture because of their inherent limitations in providing information only on the characteristics of people, households and (to a lesser degree) dwellings. They will need to be supplemented by a consideration of changes in employment opportunities, commercial investment, the general character and condition of the built environment, etc. In addition, a truly sensitive profile of the area's changing functions and fortunes in, for instance, the employment and housing markets would require some assessment of what had been going on in other parts of the city with which the area in question might have exchanged functions. Most of the information, if not all, necessary to establish these broad patterns is quite readily available in various council departments, government regional offices and local branches. Its extraction calls for a reasonable system of information retrieval and communications (which need not be technically sophisticated) and a commitment to use the information which is gathered.

Size of area

If the selection process is to operate in favour of areas in greatest need, information must be gathered in relation to common spatial units to enable meaningful comparisons between areas. For a number of reasons we rejected the use of the enumeration district (ED) as the minimum common spatial unit; apart from the tendency of ED boundaries to split 'street communities', as a unit it is basically too small both for sensitive data analysis and for most area-specific initiatives, except perhaps some housing or environmental improvement programmes. In 1971 Small Heath EDs had an average population of 144 households or 484 persons. On the other hand, we also rejected the ward, the next largest unit for which census data are aggregated, on the grounds that it is too large. In Birmingham ward population averages about 26,000, ranging from 14,000 to 40,000. Analysis of 1971 census data for Small Heath has shown that variations within an area of this size are usually greater on most quantifiable variables than the difference between the average value for the area as a whole and the average value for the city, conurbation or region. Furthermore, ward boundaries do not necessarily follow natural physical 'edges' or coincide with the 'mental maps' that people have of the district where they live. This is not to say that areas of about 25,000 people are by definition too large for area-specific initiatives – in fact for some purposes they may still be too small – but it does mean that wards are too large, too arbitrary in their configuration and likely to contain too wide a variety of conditions (physical, social and economic) to serve as the basic building blocks for comparative analyses.

We concluded that the most appropriate size of basic data area – or common spatial unit – would correspond to groups of four or five full 1971 census EDs, with an average population of between 2,000 and 2,500. Such an area would have the advantage of corresponding roughly to the larger 1966 census EDs, which in Birmingham housed a median population of 2,359. In Small Heath terms this would mean localities the size of the HAAs (Little Green, Small Heath Park) or a smaller GIA (Oldknow). In most cases, areas selected for special priority initiatives would comprise more than one of these basic units. Our analyses of 1971 census and 1974 social survey data in Small Heath, supplemented by other 'hard' and 'soft' information, indicate that units of the size proposed could sensibly be combined to form agglomerations of some 10,000 people. It must be emphasised, however, that areas selected for priority treatment under urban deprivation programmes on the

228

basis of their physical, social and economic conditions would not necessarily coincide with the area of application for specific programme initiatives. For instance, within priority areas small localities might be designated for special housing and/or physical environmental action. To take a case in point, our own experience confirms that HAA and GIA programmes ought usually to be confined to areas containing not more than 300 houses. Conversely, any programme concerned with the maintenance or promotion of employment opportunities by means of area-specific incentives would have to cast its net much wider to encompass a job market zone within reasonable travel distance by public transport. In fact, any such incentives would best be applied to fairly large zones which could supply jobs to people in several deprived areas simultaneously.

Finally, there is one important question which has to be answered before a national programme of this kind is implemented: whether the same scale of aid (pro rata to population) should be available to all qualifying areas or whether aid should be graduated according to the magnitude of need above the 'qualifying level'. In principle we would favour the second approach, since any line of demarcation is bound to be somewhat arbitrary and redistributive mechanisms should, ideally, operate progressively. In practice, however, such an approach poses immense problems. For example, how are the relative degrees of hardship imposed by different combinations of individual and collective circumstances to be weighed, or the relative importance of the 'static' and 'dynamic' dimensions assessed? This is a dilemma that cannot be resolved without fully testing the method. However, since different local authorities will contain different numbers of qualifying areas (in some cases a relatively high number proportionate to their total population) there is already built into the method an element of progressive aid to the most needy authorities. Perhaps this is as far as it is reasonably possible to go.

They are managing now to get the annexe open, for children to play in, the annexe of the old school . . . The neighbours have all got together and been running raffles to try and get it and we have managed this. Just before Christmas we shall have the annexe all papered and done out for the kids.

A few records on . . ., inflated balloons and funny things, and funny people around, rather than see 100 or 200 kids unhappy . . .

Circumstances of Families

9 Encouraging innovation

After more than three years' work on the ground in Small Heath it is hard to escape the conclusion that most of what we discovered about the problems of the area and its people had already been revealed by previous research and the experience of those engaged in working for an improvement in the physical, economic, social and political environment of inner areas. There is little new to be said about problems of poverty, low pay, unemployment, poor housing, unequal educational opportunity or social stress. It is not statistical information that is lacking. We hope, of course, that our work will make some contribution to a more informed public debate about the origins of urban deprivation, its spatial aspects and the kinds of action necessary to alleviate it; but merely to express our hopes about the value of the study in such a way is to raise important questions about the role and conduct of research, the relationship between research and action, and the direction we believe research and experiment should take in future. Although such considerations mark a shift from subject-matter to vehicle of investigation we regard it as appropriate to introduce them at this point in our report where we are concluding our emphasis on the search for solutions from an area-based or local perspective (in response to objectives 2 and 3 of our brief) and turning our attention to issues that are to be resolved principally at a wider or national level.

The role and conduct of research

Despite the many subtle differences in each local situation the basic 'ingredients' of urban deprivation have by now been recognised. It is doubtful whether much is to be gained by further major research projects undertaken by independent agencies – universities, consultants or specially appointed teams – in single small area situations. If research has an important role still to perform it is, in our view, in the comparative analysis of decision-making and action by on-going agencies of urban change, at different levels of government, in the voluntary sector, at the grassroots, in a number of 'real' (as opposed to one-off) situations. The purpose of such research would be to focus on attempts at problem-solving, to disseminate knowledge of good practice, and to promote understanding of the particular conditions, organisational and operational, which appear to lead to success.

'Action-research'

In our own work we tried, from early on in the study, to put considerable effort into the development of a programme of action projects which would shed more light on the actual organisational and operational problems of getting things done, explore promising avenues for new approaches to particular issues, and at the same time provide the people of Small Heath with direct benefits in the form of new or improved services and facilities. However, because the study team had no delegated powers of decision over the size or use of budgets, were unable to make grants or hire sponsored appointments directly, and had only limited authority in controlling projects or discretion in changing their course once initiated, they had to rely on the approval and cooperation of the agencies who held the purse-strings (principally the DOE) and formally administered the programme (principally the city council). The mechanisms of a specially constituted steering committee of politicians and working group of officers meeting at roughly four-monthly intervals, sometimes less frequently still, did not facilitate a speedy or flexible response to the needs for action we were able to identify or to changing operational circumstances, particularly since the decisions of steering committee and working group required in most instances ratification by city committees and departments. In fact, most of the project proposals we submitted eventually gained approval, though we had rather less fortune in getting established projects extended beyond their period of BIAS grant, and day-to-day crises were usually settled (if sometimes after rather long delays) by more informal means of communication. We do not wish to imply that officers or civil servants were necessarily obstructive or unhelpful. The reverse was often the case. Yet the achievements of projects and their smooth running were clearly hindered by the fact that the formal funding and controlling agencies had in most cases little close involvement and that the study team, whose involvement was closer but still only at arm's length (as observers, advisers, trouble-shooters), had very restricted freedom of action.

Because Treasury funds were limited from the start of the study, the idea of a 'model' or 'demonstration' project in an area of 35,000 people was never on. The total BIAS action budget, at its peak, would have provided, for example, for the construction of only 10 new council houses. A Birmingham resident paying £100 in rates and £1,000 in income tax per year would have spent less than 3p on BIAS, all research costs and consultants' fees included. Besides, direct benefit to the area and its people was held by the DOE to be a secondary consideration, a by-product of experiment which was hopefully capable of more general application if found successful. The important criterion was 'innovation', which meant that projects could not be approved simply on the grounds they met a demonstrable demand or need. It meant, too, that extensions of existing services, on the principle of positive discrimination, were also ruled out unless they were modified in some way to satisfy the criterion. While the interpretation of what was innovative was fairly loose. both the scale of resources available and constraints on the way they should be used were liable to conflict to some extent with the interests of local residents and community groups and even with those of local councillors and council leaders who wished, quite reasonably, to see immediate returns for their support of the study in manifest improvements. They also served to inhibit the degree to which the local community could be involved in shaping the course of the study, since the longer term value of research and experiment to people of inner areas in general was bound to appear a rather shadowy conception in face of Small Heath's large and immediate problems.

In the event a series of 20 or so action projects finally were launched, some as a result of initiatives within the local community or from voluntary organisations,

232

others as the outcome of discussions between the BIAS team and various council officers. They met with varying degrees of success, from our own perspective as a learning experience and in terms of how they were received and valued by the people affected. In time links were established between projects, especially where special appointments were involved, and we began to see the benefits to be derived from the 'people networks' we have referred to in Chapter 8. We endeavoured also to fit both plain research (surveys, etc) and action initiatives into a coherent overall framework of analysis and problem-solving. Yet, because we had additionally to react to changing ad hoc pressures during the life of the study – from DOE, city council, local groups, community activists, and indeed from within the team and consultancy practice themselves, the programme tended to develop in a manner which appeared more random than planned. Furthermore, constraints of time, manpower resources, finance and the study's geographical coverage precluded the development of an action programme wide enough in scope or fundamental enough in content to test experimentally our recommendations for change in all but a few relatively marginal cases. We could do nothing, for example, by means of experimental action in a single area to deal with important issues like low pay, the investment or disinvestment decisions of national and multinational corporations, the political management of the economy, the distribution of power in society, the system of local government finance and expenditure control, or the statutory framework of planning, all of which have a profound effect on the quality of life in inner areas.

The problems encountered by area-based 'action-research' teams will of course vary from situation to situation. Much depends on the size and type of area, the resources available, the objectives of the particular study, its timespan, the personalities involved, and the organisational arrangements adopted. In our view the potential of 'action-research' is greatest where its scope is confined to a precise and fairly narrow field of intervention, where its resources are concentrated in a small enough area and spread over a sufficient period of time (at least five years from the study's inception) to make a significant and prolonged impact on the situation under investigation, and where the team planning the intervention undertakes the action itself, with the maximum degree of autonomy. However, under such circumstances close identification with the actual task of getting the job done and responding in the most tangible manner possible to the needs of the local community, which in inner areas are bound always to stretch resources to the limit, will tend to clash with the researcher's role of rigorous and objective observation, even if one or more team members are given exclusively monitoring responsibilities. We saw this happen in BIAS projects where grant aid was given to voluntary organisations who wished to try out new approaches to their work or extend the scope of their activities in an experimental situation. Before long, either the 'researcher' in the group seemed to find himself in a situation of conflict with his colleagues over objectives, methods, performance or simply keeping records, or he tended to be drawn into becoming an extra pair of hands on the 'action' side. This suggests a separation of 'action' and 'research' functions. But rather than set up individual studies composed of twin teams (say, a specially appointed action team monitored and aided technically by a smaller research team from a university department) we would favour the establishment of a larger, central research unit which would monitor by detailed documentation and participant observation on a controlled basis a number of simultaneous experiments and ongoing programmes undertaken by existing bodies – local authorities, voluntary organisations, residents' associations, cooperatives, action groups.

In this connection the Urban Programme is a potentially rich source of learning experience and could become even more so if its scope and resources were enlarged. Despite frequent shifts of emphasis and the relatively small sums available in aggregate (about a fiftieth of 1 per cent of programmed public expenditure), over 4,000 projects received Urban Aid in the scheme's first fifteen phases. Yet to date nothing appears to have been done to draw together at all systematically the lessons these projects might provide. Similarly, the successes and failures of many imaginative approaches to inner area problems in the mainstream of local authority and voluntary sector activity, together with the reasons for success or failure, go largely unrecognised outside their own locational context because there is little concerted attempt to pass on the results of experience to other agencies working in similar situations. We do not believe it is enough to rely on the circulation of project reports and magazine articles by the experimenters themselves to encourage the adoption of new practices. We recommend that central government should take a more positive line in financing the continuous monitoring and reporting of innovative programmes and projects in inner areas up and down the country and that responsibility for the control of such research across the whole range of urban services should rest with a single department, preferably the DOE.

The value of surveys

The purpose of surveys is to provide information not otherwise available which will increase understanding of the issues under investigation and therefore contribute to better decisions on the courses of action to be undertaken in pursuit of their resolution. Our own social survey, carried out by SCPR, was designed to examine inter-relationships between the circumstances in which people in Small Heath lived and their social, economic and ethnic characteristics, to explore the way people perceived their circumstances, and to help achieve comparisons over time with the census and comparisons at a particular point in time with other published data from sources like the General Household Survey. At the time the survey was commissioned (1973) the latest census information for Small Heath was seven years old and results of the 1971 census, themselves becoming rapidly out of date as a consequence of redevelopment and selective migration, were not to be available for another year.

The SCPR survey proved extremely helpful in building up a general picture of Small Heath's social structure, the functions that various parts of the area perform, especially in the city housing market, the underlying dynamics of population change, and the importance of various aspects of change in the attitudes of residents to the place where they live. It also offered some insights into relations between people and government and into the nature of community life, affording documented evidence to support the more impressionistic conclusions arrived at from working in the area.

However, with hindsight it is not difficult to point out weaknesses. It could be argued that the variety of individuals responding to the questionnaires (1,744 individuals from 854 households) was too great to permit generalisation about them as a single group while the numbers involved were too small to allow adequate in-depth study of particular sub-groups, for instance, family households in council-acquired housing, Asian furnished tenants, or even unemployed men. Similarly, although data were tabulated according to broad housing zone (renewal areas, GIAs, etc) it was not possible to distinguish within these zones, say, between one GIA and another. A structured questionnaire, indicative as it was of general opinions, could not probe very far into the reasons for those options or the meaning of people's circumstances (living on low incomes, in poor housing, in neighbourhoods of social stress) in terms of day-to-day experience. Nor could it, of course, give an indication of the actual level of services provided or of the collective opportunities available for work, leisure, etc, except indirectly through a rather broad subjective view of their adequacy.

To some extent the shortcomings of the social survey were a product of inevitable difficulties in striking the right balance between general and particular. Additionally there was the dilemma of how best to organise an information search in order to increase understanding of a situation of great complexity when the appropriateness of the questions asked, of the sample stratification and of the method of classifying and tabulating responses depended precisely on having a fairly good idea of what answers would be most significant. The devices of an exploratory study, using a small number of group discussions and depth interviews with residents from different parts of the area and of different sexes and age-groups, and of a pilot survey to test the questionnaire design only partially resolved the dilemma.

As far as the BIAS work programme was concerned, the social survey did not make a major contribution to the formulation of action project proposals but was used only in support of proposals (community advice centre, community relations fieldworker, for example) which arose principally out of the team's direct observation in Small Heath, their discussions with local community workers and other interested parties, and a more 'intuitive' appreciation of gaps which existed in service provision related to the community's needs. The main uses of the survey data were in policy analysis, especially in the field of housing and urban renewal, and in our general response to the study's first objective: to arrive at a better definition of inner areas and their problems.

Without the survey it would have been virtually impossible to meet at all satisfactorily the study's wide-ranging terms of reference and supply detailed 'hard' evidence to substantiate a case for changes in policy and in its execution. Indeed, the survey had to be complemented by a number of other investigations: into environmental quality, pre-school provision, educational statistics, unemployment records, small firm activity, industrial land availability, the structure of employment in the area's major labour market zone, and so forth. We also considered it important to conduct a series of follow-up depth-interviews with households identified as being in poverty, consisting of single parent families, or having four or more children, in order to demonstrate more clearly the objective circumstances and subjective reality of living on low incomes; for we felt it was only too easy for policy-makers and indeed the public at large to become emotionally closed and insensitive to these problems and to have little conception of how difficult life can be for poor people. Likewise, we supported the efforts of the Artist Placement Group to raise levels of awareness both within and outside the Small Heath community not only of issues associated with living in inner areas but also of the organisational and operational contexts in which different agencies were working for change. The results of most of these individual research and communications initiatives have been or are being published separately (see BIAS work programme and bibliography in the appendices).

As a study team we found ourselves caught between, on the one hand, the requirement to make generalised conclusions on the basis of Small Heath evidence and experience which might influence national as well as city thinking about inner area strategy and, on the other, the urgent need for action within the community itself. Our view, again with the benefit of hindsight, is that the greatest priority today is for action, on a broad front, and further, that the principal task of survey-type research is no longer to define problems and identify policy issues but to shed greater light on specific issues, once identified, as an aid to immediate decisions to be made in respect of the locality where the survey is carried out.

By way of example we would point to the 100 per cent resident questionnaire we designed and implemented in collaboration with Birmingham's urban renewal team in Little Green, which was to become one of the city's first HAAs. The purpose of the questionnaire was to help devise a physical plan and programme of action for Little Green which would lead to a very marked improvement in its housing, physical environment and community facilities, while taking account of the functions it currently performed in the local housing market and respecting (as far as the need for collective decisions permitted) residents' willingness and ability to pay for house improvements and repairs, their desire to stay in their present house and/or neighbourhood or move elsewhere, their wishes in respect of rehousing, and their preferences for changes in the street and neighbourhood environment. We would not claim that the survey was a model of its kind, either in design or execution. Even in this case our own role required the collection of information for purposes of policy analysis as well as for planning and action. Yet the type of situation meets our criteria in the sense that the purpose of such a survey can be made clear to residents, it concerns issues which are of direct relevance and importance to them, its ground can be prepared by giving residents beforehand accurate information about options for choice and relevant material on house prices, improvement costs, loans and so forth, and its results can be fed swiftly and directly into the process of real decision-making, so that residents' answers are part of a genuine participation. We saw advantages too in briefing urban renewal personnel (some on secondment) to conduct the interviews themselves. Although in monitoring checks we found instances where this led to undue prompting and other departures from correct interviewing method, we believe the approach is worth pursuing both because of the greater sense of the survey's 'reality' it gives residents and because of the additional insights and familiarity with residents it gives officers.

236

Innovation, risk and accountability

The emphasis of research in inner areas, we have argued, should be directed more positively to the technical support, monitoring, comparative evaluation and publicising of innovative action. But this presupposes the creation of an organisational and operational climate in which urban experiment is given greater encouragement and the lessons of experiment are more readily assimilated into common practice.

Change and innovation produce initial development and implementation costs. They also involve risk. Yet reluctance to accept risk and experiment with new ways of doing things, whether or not they have been tried in similar situations elsewhere, seem to be characteristic tendencies of all large established organisations, not least perhaps because they threaten existing hierarchies of authority, challenge the routines which govern the execution of many departmental functions, and even put some jobs in jeopardy. The institutions of government, central and local, are no exception in this respect. Indeed, they are also faced with burdens of public accountability and the close scrutiny their spending is given, especially in the media, by virtue of the pervasiveness of government activity and the huge absolute sums of money for which they are responsible. At the same time, principles of public accountability inhibit the transfer of resources to those agencies – essentially smaller-scale voluntary organisations, community groups and action teams – which are a fertile source of new ideas but usually lack the necessary resources to carry them out.

The case in favour of extending support for voluntary and community action does not, of course, rest on their innovative capacity alone but also on the fact they can often deliver services and provide facilities at lower cost than larger public organisations and in a manner often more sensitive to the life-style and preferences of the people who are to benefit. We have discussed the case of the Small Heath Self-Help Pre-School Centre in Chapter 8. Other examples might be briefly cited. Shape's approach to the use of short-life housing not only brought down the basic cost of making dwellings habitable but offered the occupants what seemed to them a more acceptable tenant-landlord relationship. Trinity Arts demonstrated how play events could make creative use of the simplest materials and the most unlikely terrains. The Community Federation mounted a very successful carnival on a modest budget. The advantages that such agencies have are a simple organisation structure, the ability to cut across 'departmental' specialisms, the flexibility to respond immediately to changed situations and operational crises, lower overheads, more detailed local knowledge, and the frequent availability of willing volunteers to supplement the efforts of full-time staff.

We are advocating essentially two things: first, that the scale of resources available in grants and other forms of aid to non-government organisations working within local communities be increased substantially, both under the aegis of a central government urban programme (in the case of inner areas) and by the independent action of local authorities, working also in collaboration with foundations, trusts and volunteer manpower agencies like ARC (Action Resource Centre); second, that procedures for the submission and approval of projects be simplified. In the second connection, we should like to see less time (and money) spent on prior evaluation of project proposals and greater attention paid to monitoring and subsequent evaluation. It appears to us that present arrangements, in relation to Urban Aid applications for instance, tend to be biased towards comparatively 'safe' projects, that is to say, those that their assessors in local and central government departments consider (largely on the basis of past experience) to be most consistent with existing policy guidelines, most soundly presented and most predictable in their outcomes. Our own experience suggests that the results of projects are rarely predictable with any degree of accuracy; nor are the best presented necessarily the most effective in execution. The more innovative an approach is, the less past experience there will be to go on. It would make sense in our opinion to decentralise the administration of central government aid to a more local level, possibly by the allocation of lump sums against which local authorities could draw at their own discretion to support projects which fell under any of a number of broad categories if they contributed their due share of the costs (say 25 per cent as at present). If area committees were established on the lines we proposed in Chapter 6, serviced in inner area wards by their small support teams, there would be the opportunity to discuss proposals face-to-face with the initiators, thus allowing an assessment of the personalities involved – a crucial factor in success or failure, and to keep track of projects' performance during their operation. In such circumstances the process of application and approval could be greatly speeded up, more adventurous schemes could be tried out, and accountability would remain within the community itself.

Whatever the contribution such projects can make to community life and to a restoration of confidence through the feeling that something is being done, that someone cares, that the future of the area is at least to some extent in people's own hands, they are not and can never be substitutes for vigorous government action in major programmes. Government policies and practice in the fields of housing, education, preschool provision, youth work, social services, environmental care, job creation, can all potentially benefit from the lessons of voluntary and community action. The realisation of this potential and the adoption of new approaches to meet changing situations throughout the whole sphere of government activity will, however, not just happen; it will demand conscious stimulation. We have suggested the role action-oriented research might play. Administrative decentralisation, of the type advocated in Chapter 6, would also help innovation, since officers based locally and given greater discretionary powers of tactical decision, under the watchful eye of an area committee, would (as we have seen in our own experience with sponsored local authority appointments and in observing the city's urban renewal team at work) be encouraged to identify more closely with the community, improvise more speedy responses to local needs and pressures, and operate together in a mutually-supportive way across departmental lines of demarcation. But even with greater decentralisation and more exposure to information about proven good practice elsewhere, the problems of inertia may still be difficult to overcome at the central core of local authority organisations unless there are more positive incentives to change in the way of selective support to councils launching a more concerted attack on urban deprivation.

A basic theme of the Inner Area Studies has been that, because the many individual problems of inner areas are so inextricably linked, strategies to deal with them must also be linked. Yet, owing to their small area focus and their particular organisational and operational contraints, they have been unable to put anything like a 'total approach' to problem-solving into practice. In theory Comprehensive Community Programmes (CCPs), as they have now come to be conceived, appear to mark a step in the right direction, even though much about them – the magnitude of resources available, the nature of their political control, the degree to which they are incorporated into the central decision making processes, the role of communities in their design and implementation – remains unclear. Their concern will be with urban deprivation in the whole local authority area; they will involve permanent agencies in a 'real world' situation; their focus will be on action, across all fields of policy; they will offer a fine opportunity to incorporate the lessons of previous action-research and embody what appears to be the best of current practice; if the monitoring aspect of the work is well designed they will be an excellent vehicle for comparative analysis. Our biggest reservation is that if they are regarded as another 'pilot project' they might easily serve as an excuse for postponing more widespread action. We would therefore welcome the grant of special central government aid to councils participating in a CCP, because of the transitional costs of organisational and operational change involved and in order to help underwrite the risks inherent in any experimental situation. However, we do not believe that such assistance should in any way prejudice the qualification of all urban authorities with severe inner area problems for positive discrimination in the form of extra rate support, specific grants or preferential borrowing arrangements on the basis of demonstrable need.

The mechanisms of allocating public resources between and within authorities are a matter we shall come back to as we turn now, in the final part of our report, to the search for solutions largely outside the scope of area-based initiatives.

PART THREE

The search for solutions: wider perspectives

Bob Marshall

I'm an employee of Chrysler and at the moment it's touch and go. We don't know whether we'll get our notice next week, which is worrying because a lot of people from Small Heath depend on Chrysler and it's a good place to work, good money . . . It's going to have a big effect on this area because for seven or eight hundred people in an area like this to lose their jobs, it's a lot of homes affected and there's nothing else really . . . BSA of course, that's gone now.

Circumstances of Families

10 Increasing employment prospects

Before proposing appropriate policy initiatives to tackle employment decline it is important to consider alternative views as to likely future developments in the economic context. An optimistic view would see the British economy recovering from its present crisis before the end of the decade, with GNP growth recommencing and an increased proportion of new resources devoted toward investment in industry. A more pessimistic outlook could see continuing stagnation in GNP with the total number of manual workers' jobs rising, if at all, much more slowly than the available adult labour force.

The policies which follow require more resources to be devoted to industry. They will clearly be easier to implement given a revival in the nation's economic fortunes. In particular, the transfer of resources to the industrial sector will be a less painful process if additional expenditure is diverted from other sectors, rather than causing an actual reduction in the resources available to them. However, since a failure of the economy to recover would intensify the need for investment in further industrial modernisation and restructuring, we feel that our policies will still be highly relevant.

Furthermore, a continuing gloomy outlook for the economy would underline the need for initiatives to direct investment and employment to areas where unemployment is exceptionally severe. On our evidence, Small Heath would certainly come into this category as would much of the rest of inner Birmingham. In times of national job shortage, attempts to level extreme disparities in unemployment can be justified by the, possibly irreversible, damage caused to a community from persistent unemployment rates of 20 per cent and more.

In the case of a continuing economic crisis, the measures we suggest might not be adequate to effect a sufficient levelling of disparity. In that case, adjustments to the present package of incentives for industrial location, which intervene in the market economy, may have to be replaced by a more interventionist strategy and a significant move towards a planned economy. Considerations of what this could involve are beyond the scope of our research. In the discussion that follows we have, therefore, examined the problem in the light of an approach which seeks to influence rather than direct and attempted to cast our recommendations within the existing policy framework.

Small Heath does not serve as a major location for industry, although there are important areas of industrial land nearby. It is likely to continue to have a predominantly residential function in the future. However, there are a considerable number of small firms within the area, many of them interspersed with housing. With regard to these firms and other, larger ones in adjacent industrial areas we have taken as our prime objective the need to secure a pattern and pace of development which will most benefit the area's present and likely future residents.

Our industrial strategy is of course linked to housing policy. For example, the stimulation of industry to meet the needs of unskilled and semi-skilled manual workers may call for policies to encourage skilled workers to remain in the area or to facilitate their daily journey to work. The availability of skilled workers is believed to be an important determinant of industrial location decisions.

Our view of the area's housing function and hence its future residents has been set out in Chapter 5. This sees a continuing role, for the medium term at least, in the provision of cheap owner-occupied and rented furnished accommodation and seeks to concentrate resources on those in greatest need. But successful implementation of other policies should have the effect of encouraging more skilled workers to stay in, or move to, Small Heath. The most important policies here are those of urban renewal, designed to restore residents' confidence in the area's future. Other recommendations that should help are those for reducing the concentration of deprived families in council housing, changing tax allowances to favour owner occupation by lower income groups and encouraging new private or quasi-public housing development.

Whatever the success of efforts to keep skilled workers in the area, its future role in the provision of low cost housing argues that there will continue to be a concentration of people who will tend to have relative disadvantages in obtaining employment, particularly in times of economic down-turn. Future strategy to stimulate industrial investment and the location of industry should recognise this fact. However, the aim should not be to discriminate against technologically advanced firms, because they are likely to employ disproportionate numbers of skilled and qualified staff. Rather these firms should often be welcomed because they can help to modernise, broaden and strengthen the industrial base of the area. They also offer indirect benefits, though the size of these will vary from plant to plant, and will tend to raise the aggregate level of incomes in the area.

In Small Heath, previous decline in population which has to some extent masked job loss, is likely to slow down significantly and perhaps even reverse. This will result primarily from the completion of ongoing construction programmes on redevelopment sites which have already been cleared. We would, therefore, look for at least a significant slowing down in the rate of job loss in order to maintain even the present balance.

Consideration of the future demand for the labour of the area's residents is inevitably closely bound up with the future prospects for the metal working sector in general and the motor vehicle industry in particular. While it might be premature to cast a general pall of gloom over the latter, particularly in view of an all-party commitment to industrial revival, the trends for employment cannot be encouraging. Evidence elsewhere suggests that the new investment and re-equipping required to improve international competitiveness will significantly reduce employment per unit of output. Total employment will only increase if lower costs of production enable British production to displace imports in the domestic market and increase the penetration of exports. Viewed in international terms, unless a 'beggar my neighbour' view is adopted, this would call for very significant increases in international demand, given the increasing trend to local assembly, with progressive development into manufacture, now found in many developing countries. Although the very large injections of public and private capital into the motor industry can be readily justified in terms of maintaining its viability, it seems unlikely to lead to an expansion of employment beyond the levels pertaining when the economy was buoyant. Birmingham and Small Heath residents benefit from the aid that the motor industry has recently received in that it has saved jobs, many of them relatively well paid, which might otherwise have disappeared. However, we feel that it would be unwise to base a strategy for increasing employment opportunities on the prospects for the motor industry and its ancillary enterprises.

The same argument applies for many of the traditional industries which are to be found in inner city areas: they need to modernise in order to reduce unit costs. This usually means a reduction in labour per unit of output and hence a loss in employment unless a proportionate increase in output can be achieved. However, for many traditional products the available national and international markets are only growing slowly, if at all. Thus essential investment will reduce employment. Given the traditional bias of the West Midlands towards employment in manufacturing, the strains on the labour market as a result of modernisation will be particularly severe. This makes it doubly important to attract new industries producing goods for which demand is still growing and where there are consequent prospects for increased employment in the future.

We believe the attraction of new industry into inner Birmingham to be an objective of paramount importance. Unless action is taken soon the opportunity to establish programmes which can check and gradually reverse the present trend may be lost. Further deterioration might well lead to a point where massive investment initiative would be needed to reach a threshold at which progress could start again.

A generalised framework for policy

If the need to stimulate new industries in inner Birmingham is accepted, then we believe that regional policy must be reviewed. Relative unemployment in the West Midlands region has worsened and during the twelve months ended 31 March 1976 it reached an average rate of 5 per cent, which was precisely the same as that for intermediate areas.[1] The rate in Small Heath and other inner areas of Birmingham was at least twice the average for the region. Although we would argue strongly for a restructuring of regional policy to redirect resources to areas of greatest need, as an interim measure, while this is undertaken, these areas we believe justify designation as intermediate areas on grounds of high unemployment and low incomes. This would facilitate implementation for many of the initiatives that we suggest below and enable a number of specific programmes to begin without new

1. See the annual report on the Industry Act 1972 for the year ended 31 March 1976, Appendix B, Table 1, HMSO, July 1976. The unemployment rate in the West Midlands in 1975/76 was 0.2 per cent above that of the Yorkshire and Humberside region, all of which falls in assisted areas.

legislation. At the same time we would see a supporting role played by the Birmingham District Council and West Midlands Metropolitan County through strategic and physical planning policy exercising positive discrimination in favour of inner area locations. This concord of policies would indicate a clear national commitment to improving the inner cities which in itself would do much to revive business confidence.

Throughout the discussion on location which follows it must be borne in mind that the disadvantage of inner city locations is amenable to change. It relates to the profitability that industry can achieve on alternative sites and not just to the feasibility of operating in an inner city location. This profitability derives from the cost of premises, investment allowances, employment subsidies and indirectly from a range of other short-term government policy variables, as well as from 'inherent' advantages. When a longer term view is taken even many of the supposedly 'inherent' advantages of peripheral industrial locations such as access to motorways or available skilled labour can be seen to derive from past policy decisions and investments. Present day policy decisions in the same spheres can be expected to increase the 'inherent' advantages of inner city locations.

Policies to increase the attractiveness of inner city locations to industry can take the form of increasing the incentives offered by the inner city or decreasing those offered at competing locations. The balance that is struck between these alternatives, which are of course mutually compatible, will derive more from wider considerations of available resources and alternative methods of stimulating investment, than from the consideration of individual inner city areas. In our discussion below we therefore take account of the incentives and programmes currently operating elsewhere.

We believe that the central argument for locating jobs within the inner city derives from considerations of equity and need. A continuing concentration of deprived people with poor employment prospects has already been postulated. Furthermore, we have argued elsewhere in this report that a concentration of individual deprivations leads to collective deprivation over and above them. There is believed to be a preference among employers for local recruitment of their unskilled and semi-skilled workforce, in that workers for whom the location of their work is convenient and cheap will have a greater propensity to 'loyalty' than those who have to travel from some distance, though we have no direct evidence on this. Thus improved employment opportunities in the inner city will tend to favour inner city residents. In times of general under-employment this will increase their chances of employment vis-à-vis those living further away, some of whom may well be equally deprived individually. The equity argument depends, therefore, on reducing the concentration of individual deprivations in the inner city and, thereby, eventually reducing the collective deprivation.

There is a school of thought which favours strategies to extend the range of daily movement of employees to work and thereby extend the boundaries of individual labour markets. Although in no way wishing to diminish the importance of this strategy, which in times of full employment would be helpful in redressing local labour market imbalances and reducing labour bottlenecks,

246

the arguments we have set out above suggest that it will not by itself go far to meet the employment needs of inner area residents while jobs are scarce. In the present economic climate it is a supplement to, rather than a substitute for, employment location in the inner city. When the argument is extended from male employment to female employment it is, of course, greatly reinforced. The labour market area for women is much smaller than for men and if there are no local jobs many women are prepared to travel only short distances even if there are jobs available further afield. This is a problem in other parts of Birmingham outside the inner city, but for deprived families living in areas like Small Heath it is particularly important that women who wish to work are able to do so. Their earnings can make an important contribution to the family budget and help to compensate for the relatively high probability that their husbands will be out of work or, even if employed, that some will be receiving low pay.

If it is true, as we believe, that inner city areas such as Small Heath will tend to suffer disproportionately in economic downswings for some time to come, in addition to other measures which will operate permanently, there is a general case for establishing a significant contra-cyclical policy which will discriminate in their favour. We believe that such a policy should be distinct from the incentives that will be made available by a modified regional policy and act directly on employment rather than on investment.

Although we suggest below that selective assistance to individual major employers may be an essential short term measure (at least in the case of Small Heath), we believe on grounds of efficiency that it should not normally characterise intervention. A general subsidy on inner city employment would be too inflationary and a subsidy for new jobs which would not otherwise have existed would be extremely difficult to administer. We therefore propose a subsidy in respect of all new manufacturing jobs created. This could either be adopted specifically for inner areas and other designated areas or be conceived as a national unemployment measure which would discriminate between areas merely in terms of the rate offered.

The subsidy could be paid over the first 7 to 10 years of the job's existence at a level that would depend on the rate declared in the year of the job's creation. After this first year the level of subsidy should taper off progressively. In a year of high unemployment the level of subsidy for new jobs should be fixed at a fairly high level (say 20 per cent of wage cost in peak circumstances) tapering off from this level in subsequent years (say 18 per cent, 16 per cent, 14 per cent, 12 per cent and so on). In a year of low unemployment the level of subsidy for new jobs would be at a lower level (say 10 per cent, tapering off to 9 per cent, 8 per cent and so on).

The case for adjusting the level of subsidy from time to time can be argued in terms both of macro-economic management of the economy (since this is bedevilled by differing conditions in the labour market in different parts of the country – so that over-full employment in the South East can co-exist with high unemployment in Northern England) and of regional policy (since cyclical fluctuations are felt particularly strongly in marginal areas of the economy). The year to year adjustment of the rate of subsidy, however, should be such as to allow firms some guidance in forward planning. More specifically, government should announce that rates in the following few years would be at least at a designated minimum level, so that firms could base their planning on this. There would thus be a compromise between helping the contra-cyclical tuning of the economy and allowing forward planning by firms.

This proposal fits in with our analysis of the employment situation in Small Heath at a number of points. In the first place, as a proposal to subsidise new jobs, it fits in with the finding in Small Heath and elsewhere in inner cities that the precipitous decline in the number of manufacturing jobs is due much less to the movement of establishments out of the area (or the absence of a countervailing movement into the area) than to an excess of 'deaths' over 'births' of plants in these areas. In the second place, it fits in with our analysis of the regional situation and our concern over the heavy dependence of the West Midlands region on one sector of the economy. By placing the emphasis on encouraging new jobs, rather than on defending existing jobs, some degree of diversification should be achieved. There are other grounds, too, for this emphasis – the defence of existing jobs can be costly and fruitless; it may overstretch the limited capacity of government for effective and intelligent selective intervention; and it may be that the slow rate of economic growth of countries like Britain is due to an excessive concentration on defensive investment with the aim of maintaining employment in obsolescent industries as opposed to investment creating jobs in new industries. These are all reasons for preferring an emphasis on jobs in new industries. But if workers are to transfer between industries, without excessive hardship, complementary policies are required in the form of educating and training the labour force for a more flexible labour market. These will be discussed briefly later in the chapter.

There is an urgent need in the inner city to adopt a more realistic view as to the balance between jobs and housing. At the present time we feel inadequate attention is devoted to the needs of employment, though in saying this we are well aware of the unfortunate consequences of swinging the balance of concern too far one way. Control of nuisances and the pollution of the environment will still be important matters for concern and control. However, the need to co-exist should not be underplayed. A survey of Small Heath planning district revealed that 68 per cent of its manufacturing concerns were classed as non-conforming uses. We feel that for Small Heath, at least, present criteria do not adequately distinguish true environmental nuisance. The net is cast too wide.

What kind of jobs ?

Most of the preceding discussion has, whether explicitly or implicitly, been concerned largely with manufacturing employment. This does not mean that we would wish to discount the role that the service sector has in the past, or may in the future, play in the development of Small Heath. Our tendency to concentrate on manufacturing employment recognises rather that the growth of non-personal services will derive from the strength of the manufacturing industry and the economic health of the city centre, while local growth in personal services will reflect the community's economic prosperity. This is in turn intimately related to the prospects for manufacturing industry.

On account of the predominant importance of a limited number of large employers to job supply in Small Heath and adjacent areas, we have suggested that in the short term they should be an object of urgent attention. However, in the medium term, when other initiatives have been established, we would favour a policy of making suitable provision for industrial investment and then taking the industries that want to come on the terms offered. Firms which elect to locate in the inner city are likely to be those which will prosper there. Although there may be a temptation to try to pick winners we do not believe this to be a sensible long-term strategy. With limited exceptions, reflecting proximity to residential development, our proposals envisage equal treatment under the rules.

Our examination of the availability of industrial land showed that, when aggregated, there is sufficient industrial land in Small Heath and adjacent areas to allow an appropriate balance between housing and employment, though its present state (old premises) and dispersion (small sites) is not generally appropriate. There may therefore be problems in rationalising the available industrial land. Moreover, land requirements per worker could alter significantly over time. Continual monitoring of industrial land availability will be called for and it may, in the future, be necessary to limit excessively land-intensive uses such as warehousing or at least ensure that their structures would permit subsequent easy conversion to industrial use.

We do not believe that a deliberate policy of directing office employment to Small Heath would be of more than marginal help to residents as a result of filtering. At present few Small Heath residents possess appropriate skills and our evidence suggests that a high proportion of office jobs are currently held by in-commuters. What is more, the area has recently seen two office relocations to the periphery, which suggests that locational factors are probably distinctly adverse, so that an unjustified level of resources would need to be expended in order to attract new office jobs. However, we would not like to see future options to respond to changes in the needs of the local labour force prematurely closed. Wherever possible, within reasonable cost grounds, the future scope for office development in or near the Coventry Road shopping centre should be preserved.

Public sector employment, by contrast, offers more to the residents of Small Heath, though the same reservations would apply to public sector office jobs as to the private sector. Policies directing employment in terms of need would suggest that inner areas should have a relatively high share of government employment. Small Heath currently benefits significantly from this source with employment from the Post Office, the East Birmingham Hospital in Little Bromwich and British Rail. The hospital and local schools offer part-time employment which is important to many of the poorer and more disadvantaged families in Small Heath. However, research by Barbara Smith suggested that public sector employers in general are not particularly sympathetic to those who are difficult to employ. Location of public utility and public sector servicing and maintenance departments in inner city locations would provide suitable jobs. A new industrial estate might prove attractive to some of these although for others, like the municipal bus depot on the Coventry Road, individual sites could be more appropriate.

Stimulating manufacturing employment

The following three sections deal specifically with proposals relating to manufacturing industry. We have divided them for convenience according to size of firm, though we do not see rigid borderlines between categories. Further, size can be defined in many ways: the two that most concern us are land use and employment levels. Our proposal for medium sized firms, which involves a programme of industrial estate development, could clearly be relevant to firms of all sizes, though we believe it to be most relevant for medium sized concerns. Similarly, there is a degree of overlap in the other sections, but we believe there are also very distinct characteristics which are of greater importance than those which are shared.

Large firms

The research undertaken by Barbara Smith indicates that the local work prospects for study area residents are dominated by relatively few large firms. In the immediate future no policies we might propose with regard to smaller firms could compensate for the loss of even a single major employer. We suggest, therefore, that an immediate priority should be to enter into discussion with firms with an initial limit of 500+ employees (unlikely to number more than 20 in the main labour market area for Small Heath). This idea has already been broached in one of our previous reports and viewed with some disquiet by government departments who might expect to be concerned. However, we believe that it is a strategy which must be made to work in some form.

To undertake the initiative we recommend the setting up of an industrial task force which we see as promoting a number of different projects on an area-specific basis. We shall develop this proposal more fully in the last section of the chapter. One of the most urgent projects would be to discuss with selected firms their future plans relating to employment and identify particular constraints which may be militating against maintaining or even expanding the present labour force. Provided that intermediate area status is granted, resources could be made available under Section 7 of the Industry Act 1972 for new projects and expansions which create additional employment (at subsidised interest rates) and for projects, eg for modernisation or rationalisation, which do not provide extra jobs but maintain or safeguard employment (at broadly commercial interest rates). In addition, 'exceptional cases' which fall in neither of these categories would be decided 'in the light of circumstances', and any expenditure on new building and works and adaptations would qualify for a regional development grant of 20 per cent, which would not be treated as reducing capital expenditure for tax purposes.

We recommend that an industrial adviser from either the Department of Industry or the National Enterprise Board should head the industrial task force. He would clearly take principal responsibility for discussions with large firms and making appropriate recommendations to his steering committee. In some cases planning controls, physical problems with site expansion or easily remedied deficiencies in the transport infrastructure will probably be identified as difficulties. In such instances other members of the task force will have appropriate skills to examine the problem and prepare evaluations and recommendations for the steering committee, on which the bodies already empowered to take the appropriate actions will again be represented.

Interest is currently being expressed in the possibility of planning agreements. Although this approach has been considered for some time, it is not yet fully tried. It is as yet too early to evaluate whether planning agreements will offer scope for influencing the spatial location of investment in the case of multi-plant and even international firms. However, in spite of these reservations, we believe the possibility of planning agreements should be borne in mind in considering employment policy for inner areas. Prior to the exercise starting, it is difficult to identify, for individual firms, either the magnitude of their problems or even what the effective constraints may prove to be. However, we do not believe that the exercise will, taken as a whole, impose an intolerable burden on resources.

The inner city is still a viable location for many large firms and such limited evidence as we have from the Small Heath exchange area suggests that there has been a significant correlation between the size of a firm and the tendency to remain in the same premises. Although the size of the sample at the upper end of the scale dictates caution in generalising the results, they at least suggest that in the short-term interventionist policies with regard to large firms may be directed at the target offering most chance of success. The following data relates to the Small Heath employment exchange area.

Size of firm (number of employees)	Number of firms in category, 1973	% of firms in 1973 remaining in same premises as in 1967
11–24	1,061	57
25–99	402	64
100–499	131	60
500–999	24	83
1,000–1,999	7	86
2,000+	11	91

The above discussion is specifically concerned with the maintenance of employment at large firms in the area. The priority we have accorded it reflects our view that it constitutes, in the industrial sector, the most immediate way in which government's commitment to allocate more resources to inner areas can be implemented. We see this in terms of an essential holding operation to provide a breathing space in which longer term initiatives can begin to have an effect.

In the longer term, strategy should not, we believe, seek to discriminate in favour of large firms. They should be as well placed as any others to take advantage of the new incentives we are proposing to increase the attractiveness of industrial location in the inner city to all firms. In particular, large firms stand to benefit from a more flexible attitude toward rescheduling housing land for industrial use, in that this should help to make more large freehold sites available. It is the larger firm which is best placed to develop an individual site, given the requirements for management expertise and access to financial backing.

Medium size firms

There is a need to strengthen the economic base of inner Birmingham through the provision of new industrial estates particularly catering for medium and small sized firms. This is not to belittle the importance of an adequate supply of older premises, but to recognise their inevitable decline in attractiveness to firms when compared with the convenience of modern buildings and the greatly improved working conditions they can provide. We believe that the availability of modern premises for rental on an industrial estate is in itself an attraction for new firms to develop. Indeed it may have an importance for some firms which outweighs the balance of locational considerations.

In making this proposal we are supporting Birmingham's structure plan proposals. The council has already examined a number of possible sites for future development, including an old brickworks at Adderley Park, Yardley Sewerage Works and Gas Board land at Saltley. None of these sites is easy to develop, but their redevelopment would provide employment within easy reach of inner city residents (somewhat less so in the case of Yardley). What is more, in the case of at least the Saltley site, there is the possibility of increasing the size of the development from 30 acres to 60 acres if land presently designated for residential development is rescheduled. In addition to other considerations, development of sites such as these could help to improve the surrounding areas by removing at least one element of dereliction.

We would argue that the proposals for development of industrial estates in inner city areas should be accorded a high priority in the implementation of Birmingham's structure plan since this will help to improve the inner city's economic and physical environment and to assist in the urgent task of modernising British industry. Part of the funds for this and other initiatives to provide employment and increase incomes should come from savings realised by the cut in council house construction on the periphery of the city that we proposed in Chapter 5. We would expect this to be supplemented by financial and technical assistance from the English Industrial Estates Corporation. The EIEC is responsible for the mechanics of the advanced factory building programmes which are undertaken in the areas for expansion. It has developed expertise in constructing modern buildings, to an acceptable standard, which are reasonably priced. As yet its activities in inner city areas are confined to a small project in Liverpool but we feel that the accumulated experience acquired elsewhere would be of material assistance.

Gordon King

If I was out for another year . . . you'd have to go to the mental hospital to see me. I couldn't stand it. I'll stick out over Christmas all right – being unemployed. But next year, I'd have to get work somehow . . . anything.

If you're not working, you're socially inferior, everybody seems to be looking down at you. I was never out of work before . . . This year, there's that many laid off work . . . You've got to be very lucky, very, very lucky.

Circumstances of Families

The level of subsidy which may need to be provided in the form of rents or purchase terms will depend crucially on site development costs and on the price which has to be paid for the land. The price will vary considerably from place to place and will probably reflect arbitrary and historical considerations as well as true use value. Therefore, we do not think profit maximisation (or loss minimisation) should be the prime factor in determining which inner city site to develop. An authority seeking to maximise its profit from operating the Community Land Act would in fact tend to develop peripheral, green field sites.

The financial implications of inner city industrial estate development depend partly on supply factors — where the cost of acquiring and developing the land is crucial — but demand factors will be equally significant. In this respect present indications are encouraging. The Gravelly Hill development, though providing potential jobs for inner city residents, must be considered as exceptional given its outstanding attractions for transport access. However, it does suggest that our proposal will be pushing forward a trend which might slowly have developed of its own accord, providing land assembly were possible. This should mean that current local market values are at a level such that subsidy levels need not be particularly high. Of course the incentives that will be needed to keep or even attract firms to inner Birmingham will depend on the incentives offered at alternative locations in the region and elsewhere.

Government and the local authorities should launch the initiative and implement the first phase as a seeding operation. There may well be an opportunity to involve the private sector in the development, management and implementation of subsequent phases, releasing officials to proceed with the preparation of subsequent schemes. We would welcome this and would in any case feel that, irrespective of who handles development, they should be enjoined to do so in a commercial manner, once the social guidelines have been set. Attempts to fine-tune policy through continually changing the social guidelines will, we believe, prove counterproductive; they should therefore be set for a known fixed term.

Once the strategy has been accepted in principle the district council planning department should be requested to prepare a pre-feasibility statement identifying those inner city sites which it believes justify consideration as possible industrial estates. This selection should be subjected to the widest possible scrutiny consistent with avoidance of land speculation, and be reviewed by the local authorities and by the Department of Industry in conjunction with other interested ministries such as the Department of Employment and the Department of the Environment. They would jointly make a formal selection of one or more sites for detailed feasibility investigation to be prepared by an independent body, either in the private or public sector, with specifically relevant commercial expertise. The terms of reference should allow the body to consider politically sensitive issues such as rezoning adjacent housing land, from the point of view of commercial considerations. It should also be encouraged to comment on any sites in addition to those identified by the district council and to examine ease of access to inner city residents in terms of current and realistic future public transport provision.

A feasibility study should, we believe, be able to establish land and development costs and operating costs within a reasonable margin of error. It should also propose an efficient procedure for speedy implementation. The revenue calculations will inevitably be only approximate given the uncertainty of the present economic climate. They can, however, provide an important basis for decision making: strategies recommended should be flexible and allow a phased implementation that reflects market conditions while being sensitive to the project's cash flow and profitability under alternative assumptions about demand.

While the inner city sites are being developed, we believe that other developments at competing locations should be carefully monitored so that the launch period does not come at a time of overwhelming supply. However, great discretion will have to be exercised during the interim period to see that development control does not hamper industries' new investment plans. Once the inner area sites are ready for occupation, we feel that development elsewhere should be restricted, particularly in more prosperous peripheral locations.

In justification for the above recommendations we feel that the industrial activity still remaining in inner Birmingham confirms that these areas can provide economically attractive locations to private manufacturing firms. The precise cost of developing new industrial estates will only be established on a case by case basis as feasibility investigations are undertaken. However, such industrial land as is currently available is offered at prices comparable to or in some cases marginally higher than on the periphery, which suggests that there will be a possibility of offering new premises at rents comparable to those elsewhere without excessive subsidy. Furthermore, although motorway access may be a problem for developing new industrial sites in other cities, inner Birmingham has already borne the cost of driving a motorway right into the city and is now well placed to derive compensating benefits. Our evidence suggests that, even with present transport facilities, many of the firms operating in and around the study area are satisfied by their location, though there may be a need for further local improvements to the inner and middle ring roads.

Finally the argument that new and growing firms will reject inner area locations because of inadequate skilled labour is in fact an argument for changed housing, educational and other policies, not for writing off the areas. In the short term it will be necessary to ensure, and then to assure potential investors, that skilled labour will be able to travel easily to the new industrial estates. In the long term housing policies may need amending. Between the 1966 and 1971 census Small Heath lost its relative advantage, vis-à-vis the Birmingham average, in the proportion of skilled workers in its labour force. But in 1971 it had still the same proportion as the average for the city. This position may of course have deteriorated over the last five years. However, we believe changed housing policies can slow down, and perhaps even halt and reverse the process, providing that continuing employment opportunities and an improved general environment help to make Small Heath a more attractive place in which to live.

Small firms

Small firms are a characteristic of our study area and it is, therefore, to be expected that our area-specific research should have been more particularly directed to them. Our research has shown that small firms are liable to be particularly affected by local government policies in general and by redevelopment in particular. In general terms it suggested that there was a genuine opportunity for officials to approach problems with small firms in the spirit of mutual cooperation to a joint objective rather than as enforcers of bureaucratic controls. Our analysis of an individual HAA (Little Green), although permitting only limited generalisation, showed that there are some uses that are perceived by residents as imposing unacceptable environmental burdens, but they were the exception. We felt in this particular instance that local traffic management potentially had an important role and might enable firms to coexist more amicably with housing.

If firms are located in urban renewal areas there should be a careful analysis of the possibility of allowing them to remain and of the economics of giving improvement grants for investment to reduce adverse impacts, rather than paying compensation for relocation. Grants to rehabilitate existing premises might also be made to assist in achieving standards set by safety and health regulations. Such projects could also offer suitable scope for the present job creation scheme. Compensation payment has in many instances been unsatisfactory. The small firm is likely to be particularly short of the expertise needed to cope with the problems of redevelopment. Part of the problem is inadequate information; speedy appointment of an agent can help in overcoming this. More importantly, the level of compensation provided is inadequate and should in future be increased to reflect the inconvenience and cost of setting up in new premises. It is also essential that it be paid promptly.

Our research has also suggested a shortage of premises of up to 3,000 square feet. Many firms forced out by redevelopment may wish to find older premises which offer cheap rents and we have identified a need for giving them significant assistance in doing so. At one time Birmingham was supposed to be well organised in this respect, but the system no longer appears to function well. Other firms will want to use the enforced relocation as an opportunity to move into modern premises, perhaps elsewhere in the redevelopment area from which they have been displaced. There is presently a reluctance on the part of the private sector to undertake developments geared to the small firm, since they are not particularly profitable. Birmingham has helped to meet this need in the past and we suggest that there is now scope for the district council to undertake a trial small factory project near to an area where redevelopment has caused or will cause firms to close. There might be arguments for encouraging the relocation of small firms whose operations are noisy, smelly and dirty and who are unable to face the cost of reducing environmental nuisance. However, since relocation does not allow them to improve gradually over time, they could be assisted in becoming more environmentally acceptable through a short term subsidy, whether in the form of subsidised rental, rate rebate or some analagous scheme.

256

Supply considerations

The strategy that we have outlined above has implications for labour supply policies. However, we have not undertaken specific research on this subject and the following comments should be read with that in mind.

We recommend above that industrial policy should be essentially laissez-faire with regard to what type and which firms are encouraged to locate on inner city sites. This means that it will be difficult to determine in advance the balance of skills which would be most appropriate. Moreover, if the strategy succeeds in attracting firms which are innovators in growing and changing markets, requirements will change over time at a faster rate than they have in the past. We feel that a flexible labour force capable of accepting and profiting by changing demands should be the aim for inner areas.

In achieving this aim education in the schools and training programmes have important roles to play. Employers have voiced concern about the level of competence in reading, writing and basic numerate skills. In addition to increased effort in this respect, which would require more teachers, we feel that there is also scope for the introduction of a wide variety of craft education within the area's schools. Such education can introduce basic skills and provide school leavers with a much better basis for deciding where their strengths and inclinations lie. Properly taught they are also free of many of the pressures inherent in vocational training and can help contribute to the objective which we believe should permeate all education and training – the fostering of flexible attitudes and aptitudes, and instillation of the ability and inclination to continue learning through life, whether formally or informally.

Poor attitudes to school may be found to continue to handicap efforts within the school, whereas motivation towards training will be considerably higher. In that case it might be beneficial to introduce a general craft training (education) course outside the school system. However, there is a strong case against offering only highly specific training to those who, whether because of aggregate demand deficiency or personal aptitude, have little prospect of finding work in the near future. An important element of training lies in acquisition not just of basic skills but of the speeds required from skilled workers. If trainees do not find suitable employment within a reasonable time there is a very real possibility that they will lose the speeds that they have acquired and require retraining which would be wasteful and could prove seriously damaging to morale. Clearly an upturn in employment opportunities would modify the force of this argument but we still feel there to be a strong case for training those in work through day and block release for specific skills.

In relation to assistance in job search we feel that more attention should be paid to the fact that policy changes toward the operation of the employment offices have reduced the discretion that they are able to exercise in favour of the disadvantaged. The new provision of self-service display boards means that placing individuals with special needs by exchange officers is more difficult. The opportunity may have

257

been snapped up by a 'self-server' before the officer can contact his client. This may prove to be justified in terms of persuading employers to register more vacancies, but we feel that the new policy should be subject to a critical review after a trial period, with attention focusing on the impact it has had on the disadvantaged.

Finally, our research has identified two areas where more resources should be directed:

Into language classes and instruction in application for jobs for immigrants with little or no command of English who are especially disadvantaged in the employment market

Into the increased provision of day care facilities which in Small Heath are inadequate and indeed lower than the city average. This would enable an increased proportion of married women and also the heads of single parent families to seek work – a theme to which we shall return in the next chapter.

Industrial task force

In the above sections we have discussed ways in which industry can be developed in our study area and the surrounding areas so as to benefit inner city residents. In implementing specific initiatives we have mentioned the desirability of an industrial task force which would be able to tackle the problems of a particular area, identified as having priority, in an integrated manner. However, in relation to the industrial development of other parts of Birmingham, not selected for priority action, we believe that a significant contribution can be made by improved procedures and more particularly by the adoption of a positive attitude towards industry throughout city and county government. We believe changes in attitudes, particularly at the less senior level, can best be effected by education to increase awareness of problems and relationships. An important first step in this process has been taken by the publication of Barbara Smith's working paper 'What can Birmingham Metropolitan District Council do that will benefit employment and the economic situation in an inner area like Small Heath?' We hope that the evidence in this report will constitute a further stimulant to discussion.

In order to bring about the speedy implementation of the initiatives we have recommended, an increased awareness and concern will not in itself be sufficient. Even if the necessary resources can be made available, we doubt the ability of the system as presently constituted to deploy them effectively, given our belief that they should be focused on areas in greatest need. The proposals for industrial development, as set out in Birmingham's Corporate Policy Review (January 1975), illustrate the problem. They envisaged responsibility divided between the land committee, planning committee, general advisory committee, industrial liaison group and management team. These were in addition to work in conjunction with the education committee, social services committee and environmental services (urban renewal sub-committee).

Our proposals for an industrial task force do not avoid the need to liaise with local and national government departments but we believe they do clearly identify the responsibility for industrial promotion and offer a reasonable chance of effecting an integrated approach to the problem. If this proves effective within the chosen area then we would hope that, in the longer term, the metropolitan county and the district council would decide to make all aspects of industrial promotion the responsibility of one department. At present the planning department would appear to be a good candidate in Birmingham.

In order to deal with an area such as Small Heath and the adjacent employment locations, we would envisage a task force composed of both full time and part time members. The full time members would be seconded for a period of, say, three years from their authority and the part time members would be individually nominated officials with an agreed time allocation for assistance to the task force.

The proposed composition reflects the nature of the principal tasks that we have already outlined above:

Enter into discussion with selected large employers to identify constraints, problems and possible appropriate assistance

Develop and promote (an) industrial estate(s)

Provide assistance and advice to small firms when relocation is unavoidable but pursue alternative courses of action wherever possible, so that their coexistence with a predominantly housing function can be maintained to the mutual benefit of both.

A suggested staffing list, identifying specific skills required, is shown below.

Member	Specific skills	Seconding authority
Full time members		
Industrial adviser*	General knowledge of industrial policy and legislation, experience in close and direct liaison with individual firms	Department of Industry or National Enterprise Board
Planner	Specialist knowledge of land assembly in Birmingham, preferably in the selected area	Birmingham District Council or West Midlands Metropolitan County
Civil engineer	Broad expertise in all branches of engineering, with particular capability in soil mechanics	West Midlands Metropolitan County or Birmingham District Council
Estate planner	Experience in the design and layout of industrial estates	English Industrial Estates Corporation or a new town corporation
Estate marketing officer	Experience in the promotion of industrial estates and negotiation of agreements with firms	New town corporation or English Industrial Estates Corporation

*Team leader.

Member	Specific skills	Seconding authority
Part time members		
Traffic engineer	General knowledge of transport planning and management, preferably with specific experience of selected area	West Midlands Metropolitan County or Birmingham District Council
Solicitor	Expertise in legal aspects of land assembly	Birmingham District Council
Small firms adviser	Experience in dealing with a wide range of small firms' problems in Birmingham	Small Firms Information Centre

We recommend that the task force should be responsible to a steering committee containing representatives from both sides of industry, from elected members of local government and from regional offices of certain ministries. The steering committee would meet monthly as a general rule, although it might choose to convene extraordinary meetings during the launching of the programme. The chairman of the committee could be provided by one of three bodies – the West Midlands Metropolitan County, Birmingham District Council, or the Department of Industry. If a three year programme is envisaged in the first instance, it might be helpful to agree a rota for the chair at the outset. The composition of the steering committee should be as follows:

West Midlands Metropolitan County	1 representative
Birmingham District Council	1 representative
Department of Industry	1 representative
Department of Employment	1 representative
Representatives from selected area	2 representatives
Trades Council	1 representative
Chamber of Commerce	1 representative

The task force team leader would be responsible for preparing advisory briefs for the steering committee which would be fully discussed and amended in so far as agreement could be reached, or dissent noted on points which could not be agreed. The representative of the authority on which action devolved would then be enjoined to submit the recommendation on behalf of the steering committee and report back at the next meeting as to the progress made. We suggest that, to inject a proper sense of urgency, such reports should automatically be submitted at each meeting for all outstanding recommendations. Confidentiality should only be imposed when the position of individual firms seeking assistance of a financial nature is being considered. Since the task force would itself be given only very limited executive powers, its effectiveness would only be secured through a firm commitment from all participating bodies.

We are aware that the above suggestions, in so far as they relate to a single area-specific programme, will only address part of the problems of inner Birmingham. However, if one of the principal criteria in selecting the area for the programme is that of need, then at least the effort will be well directed. A step by step approach will enable experience to be gained which will guide the expansion of the programme and permit revisions to be made in the light of experience. Moreover, although we would ideally like to see action throughout the inner city, we believe that the dilution of effort and resources that this would require might prove counterproductive.

Bob Marshall

Social security. That's just enough to survive on . . . They reckon that what they give you, it's supposed to cover for all you need. That's what they reckon. But of course they don't have to live on it; you have to live on it.

It's just a hateful thing to be out of work . . . You come to a dead end. You don't know what to do. You can hardly meet the bills that are coming in.

Circumstances of Families

11 Raising incomes

Measures to raise household incomes are crucial to any strategy to alleviate deprivation in inner areas. This chapter is both central and peripheral to the case that we are making. It is central because issues of income generation and income maintenance lie at the centre of the problem of inner areas, as is now – perhaps belatedly – widely recognised. This is primarily an economic issue, not one of social work or the delivery of local authority services, and policies are needed that reshape the workings of the labour market and the housing market so that people can use their labour productively and get income for themselves. The sense in which the issue of low income is peripheral to an area-based study such as ours is that the causes of low income lie outside the area itself and (a distinct point that does not follow logically from the first) that action to raise incomes must be taken through wider national policy, aside from more limited changes in local policy to facilitate industrial location and the working of the local labour market. The scope for area-based policies directly aimed at tackling low incomes is limited. Moreover research has repeatedly shown that it is easy to exaggerate the extent to which most poor people live in areas where poor people are most concentrated.

The importance of income generation

Our analysis of the problems of inner areas points to low incomes as one of the crucial and fundamental problems, determining other problems. It is fundamental to why people live in the area, and why they live in bad housing, and it is fundamental to policies seeking to improve people's housing. The inner areas, including Small Heath, are accommodating increasing concentrations of people who are weak or marginal in relation to the labour market, or who are outside the labour market altogether, or whose earnings have to cover the needs of exceptionally large numbers of dependents. This has come about, at least in the case of Small Heath, principally through the operation of the housing market, though it has been exacerbated by the trends in employment and employment location. As noted earlier, it has resulted in a range of problems, including lack of confidence in the area among residents and among potential investors. It underlies the lack of choice that residents have in the various realms of their lives – housing, employment, leisure and consumption.

The issue of private sector investment is an important one. We refer not only to investment in housing but also to investment in a whole range of commercial facilities – shops, cafés, pubs, cinemas, launderettes and so forth. In Small Heath such facilities are often either run-down or non-existent. The only real exception is cheap basic shopping. Investment is desirable, both in its own right and as one in a series of cumulatively reinforcing factors to restore confidence and redress the tendency for the young, the enterprising and the better-off to leave the area. But such investment must pay for itself and this means that there has to be surplus spending power in the potential user population who will in most cases be living locally. At present few Small Heath residents have much income left over after they have paid for housing, transport and the bare necessities. Raising incomes, and so the power to spend on local services and facilities, should help to attract commercial investment back to the area, as well as making it more economically possible for local residents to take advantage of what the city centre has to offer.

Earned incomes

Recommendations for policy in the labour market were made in the preceding chapter. These have the implicit aim of raising the incomes of people living in the area through stemming the loss of job opportunities (by easing constraints of land and premises, etc) and, to a lesser extent, through enhancing the ability of local people to use those opportunities (by education, training, etc) and so to earn more money.

People can also earn money outside their primary job, though we did not find that this was at all common in Small Heath. It could be encouraged, particularly in the field of housing policy, by a more sympathetic treatment of residential landlords as discussed in Chapter 5, and by providing financial incentives to council tenants who undertake work to maintain or improve their own houses and to sublet to lodgers.

This emphasis on raising earned incomes is crucial to the future social and economic viability of the area, and should ultimately strengthen the position of the most deprived, who, because of the lack of earnings opportunities, are now dependent for the most part not on earned income but on benefits. As we showed in Chapters 1–3, the causes of poverty are extremely complex and are embedded in a multiplicity of factors of disadvantage (to which there is often a spatial dimension), but it is clear that the probability of poverty in a family's life history, whether as an almost normal experience at points of its life-cycle or as a heightened risk at other points of the life-cycle, is much higher among the less skilled manual classes than among other social classes. To attack the underlying structure of disadvantage and poverty, therefore, means to transform the life chances of people from these social classes, and particularly in employment. It is in this context that measures to attack low pay, such as those advocated by the TUC, are of urgent importance even though (as we show below) low pay does not stand out as a major direct cause of poverty in Small Heath.

Income support

In the shorter term improving opportunities in employment is not sufficient from the point of view of raising the conditions of the most disadvantaged people. The reasons for this are:

Most structural change affecting earnings is bound to be a long drawn out affair, leaving a need for immediate action through fiscal and welfare policy

Most of the poorest and most disadvantaged families rely for their income on benefits rather than earnings

There is no very close connection between individuals who receive low pay (defined as less than £33 a week in spring 1974, equivalent nationally to the lowest quintile of earnings of full-time male workers) and households who are in poverty (defined as an income less than 140 per cent of the household's notional basic supplementary benefit entitlement, an arbitrary criterion whose use introduces its own distortions to the analysis).

In Small Heath most of the poor are not low paid and most of the low paid are not poor. Moreover only 2 per cent of the households in the SCPR social survey were both in poverty and had a main earner earning less than £33 a week. These households accounted for only 13 per cent of households in poverty; other causes of poverty are much more important, in the short term, than low pay.

Making it possible for mothers to work

Raising the incomes of the poorest families therefore depends mainly on the government's income support system and on the relation between gross and net pay through taxes and allowances. It depends also on reducing unemployment and, to a lesser extent, on drawing women into employment, because of the importance of having a second earner in the household. This last point shows up, for instance, in the much greater likelihood of a family being in poverty if there is a young child in the family, making it unlikely that the mother would work. In the data from the SCPR survey 21 per cent of households with children (accounting for a quarter of all children in Small Heath) could be identified as being in poverty. For households with exclusively older children the proportion was only 12 per cent, and even of this 12 per cent almost two-thirds were households without a full-time earner. For households with a young child the proportion in poverty was as high as 32 per cent, as Table 24 shows.

Table 24: Households in poverty containing a young child

	Number of children in household		
	All households with children (No. = 391) %	Households with 1–3 children (No. = 306) %	Households with 4+ children (No. = 85) %
All households with children (No. = 391)	21	16	42
Households with child aged 0–4 (No. = 190)	32	23	52
Households without child aged 0–4 (No. = 201)	12	11	22

Note: Poverty equals income less than 140 per cent of supplementary benefit entitlement.
Source: SCPR social survey, manual analysis.

The data demonstrate the importance of giving mothers with young children the opportunity to work, if the number of children in poverty is to be reduced, and also the importance of making it possible and worthwhile for single parents to work. This is not a really new finding. The DHSS in 1970 found that the number of poor two-parent families with fathers working full-time would have been nearly trebled if the father's earnings had not been supplemented by the mother's.

There would be little advantage, however, in enabling mothers to compete for jobs that do not exist. The recommendations that we make below should therefore be seen as complementary to policies to reduce unemployment and to provide part-time jobs with flexible hours. Our recommendations are that:

Day care provision should be substantially extended – perhaps on the lines of the Small Heath self-help pre-school centre discussed in Chapter 8

More imaginative use should be made of childminders – for instance on the lines of the Borough of Lambeth's experiment in paying women who will train as minders and take three or more children, including their own

Incentives should be extended to firms, or groups of firms, to provide crèches for their employees.

Action to enable women to work would have the additional advantage of reducing the extreme isolation and loneliness of some young mothers, as revealed in the Circumstances of Families interviews. It should be accompanied by more research and monitoring on the effects of minding young children and on the costs of alternative ways of providing minding. As for single parents, some of them with older children, there are financial disincentives for them to work. The same Circumstances of Families interviews suggested that many would like to work, were it worth their while, for the company and for reasons of self-respect as well as for the money, but that they received as much money staying at home and drawing social security. This problem is linked to the issue of taxation and benefits reform discussed later in the chapter.

Raising benefits

Chapter 2 gave a very brief picture of what it means to live on an income at or little above the official poverty line as recorded by the Circumstances of Families survey and concluded that what these people needed in most cases is simply stated: more money. Moreover our own experience interviewing these people, and hearing their problems at first hand, was that raising the levels of supplementary benefits and pensions should be given a very high priority in any strategy to combat disadvantage – without it any strategy would have a hollow ring.

The Circumstances of Families interviews give some indication as to what groups among the poor would, in terms of their need, have the highest priority for any available resources. The first group, again, are women – and it is important that money should go directly to them. In our survey, the financial situation of the housewife and so of the family depended on how much her husband gave her, as well as on what he earned. There seemed to be no rules for this – or rather the rules seemed mostly to be set by the individual man. Some men were generous;

others were not. This was one reason why single parents were not more bitter about their financial position; very often the man's meanness over money was one cause of splitting up, so they were better off alone. It also seemed to apply where families were claiming social security illegally since the man was working. In the small (but proportionately not negligible) number of cases that we came across the woman got little of these earnings and it was hard to see how she and her children would get by at all if not from supplementary benefits.

The second group are both the 'short term' beneficiaries and those who are officially classified as 'long term' beneficiaries (pensioners and people who no one could suggest with the remotest plausibility should be working). The accidental effect of government policy has been that the level of benefits of the long term beneficiaries have progressively risen relative to those of short term beneficiaries. Our own interviews suggest that this is wrong, judged by the only criterion that can in the end be justified – that of how much people need.

The people who were finding it hardest to get by, on the whole, were people having to adjust their living standard downward from a higher level (unlike those who had been on benefits for a long time) and people with children at home (especially with older children) as opposed to pensioners. Moreover, the SCPR survey showed them to be the most multiply-deprived group among the poor in Small Heath, living in poor housing as well as having low incomes. We would therefore recommend that all beneficiaries should receive parity of treatment without regard to whether they are long term or short term, and regardless of age.

This should, in our view, be seen as a step towards treating all claimants on an equal footing, without distinction between those who have supposedly contributed to a notional fund for their benefits and those who have not. One disadvantage of the present distinction as to whether or not benefits are 'contributory' (a distinction that was very much alive in people's minds in Small Heath) is that antagonism to immigrants is fuelled by the idea that they are getting benefits for which they have not 'contributed'. Another disadvantage shown up by our Circumstances of Families interviews was that some people in poverty were reluctant to approach the social security office at all.

Suspicion and resentment about benefits paid to neighbours was one factor in the decline of good relationships between neighbours (especially those of the most disadvantaged people) and so of community in Small Heath. Some part of this seemed due to publicity in the press about 'scroungers'. The increased use of discretionary benefits was another cause, especially as many people had a confused and exaggerated idea about these grants (which in 1975 amounted to only 14 per cent of the total supplementary benefit bill) and since their existence encouraged the largely mistaken but still prevalent idea that social security provided a soft option at the expense of working people. For reasons set out in greater length in our report on the interviews, we recommend that the DHSS should attempt to substitute benefits claimed as of right for the greater part of these discretionary grants.

Above all, resentment was due to the overlap betwen incomes from benefits and those from work, and the high tax rates on the latter, which led people to be very aware that people on benefits might be receiving larger incomes, while not working, than they themselves received by working. None of the unemployed claimants that we talked to seemed to be in this position and in fact it seems rarely to happen, but people who were working and who had large families to support nevertheless often suspected that they would receive more from social security than they got in their pay packets. It was in this rather indirect way that working people seemed to be most aware of the real 'poverty trap' facing them, that of high effective rates of marginal taxation and withdrawal of benefits. The answer to this lies principally in higher child benefits, particularly for large families.

Many large families were living in very difficult circumstances, and indeed we would argue that more of them did not fall below our poverty line only because the criterion of 'needs' that we used to calculate whether a family was in poverty embodied the particular lack of generosity of supplementary benefits rates to people with children (especially older children). There is an overwhelming case on the grounds of need for early implementation of higher child benefits. This would have additional advantages; first, because these benefits raise the incomes of families with earners above what they would be able to claim should they stop mother directly and, third, they help the considerable number of people who are in mother directly and third they help the considerable number of people who are in poverty but who are deterred from approaching the social security office for help. As compared to a raising of income tax thresholds, higher child benefits would be much more selective in helping those in need and much more effective in reducing the problems of overlap between the systems of earned income and income support. This would be particularly so if a higher level of child benefit were paid to large families, to families with at least one child of pre-school age (making it difficult for the mother to work) or to families with older children (whose heads of household if unemployed receive more from social security).

Most of the interviews in the Circumstances of Families survey suggested, in one way or another, that there was a crisis in the benefits part of the welfare state. In addition to the long familiar, but no less serious, problems of stigma, administrative complexity and low take up, there is underlying this crisis the overlap that we have referred to between the system of earned (and taxed) income and that of government income maintenance. The most important step needed is for higher child benefits; this would eliminate or at least reduce the biggest anomalies. The next step should be for action to follow up the proposals that should be reached within a year or so by the DHSS's current working party on supplementary benefits, particularly if these lead (as we believe they will) to fewer and simpler benefits. It is essential that wider debate about more fundamental reform does not delay such decisions. For this reason it may be that the plea for a 'new Beveridge' (which we made ourselves in our summary report published prior to the completion of the present volume) is mistaken in its timing. Even so, we would still urge government to increase its capacity to undertake fundamental reform. Acquiring the ability to predict and monitor the effects of tax and benefit changes on a range of household types is an obvious but important example.

In the longer term we believe the government should work towards a 'negative income tax' or 'tax credit' system of income support. This would offer great advantages to the recipient and should (once set up) be administratively more efficient, but it could probably not be implemented for several years. Apart from the difficulties of designing and planning the changeover to a new system, reform would demand a considerable increase in transfer payment. This is firstly because there seems little scope to achieve greater efficiency by alterations within the existing system of benefits and secondly because most schemes of combined tax and benefit reform would initially be extremely expensive in terms of the money paid out, assuming that no households were to be made worse off by the change. The Heath Government's tax credit scheme had an estimated net cost equivalent to almost $2\frac{1}{2}$ per cent of the gross national product.

Increasing take–up of benefits

BIAS has not itself been directly involved in projects primarily aimed to raise take-up of benefits. It has however funded and monitored two advice centres, the more interesting of which in this respect was the 435 Centre in Bolton Road. The experience of the centre suggests strongly the usefulness of a claimants' union function located in neighbourhood centres established in areas of rapid housing transition where there is a large population of families dependent on benefits. Another point, suggested by the Circumstances of Families interviews, is the importance of the point of first contact with the DHSS office, both from the retrospective point of view of those who have claimed, been rebuffed and will not approach the office again, and from the point of view of those (and they include people living at income levels below basic supplementary benefit levels) who prefer not even to enquire about what they may be entitled to for fear of a rebuff. In general it is important that information should be easily available in a form that does not bring fear of exposure or rebuff to people wanting to obtain it. What is needed is simpler benefits (which will cost more – discretion is cheap, which is why it grew); then fewer and better leaflets; more advertising campaigns on TV, backed up by detailed information in post offices and advice centres; and more staff in areas where the work is hardest, when simplification of benefits allows some economies elsewhere.

Our experience with the Circumstances of Families interviews suggests that it should be quite possible for voluntary groups, if funded and backed by the local authority, to survey the population in an area with a view to identifying people entitled to but not taking up benefits. This could be done as a two step process with volunteers making an initial door-to-door approach, to be followed up by people with information and advice as to opportunities. It would be particularly valuable as part of an effort at positive discrimination in an area, and could be backed up by the provision of nursery school and child-minding places, home helps, etc, as required. It would probably be more successful if combined with asking people their views on local needs, not only because these should be of value in developing community services and facilities more sensitive to local preferences, but because it would help win people's confidence to feel they were able to have some say in shaping council activity.

Giving people the opportunity to accumulate assets

This chapter has so far worked to a very limited definition of income. There is wide agreement that a strict distinction between income and the acquisition of wealth in the form of assets is untenable: both refer to the command over resources over time. There is also agreement that, with the extension of the welfare state, it becomes increasingly meaningless to think of income divorced from access to communally owned or provided resources, what has been called the 'social wage'. The Circumstances of Families interviews found that poorer families in Small Heath had little chance of accumulating assets (in contrast to rather better off owner occupiers) and that when they drew on the command of resources implicitly ceded to them through the welfare state, these resources were frequently devalued or demeaned through feelings of dependency, loss of self-esteem and stigma. These are both major problems in any discussion of income.

The main, and increasing, forms of asset accumulation in our society are pension rights and owner-occupied housing. The system of pension rights is crucial to the relation between low pay and poverty over the life-cycle (and to whether the low paid while earning become the poor when retired), but more relevant to our area-based study is housing. As already cited, the Circumstance of Families interviews found a marked contrast between council tenants and owner occupiers in their attitude to their homes, in their willingness to maintain them and to improve them, and in their satisfaction with their condition and with their homes generally. This could not be explained either by the greater income of home owners or by the physical conditions of the houses. The implication is that with more tenure rights existing tenants would become more improvement-minded. This is not quite conclusive, however, since we were unable to judge how far the difference between owner occupiers and tenants could be explained by a process of self-selection – those who started out most predisposed to improve their homes becoming owner occupiers.

One of the key arguments for raising incomes in areas like Small Heath is to stimulate investment in the area. It is therefore important that steps to raise incomes are accompanied by changes that encourage people to invest in their homes. We also argue that measures to raise incomes and to encourage investment should in the long run be cumulatively self-sustaining. A key element here is the hope that by giving people the opportunity to accumulate assets, they may come to feel that there is point and possibility in having a longer time perspective to improve their circumstances than people living from day to day in difficult conditions have had in the past. This may be crucial in breaking the 'cycle of deprivation' and underlines the importance of the measures to encourage home ownership that are discussed in Chapter 5.

This argument also suggests the need for some sort of tenure reform to give council tenants some of the advantages enjoyed by owner occupiers. We see a role for new

270

forms of tenure, such as tenants' co-operatives, and also for the sale of council houses to their occupiers provided that this is on fairly strict conditions. In particular, as noted in Chapter 5, questions of the quality of housing management and maintenance are not as central to the relief of housing deprivation in Small Heath as is the council house allocation system and the ability of the council to allocate housing according to need. The devolving of property rights across the board is not likely to benefit the most deprived directly, and could lead to them being increasingly concentrated in residual estates. We therefore recommend that any policy to sell council houses should include careful monitoring of its effects on the council's ability to allocate housing according to need, and should be designed to encourage the sale of less good houses (or those in less popular estates) to less well-off families. The financial benefit from the sale of council houses, which may include substantial saving in management and maintenance costs, should accrue to the remaining tenants (through the local authority's budget) at least as much as to purchasers, except where purchasers receive an explicit subsidy in consideration of their ability to pay. One use to which savings could be put would be improved maintenance and repair of older properties and estates, a measure that would particularly stand to benefit lower-income tenants.

Gordon King

Small Heath is such a drag. I mean, you look outside my front door, you look outside my back door, and what do you see? Rubbish, absolute rubbish . . . I got a football team, right? We went out to Wythall with my mates, we all went, and we were absolutely in our glory, because there was green grass, absolutely green beautiful grass, apples growing on the trees, acorns . . .

Circumstances of Families

12 Finding the resources

The scale of resources needed to deal effectively with individual and collective deprivation in inner areas is daunting. Small Heath's needs are considerable and many other large cities have inner areas with claims as great or greater. Using a combination of indicators along the lines suggested in Chapter 8 to select priority areas, a national urban programme which gave special assistance to, say, 10 per cent of urban EDs (housing roughly 4 million people) would probably not incorporate more than a third of Small Heath.

The case for more resources rests not simply on present disparities between inner areas and other areas but on the urgency of reversing trends of decline. If these are allowed to continue, either in the form of the present unplanned downward spiral or of a phased rundown, society and government will be faced with very major economic and social costs. An increasingly marginal community, with continuing high unemployment and a growing concentration of disadvantaged people, would be more prone to crime, vandalism, racial tension and other symptoms of stress. This would necessitate higher spending on welfare benefits, health and personal social services, police and probation services and remedial education. It would deprive society of valuable productive potential. Most of all, it would bring severe hardship and suffering to many thousands, indeed millions, of people.

Small Heath's problems have already been exacerbated by economic recession and accompanying unemployment rates at an intolerable level. Recession has had two effects: it has made resources harder to find and it has increased the urgency for programmes and mechanisms to increase the amount of them going to inner city areas and their residents.

The resources required

The resource implications of the recommendations made in preceding chapters have many different dimensions, relating both to the scale and timing of expenditure.

The success of programmes to raise incomes is crucial to increasing owners' expenditure on renovation and increasing the ability of tenants to meet the higher rents inherent in improvement. Given such success, the switching of investment from new construction to rehabilitation will in future years reduce the required pace of capital expenditure on clearance and redevelopment. In addition to increasing the resources devoted to rehabilitation, we have also suggested a change in the rules governing subsidies to the local authority for house and environmental improvements, which would tend to encourage greater selectivity in expenditure by the local authority, with increased incentive to reject low priority applications.

In our consideration of the ways in which local and national services could better meet the needs of places like Small Heath, we have identified a number of requirements which are specific to inner areas. These would call for recurrent expenditure to employ, for example, community education development officers, fieldworkers with knowledge of immigrant languages, specialist teachers to provide English language and practical classes for Asians, and staff for small support teams responsible to area committees. We have also advocated increased support for voluntary organisations and community groups. However, the main claim on resources is not for innovation or supplementary programmes but to provide more adequately the services that are found in all areas of the United Kingdom. Our central thesis is that the overall national budgets for services such as education and health should discriminate positively in favour of areas with greatest need. For instance, to help redress the disadvantages of inner area children we see a need for better pupil/teacher ratios and more specialised equipment, on the principle of 'unequally generous treatment' in comparison with less needy areas. The first priority in Small Heath is in the case of most services, recurrent expenditure rather than major new capital projects. This reflects the fact that a considerable amount of investment has already been committed to residential redevelopment and to a new comprehensive school and leisure centre. Some capital spending will, however, continue to be required to replace physically obsolete buildings which are uneconomic to repair and maintain.

In addition to these strategies aimed at increasing the 'invisible' social wage, we have identified the need for a simplification of the system of income support which would aim to substitute benefits claimed as of right for the greater part of present discretionary grants. Our examination of the circumstances of low income families in Small Heath revealed the urgent need for benefit levels to be raised and for additional investment in programmes to increase awareness of entitlement and improve benefit take-up. This latter point applies also to rent allowances, rent rebates and renovation grants, where lack of knowledge was preventing some of the most deserving cases from obtaining benefit. The amount of resources which increased benefit take-up and increased levels of income support can absorb are very substantial indeed.[1]

Finally we have made proposals directed at maintaining and renewing manufacturing industry in the inner city. These are integrally related to preceding recommendations for housing, social services and income support. A successful programme to provide employment opportunities at locations offering inner city residents a competitive advantage will help to reduce future expenditure on income support. It is also an important component of the strategy for switching the emphasis of housing policy toward renovation. The economic arguments are reinforced by the social problems that arise from high concentrations of unemployment. However, our proposals will require a substantial initial expenditure and a commitment to providing such recurrent subsidies as are found to be necessary.

1. The National Consumer Council estimated in a paper published in January 1977 that between £367 millions and £645 millions of means tested benefits lie unclaimed by people entitled to them.

The benefits from investing in inner areas

In considering the case for devoting more resources to inner areas, it is important to establish whether the proposed policy will, in the longer term, increase their self sufficiency and reduce their dependence on economic subsidy.

In order to answer this question we must consider two basic accounting methods:

The conventional capital and revenue accounting of central and local government which sets directly relevant costs incurred (including debt service) against additional public incomes created

The social accounting method which also takes into consideration: direct expenditures which would be incurred if certain actions were not taken (eg, unemployment and supplementary benefits); indirect costs which are difficult to measure (eg, worsened community relations, loss of social capital through collapse of existing institutions); much longer term advantages resulting from, say, increased disposable incomes, higher educational standards, a more balanced socio-economic mix of residents, and consequential attraction of private and public investors to the area.

We believe there is a strong case for applying to inner areas the social accounting method in addition to conventional capital and revenue accounting.

A continued run-down of the inner city would undoubtedly call for greater direct expenditure. Increasing unemployment would mean more people receiving supplementary benefits, family income supplements, rent rebates and allowances. Such support systems are expensive. In the early part of 1976 it cost an average of £3,000 per annum for each unemployed person, in terms of unemployment or supplementary benefit and revenue foregone. More adequately paid jobs would reduce the inner areas' dependency on welfare benefits. Moreover, the savings would be immediate.

Our recommendations foresee an increase in the expenditure on social services in the inner city. We see positive discrimination in public expenditure on housing, education, health and community welfare programmes. However, these should be regarded as investments which would, in future years, reduce the amounts spent on policing, prevention and repair of vandalism, and on maintenance of the area's infrastructure. It has been shown that poor educational performance and deviant behaviour are strongly linked with bad housing, poverty at home and poor job prospects (which discourage effort). The simultaneous and interrelated programmes that we recommend offer the best hope of breaking this wasteful self-reinforcing mechanism.

Increased economic prosperity in the inner city would lead to direct accretions of revenue as well as reduced costs, though the magnitude of the revenues will be determined by the taxation regime in operation at the time. The national exchequer would benefit from additional direct and indirect tax revenue. The local authority would gain from the increases in rateable value which would accompany an improvement in the economic, social and physical environment. Increased spending power would attract commercial and other forms of private and public investment. Theoretically valuable land (now lying idle) would be brought into productive use.

Finally, in assessing the benefits to be derived from investment in inner areas, account has to be taken of equity considerations. We have identified collective deprivations deriving from a concentration of disadvantaged people which interact with and increase individual deprivations. The social benefits from successful inner area programmes would be greater than devoting the same resources to alleviating individual deprivations without regard to their concentration. Similarly, we believe the benefits gained in inner areas would more than compensate, on balance, for benefits foregone in other locations where the effects of, say, a withholding of investment or a relative loss in rateable value woud be more diluted.

Where the resources must come from

Some of the resources could be sought from within the cities by, for instance:

Achieving the same output with fewer resources: there is some scope for this by employing more local and fewer non-operational staff and by streamlining the implementation of programmes

Switching resources from less to more cost-effective uses: transferring resources from new construction to house improvement; the extension of the principle of rehabilitation to factories, schools, libraries and government offices; making fuller use of existing buildings and space

Mobilising resources in society that are not now tapped: this could be done immediately through giving people better incentives to maintain and improve their own houses and, in the longer term, as part of the process of the community becoming more self-reliant through playing a greater part in the planning and management of its own activities and facilities.

However, we do not believe that these sources will be sufficient to meet the scale of need and others must therefore be found.

There is an appealing line of argument which suggests that the best way to provide the resources needed for social programmes is to generate wealth (primarily through increased industrial production) as quickly and efficiently as possible and then redistribute it appropriately. However, this approach ignores the fact that social needs derive from the organisation and location of production. Production is an important variable in determining the demand for social resources as well as their supply. Efficiency arguments are partial. They are preoccupied with short-term considerations. The organisation and location of production must respond to social as well as economic considerations. It will therefore be necessary to redirect resources (especially within regions) from better off areas and people to deprived inner areas and their residents.

There have already been moves in this direction. The rate support grant has been used as a mechanism of redistribution and in 1975 its needs element was adjusted to direct more resources to local authorities with severe inner area problems. In the housing sector GIA and HAA policies have been specifically designed to help the rehabilitation and gradual renewal of the inner city. However, greatly welcome as they are, these efforts to discriminate positively in favour of the inner city have not gone far enough. They need to be strengthened by complementary strategies to guide more new development into inner areas rather than to outer areas or out of town locations.

We should now modify the range of policies, operated for many years after the war, supporting growth in outer areas and out of town locations and making the new settlement areas more attractive, environmentally and economically, than the inner areas of old cities. Not that the strategy was necessarily wrong in its time. There seemed to be an irresistible urge for people and jobs to pour into the cities; they seemed to attract all the public and private capital which was being created, and they were suffering from overcrowding, congestion and overloading of their construction industries. Their average incomes were rising, and unemployment rates falling, compared with the areas outside the cities. We believe, however, the pendulum has swung too far the other way. The relative positions of the cities and the non-metropolitan areas have been almost exactly reversed. Now we must adopt policies and allocate resources to make the inner city more attractive again in relation to other locations, so as to inspire a renewal of confidence in its future.

The attractiveness of inner areas can be increased either by increasing their absolute attractions, or by reducing the advantages of competing locations, or by a combination of both. The appropriate balance touches on many issues of national policy which are beyond our purview, in particular the proportional share of taxes in national income. Increasing the absolute attractions of the inner city, with all else remaining equal, would require more taxation, whereas increasing their relative advantage could in theory (though it is perhaps unlikely in practice) be consistent with a reduction in taxation.

In the section which follows we offer some comments relating to mechanisms for transferring resources. They do not prejudge the balance between reallocation of government spending and the raising of additional revenue. For convenience of presentation the discussion of a particular topic may consider both increases in expenditure which we consider necessary and savings which we feel could be made. For instance, we mention that increased allowances in line with inflation could reduce the yield of income tax, but that only allowing mortgage interest relief at the standard rate could increase it. This presentation does not mean that we see redistribution of resources as being balanced within budget headings. Savings in the road programmes on the urban periphery might, for instance, be put towards raising income support or financing pre-school facilities. There is no reason why savings in area-specific expenditure should not be devoted to household-specific programmes or vice versa. The fundamental criteria in resource generation and distribution are not technical; they relate to equity and to securing political acceptability in society at large.

Transferring resources to and from the individual

At the level of the individual the prime concern is to ensure the opportunity to work, an adequate level of pay and support mechanisms in case of exceptional need. The issues are discussed in Chapters 10 and 11. However, when these goals are met, it is still important to consider the impact of revenue generation upon the individual and to ensure that policies are sensitive to its incidence on the less privileged.

The main area of concern would be the balance to be struck between direct and indirect taxation, bearing in mind the tendency of the latter to be regressive. In respect of income tax the effect of inflation upon the spending power of the poorer paid should be borne in mind and allowances regularly reviewed to maintain their real value. Additional measures should be considered which would tend to benefit the disadvantaged, such as a raising of child benefits, together with modifications to allowances which most benefit the well-to-do. For instance, tax relief on mortgage interest could be restricted to the standard tax rate and, if there is concern about the disincentive effect of higher income tax rates, greater priority could be given to the introduction of a wealth tax. Its operation would have no incidence upon the vast preponderance of inner city residents.

It is doubtful whether the effect of indirect taxation could be made much less regressive without raising administrative costs disproportionately in relation to yield. However, the social role of the nationalised industries in modifying utility tariffs to benefit the poor consumer might be accepted as a constraint in setting their profit targets and reviewing their performance.

In the longer term domestic rate relief might be incorporated into a system of tax credits (see Chapter 11). In the shorter term consideration ought perhaps to be given to the introduction of a scale into the domestic element of the rate support grant, so that owners of houses whose rateable value is low get proportionately greater relief than owners of higher value property and relief is spread more equably between high poundage and low poundage areas. Relevant here is the extent to which rates are regarded as a tax on one aspect of wealth, the proceeds of which are to be redistributed according to social priorities, or simply as a contribution which entitles the ratepayer to a standard of public service he considers adequate value for money. It has been argued that the more rates are used redistributively the more they will tend to be capitalised and reflected in lower property values.[1] In view of this it would seem that, in principle, the introduction of local income tax (LIT) together with reform of the rating system itself and more selective positive discrimination through the rate support grant, if more progressive in their combined effects, would assist local authorities in gaining electoral acceptance of more redistributive policies.

The spatial allocation of resources

An effective transfer of resources between areas requires a commitment by both central and local government. Central government can and should make more

1. See Department of the Environment submission to the Layfield Committee in *Local Government Finance*, *Report of the Committee of Enquiry*, Annex 18, HMSO, May 1976.

resources available to authorities in which areas of deprivation are concentrated. It is, however, at the local authority level that resources are spatially distributed to a degree which can secure effective positive discrimination favouring areas in greatest need. Central government grants can provide them with an important incentive but will not by themselves guarantee that local authorities use the resources progressively as intended. If the process of local democracy is insufficient to ensure that central government funds are employed to raise levels of service in inner areas, rather than in substitution of locally-generated revenues, then appropriate safeguards will have to be instituted by central government to make positive discrimination mandatory.

Regional industrial and urban policy

We have already recommended, in Chapter 10, an urgent review of the Industry Act 1972 so that the considerable resources it deploys can be directed more selectively. Similarly, we believe that regional and sub-regional urban policy needs to be reviewed. In the climate of limited national growth which is likely to prevail for some time ex-urban developments and new small town expansion schemes will have to be reduced, especially in respect of new housing. This reduction in resource allocation would take some time to achieve savings as existing commitments would normally need to be honoured. Moreover, exceptions may well have to be made for major new industrial developments on the urban fringe for which more socially desirable locations may be physically infeasible and which, if reasonably accessible to city residents, could lead to a more efficient use of roads and public transport by reverse commuting. Nevertheless curtailing out of town and new small town developments could be a major source of funds for reallocation.

The review of regional urban policy should pay particular attention to new and designated expanding towns as places to which inner area residents could move if they so wished. Potentially they have a positive complementary role in alleviating deprivation, particularly in regions where inner areas are physically overcrowded and planned outmigration is desirable. As yet new towns do not appear to have functioned to any great extent as reception centres for the unskilled, the poor or for immigrants. Development corporations are, however, as landlords in a good position to match homes with jobs and to provide rented accommodation. If more generous funds were made available to held lower skilled workers meet the costs of moving and incentives were extended to firms undertaking to train them, we see no reason why planned dispersal should not be more successful. We suggest further efforts be made to explore, by carefully monitored programmes, the contribution that new towns can make to alleviating the problems of inner areas.

The results of such programmes would be an important factor in reviewing each new town's investment programme. They would need to be assessed in the light of such economic factors as capital investment thresholds and the role of the particular town in regional policy. We believe, further, that attention must be paid to honouring the expectations which were encouraged in attracting existing new town residents and investors. If confidence in the new town programme is undermined, it could be both difficult and costly to rebuild. Thus, in a national strategy of urban resource allocation new town programmes merit careful consideration on a case by case basis.

Local authority spending

Local authorities which contain a high proportion of deprived areas will be characterised by low and falling rateable values, a high proportion of rate rebated properties, declining industrial and commercial activity and low personal incomes. Irrespective of whether rates and/or a local income tax are seen as the future major source of local revenue, such areas will continue to receive support for their finances from central government. This may take the form either of a block grant, such as the current rate support grant, over which the authority can exercise discretion, or funds allocated to specific programmes and projects.

The rate support grant has already been used as a means of discriminating in favour of authorities with severe inner area problems. We believe that there is a strong case for further adjustments to the needs element formula, so that it reflects to a greater extent present and future needs and puts less emphasis on past expenditures. A block grant has the advantage of allowing local authorities to respond flexibly to their particular combinations of needs and priorities. But disbursement of the grant in a manner favouring the deprived areas within an authority is dependent upon the political commitment to do so. This will need to be strong enough to revise existing procedures and reject past precedents in administration, many of which may impede positive discrimination.

Securing the necessary acceptance by the electorate at large will not be easy, though there are examples of positive steps in this direction.[1] Outer suburban ratepayers may well welcome the postponement of new council house construction on the periphery in favour of inner area rehabilitation, but they may be less inclined to look with favour on the principle of more progressive spending in, say, education, environmental or leisure services. The problem of raising the general awareness of the electorate of the urgency of tackling urban deprivation is a matter we shall take up in Chapter 14. At this juncture we would simply make the point that the difficult dilemmas of political choice should be made more explicit through the local democratic process. The measures we advocated in Chapters 6 and 7 to give inner areas a stronger political voice should help to achieve such an end. They will certainly ensure closer monitoring of the extent to which central government resources are used for the purposes intended.

Central government can and should assist positive discrimination through national programmes which will tend to benefit deprived areas (eg, support for housing renewal) and specific programmes for designated priority areas (eg, grants towards increased pre-school provision and additional community support services). Specific grants should be envisaged as topping up resources, though we believe their scope should be extended on the basis of budgeted expenditure on broadly agreed

1. See, for instance, *Top Priority, Newcastle's Approach to Priority Areas*, City of Newcastle upon Tyne, a Council Green Paper, 1976.

programmes. To guard against a corresponding reduction of expenditure in priority areas from other sources and to prevent central government resources being used merely to hold down rate poundage, certain controls will be necessary. More use might be made of the device of matching local authority expenditure with central government funds, though this too has certain disadvantages, as we pointed out in Chapter 5. Alternatively, the level of central government support might be made contingent upon an agreed rate adjustment. There is a precedent here in tying the amount of central government housing subsidy to council rent policies.

With regard to capital spending, we suggest that consideration should be given to modification of loan sanctions so as to enable local authorities to play a more effective role in employment creation. They could also be encouraged to direct capital investment towards designated deprived areas through either a differential interest rate structure at the Public Loans Board or supplementary capital grants for projects making an especial contribution to the alleviation of inner area problems.

Finally, a general commitment to the principle of 'unequally generous treatment' means that not only would priority claims on limited capital or current expenditure resources be decided more strictly in accordance with need but those resources themselves should be stretched by adopting more positive cost-saving and asset-conserving approaches throughout the whole local authority territory. Self-help schemes and schemes involving collaboration with private resource agencies and foundations or with voluntary organisations should be encouraged as much in 'outer' as in 'inner' areas. Indeed, there is every good reason for doing so, since the private investment reserves in more affluent areas are that much greater. Part of the encouragement could be the more selective use of local authorities' discretionary powers of fully de-rating charities. Consideration should also perhaps be given to extending the categories of organisation qualifying for de-rating.

*

Our central proposition is that remedial action has to be started simultaneously on a number of fronts and by a number of agencies working to different time scales. Initiatives should range, in their characteristics, from first-aid types of activities to the promotion of very long-term changes in social structure. This proposition rests on the assumption that the 'causes' of urban deprivation are not to be listed in any simple linear sequence, but that its origins are extremely complex and each manifestation interacts with every other, to such an extent that concentration on any of them, without equal attention being paid to all others, is nugatory. For example, if we provide better housing but the people who live in these houses have no jobs and no access to education, recreation, shopping and other services and have no mobility, the effort is largely wasted.

This need for a coordinated approach on an area by area basis underlines the essential role of the local authority. Central government can propose and facilitate; it cannot dispose and achieve. Without a commitment from the local authority it is difficult to see how the problems of inner areas can begin to be seriously tackled, let alone solved.

Once they've started to plan, everything goes. Now they've made it so you want to get out anyway.

SCPR Exploratory Study

There's been a couple of years of planning, but the corporation . . . They haven't got a clue, that's the planners.

Circumstances of Families

13 Improving urban planning

Urban planning could and should play a more positive role in the alleviation of inner area problems. Reflection on our experience in Small Heath has led us to conclude that the current planning process is not geared to respond effectively to these problems, despite changes during the past ten years aimed at making both the system and process more sensitive to needs and changing circumstances.

The changes we propose in this chapter extend themes pursued in earlier chapters, where we have advocated a more open style of urban government, with much greater local influence on the decision-making process. Our proposals, which we believe can be implemented within the existing legislative and organisational framework, entail two complementary approaches: streamlining and modifying the strategic planning process to make it more flexible and more sensitive to local issues, and the development of participatory local community planning as a continuous activity within a context of devolved political accountability and decentralised administration. We believe that our proposals – which have derived not only from our study of Small Heath, but also from a reflection on other planning studies with which we have been concerned – could have general applicability. However, mechanisms for their implementation will require detailed government consideration.

The purpose and nature of planning

Before setting out our specific proposals for changes in the planning process we wish to make clear what we understand to be the purpose and nature of planning and, in the light of this, why we are advocating change.

Looked at from the perspective of dealing with the problems of inner areas, the fundamental purpose of planning becomes the resolution over time of conflicts between different interest groups concerning the equitable distribution of resources and services throughout the whole urban system. We find the share of social goods and opportunities available to different sections of the community to be disproportionate to their needs and that residents in deprived areas have insufficient a say in major decisions which affect the quality of their lives. Existing resources are often used wastefully and are not sufficiently directed to groups and areas which should have the higher priority claim upon them. We therefore see the three main goals of planning in respect of inner areas as:

Improving the relative quality of life of disadvantaged sections of the community

Providing greater scope for deprived communities to participate actively in the planning process

Better husbanding of existing resources and redistributing existing and new resources in response to priority needs.

The pursuit of these goals must, in our view, entail:

A better integration of economic, social, and environmental planning with resource planning

Greater responsiveness and sensitivity to the needs of communities, based on collaboration between government and the people, their institutions and associations, both public and private

More purposeful and better organised resource planning, particularly at national and regional level, governing the allocation of resources between and within regions as well as the determination of the size of the resources and from where they should come.

There are two distinct aspects to all planning activity – 'demand' and 'supply' planning, a distinction already embodied for example, in the terminology of the 'needs' and 'resources' elements of the rate support grant. The concept is developed in a discussion paper of the RTPI[1] upon which we have drawn since we consider it relevant to our study. While we find it helpful to distinguish between demand or community planning and supply or resource planning, we see these as mutually complementary parts of the same cyclical process. 'Demand' planning is concerned with the identification of needs and issues for priority attention, while 'supply' planning is concerned with the harnessing of resources to provide for those needs.

One of the links between demand and supply planning is land and its utilisation. In locational decisions, for example, regarding industry and commerce, land is a vital factor in production and is critical for the shaping of the environment in terms of housing, recreation and so on. These investments are often determined by central government grants and have as much to do with distribution of prosperity between regions as within regions, which in turn can have a direct bearing on the alleviation of inner area problems. The development of a flexible strategic framework for controlling the use of land is a key element in maintaining a balance between 'demand' and 'supply' planning, in turn a vital aspect of local and structure plans.

Current defects of the planning process

Structure plans, as conceived in the PAG Report,[2] were to take the form of policy statements dealing with population, housing needs, employment, transport, education, leisure and environmental issues; they were to be made flexible to respond to changes in population, economic activity, technological conditions, etc, by frequent re-evaluation and up-dating. At the local level, district plans would be prepared which would include areas for action within 10 years. Greater public involvement was also advocated, which at the local level would be concerned with detailed planning questions but at the structure plan level would focus on issues rather than on minutiae of land use. In 1965, and in 1968 when the PAG proposals were enacted, we were still (or so it was thought) in a growth situation. Unemployment was seen

1. *The Future and Planning*, a discussion paper, Royal Town Planning Institute, November, 1976.
2. *The Future of Development Plans*, Planning Advisory Group, HMSO 1965.

as a purely regional phenomenon and the problems of the inner city were seen simply as a back-log of unfit housing which could be remedied largely by new construction in 10 years or so, and there was little, if any, awareness of the complex economic and social issues of the inner city. Last, but not least, no constraints on public expenditure were foreseen right up to 1973 as plans were prepared for massive investments like a third London airport and a Channel tunnel, extensive urban motorway systems for our major cities and the doubling of the national motorway system within 10–12 years. However this is not to say that strategic planning in a little or no-growth situation in which we find ourselves now is not necessary or that structure plans in the modified form suggested later on could not deal with decline. Indeed, it could be argued that such a situation calls for even more sensitive and perceptive planning than planning for growth.

Defects in the way the planning system operates which have emerged from the first structure plans[1] can be grouped into three broad categories: focus, procedures and implementation. With regard to focus, the planning process is too remote from people and insufficiently area based. This is because local government tends to look at problems in an aggregate way and does not readily make allowances for needs of particular areas or client groups within the community. Hence planning is often inadequately related to local issues, still over-concerned with physical planning at the expense of social, economic and resource planning, too concerned with plan making, insufficiently focused on local programmes for action and therefore insufficiently action oriented.

Procedurally the planning system is too fragmented between various authorities and too cumbersome. It is therefore confusing in relation to other plans and too slow in its process. Because it is so slow and so cumbersome it becomes too static, tends to be overtaken by events and loses the essential flexibility PAG envisaged. It also leads to considerable uncertainties about current policies and plans. With regard to implementation, since the present form of structure plan is not designed to allocate resources but only take them into account, it is difficult to effect a redistribution of resources via the planning process. There is also no clearly identifiable role for the private sector of the economy and respective roles and responsibilities of different authorities at the various levels are ill-defined. For these reasons implementation of planning policies is often slowed down and frustrated.

In addition, the operation of the new planning system suffers from two major disadvantages outside its control: the two-tier local government structure introduced in 1974 has greatly exacerbated operational difficulties, and the general consensus about planning as an activity for the benefit of the public as a whole has broken down as questions are being increasingly asked about who benefits and who loses by planning. With regard to the latter point, the breakdown of consensus, this might perhaps have been foreseen if planners had been more aware of the fact that planning as an interventionist activity was inevitably concerned with value

---

1. At the time of writing only 6 structure plans have so far been approved by the Secretary of State for the Environment. Another 27 have been submitted with 44 to come.

judgements and conflicts between different groups in society. This increased awareness of planners that their activities are concerned with differential benefits and disbenefits to different interest groups is especially essential if they are to plan effectively for people in inner areas.

Improving strategic planning

First and foremost, greater flexibility should be aimed at in strategic planning so it can respond more readily to fast changing circumstances such as we have had since 1973. This could be achieved through a modified form of structure planning by producing less elaborate 'strategic statements' which would be issue-oriented and consider alternative assumptions, about economic performance and social change.

Arguably, the strategic planning process should begin with two types of situation report: a community appraisal by lower-tier authorities setting out the key issues they consider need to be resolved, service by service, area by area. Those areas where economic, social and physical characteristics cause serious concern would be identified with supporting evidence. The higher-tier authority could at the same time produce a report assessing the effects of national and regional trends and policies on the strategic planning area as an industrial and commercial base, source of employment and housing, and on educational and recreational facilities. From these two sets of documents the higher-tier authority would produce a 'strategic statement' on the lines we suggest below.

The strategic statement would synthesise the main factors likely to influence local government activity in the strategic planning area, within the context of the national situation, over a period of up to 10 years,[1] with more emphasis on the first 5 years. It would also assess the impact of these factors on key issues raised in the situation reports; single out geographical areas suggested for special priority programmes; indicate the broad strategy and actions proposed at the local level to achieve an appropriate balance between demand for jobs, housing, education etc, particularly for the economically most disadvantaged and least mobile sectors of the community; and identify the immediately available opportunities for change and development.

The statement would also give a better indication of when and where it is necessary to undertake more detailed work. It should take less time to prepare than over-elaborate structure plans, should be a more effective guide for district authorities and would be more easily comprehended by a lay public who could then play a more effective role in the discussion of strategic issues, usually by means of a non-legalistic inquiry. In fact, some of the more recent structure plans[2] have already adopted modified approaches pointing in this direction.

Strategic statements would be kept under constant review and be periodically updated in the light of new information on changing circumstances. Their chief

1. Since the rate of change has been accelerating in recent years, we believe that the 15 year time span suggested by the DOE for structure plans is excessive and therefore propose a 10 year period for strategic statements.
2. Examples of this approach are the Oxfordshire and Peak Park structure plans.

286

purpose would be to provide a common policy framework for the strategic plans of all services of the county and its constituent authorities and serve as a basis for identifying priority programmes attracting special central government funds.

This raises the question of the relationship between the strategic planning process outlined above and corporate planning. We see corporate planning as the attempt to make best use of an authority's potential resources by reconciling competing demands from its various functional and geographical constituents, in such a way that overall performance, measured against major strategic goals, is optimised. Since strategic planning must be concerned with resource allocation it and corporate planning should really be regarded as one and the same thing. Before local government reorganisation, the then all-purpose county borough of Coventry produced a combined structure/corporate plan. Unfortunately, local government reorganisation, resulting in a two-tier system in which functions are split between the upper and lower tier, has now made such an approach much more difficult. In any case, as a report by the Home Office Urban Deprivation Unit[1] points out, a corporate approach at local level is only of limited value unless it can be paralleled at regional and central government level, a point we take up later in this chapter.

The existence of two tiers of local government planning for the same territory is likely to lead to conflict, especially where political control is by different parties committed to different goals, values and national policies. Indeed, it is because of these difficulties that we advocate a system which gives more prominence to local planning, leaving the county to exercise its control over local plans through its assessment of priorities in its strategic statements, which would be taken into account, via regional and sub-regional authorities, by central government in making special grants. The county should also have a right of objection, which should be made public, to strategic plans produced by districts for main services. Such objections would again be taken into account by regional authorities and central government when they consider loan sanctions and rate support grant allocations. We believe it is perfectly right and proper that strategic conflicts which cannot be resolved by the normal political processes of local government should be arbitrated upon by central government exercising its prerogatives.

If the approach we advocate were adopted, strategic planning would then focus more sharply on public intervention (within national and regional resource allocation policies) to resolve issues which are manifested at the local level. Land use, transport and environmental planning would be the means of translating into physical form judgements about the distributive consequences of the location of various facilities, and about communities' needs and preferences. Central government would simultaneously refine its national urban strategy, so that, for instance, incentives in older urban areas and in new and expanded towns' programmes worked in a complementary way and were more closely linked financially. At the same time, the input from strategic planning authorities would help central government to adopt policies which would be sensitive to variations both within and between regions.

1. *Local Government: Approaches to Urban Deprivation, Occasional Paper No. 1*, Home Office Urban Deprivation Unit.

Central government's role

Central government's principal role in relation to strategic planning is concerned with supply or resource planning – the allocation of available resources according to priority demands from different areas. The response is already conditioned and, we would argue, should be even more so, by the demands for resources placed upon it by local communities via metropolitan counties or groups of shire counties advised by regional economic planning councils and the DOE regional offices.

There is a clear need for central government to develop a distinctive role with regard to strategic resource allocation and the co-ordination of policies of the various agencies responsible for resource planning. There is, at present, no single government agency responsible for comprehensive resource planning, allocation and control. Individual major organisations whose decisions have an important effect on the distribution of resources are numerous and fragmented: nationalised industries, many government departments, the major multi-national firms and the unions. However, central government has already moved in the direction of establishing bodies which would be responsible for a joint approach in certain policy fields, such as social policy, by the creation of a high level group to develop a Joint Approach to Social Policies (JASP) with committees of ministers and senior civil servants from all relevant departments. This approach should be extended to include economic and environmental policies and be strengthened to comprise budgeting, particularly for resource planning policies and special grants related to inner areas.

In recent years, central government has been showing increasing concern about the inner city by providing special funds through urban aid, and setting up community development projects, inner area studies, comprehensive community programmes and the Urban Deprivation Unit in the Home Office. But these all amount to a fragmented approach. The mechanisms of the Public Expenditure Survey Committee could be used to take a necessary overview of inner area needs. In September 1976, the government set up an Urban Affairs Ministerial Committee under the chairmanship of the Secretary of State for the Environment. We suggest that this committee should be developed to become the permanent government body responsible for the co-ordination of public and private resource planning and for advising the Cabinet on the resource allocations necessary for the alleviation of inner area deprivation. In addition to the DOE the Home Office, the Departments of Employment, Education and Science, Industry, Health and Social Security, Transport and the Treasury would be represented on such a government body and serviced, we suggest, by the DOE's Inner Cities Directorate and civil servants drawn from the departments concerned. This Urban Affairs Committee should also have regular contact with representatives of local authorities with serious inner area problems as well as with the unions and management from public and private industry.

The role of regional planning authorities

National resource planning decisions would be reflected within each region according to its special problems and requirements. Existing regional authorities like the metropolitan counties, groups of shire counties, regional economic planning

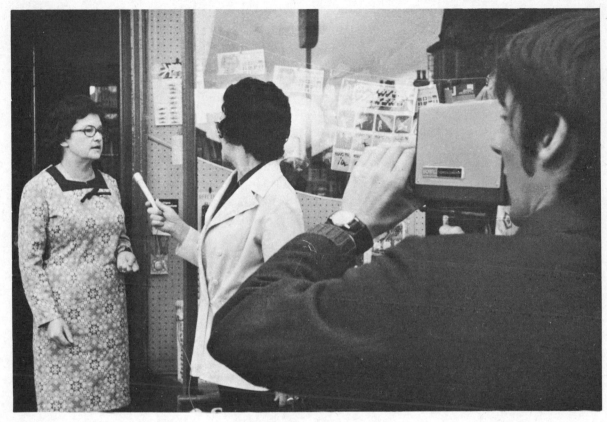

Us people, people who live in Small Heath, are not expected to take in what the council are putting forward.

SCPR Exploratory Study

You can't get to know nothing. If you go into town they say all the plans are squashed, and the next thing you read in the paper they've drawn it up again. One minute they're putting in a new road, the next minute they're not. We can't find out nothing.

Circumstances of Families

councils and DOE regional offices would be better informed and made more aware of community needs within their region through district councils' community reviews and plans (discussed below) and the county councils' strategic statements, while at the same time they would be involved in discussions with national government about regional resource allocations. Their regional strategies and programmes would then be matched to the allocation of central government funds and proposed regional priorities for funding economic social and environmental programmes, and they should have a measure of discretion between spending programmes. We are, of course, aware of the fact that the whole question of devolution of power and responsibilities to regions is under discussion and that as a result there may be changes in the structure of regional government.

However, whatever form regional government may eventually take, we would like to see a greater response at national and regional level to the problems of inner areas by the allocation of resources commensurate to their needs. Once priority areas have been identified, possibly on the lines proposed in Chapter 8, and the size of these allocations has been determined it could be argued, as does the Layfield Report, that there needs to be greater freedom for district authorities to use allocated resources for local action programmes, particularly with regard to the alleviation of problems in their inner areas. On the other hand, a central government determined to make priority allocations for inner areas may be frustrated in this by a local authority unsympathetic to those objectives. Thus there is a genuine dilemma between allowing local authorities greater freedom in the use of government resource allocations and necessary government control to ensure that its funds are used by local authorities as intended nationally. The special programmes and grants proposed in Chapter 12 would be a positive step towards overcoming this dilemma, especially where organisational measures were adopted to give inner area councillors and the people they represent a greater opportunity to influence the distribution and use of local authority resources.

Improving local planning

Local planning is about resolving conflicts, tackling problems and realising opportunities which are understood as relevant issues by local residents. From the outset it should be undertaken in collaboration with representative local groups – an approach made much more possible in a context of area committees and active community organisation – and should be seen essentially as an ongoing political activity supported as necessary by technical exercises.

Community reviews and plans

The first task is to assess a community's needs at a particular point of time and over time, as seen by residents, local institutions, private investors and by the local authority's elected members and officers. This could take the form, for example, of community reviews as suggested by the Sunderland Study[1] and would consist

1. *The Sunderland Study*, DOE, Sunderland BC, McKinsey & Co Ltd; HMSO 1973.

essentially of a stocktaking of community problems, both clearly identifiable ones and those which might be hidden because they are not part of any agency's defined responsibility. They would spell out the community demand aspects to which not only the local district council, but also the county councils, the respective regional economic planning councils, as well as national government, should respond. At the same time, financial and other constraints at city, regional and national level would be made known so that the participants in community reviews would be aware of this context.

The key problems identified by these community reviews should be continuously monitored and the reviews up-dated in the light of changing circumstances, with revisions consolidated annually in published statements. A rolling programme of demand reviews and of policies and programmes to meet these demands would be the appropriate means whereby social, economic and environmental policy and action could be integrated. This could be done, both at the local level and at the level of strategic planning, by providing inputs to periodically updated strategic statements. The reviews should also be integrated with land policies arising out of the five-year rolling programme under the Community Land Act 1975 for land acquisition and disposal. Annually up-dated community reviews would also provide the opportunity of a more critical assessment of the distributive effects of annual budgets when these are discussed between local authorities and central government.

The review process would be followed by a selection of priority programmes for action – a mainly political process at the local level. The selected priorities and programmes would form the basis for the development of local district plans which we see as 'area community plans'. The reason for proposing this change in terminology is two-fold: the term 'district plan' was coined before district authorities were established and local district plans can be confused in the public mind with plans for whole metropolitan districts, and by adopting the term 'area community plans', their community based character is emphasised.

We would argue that district plans, in the form of area community plans, should be seen as essential links between local action area plans and strategic planning documents at city and county level and that they thus require a comprehensive approach to economic, social and physical issues. Naturally, there will also be a strong emphasis on environmental issues. These area community plans for local districts like Small Heath should ideally provide a programme for physical, institutional, economic and social development and for private investment based on available resources, and a realistic timetable which enables all agencies to cooperate in the realisation of the plan. If this proves either too ambitious or inappropriate, area community plans should at least identify key issues and a series of guidelines for public and private investment, taking into account the likely available resources over time. The Birmingham Project Report for the Small Heath Study and Plan envisages an approach along these latter lines which is appropriate in the case of considerable future uncertainty, as in Small Heath. The report recognises that there is only limited scope for significant land use change in the area and has identified the major physical issue as the renovation of existing housing stock. The prime economic issue is the improvement of the economic viability of the area by providing increased job opportunities coupled with the need to assist community development.

The production of these community plans, like the community reviews, would be undertaken from the outset in collaboration with representative local groups and would, of course, draw on information from the county's strategic statements; it would consider wider issues of locational strategy and communications as well as expenditure constraints in the district, county and region as a whole; it would review relevant aspects of the strategic plans of major spending services; most of all, it would enable people to express informed and significant preferences through collective action and via normal constituency process – particularly where area committees and neighbourhood organisation were well developed and played active roles (see Chapters 6 and 7). Within the framework of these area community plans, action area plans would be prepared as required for relatively small areas, like HAAs, where action would take place in the next few years.

The preparation of area community plans and strategic statements should be seen as complementary elements in a single, continuous planning process. The 1968/71 Town and Country Planning Act stipulates a hierarchical order for the preparation of plans: structure plans, district plans, then action area plans. This reflects the hierarchy of the plans themselves – the structure plan being the intended key policy statement – but the apparently logical sequence of preparation has in practice been found not only undesirable but frequently unworkable. Largely this has been due to the different timescales involved, district plans often being required to deal with pressing local issues before lengthy structure plan preparation is completed. The principal disadvantage of this situation is that although the district plan is in effect a valid statement of policy, it in fact has no statutory force until formally approved, which must await approval of the structure plan. On the other hand, by treating issues of both local and strategic significance in depth, a district plan can and does provide a valuable input to strategic planning.

We consider that the notion of sequential preparation of plans at strategic and local level should be dropped; instead all planning activity (whether geared to the preparation of detailed plans, broad guidelines or statements of intent) should be regarded as iterative, aimed at the speedy identification of changing priorities and the development of strategies to tackle them effectively. Furthermore, statutory approval of area community plans should not await production of the relevant strategic statement; certification by the county that the plan is broadly compatible with the trend of strategic thinking at a particular time should qualify the plan for approval by DOE.

Land use regulation

If planning is to be made more relevant to the needs of inner areas, then there is a need for certain changes in applying specific controls to the use of land. In the first place, there is the question of zoning and mixed uses. Planning dogma decreed

292

several decades ago, when most industries were dirty, noisy and smelly, that in residential zones only residential uses can be permitted, that other uses like workshops, however small and innocuous, must be treated as non-conforming uses and so be eliminated. This policy has in fact been so successfully implemented that many businesses, large and small, which might otherwise still function have disappeared altogether. Others, of course, have gone out of existence on their own account. This has resulted in a particular dearth of those small scale employment opportunities in inner areas which would be so welcome in providing jobs close to the homes of potential workers. This does not mean that we wish to advocate an indiscriminate mixture of residential and industrial/commercial uses. We believe, however, that there should be a clear distinction between uses which are functionally incompatible with housing, and small scale work places which are environmentally acceptable in or close to residential areas. Such uses should be allowed and encouraged according to this criterion. We proposed in Chapter 10 that grants should be made available to industry (as in GIAs) for improvements to meet encouraged to make greater use of class III industry.[1] Furthermore, mixed use zoning should be adopted wherever appropriate.

The other principal change required is in the application of the Community Land Act 1975. Provided planning considerations predominate, the Community Land Act 1975 could open up new opportunities for local planning, since it enables local authorities to purchase land under more favourable terms than was the case before the passing of the Act, and gives them greater scope to initiate the development of new employment opportunities. Local authorities should be able to exploit to the full these new enabling powers and the DOE should encourage them to concentrate on the pressing needs of inner areas, rather than on quick and easy gains on green field sites.[2] With this in mind some amendments to the Act may be required to enable local authorities to acquire land at existing use value in advance of the second appointed day, whether or not planning permission exists for that land. Earlier in this chapter, we have suggested that a rolling programme of demand reviews, and of policies and programmes to meet these demands, should be integrated with land policies arising out of five year rolling programmes under the Community Land Act for land acquisition and disposal. If these proposals were accepted, specific policies and programmes, like the industrial development initiatives which we proposed in Chapter 10, could be more readily implemented than was the case before this Act was passed.

Public participation

We have already discussed (in Chapter 4) the pervasiveness of 'government' in Small Heath, yet active, meaningful resident involvement in policy formation is currently restricted to liaison between the community federation and the local

---

1. Class III as defined in the Town and Country Planning (Use Classes) Order is the use as a light industrial building. Such uses have already been incorporated, for example, in the Chelmsley Wood development in Birmingham.

2. These are the implications of paragraphs 60 and 61 of *Community Land – Circular 1, General Introduction and Priorities, Circular 121/73*, DOE.

authority concerning the use and management of the community school and, on a wider scale, between residents' associations and the local authority in the development of GIA and HAA plans. The community federation was involved in consultations with officers preparing the Small Heath Study and District Plan but excluded from the study's working group and steering committee.

We strongly support in principle the energetic and extensive efforts of Birmingham's urban renewal team in fostering public participation and the innovation of using street meetings to facilitate the work of the local authority's house improvement agency. Residents' participation in urban renewal in this way is 'meaningful' in that it involves them, individually and collectively, in decisions affecting their homes and immediate environment. Though public participation in urban renewal is administratively costly and time-consuming (we estimated up to 25 per cent of the total man-months required for GIA/HAA plan preparation in Birmingham) and does not provide a model for participation on wider issues, the experience in Small Heath and elsewhere in the city is certainly relevant to the general issue of 'participation'.

The process of resident involvement in urban renewal, as we have observed it, has shown quite clearly that where a dialogue between residents and the local authority can be established on the basis of an exchange of information and ideas, public participation becomes much more than simply 'rubber-stamping' or rejecting a proposal by the authority. It becomes increasingly a matter of informed consultation and cooperation – though, of course, not without some (often considerable) conflict along the way. The more frank the dialogue, the better the end product is likely to be; at present, as we have pointed out in Chapter 6, one of the problems which persists is that local project teams do not always have either the information or authority to be as frank or open as they or residents would like. Nonetheless, in both Little Green and Nechells (the two HAAs we observed) conflicts were ultimately resolved. The plans produced, and approved by committee, strongly reflected residents' wishes and ideas.

All of this points to a key element in public involvement in the decision-making process: the degree of public awareness concerning the relevance for the community and the individual of the issues presented for discussion or comment. Hence, a high degree of involvement in the urban renewal process and a very low response to strategic planning issues. This pattern is generally observable and not confined to inner areas, and is largely attributable to the way in which issues are presented. Unless the possible consequences of strategic options are translated into specific, local terms, most people are unlikely to understand their relevance or potential impact, yet strategic decisions condition the distribution of resources and for inner areas there is no denying the important consequences of these decisions.

Finally, if public participation is to be successful, it must be a process of ongoing consultation and information. For example, the federation, having been consulted in the initial stages of the Small Heath District Plan, were then left in the dark for over three months and had no firm information about what was happening in terms of committee submissions or steering group meetings or the progress of work generally. They became frustrated and disillusioned, feeling that though their initial opinions had been sought, their influence was likely to be negligible.

Organisational and manpower implications

The approaches to strategic and local planning advocated in this chapter imply certain changes in the organisation of planning activities and the deployment of manpower. At both county and district level the emphasis would be on the coordination of planning by individual departments and agencies, rather than the production of all-embracing plans by specialist planners. Elaborate data-gathering exercises, which so often precede the preparation of these plans – especially at strategic level, should be considerably reduced; data collection and analysis should be directed more selectively towards the identification and resolution of key issues. In this connection maximum possible use should be made of information already existing within departments. On the other hand, much more emphasis on monitoring would be required for the planning process to respond more quickly and effectively to changing circumstances. Again, this should be done selectively, focussing on the key elements of strategy.

While these changes would probably necessitate an increase in manpower in some areas of planning activity, a reduction in staff might well be achieved in others. We see many of the alterations in staffing being achieved by redeployment between departments and authorities, often by secondment. At strategic level there would certainly be scope for a reduction in manpower in authorities which are fully geared to structure planning requirements. At the local level a more open, participatory style of planning indicates an increase in staff as does the recommended general shift in emphasis from strategic to local planning activity. These additional staff requirements should be minimised by streamlining planning processes wherever possible; necessary increases should be met largely through redeployment. Furthermore, where there is a significant measure of decentralisation within the local authority, and in particular where community development teams or local support teams serving area committees are established, the process of assembling information would be considerably eased, as would the process of forming and maintaining close contact with residents. Thus, overall, we do not envisage an increase in manpower involved in urban planning.

*

Our main argument is that planning for deprived inner areas must be based upon the principle of positive discrimination in their favour and, at both the strategic and the local level, must be particularly sensitive to the needs of local residents. If it is to be effective, planning in its widest sense must take place by cooperation between the local authority and the local community. However, effective participation by the community suggests the need for an educative process leading to a widespread change of attitudes within society, which we shall discuss in the following chapter.

I want my children to better themselves . . . There was no opportunity for us; we had to come out of school and go into a factory 'cause that was it . . . I'm hoping that my children are going to stay at school. But not only that, there ain't goin' to be the jobs anyway without education.

When they leave school now, it's on the dole . . . Well, that isn't very nice for a young kid that's just left school, is it? . . . I mean, all he does in one day is mosey round the streets. Well, what's in Small Heath, lately?

Circumstances of Families

14 Educating for change

The kinds of policy we have been advocating in preceding chapters will not be easy for government to adopt at the present time. Nor will it be easy, even assuming political will on the part of government, to persuade powerful interest groups and large sectors of the electorate that such policies are necessary. We have already seen, in Chapter 4, how 'public opinion' appears to have been shifting against increased public spending on social services. It is hard to envisage how measures designed to bring about substantial redistribution will be readily accepted without widespread changes in attitudes, indeed without a reversal in the trend of certain popular attitudes which have been fostered by the diffusion of assumptions underlying past economic and social policies.

Changes in attitudes will not just happen. The more privileged people in society (most of whom live in collectively more privileged environments) cannot reasonably be expected to make concessions of privilege, either by the sacrifice of present advantage or by foregoing future opportunity, unless, first, they are made more aware of the 'unfairness' of the great disparities that still exist in the distribution of social goods and opportunities and, second, the disadvantaged themselves become more organised and articulate in pressing for a better deal. We believe the achievement of a substantial planned redistribution will depend on both conditions being met. In the first place, while traditional class deference may well be to all intents and purposes a thing of the past, there is considerable evidence to suggest that the aspirations of the most deprived remain very restricted and their political attitudes characterised more by passive acquiescence than by the kind of consciousness which would pose a real threat to the established order of things.[1] Faced with powerful and more organised groups whose interests appear to inhibit change, what political activity is currently generated tends to be confined to the pursuit of essentially short-term and fragmentary gains which can usually be accommodated within existing political and economic arrangements, only for the balance of privilege and disadvantage to readjust itself in other ways and the basic structure of inequality to be left unaffected. In the second place, although the dominant set of political and economic assumptions and values which influence the allocation of the nation's resources are under constant fire from many sources, a substantial shift in assumptions and values towards a rather more egalitarian position is unlikely to come about in the absence of a clearer demonstration of how far many common assumptions about the welfare state fall short of grasping the harsh reality of poverty and disadvantage. While political action by the disadvantaged alone could not be expected to provide the necessary stimulus, it is hard to imagine how the stimulus could be provided entirely without such political action, if for no other reason than to gain the increased support of potentially

---

1. In this connection we would single out W. G. Runciman's classic study of reference group structures in *Relative Deprivation and Social Justice* (Pelican edition, 1972).

sympathetic lobbies and pressure groups, in particular within the trade union movement, political parties, professions and press.

For the expectations of both disadvantaged and privileged groups to change determined educative efforts will be called for, promoted by a wide range of different agencies. Expectations are moulded not only by formal education in schools and colleges but by informal education in home, workplace and community and by the many media of communications. To change expectations – which means changing the image that child and man have of their place and purpose in society, the view they take of their rights and responsibilities – educational strategy must concern itself with all major influences on the social development of the individual: the curriculum and organisation of schools, television programming and the uses of advertising, political communications and public relations, the extent and content of community education, the role of the press, and so forth; it would be concerned with the relationship between the learning experience the child undergoes in school and that to which he is exposed in his family, social and cultural group, community and neighbourhood; it would pay attention to the transition from school to work, the relationship between promised and real opportunities.

Central government already plays an important role as public educator. It has acquired powers of influence over formal educational practice, the use of media and marketing behaviour. It is responsible for the brand of political and economic philosophy and the vision of the good or just society it communicates to the electorate. In its management of the economy and control of public expenditure it can help to determine, selectively, the level of resources going into various forms of educational activity, thus affecting not only the quantitative provision of opportunities, and their location, but also the quality and variety of provision. In Chapter 8 we argued that present programmes of positive discrimination in the allocation of educational resources do not go far enough, that too little is being spread too thinly for any significant benefit to be derived. However, in terms of the form and content of education, which in the end have most to do with the efficacy of whatever resources are available, we believe that government's role should be that of facilitator rather than director. Increased state control over what is to be learnt and the way it is to be learnt would in our opinion inhibit motivation, stifle experiment, and present very real dangers to individual freedoms, of both educator and educated. Consciousness will not be changed by act of government but by the acts and example of many individuals – teachers, community workers, union officials, professional communicators, managers (whether or not guided simply by 'enlightened self-interest'), residents and workers themselves – working alone and collectively. In the final few sections of our report we consider some of the approaches we should like to see adopted and how in certain instances government might encourage them.

Learning and teaching in the urban school

Educational research and practice have clearly demonstrated that children (and people in general) learn best when they are motivated – by encouragement, especially from within their own family, and by the incentive that the end-product of their learning effort holds for them – and when the content and context of what they are learning have real significance for them, in that they reflect their own personal experience, interests and concerns. The apathy, if not open hostility, of so many inner area children to their schooling, which is illustrated in their low educational performance as well as in behavioural problems and truancy rates, testifies to the fact that their parents have often little conception of what goes on in the schools or how they might aid their children's progress, that few (if any) expectations are held as to the benefits of the experience in later life, and that the curriculum and organisation of the school mirror largely the values, attitudes, language styles, cultural meanings and preoccupations of a different social reality, essentially those of the middle class.

If children in inner area schools are to acquire the basic skills, information, attitudes needed to enlarge their opportunities of formal educational achievement and self-fulfilment, then the first requirement is for barriers between home and school to be dismantled, so that the school functions as part of the community, attuned to its social, economic and cultural environment. Understanding of the children's environment and its cultural meanings is doubly important for teachers because not only will it condition attitudes to curriculum and school organisation but it will also affect their expectations of children's performance, which a number of studies have shown to be a significant factor in pupil achievement and a further source of disadvantage to lower class children, of whom teachers have been found generally to expect less, quite irrespective of their actual intelligence.[1]

It is too early to assess the value to Small Heath schools of the environmental education kit, proposals for which emerged in discussions with local teachers following BIAS/CURS work on children's perceptions. Results will depend in any case as much on the skills of individual teachers and the particular school or class setting in which they are working as on the intrinsic quality of the kit itself. The case, however, is well established for the potential usefulness of taking the neighbourhood, its physical form, life and activities as the starting point for the successful teaching of 'subject' work in geography, history, language . . . even mathematics and the physical sciences. Environmental education or 'community studies' should not be regarded as a separate item on the curriculum or something to keep ROSLA pupils occupied, however much interest may be temporarily aroused by particular projects like the series of classroom sessions devised by CURS for us in the interests of both research and a stimulus to teaching; it should be seen rather as a theme or principle pervading the whole of school and classroom activity, at all age levels.

Links with the home must begin early on in the child's school or pre-school life. Indeed, the first target is the child's parents. We have witnessed at a fairly simple level through two of our own action experiments (pre-school community worker,

1. For a useful short review of the evidence, see Sylvia Mills, 'Teacher Expectations and Pupil Performance', in *Successful Teaching in the Urban School*, introduced and edited by Paul Widlake, Ward Lock Educational, 1976.

community education development officer) how much benefit mothers in particular feel they derive from learning to understand their children's development and to communicate more effectively with them through language and play. Research has demonstrated that the effects of nursery school or playgroup, so often praised per se as a means of giving disadvantaged children a 'head start', are soon eradicated if continued individual support is not forthcoming in the home and/or primary school. Measures like the appointment of home-school liaison teachers, as our own experience confirms, will have only marginal impact unless the general conduct of school life reflects a recognition, especially on the part of the head, of the cultural and educational interdependence of school and home. In a situation where, for example, parents are prohibited access to the school except by invitation or where the form and content of 'education' and the institutional context in which it takes place are viewed as the exclusive preserve of professional educators, the liaison teacher will almost inevitably be pressed into functioning simply as an extra pair of hands, to fill in for absent staff or undertake remedial teaching, and as a problem-chaser in individual cases of poor attendance, discipline or performance. In fact, there is a danger that in an unfavourable operational situation such an appointment will encourage regular teaching staff to draw still sharper artificial boundaries between teaching and other roles in relation to the child as a developing personality.

In multi-racial communities the importance of the home-school link is greater than ever. The cultural diversity of a school population including many children of Irish, West Indian, Pakistani, Bangladeshi, Indian and African Asian descent, whose parents are often newly-arrived in this country, presents teachers and other school staff with an immense additional challenge. In some Small Heath schools cultural minorities make up the majority of pupils. The heterogeneity of languages, dialects, religions, taboos, dietary habits, customs, values, expectations of school and society is daunting, even to teachers with long experience of working in the most difficult conditions. Many children, especially Muslim and Hindu girls, face considerable personal stresses in adjusting to the entirely new cultural environment they encounter in school. The 'better' they adjust, the greater the risk of cultural conflict within their home and sub-community.

Cultural diversity can be a rich source of learning experiences if children are encouraged to explore and compare their different backgrounds, traditions, art and dance forms, social attitudes, etc; but even more than the need it creates for specialised equipment (language laboratories, for instance), for smaller class groups and for new organisational approaches like team teaching, it demands a great deal of awareness and sensitivity, quite special interpersonal and teaching skills. We would certainly advocate more initiatives along the lines of the course in Asian cultures for professional workers and the various English language and practical classes for Asians set up by the BIAS-sponsored community educational development officer and community relations fieldworker. However, such initiatives on their own will reach comparatively few teachers and parents. Only a much more positive effort by education authorities and individual schools to involve parents directly in the activities of the school and encourage teachers to enter more fully into the life of communities will open the door to greater mutual understanding.

300

Central government could do more to stimulate the development of special curricular programmes for urban and multi-racial schools through bodies like the semi-independent Schools Council and to fund (directly through DES or by way of the Urban Programme and provisions under Section 11 of the 1966 Local Government Act etc) experimental projects and additional appointments concerned with broadening the scope of good practice and relieving part of the burden on hard-pressed staff in schools in disadvantaged areas. We have already argued in Chapter 9 that central government (in this case DES) should play a more active role in monitoring experiment, as opposed to financing more academic research, and in disseminating the results of good practice. It is, however, in its control of the expenditure of local education authorities that it can and does exert the greatest influence on what may or may not be achieved. In this connection it is unfortunate, to say the least, that a training college like St. Peters, Saltley, one of comparatively few specialising in preparing teachers for work in inner area situations, should be threatened with closure because of projected falls in the child population when such an eventuality offers precisely the much-needed opportunity to increase teacher-pupil ratios, which in areas like Small Heath are much too low in relation to the task in hand to permit teaching of comparable effectiveness to that in more privileged areas. If cuts in educational expenditure have to be made, it would seem to us that this is the last place in which to make them.

The implication is that more selective mechanisms are needed to ensure that an appropriate balance is achieved between capital and current spending and that both are directed more positively to the benefit of schools whose needs should have highest priority – an outcome which will not be realised simply by minor increments to teacher salaries and capitation allowances. In our view, this again supports the case for shifting the focus of control from the detail of individual loan sanction requests and from crude retrospective RSG adjustments to the assessment of objectives and strategies as set out in local authority long and short term service plans and budgets/cash flow estimates (see also Chapter 6).

Little purpose is to be gained by attempting to intervene directly through more frequent inspections and tighter controls in the curriculum, mode of organisation and teaching style(s) of individual schools. The ratio of administrators to teachers is arguably already too high. We believe too that schools should be allowed considerable autonomy in responding to their own specific environmental circumstances and building on the particular range of understanding, aptitudes and skills commanded by their own staff. On the other hand, our experience with the formation of a teachers' working group in Small Heath, even though it met infrequently and suffered from a lack of direction and focus due to changing pressures on the scarce time of BIAS team members, suggests that much might be achieved through the encouragement of local forums, workshops or resource centres[1] where teachers from different schools in the same area – nursery, primary, secondary, special – could meet to explore common problems, exchange views, learn of successful experiments elsewhere, receive special training, loan or use specialised equipment, and prepare

1. The idea is, of course, not new. See for example the report of an experiment along these lines, with its organisational and operational problems, *The Evaluation of an Educational Programme*, West Glamorgan CDP, July 1974.

joint projects. These activities, which could be based entirely in existing buildings (in Small Heath the new community school would be ideal) and would demand only very limited resources to meet the running costs of courses and similar initiatives, might usefully be planned in conjunction with a training college or university department of education specialising in inner area/multi-racial work.

Community education, community school

The case for a 'relevant' education is a strong one purely on the grounds of the improvement it offers in conventional educational performance. But it does not rest solely on that, nor even on the personal satisfaction to be derived by children from the acquisition of intellectual, artistic and manual competences. Another important objective is to increase children's understanding of the processes that shape the environment in which they live, so that as active members of society they may participate individually and collectively in transforming that environment. Thus educational strategy joins those of urban renewal, employment maintenance, community organisation, political devolution and administrative decentralisation in fostering a stronger neighbourhood identity, a greater sense of confidence in its future, and a firmer belief in residents' own power to influence that future.

Much effort in the recent past has been directed towards making inner area schools 'better' schools. This is usually taken to mean more like schools in relatively privileged areas: more modern, better equipped, better staffed. And certainly we should like to see more modern, better equipped and better staffed schools in inner areas. But we have taken the position that inner area schools should first and foremost be different schools, in terms of what goes on within them[1]. Under present circumstances, where educational objectives, curriculum, teaching methods, language of instruction and organisational forms in most inner area schools (and Small Heath is no exception in this respect) are virtually indistinguishable from those in schools generally, the very few children who succeed tend to become alienated from their social and cultural background which they leave at the first opportunity, thus depriving disadvantaged communities of their potentially most talented and resourceful members, while the vast majority who fail are on the whole ill-prepared for the life they will have to face.

The 'relevant' education we advocate is a 'community' education not only because it draws on the communities from which the children have come as a rich source of learning experience but because it aims to equip the learner to cope successfully with the problems and opportunities he will meet at each stage of his life, during and after his time at school, in the communities in which he lives and will work. This does not mean we are advocating that working class children should be educated for their

1. In this we are following the line of argument adopted by Norman Garner, Eric Midwinter and other proponents of 'community education' in this country. See, for example, *Teaching in the Urban Community School*, Norman Garner *et al*: Ward Lock Educational, 1973. Our intention, here as elsewhere, is not so much to develop new theories and approaches, for which we would not claim the competence, but to show what kinds of theories and approaches we hold to be consistent with our overall concept of inner area strategy.

'station in life'. On the contrary, the aim is to increase their skill levels, employment options and their chances of mobility but without necessarily increasing the desire to move.

Community education, in the sense we use the term, is concerned with building on the positive features of inner area life and culture, with encouraging feelings of belonging, commitment and solidarity (inherently there already but so often turned by the school and other societal influences into rejection or a negative attitude of resignation) while simultaneously focusing attention on means whereby what is in urgent need of changing might in fact be changed. This means, for example, actively inviting children in and out of the classroom to ask 'why' and 'how' questions about the world around them, to explore local issues of concern and become involved in problem-solving situations. On one simple level the 'litter event' organised by the BIAS – sponsored area caretaker with the cooperation of a local primary school was an attempt to raise children's awareness about the origins of a source of widespread discontent, revealed through our work on both children's and adults' perceptions, and about simple ways of tackling it.

On a different level we might cite activities undertaken by the Birmingham Young Volunteers youthworker, as part of another action project, to help school-leavers through discussion, visits and/or participant observation achieve a greater under-standing of issues of housing, employment and unemployment, child development and play, care of the aged, etc, though success here was clearly inhibited by the fact that the students concerned were already on the point of leaving school, in many cases with reputations as trouble-makers, habitual truants and 'non-achievers'. More striking results have been obtained elsewhere in situations where such concerns are integrated into the mainstream of the school's curriculum content from much earlier on.[1] Of course, such an education is intrinsically political – not to be confused with partisan – and has been attacked on those grounds by some educationalists. But we would contend that, in reality, so too is an education whose implicit values, by stressing competitive individualism, ignoring cultural differences and mistaking nominal equal opportunity (in terms of resource inputs) for equal chances of educational achievement, favour the perpetuation of disadvantage.

There is a slowly growing recognition that the school as an important neighbourhood resource with which most households have been or are associated in some way (as pupils or parents, relatives and friends of pupils, past, present and future) is potentially ideally placed to perform the function of a focus of community activity – educational, recreational, political – for all age-groups. The Van Leer educational and social development project in Birmingham, jointly funded by the LEA and a private foundation, is centred on the primary school, having as one of its objectives 'to help parents with active involvement in the understanding . . . of the contribution and satisfaction to be made and obtained from the involvement of the whole community in its own affairs'. In Small Heath the designation 'community school' has been applied to the new comprehensive school due to open for the 1977 autumn

1. On the theme of community action and the school we would recommend Colin and Mog Ball, *Education for a Change*, Penguin Education 1973.

term. This, too, is planned as a resource centre with facilities (swimming pool, library, workshops, meeting rooms, etc) for use of the general public.

However, the concept of the 'community school', primary and secondary, will only become a reality if the school genuinely serves the interests and aspirations of the community – in all its cultural complexity – and is in turn served by the community. This means, as a first condition, that the community itself must be directly represented in determining how the school is run. The community federation in Small Heath has pressed for such representation, making a videotape to help publicise and raise local awareness of the issue. In particular it has been concerned to ensure that the management of the school is made responsible to a committee controlled by local people, that priority claim on leisure facilities is reserved for Small Heath residents, and that events and activities respond to needs and wants expressed by residents themselves. The latter principle was strongly endorsed by the BIAS-sponsored community education development officer whose approach has been to work closely with residents' associations and other local groups in identifying demand for educational and leisure initiatives, such as do-it-yourself home improvements, urban renewal policy and procedures, communication skills, nutrition and sewing for Asian ladies etc, geared to their own interests and concerns and largely unprovided for by nearby adult education centres. Agreement in principle has been accorded by the local authority to a management committee composed predominantly of representatives from the community. However, it is by no means clear how much influence the committee will be able to exert upon the consortium governing body, nor do the federation's other proposals appear yet to have been given the serious consideration its members feel they deserve. It is regrettable too that the appointment of community education development officer has been allowed to lapse as part of local government economies.

It is interesting that very little of the discussion between federation and local authority seems to have related to the 'school' itself, merely to the leisure centre or what Education Department referred to in its draft terms of reference for a management committee as 'the community aspects of the complex'. If the concept of community school were to be more fully realised, such a distinction would largely disappear. Parents, local employers and craftsmen, union officials, community leaders, other residents and workers would contribute actively to the life of the school by becoming involved in the classroom as well as in extra-curricular activities, sharing their skills and experience, and learning a good deal in the process about the children's needs, aspirations, interests, attitudes. In turn, a greater part of the life of the school would be spent doing and learning things out in the community – 'orthodox' community service, special projects, observation, with or without direct participation, in workshops, playgroups, hospitals, residential care homes, government offices, etc. Parents, other community representatives and children themselves would be closely involved alongside teachers and professional administrators in planning the school programme.

There is room for hope that the new Small Heath comprehensive will in time become such a school. Although the local authority committees (education, leisure services) and departments concerned seem not to have looked much beyond the essentially

304

Roland Lewis

I can imagine a new city where coloured, white and catholic all . . . get together and sort out this mess and untidy situation.

A Child's Eye View of Small Heath

I think that when the children of our people will get education then there will come some changes . . . Education is a must for the children.

Circumstances of Families

'managerial' problems of integrating a secondary school and a community leisure centre within the same premises and (at least initially) not to have envisaged more than token local participation in planning and control, the headmaster himself, sensibly nominated some two years before the formal opening, has shown a willingness to discuss ideas and intentions with local people, has expressed support for the principle of a community education based on local priorities and preferences, and appears sincere in his determination to make the new complex a real centre of neighbourhood life 'round the clock'.

The community school offers the opportunity of breaking down some of the rather artificial distinctions between pre-school, school, adult and further education, youth work, vocational and pre-vocational training, so that 'education in community' comes to be a continuum, not merely in the sense that easier transitions are achieved between different stages and aspects of the process of educational, social and occupational formation but also in the sense that different age-groups may become involved in mutual help. We have seen in two of our own projects (BYV youthworker, pre-school playgroup development officer) that some of the most 'difficult' schoolchildren can be valuable helpers in playgroups and playschemes with under-fives, both enjoying and learning from the experience.

One case comes to mind of a black secondary schoolboy, with a long record of 'troublemaking', who so looked forward to his visits to a playgroup during 'community service' time that preventing his attendance was used as a punishment for/deterrent to his bad behaviour in school. Unfortunately, his punishment also punished the toddlers in the playgroup who equally cherished his visits. In fairness we must mention, too, that one scheme to involve a group of girls in a nursery school and playgroup was terminated at the request of professional workers who considered the language/communication skills of the girls too low for their assistance to be of value to the infants. That is perhaps a sad reflection on the particular girls' fitness as future mothers and it may well reflect an over-zealous professionalism on the part of the workers in question. Yet, if anything, it strengthens the case for this type of interchange, albeit more carefully prepared, and stresses the importance of instruction in child development and practice in child care as part of the education task in communities where verbal communication within the home is likely to be especially limited and thus another factor in the pattern of disadvantage.

But pre-school is not the only point of interchange we have in mind. Other examples would be: the more academically gifted children as one-to-one adult literacy instructors, older children tutoring younger children in very small groups, children and adults working together on community newspapers and video programmes or on planning community and school events, teams of student teachers as 'task forces' on special in-term and holiday projects . . . All of these have been tried, all have met with sufficient success to justify further experiment and incorporation into ongoing programmes.[1]

1. In addition to sources already quoted (Ball & Ball, Garner, Widlake), see *Equality and City Schools, Readings in Urban Education, Vol. 2*, RKP in association with The Open University Press, 1973. Section 3 – 'New Ideas for City Schools' – is a useful introduction to 'a radical reorientation towards education based in and on individual communities'.

In the present situation of high unemployment (including teacher unemployment), growing numbers of early retired and cuts in public investment programmes, and faced with the uphill struggle to hold current spending in check despite constantly rising costs (a pressure particularly marked in education which is far and away local government's biggest rate account budget), it makes eminent sense to embrace the kind of community education approach we have sketched, employing the wide range of underutilised human resources and fixed assets within the community, quite apart from its intrinsic value as a potent force in the longer run for urban change. What that requires on the part of government, central and local, is a more flexible attitude towards educational provision, both in terms of facilities and the activities which go on in and around them.

We do not wish to imply by this that new school construction in older urban areas should cease to be a high priority; indeed, we would favour mechanisms for ensuring that capital investment levels between and within local authorities are more strongly biased towards that end. But within the general pattern of positive discrimination and depending on local population movements and other considerations, it will sometimes make more sense to improve and convert an older building and make it available for wider community use than build a new one, for either educational or leisure purposes. It may also be a preferable option, as we argued in Chapter 8 in the case of the Small Heath Self-Help Pre-School Centre, to aid a voluntary nursery or day-care initiative run by local people themselves out of improvised premises, than insist on DES or DHSS minimum standards at a time when resources are not available to provide nearly enough places to meet demand. Similarly, 'free schools' outside the formal education system deserve support as a means of offering a wider range of educational provision to children who would benefit more from a qualitatively different learning context. By doing so they can also help to relieve the excessive burden on the teaching staff in formal schools.

One final word in this connection on the position of the ordinary primary or secondary school teacher. In advocating a more open system of schooling which makes greater use of non-professionals, that is people without formal teacher training qualifications, we are in fact recognising that the trained teacher has quite special skills which make him most suited to exercise certain teaching functions, especially those concerned with systematic, planned instruction and with acting as motivator, facilitator, guide to the individual's and group's overall development, but that other people within the community have complementary skills and experience in various fields of task- or problem-oriented endeavour, from repairing a TV set to bringing a case before the Race Relations Board, which could be tapped to the mutual benefit of child and teacher. Each school should, of course, make its own choice as to how far it is prepared to go in the direction of reform. It is, however, within the powers of LEAs to encourage experiment along the lines suggested, especially in planning new or replacement provision, and of central government to enable such encouragement to be given, where this might entail some form of special financial or administrative arrangements.

Education for social responsibility

Inner areas are not islands. What happens in them and in their schools affects the rest of society. What happens in other schools and parts of society also affects inner areas. The task of educating for change is not confined to disadvantaged communities; it is concerned too with raising consciousness about problems of deprivation among relatively privileged groups, with increasing their sense of social responsibility.

School children in relatively affluent, more middle class areas not only benefit generally from greater parental interest, help and encouragement in their education, they also have the advantage of learning at home and in school in a similar cultural environment, which makes for higher educational performance as conventionally measured and greater economic success even if it does not by itself necessarily prepare for a qualitatively rich life experience. We concede that affluent suburbs and more privileged groups have their social problems too. But, whatever its intrinsic merits and demerits, the relatively 'closed' nature of this learning environment, reinforced by the tendency for higher-income areas to attract a proportionately large share of resources spent on more advanced (elitist) secondary education, can quite easily engender a distorted view of social reality which, if it acknowledges the existence of deprivation at all, equates it with individual misfortune or failure and does not therefore regard it as a remediable condition in society. We would argue that teachers in more privileged schools, no less than those in disadvantaged schools, have a responsibility to stimulate problem-oriented thinking about contemporary society, just as they have the opportunity to contribute through their teaching methods and the values they apply to school organisation to the cultivation of a spirit of cooperation and collective duty rather than of competitive individualism.

Many individual teachers are of course already attempting to put such principles into practice. The visit of a group of boys from a famous public school in the south of England to Small Heath could certainly be looked on as a step in the right direction. We should like to see more of that sort of intiative, not as a one-off event but integrated into schools' curricular programmes. The examination, analysis and criticism of social, economic and political structures, with a consideration of the personal implications of issues and options for the students themselves, should in our opinion be part of any common core curriculum developed in furtherance of national educational policy, even though ultimate choice of subject-matter and material might best be left to the individual school. For widespread changes of attitude to result, however, the efforts of individual teachers and individual schools will require a great deal of reinforcement in society at large and within all its major institutions.

The obstacles to more widespread acceptance of greater redistribution and of consumption restraint among the more privileged are considerable, not least within what is arguably society's most powerful institution, the business sector, whose interests have till now been served by the continued and general rise in public expectations and aspirations (inflationary though it may be) and whose marketing practices have encouraged 'consumer dissatisfaction'. There are close links between

308

a thriving business sector, the health of the economy as a whole (and thus the total wealth of the nation), and the economic well-being and social status of those who depend on the success of individual industries and firms for jobs and incomes. Giving a higher priority to wider issues of social justice would demand major adjustments in business philosophies, in product and marketing mixes, in the pattern of collective bargaining. Although mechanisms are available to government – changes in company law and taxation, in the range and scale of investment and employment incentives, in prices and incomes controls – which could both stimulate and cushion the effects of adjustment, we believe that even the effective use of such mechanisms would require first a greater degree of consensus within society on their necessity. This, in turn, could only be brought about by political action, informed argument, and harnessing whatever reserves of goodwill are to be found among people as individuals within institutions.

The success of Action Resource Centre has been impressive in placing full and part-time secondments from the business sector with community organisations and projects, many in deprived areas, at no cost to the community agencies concerned.[1] We also find encouraging the widening discussion in recent business publications of the case for a more socially conscious approach to corporate behaviour. We see these as signs that many corporations – that is, influential individuals within them – may be coming to take a wider view of their social responsibilities and role within the community, and to involve themselves in action beyond the simple donation of funds to 'charities'. However, it would be mistaken in our view to rely merely on what is, at best, a very gradual process of changing attitudes, reflecting perhaps as much a defensive reaction to new economic and social realities as a positive initiative to embrace new social values. In the final analysis there can be no substitute for vigorous campaigning by movements, organisations and individuals representing or sympathetic to the interests of inner area residents and disadvantaged social groups in general, utilising not only the usual modes of political action but also the wide range of media opportunities now open.

Use of media

For inner area residents to become politically more active and more effective in communicating with agencies of government and the public at large, two conditions will, we believe, have to be met. First, 'advocacy planners' and experienced community workers will be needed to work within the community and help residents acquire greater understanding in the use of the processes of political representation and local government. Much of what we said in Chapters 6 and 7 and in discussing community education earlier in the present chapter had this end in view. Second, professional communicators must be prepared to put their knowledge of the capabilities and techniques of different media in the service of communities, to act as 'facilitators' of a genuine grassroots participation in determining the coverage of television, local radio and the press and in bringing a clearer exposition and critical examination of key issues of concern to the general public.

1. See, for example, the list of almost 90 projects matched or given material assistance in *Action Research Centre Annual Report 1975/76.*

Interesting and important experiments have already been made in this direction. The BBC's 'Open Door' programme is a case in point. The Trinity Arts Playvan project in Small Heath has already been featured. Victoria Residents' Association, having made a video film on changes in local community life with the assistance of the Artist Placement Group team, were discussing the possibilities of making a second tape entirely on their own initiative for 'Open Door'. As part of the Liverpool EPA project, Radio Merseyside and the Workers' Educational Association collaborated on a series of six fifteen-minute discussion programmes on the problems social change was producing for people in the EPA. Involvement in the programmes within the community was ensured by the formation of a dozen 'listening groups' meeting in pubs, community centres and local houses. The potential for this kind of community education activity has scarcely started to be tapped.

Our own experience in Small Heath has shown that there is plenty of talent, energy and enthusiasm latent in what are frequently considered to be 'inarticulate' communities. We have seen local working class people produce their own community newspaper, record their own video films, group-author (without any previous experience) their own stage production. Examples have been cited elsewhere in this report. VTR (video tape recording) seems to be a particularly promising medium, both for raising the consciousness of local people themselves – consciousness of issues, of their own attitudes to them, and of their 'performance' in seeking their resolution – and for communicating vividly with political representatives and official agencies. The 'truth' of a video tape is difficult to ignore in the same way as a letter or report. The directness of the medium also seems to have a strong appeal for residents whose education may have alienated them from (or failed to develop in them a feeling for) the written word but who often have a powerful sense of the visual image and the spoken word, in no small way due to the influence of television and radio. We see considerable scope for using video tapes produced by community groups as inserts in regional and even nationally networked current affairs programmes rather like local radio 'talk-in' or 'phone-in' sessions. Indeed, in America programmes have been devised combining TV documentary, group discussions in viewing posts, 'phone-in' of questions and comments from viewing posts, and follow-up TV discussion in the studio.[1]

The role of the professional

As participants in an 'urban experiment' it is worth concluding with a brief reflection on our own role in the process of educating for change. We have argued (in Chapter 9) that little is to be gained from further research into the nature of inner area problems. There is already an exhaustive amount of evidence compiled by researchers, academics, consultants, community activists and, naturally, by local and national government departments themselves. Yet, if the problems are well enough known to professionals and politicians working in the field, this knowledge does not seem to have been adequately communicated to the public (electorate) at large.

1. The illustration is owed to Brian Groombridge, in *Television and the People, a Programme for Democratic Participation*, Penguin Education, 1972.

Part of the explanation for this is that so much of professionals' work appears to be destined primarily for other professionals, while politicians understandably tend to play down the seriousness of issues which they feel they cannot grant top priority but which, should their reality become more widely appreciated, might prove an embarrassment. One cannot really expect politicians to behave otherwise, unless priorities are changed as a result of sustained and powerful pressure. There is no reason, on the other hand, why professionals should not adopt a more positive 'advocacy' stance, utilising the results of their experience to increase public awareness of deprivation, its consequences, and ways in which it might be combatted.

A discussion of issues like poverty, bad housing, widespread unemployment, educational disadvantage, economic and political inequality cannot be 'value free'. They demand not so much a detached appraisal as the more impassioned language of political choice. Nevertheless, a study team commissioned to make practical recommendations for government action, now as well as in the more nebulous 'long term', is obligated to present its evidence and argue its case in a rational manner, so as (hopefully) to convince the uncommitted reader. Our dilemma has been to address the task of problem-solving as consultants and, at the same time, communicate something of the urgency with which we view the situation. If, in trying to resolve that difficult dilemma, we are successful in helping to stimulate a wider and more informed public debate, then we shall have brought a little nearer the possibility of swift and determined action to alleviate the plight of inner areas.

Summary

Summary of principal recommendations

In this summary we draw together those major recommendations we believe must be implemented now if the decline of inner areas is to be halted and eventually reversed. They are grouped according to the broad field of policy to which they relate.

Since low incomes are at the centre of inner area problems, our recommendations begin with policies for maintaining and improving earned incomes. These policies must be complemented by income support measures to reduce individual household poverty. Housing is the next major area for which we make recommendations and this is followed by a call for improvements in urban government. The sensitivity of those who govern to the needs of the governed must be increased and weaknesses in planning and policy execution must be overcome. Finally, we turn to the question of finding the resources to carry out our recommendations and suggest that the principle of positive discrimination in favour of those in greatest need should be applied simultaneously to individual households, wherever they live, and to areas where they are concentrated.

The resources required to deal effectively with collective deprivation in inner areas, as well as with individual deprivation nationwide, are considerable. Since the additional resources needed are likely to be hard to come by in the short term, it is of vital importance too that existing resources are used with utmost efficiency and, where possible, savings are made: for example, in some sectors of housing and (though to a much lesser extent) through improved methods of urban government and better management of existing resources.

To have the greatest impact, programmes adopted now should be directed to areas in greatest need and allow for incremental implementation and expansion as and when resources permit. They should be accompanied by specific measures to unblock the constraints which currently hinder the transfer of resources to deprived areas and people, who suffer disproportionately in times of economic recession. Hence the importance of action in the fields of community organisation, political representation and education. People should be given the opportunity to exercise greater influence over major decisions that affect their lives and the incentive to take action for themselves rather than become increasingly dependent on government for services.

Employment and incomes

In Chapter 10 we advocate a policy for employment which operates on the preservation and creation of jobs in, or readily accessible from, inner areas, which subsidises employment directly as well as through subsidising investment, and which takes account of the vulnerability of inner areas to the trade cycle.

As a first step, use should be made of 1972 Industry Act provisions to give additional incentives to industry to locate in selected inner area employment zones pending a more basic restructuring of regional policy. In the West Midlands this would mean their designation as intermediate areas. A job subsidy should be paid on all new jobs in the manufacturing sector – in the first year at a declared rate and over the next six to nine years at a tapering rate. The declared rate applying to new jobs would be graduated annually by central government according to unemployment conditions nationally. The rate could be varied for each region to reflect differing industrial structures and market circumstances.

When planning their particular employment strategy to alleviate very high current unemployment, city authorities, together with the county, should:

Pay vigilant attention to the balance between housing and employment, eg by improving the quality of housing in inner areas so that fewer skilled manual workers are lost to the local workforce

Develop modern industrial estates in inner areas

Rethink planning and zoning policy, including the treatment of non-conforming uses

Make grants available for the rehabilitation of industrial premises and their upgrading to meet safety and environmental protection standards

Respond more effectively to the needs of industry, particularly where there is disruption from redevelopment

Examine educational policy to see whether the provision of manpower for new industrial enterprises is being given sufficient attention by schools.

To give initial momentum to industrial investment and the creation of employment in the inner city, we recommend the experimental establishment of an 'industrial task force'. At first this body should be autonomous under a multi-authority inter-departmental steering committee, chaired by a representative of the Department of Industry, the county or the district as appropriate. On-going programmes would then be handed over to either the metropolitan county or the district authority.

The task force would have two prime functions: to plan the establishment of industrial estates in the inner city and set in motion a programme of advance factory provision, and to discuss with selected larger concerns their plans for the future, with a view to identifying any problems that constrain the maintenance or expansion of jobs. Funds would be received predominantly from central government who would remain responsible for policy relating to major resource allocation: for example, by vetting industrial plans to ensure funds were directed to the most needy areas. However, the task force might have a discretionary budget for dealing with the problems of small firms, where the amounts involved are not large and speed is of the essence. The task force would be staffed from county and district officials, from government departments, and might be strengthened by staff from either the English Industrial Estates Corporation or from new town development corporations.

316

Raising incomes of inner area residents through more and better paid jobs is, of course, the most important of a family of solutions necessary for helping inner areas, but we realise that it will take time for such policies to have much effect on earnings and household poverty. There are more direct means of raising incomes, however, that ought also to be implemented nationally as soon as possible. These we propose in Chapter 11. Most urgent is the need to raise levels of child benefit, next the revision and simplification of supplementary benefits, without distinction between different categories of claimants. Higher take-up rates should be encouraged by better staffing of social security offices in areas of greatest need and a wider publicity of the range of benefits available. Central government should meanwhile increase its capacity to undertake more fundamental reform in the longer term, on the lines of a 'negative income tax' or 'tax credit' system.

At the local level, the city's most effective contribution would be to provide more day-care for mothers who wish to work, since those prevented from seeking work are often those in most need of it. In addition there should be greater coordination of various pre-school services and financial support given to private minders and to firms willing to establish crèches. For such measures to be successful, however, they would need to be linked to strategies of job maintenance and creation.

Housing

Our recommendations for improving housing conditions, which we put forward in Chapter 5, are specifically aimed at three problems:

    The avoidable human misery that has been involved in the process of redevelopment and in Birmingham's extensive use of short life housing

    The failure of housing resources to reach people and houses in greatest need

    The imbalance in investment between new construction and rehabilitation.

Redevelopment

Birmingham (and other local authorities with uncompleted redevelopment programmes) should try as a matter of priority to adhere more closely to stated redevelopment dates and reduce the time spent by families in short-life housing. Central government should help by a speedier handling of CPOs. At the same time, more money needs to be spent on maintaining shortlife housing. In clearance areas (which in future should be very much smaller) there should be temporary community support services, including play provision and centres for advice and information. We further recommend that management of housing in areas of stress be decentralised to the local level.

Resources for people and houses in greatest need

The renovation grant rules should be changed to secure a better direction of expenditure to the worst houses intended for retention. There should be more grant aided expenditure on improving sharing arrangements and encouraging low income owner occupiers to sub-let. Local authorities should acquire more of the worst tenanted property with sitting tenants, although, depending on local circumstances, not necessarily for continued local authority management.

Low income house purchasers should be given more help at the expense of high income purchasers: for example, by a revised option mortgage scheme offering specially low interest rates on small loans to purchase cheap properties. Birmingham's programme of selling unimproved houses coupled with a renovation grant arrangement should be extended. To permit this, council mortgages (including Birmingham's innovative 'half and half' mortgages) should be restricted to pre-1919 property, at least for the time being.

Environmental improvements in Housing Action Areas should qualify for the higher levels of grant aided expenditure allowed in General Improvement Areas.

Local authorities should make greater use of criteria based on need when allocating council dwellings.

Balance between new construction and improvement

We believe that there is a case in Birmingham for expenditure on building new council housing to be reduced on the periphery of the city. The funds released should be redirected to increased investment in and the speeding up of rehabilitation, and to boost parallel industrial investment within the inner city, to increase employment and raise incomes. If the 1975/76 construction programme had been halved in this way, the city could have tripled its rehabilitation programme in declared and proposed GIAs and HAAs, reallocated some £9 million to employment generating uses, and still have reduced the aggregate excess of households over dwellings.

Transferring some resources to industrial development would be justifiable in terms of housing policy since fundamental change to end housing and environmental deprivation in inner areas will depend on raising household incomes. Increased incomes would enable more owner occupiers to pay for improvement, more tenants to pay the higher rents inherent in improvement and more large families to afford the larger dwellings which already exist.

Urban government: sensitivity to needs

We consider that the processes of urban government must be modified to enable a more sensitive response to local needs, principally by greater devolution of political responsibility and by greater decentralisation of administrative activity to the local level.

In Birmingham we recommend (in Chapter 6) that, without changing fundamentally the existing committee structure, informal area committees be established, each covering an area roughly the size of Small Heath, say, one or two wards. The committees would be 'informal' in the sense that they would not be responsible for major service budgets. Their membership would comprise ward councillors and ex-officio representatives of local community groups. Their main role would be to act as representative and advocate, within the local government system, on behalf of the local community. Committees for parts of the city with serious problems of urban deprivation (say seven in all) would enjoy positive discrimination in the provision of special support teams and would have the additional function of acting as a channel for central government programmes for inner areas outside the major fields of housing, education and employment, with some discretionary use of funds. Allocation of special central government aid between areas of urban deprivation might be decided by a central sub-committee (most appropriately of Policy and Resources) composed of delegated members from the area committees concerned. The provision of area committees concerned with local planning and with delegated responsibility for certain aspects of policy execution would allow main committees to meet less frequently, to have smaller memberships, to concentrate on major policy issues and resource allocation, and to be serviced by a smaller central staff.

We recommend (in Chapter 7) that community organisation and development be actively encouraged in inner areas, so that residents may exert greater influence on the decisions which affect their lives. Sometimes, as in Small Heath, a local programme such as urban renewal, will provide the necessary catalyst for organisation. In other cases, the local authority may have to create a catalyst where apparently none exists. We consider this would best be achieved by the appointment of a small community development team, taking a fairly clear issue of local concern as their starting point. Either way, local groups should be given support by financial (grant-aid) and practical assistance, particularly in the early stages of their existence.

One of the aims of community organisation should be to enable local groups progressively to take on responsibility for planning and managing their own facilities and activities, such as youth and old people's clubs, playgroups or childminding schemes. This would not only give residents greater choice and control over their type and style but it would also allow the local authority to concentrate more of its attention on major programmes such as housing, education and employment. Also, as the community becomes more organised, a federation of residents' groups could play a valuable role by helping to resolve conflicts of interest and competing demands for scarce resources (grants and premises); by acting as a lobby on issues of common concern; and by undertaking activities on a wider front – such as producing a community newspaper or organising social events.

Urban government: planning and implementation

In terms of a general approach to urban planning we recommend in Chapter 13 that to make the planning process more responsive and relevant to the needs of inner areas, there should be a much greater emphasis than now prevails on local planning, as compared with the production of formal long-term plans at the strategic level. Structure plans should be replaced by simpler, more flexible 'strategic statements' and concentrate on key regional issues. Local district plans should take the form of 'area community plans' reflecting the key issues at local level. These local plans should be prepared with close cooperation between local authority elected representatives, their planning staff and local interest groups. They should be regularly monitored and up-dated.

We propose that at the national level, central government should assume responsibility for strategic allocation of resources and the coordination of policies of all major agencies engaged in urban resource planning. The machinery of the Public Expenditure Survey Committee should be used to take an overview of inner area needs. The Urban Affairs Ministerial Committee under the chairmanship of the Secretary of State for the Environment, which was set up in September 1976, could become the permanent body responsible for supervising public and private resource planning and for advising the Cabinet on the resource allocations necessary.

Apart from the DOE, there would be represented on such a body the HO, DES, DE, DI, DHSS, DT and, most importantly, the Treasury.

The DOE already vets annual housing investment plans. Vetting annual local authority housing, education and industrial investment plans – as a total proposition – would be a very important tool for central government to ensure that inner area needs are more effectively met.

Too detailed a control by central government of local authorities' activities can be both costly and time consuming. For example, by the time that the average GIA proposal in Birmingham is forwarded for DOE approval over £13,000 of administrative time has been spent, which would be wasted if approval were to be withheld. An equally important improvement to urban government should therefore be for central government to allow local authorities greater freedom with regard to detailed decision-making. In this we are confirming our support for recent government moves permitting local authorities greater discretion to decide priorities within explicitly stated constraints of national policy.

At the local authority level too, changes are needed (Chapter 6). One extremely important management task is financial appraisal. We recommend that all major policy proposals requiring funding should undergo financial analysis: for example, by spelling out the financial implications of alternative programmes and actions. Such an appraisal would reduce inter-departmental problems by relating basic discussions concerning different types of service to a practical consideration of resources (buildings, staff and money) which each department has at its disposal.

Another weakness in local government is the rigidity of established posts, which inhibits flexibility of staff deployment. We recommend that for all inter-departmental projects there should be teams of wholly seconded locally based staff. They should report to a 'projects officer' of chief officer status, not connected to any one department; this should result in a substantial cut in the length of reporting chains between officers and in a reduction of centrally located staff. Since many inner area needs are temporary, flexibility should be the keynote and, in addition to

320

secondments, more use should be made of peripatetic officers in permanent posts – as already exist in Birmingham Education and Housing Departments.

The public is often confused and greatly inconvenienced in trying to deal with the many different departments of the city's administration. We therefore recommend combined local reception points which would provide basic information and advice on council services. These should be accommodated in the most suitable existing council building, irrespective of which department is the main occupant. Alternatively, a large house or shop might be bought for that purpose.

Finding the resources

In Chapter 12 we put the case for new resources for inner areas: it rests not only on disparities between inner and other areas but also on the need and urgency of reversing the present trend of accelerating decline. If the downward spiral were allowed to continue unchecked, the social, economic and political costs could escalate to an extent which would put retrieval out of reach altogether.

Implementing our proposals will require substantial new resources. Some resources could be found from within cities by:

Achieving the same output with fewer resources – by streamlining implementation and by employing more local and fewer non-operational staff

Switching resources from less to more cost-effective uses – transferring resources from new house construction to house improvement and to income generating measures, making fuller use of existing buildings and space

Mobilising resources in society that are still untapped – through giving people incentives to maintain and improve their own houses and, in the longer term, by enabling communities to become more self-reliant.

However, resources found in these ways will not be sufficient. There is in our view no viable alternative to a large-scale switching of capital and current expenditure from more prosperous areas outside the inner areas, particularly from peripheral city growth areas and expansion of towns outside conurbations. A greater share of the rate support grant will have to go to deprived areas. To release resources for capital expenditure there will have to be restraint, at least temporarily, on further public and private development in better-off areas.

Even if conditions in inner areas are improved, some outmigration is likely to continue, and new and designated expanded towns can play an important complementary role as reception areas. New town development corporations, as landlords, are in a good position to match homes and jobs; they should therefore increase their efforts to provide for the less skilled workers and otherwise disadvantaged inner city residents. However, each new town's capital expenditure programme should be evaluated according to its regional context, investment thresholds, the need in some cases to maintain momentum, and its ability to match homes with jobs.

Whilst adjustment of the needs element of block grants would give local authorities more discretion as to the allocation of extra resources between different services, it would not ensure that extra resources are distributed spatially as is intended. Therefore, if central government wants to ensure that specific areas obtain particular aid, a substantial proportion of this would have to come through special programmes and grants. With the objective in mind that inner areas should eventually be less dependent on public subsidy, central government aid might take the form of:

National programmes which will tend to benefit deprived areas (eg support for housing renewal)

Specific programmes for designated priority areas (eg grants towards increased pre-school provision and additional community support services).

Within this context central government should allocate a greater volume of grant aid to local authorities with major inner area problems, and local authorities themselves should devote a larger proportion of their own resources to inner areas. Authorities with a high tax base relative to their needs might be required to contribute from their own taxation a levy to be distributed to poorer authorities.

Our final series of recommendations all relate to the general principle of positive discrimination. We recommend that this principle – unequally generous treatment for those who start with the greatest disadvantages – be extended across the whole field of policy-making. Funds should be allocated to local authorities and then by them, within general constraints set by government policy, to areas in greatest need. Allocation between local authorities should be according to fixed, and fairly simple, criteria of needs (Chapter 8). The size of areas covered should be smallest for physical programmes such as housing, larger for social programmes and larger still for employment.

To effect this principle with any real sense of commitment there will have to be a parallel educative effort (Chapter 14) to give the deprived and mainly powerless people who live in inner areas a greater say in the shaping of their social, economic and physical environment, and in more prosperous areas to increase public acceptance of the transfer of resources in a form that can be shown to be fair. If, however, the process of local democracy proves insufficient to ensure that central government funds are employed to raise levels of service in inner areas, rather than in substitution of locally-generated revenues, then appropriate safeguards will have to be instituted by central government to make positive discrimination mandatory.

Priorities

To secure the necessary commitment to deal effectively with the problems of inner areas will call for informed, widespread public debate about national priorities. The following short list of recommendations identifies what we see as the steps which need to be taken immediately.

At central government level

Review national and regional patterns and mechanisms of resource allocation with a view to channelling more resources into deprived inner areas.

Extend the principle of positive discrimination across the whole field of policy making.

Select jointly with cities and counties priority inner areas with the most acute employment and housing problems for special programmes and grants.

The Department of Industry to review critically its policies to ensure that they are consistent with social policies for inner areas and to develop its own initiatives to that end.

Irrespective of geographical location, improve income support for those in greatest need, particularly by an early increase in child benefits.

Strengthen the Secretary of State for the Environment's Urban Affairs Committee and make it into the government body responsible for coordination of resource allocation throughout the whole urban system.

Develop further the approach whereby central government concentrates on major goals of policy, particularly in the field of housing, while allowing more freedom to local authorities with regard to the choice of detailed strategy for implementation.

Help authorities to adhere to their redevelopment and rehabilitation schedules by adopting a more consistent policy on housing finance over a committed time span which allows local authorities to plan effectively for implementation.

At local government level in Birmingham and other cities where applicable

Reduce new council house construction, at least temporarily, on the periphery and use savings to accelerate GIA and HAA programmes and, where appropriate, inner area redevelopment to a firm and realistic timetable.

Adhere firmly to redevelopment schedules and thereby reduce the time people have to spend in short-life housing.

Increase expenditure on the maintenance of short-life housing and on community support services in clearance areas.

Extend purchase and improvement arrangements for council acquired unimproved housing and increase the availability of council mortgages for pre-1919 houses generally.

Reconsider zoning policies with regard to 'non-conforming' uses in residential areas, to enable the retention and expansion of environmentally acceptable work places.

Establish an industrial task force to initiate programmes of industrial development in a selected priority area (as a pilot experiment).

Extend childcare facilities to enable more mothers to seek work.

Set up area committees, supported in deprived inner areas by a small staff team, and decentralise the administration of service delivery to a more local level.

Place greater emphasis on the process of local planning within this system of devolved political responsibility and decentralised administration, so that residents may exercise greater influence over major decisions which affect the quality of their lives.

Establish inter-departmental local information and advice centres.

Encourage community organisation and development by financial and other assistance to voluntary organisations and residents' groups, to enable them progressively to take responsibility for planning and management of local activities and facilities.

Employ local residents, like area caretakers, for local environmental care and facilitate do-it-yourself house repairs and maintenance by residents wishing to do so.

Encourage inner area schools to ensure that their curricula and teaching methods are relevant to children's needs and circumstances; promote stronger links between homes and schools; and facilitate the use of schools as neighbourhood activity centres for all age groups.

The most important short-term objective is to restore the confidence of residents and potential investors in the future of inner areas. What is essential is that action to set revitalisation under way is taken now while retrieval is still possible.

Appendices

Appendix A

The BIAS work programme

	Research/Study	Experiment
General (Perceptions, Images, Attitudes . . .)	SCPR Exploratory Study	APG Community Video
	SCPR Social Survey	APG Stage Event
	Circumstances of Families	
	The Labelling of Small Heath	
	APG Film	
Housing and physical environment	Housing Policies for the Inner City	Shape Housing and Community Project
	Little Green: A Case Study in Urban Renewal	Home Environment of the Elderly and Disabled
	The Management of Urban Renewal	Area Caretaker
		Area Co-ordinator
	Industrial and Commercial Premises in Housing Action Areas	Talfourd Street Improvements
	APG Video	St. Andrews Public Open Space
	Environmental Quality Assessment	Anti-Litter Project
Health	Health Services Study	
Employment and Industry	Employment Opportunities (CURS)	
	Small Firms	
	Small Firms: Industrial Relocation and Urban Redevelopment (ARC)	
	Industrial Employment and Property Availability	

	Research/Study	Experiment
Education, Recreation and Play	A Child's Eye View of Small Heath (CURS)	Environmental Education Projects
	Adult Education in Small Heath	Home School Liaison Project
	Survey of Preschool Facilities and Play Provision	BYV Youthworker (and Youth Centre)
		Community Education Development Officer
		Trinity Arts Playvan (and People's Pottery)
		Small Heath Self-Help Pre-School Centre
		Pre-school Community Worker
		Pre-school Playgroup Development Officer
		Area Consultative Committee on Under Fives
Community Development		FSU 435 Neighbourhood Centre
		Small Heath Community Advice Centre
		Small Heath Community Federation
		CRC Area Fieldworker

Abbreviations:

APG	Artist Placement Group
ARC	Action Resource Centre
BYV	Birmingham Young Volunteers
CRC	Community Relations Committee
CURS	Centre for Urban and Regional Studies
FSU	Family Service Unit
SCPR	Social and Community Planning Research

Appendix B

Small Heath: An annotated bibliography

General

Jean Morton-Williams and Richard Stowell,
Small Heath Exploratory Study, Social and Community Planning Research, 1973.

A forerunner to the detailed social survey in Small Heath, which explores residents' attitudes to the area, their perceptions and concerns, by means of a limited number of group discussions and depth interviews.

Jean Morton-Williams and Richard Stowell,
Small Heath, Birmingham: A Social Survey, DOE 1975.

This survey, covering 854 (or roughly one in thirteen) households in Small Heath, was designed to provide three kinds of information about the area: data on residents' demographic and economic characteristics that would augment the data from sources such as the 1971 census; data on housing conditions and needs, both for individual households and for the area as a whole; and data on residents' attitudes to Small Heath as a place to live and to policies for improving it. The report on the survey presents the major findings, while the four hundred tables of detailed information have provided essential local data throughout the Birmingham Inner Area Study.

Matthew Melliar-Smith,
Circumstances of Families Survey, DOE 1977.

This survey, carried out by means of over 100 depth interviews, was designed first to assess levels of material deprivation in Small Heath as a step towards the design of policies to protect and raise living standards, particularly among the most vulnerable and deprived members of society, and second, to identify and evaluate the importance for planning of traditional institutions, networks and supportive systems whose continuance (in Small Heath) is threatened and whose loss is (or would be) felt as a deprivation by at least some local residents. The survey covered families 'in poverty', ie whose incomes were no more than 140 per cent of their basic social security entitlement, large families, single parent families and households in short-life dwellings.
The findings vividly demonstrate the subjective reality of poverty and hardship. They show that the greatest single concern is lack of money, though people in extremely bad housing are primarily concerned about their living conditions. The urgent need for more effective means of income support and for greater sensitivity within both central and local government to the needs and circumstances of vulnerable minorities are undoubtedly the most important conclusions drawn from the survey. An unpublished draft report in seven volumes, has been produced, to be followed by a single-volume final report, due for publication in mid 1977. Both make considerable use of direct quotation from interviews.

John Lloyd,
The Labelling of Small Heath: The Role of the Press, Unpublished, 1975.

Much of the work on the Birmingham Inner Area Study was concerned with the way in which different groups and individuals perceived the problems of poverty and deprivation. This report discusses the role of the press in creating the image of Small Heath as a 'deprived' or 'slum' area. It was prepared as a dissertation for the City of Birmingham Polytechnic, and the discussion is set in the framework of an examination of deviancy theory.

Elizabeth Crowther-Hunt,
Small Heath: Area Profile, Unpublished Draft, 1975.

The area profile draws together the principal results of research approximately half way through the study. The draft, which contains a wide range of information, comprises four volumes dealing with 'people', 'place', 'perceptions' and 'policy' respectively.

Rev. W. A. Dixon,
Small Heath: A Survey, Small Heath Baptist Church, 1973.

This independent survey was carried out in order to document and draw attention to the hardship and uncertainty faced by the 500 households in the clearance area adjacent to the Small Heath Baptist Church, and the report makes recommendations for improving both the process and outcome of redevelopment in the western part of Small Heath.

Peter Walding and Roger Coward,
Artist Placement Group Project: You and Me Here We Are, DOE 1977.

APG was formed in 1966, with the basic aim of 'involving art once more in the fabric of daily life', and has had artists placed in both nationalised and private industry and, more recently, government. Their concern is with the broad relationship between individuals and organisations. The four-month BIAS placement preceded by a two-month feasibility study, involved a group of five artists whose work focussed on exploring the process of communication between individuals and groups, with particular (though not sole) emphasis on how this affects the public decision-making process. The group facilitated the making of three video-tapes by local residents' groups; they video-recorded the decision-making process at work in a Housing Action Area; they mounted a stage event, comprising four group-authored plays, including one by a local residents' association; and they made a two-hour film which explores the use of images in public decision-making, from the perspective of the artist.

Housing and physical environment

Peter Wickenden, Anne Apgar, John Freeman,
Housing Policies for the Inner City, DOE 1976.

Poor housing conditions were one of the main reasons for the selection of Small Heath for the Birmingham Inner Area Study. This report analyses the incidence of housing deprivation in the area and the impact of national and local housing policies, and identifies shortcomings in legislation and its application. Recommendations to both central government and local authorities are based on the main conclusion that available public resources are not at present being directed to people with the greatest housing needs.

Anne Apgar,
Little Green: A Case Study in Urban Renewal, DOE 1975.

This report examines the problems and opportunities arising from HAA legislation. Little Green, Small Heath, was used as a case study, and the report presents guidelines for local authorities considering and undertaking HAA work. The guidelines cover HAA selection, establishment of project teams, action programme development, community involvement and monitoring.

John Freeman,
The Management of Urban Renewal, DOE 1976.

The focus of this report is how action for the renewal of older inner city residential areas can best be managed by central government, local authorities and residents. It is based on an analysis of urban renewal administration in the study area and the city as a whole, and includes comparative data for the 11 largest metropolitan districts in the country. Recommendations are made for changes in the management of expenditure, staffing, procedures and central government guidance to local authorities.

Laura Stieg,
Industrial and Commercial Premises in Housing Action Areas: A Planning Guide,
Unpublished, 1976.

The Housing Act 1974 provides no guidance for the treatment of non-residential properties in HAAs. This study had two objectives: to develop a policy for the industrial and commercial premises in Little Green HAA and to develop a methodology applicable in other HAAs. The report concludes that the majority of industrial and commercial premises in Little Green should be retained and suggests procedures for similar exercises elsewhere.

Sharon Fingland and Gordon King,
Environmental Quality Assessment, Unpublished, 1975.

This study developed and tested a technique which was designed to provide a source of information back-up to GIA and HAA programmes. A representative sample of 42 streets in the study area was surveyed, in terms of character, condition and potential land use conflict. The elements surveyed were selected to cover the range of improvements possible under a GIA or HAA programme, and the technique employed was designed to ensure as much objectivity as possible by making value judgements explicit, systematic and consistent. The report describes the method in detail and discusses the merits and limitations of the approach.

Robert Skinner,
The Coventry Expressway and the Small Heath Community, a postgraduate dissertation submitted to the Department of Transportation and Environmental Planning, University of Birmingham, 1974.

This study, carried out in collaboration with BIAS, examines the impact upon Small Heath of the proposal to route the Coventry Expressway through the southern part of the area. It analyses the advantages and disadvantages, including the blighting effects of delay in implementing the proposal, and suggests that the route design could be modified to minimise adverse impacts, and that the history of the proposal points to the need for an approach to transport planning which is more sensitive to community needs and preferences.

Reg Alcantara,
Small Heath Park: An Investigation of its Pattern of Use, a postgraduate study submitted to the Department of Transportation and Environmental Planning, University of Birmingham, 1974.

The material presented in this project report provides detailed information on how Small Heath Park is used and by whom. It shows that the park provides a valued amenity for many people, but also that its catchment area is limited, indicating the importance of providing smaller open spaces, especially for children's play, throughout the study area.

Alan Clawley,
Shape Housing and Community Project, DOE 1977.

The Shape project, set up in 1973, was grant-aided through BIAS for two years from 1974. It was conceived as a unified approach to problems of homelessness, community disintegration and the alienation of young people in the inner city. Through the renovation of short life housing it sought to relieve these problems by providing accommodation for those in need, by providing work and a stable, supportive base for young people alienated by unemployment or family difficulties, and by involving tenants in helping to establish support systems in the wider community. A further aim was to assist current urban renewal policies by temporarily rehousing people who wish to remain in the area. For a variety of reasons, which are examined in the report, the project has been unable to fulfil all its objectives, but has developed its work with short life housing. The evolution of both the project's work and organisation provide some interesting and valuable lessons.

Paula Jones,
Home Environment of the Elderly and Disabled, DOE 1977.

The aim of this action project was to develop a comprehensive approach to improving the comfort, safety and convenience of the homes of elderly and disabled people, through the urban renewal process. An occupational therapist, working with a local project team, explored means by which the provision of special adaptations can be effected as part of improvement and repairs under the 1974 Housing Act, using as far as possible the normal financial arrangements for renovation grants.

Alan Clawley,
Area Caretaker, DOE 1977.

The objectives of this action project were to help residents in a stable residential area to raise the standard of maintenance of the physical fabric; to encourage residents to invest time, money and effort in their own property; and to obtain a swifter response to small problems of a physical nature (eg blocked gulleys). The project involved the employment of one man (reporting to the local urban renewal team), working within the GIA covered by the Grange Park Residents Association. He worked closely with the association, and his work has proved effective in supplementing existing council services. The appointment has been continued by the city council. There is considerable interest in the possibility of making similar appointments in other urban renewal areas in Birmingham and the environmental department has sponsored the making of a video-tape showing the caretaker's work and his approach to it.

Nobby Clark and Alan Clawley,
Area Co-ordinator, DOE 1977.

This project involved the appointment of a locally-based officer whose duties would involve short-term action to ameliorate the poor environmental conditions in an area affected by the redevelopment process. Whereas the Area Caretaker's work in a GIA was concerned with carrying out maintenance work, the Area Co-ordinator's role was to identify problems by observation and contact with residents and to initiate action by the relevant council department. The appointment was discontinued after the one-year experimental period, having made only a marginal impact upon the environmental problems in the area covered.

Alan Clawley,
Talfourd Street Improvements, DOE 1977.

This project was one of five BIAS proposals designed to tackle areas of public space not covered in the urban renewal programme. The Talfourd Street Estate is within Little Green HAA, but is excluded from environmental improvements under the Housing Act 1974 because it is council-owned. The principle behind the project was that tenants should be given an opportunity to determine priorities for the spending of a fixed sum of money in order to improve the physical environment within the estate and provide adequate neighbourhood play space. A number of improvements were made, and tenants clearly valued most those which made a practical contribution to the safety and maintenance of the estate.

Claire Glasspoole and Alan Clawley,
Public Open Space Project – Sara Park, DOE 1977.

This project was concerned with the experimental development of cleared ground in part of the St. Andrews Redevelopment Area. One of the main objectives was the provision of recreational space in a clearance area before the completion of redevelopment. Using a 'low-soil/high-fertiliser' technique (the Bradshaw technique), it was found possible to do this within a year. The technique used has relatively low initial costs, and this fact coupled with the positive reception of the project by local residents points to the feasibility of approaches of this kind in alleviating adverse environmental conditions in clearance areas.

Trevor Fisher and Nick Wigg,
Anti-Litter Project, DOE 1977.

Early in the study both children and adults had identified litter as a major problem in
Small Heath. An 'anti-litter campaign' was therefore incorporated into the BIAS environmental education programme, aimed both at a short-term 'clean-up' operation and longer
term effects through making children more aware of means of litter prevention. The
campaign was not mounted on the scale originally envisaged, but the project was taken
on by the Area Caretaker, who organised an anti-litter march in conjunction with a local
school. It was successful in attracting a large number of children and seems to have
increased to some extent their general awareness of the importance of litter prevention.
A second march has since been held (on request) in a neighbouring area.

Health

Linda Darke,
Health Services Study, Unpublished, 1976.

This report looks at the organisational and functional arrangements for health services
provision in Small Heath, and makes suggestions for the direction of future efforts to
improve the delivery of these services in inner areas.

Employment and Industry

Barbara Smith,
*Employment Opportunities in the Inner Area Study Part of Small Heath, Birmingham,
in 1974*, Research Memorandum No. 38, Centre for Urban and Regional Studies, University
of Birmingham, 1974.

The report presents data both on employing units within the study area and on the employment characteristics of the local population, in relation to the existing situation and to
changes over time. The material is presented in eight working papers, each dealing with a
particular topic.The data in the report formed the core of the study's employment work,
and was subsequently extended and updated where appropriate.

Martin Pinder,
Small Firms, Unpublished, 1974.

A study of the nature, problems and opportunities of small industrial firms in
Small Heath. The 'small firm' in this study has no more than 40 employees; up to 7,000 sq ft
of floorspace; a maximum turnover of £150,000 pa; and was in single, family or
partner ownership. The study shows that while the area has certain advantages for small
firms, many are adversely affected by zoning policies and redevelopment, the latter often
resulting in closure of the firm.

David McDiarmid,
*The Problems of the Small Firm Facing Industrial Relocation due to the Effects of Urban
Redevelopment*, Action Resource Centre/Birmingham Inner Area Study, Unpublished, 1976.

This short report, prepared by a working industrialist for the Inner Area Study under the
auspices of the Action Resource Centre, is a practical guide for small firms faced with
relocation as a result of redevelopment. Based on the author's first hand experience it is
aimed at minimising the procedural and financial difficulties encountered by firms faced
with compulsory relocation.

Anne Apgar,
Industrial Employment and Property Availability, DOE 1976.

This report presents the findings of a study which explored the extent to which restrictions on available industrial property, both locally and city-wide, might constrain employment opportunities for Small Heath residents. The principal finding was that industrial property availability will probably not constrain residents' employment opportunities until after 1986. Other factors are likely to be far more important in this respect, and the report suggests means by which approaches to industrial development might be made more effective in improving employment opportunities for people in Small Heath.

Education, Recreation and Play

David Spencer and John Lloyd, with a technical appendix by Brian Goodey,
A Child's Eye View of Small Heath Birmingham: Perception studies for environmental Education, Research Memorandum No.34, Centre for Urban and Regional Studies, University of Birmingham, 1974.

Developed as part of the BIAS education programme, this study investigates how children in Small Heath perceive and relate to the environment, evaluate their localities and are aware of environmental issues. A secondary purpose of the study is to illustrate the usefulness of perception studies and related techniques to teachers involved in environmental education.

Rex Bird,
Adult Education in Small Heath, Unpublished, 1975.

This review of non-vocational education looks at its relevance to the needs of people in inner areas, by specific reference to local authority policies and provision as they affect Small Heath, and by wider reference to research and writing on the role and concept of adult education. The report's conclusions echo those of the Russell Report on adult education, and it makes specific recommendations for the provision of a service more closely geared to the circumstances of people in Small Heath and inner areas generally.

Elizabeth Crowther-Hunt and Bryan Helm,
Small Heath Survey of Play Activities and Pre-School Facilities, Unpublished, 1974.

This survey provides basic data on the number and type of play and pre-school facilities in the study area, and draws conclusions as to their adequacy in terms of known needs at the time of survey. A number of deficiencies were identified, and the report puts forward options for BIAS action projects in the play and pre-school fields, some of which were subsequently developed and implemented.

Trevor Fisher,
Environmental Education Project, DOE 1977.

Following the work on children's perceptions in Small Heath ('A Child's Eye View of Small Heath') a teachers' working group was set up to carry the work a stage further within schools in the area. This involved the preparation of an 'environmental education kit', a well-researched and catalogued body of source material on Small Heath upon which teachers can draw in developing environmental studies in both primary and secondary schools.

Trevor Fisher,
Home/School Liaison Project, DOE 1977.

Recognition of the importance of the home environment in the education of the child, and of the problems that a poor home environment poses for both schools and children, led to the two-year sponsorship of two home/school liaison teachers to work in Small Heath primary schools. The rationale for the appointments derived from similar work in Educational Priority Areas, and the intention was to experiment with home/school liaison on a somewhat wider basis than had been tried in EPAs by emphasising the community work aspects. While the project confirmed that home/school liaison teachers can and do play a valuable role in the life of the school and in establishing wider links with parents and the community, it also demonstrated the need for a general acceptance within the school of the value of such links if the work of liaison teachers is to meet with any real success.

Trevor Fisher,
Birmingham Young Volunteers Youthworker Project, DOE 1977.

Birmingham Young Volunteers (BYV) is a voluntary agency concerned with stimulating voluntary social and community service among young people in the broad age range 15–25 years. This project was an experiment in developing voluntary service among the less academic, both in a school setting and in the period after school. A full-time youth-worker was appointed to work in Small Heath, and worked mainly with pupils from two secondary schools. A disused garage was converted into a youth centre, and a number of community service projects carried out with school leavers. The project has demonstrated that valuable educational work can be carried out by a detached youth worker operating in a secondary school setting, but that the response of the schools is a crucial factor in stimulating the work.

Trevor Fisher and Barry Martin,
Community Education Development Officer, DOE 1977.

The CEDO action project developed from BIAS research into adult education in Small Heath. The principal objective set for the project was to increase the effectiveness and relevance to local needs of the existing adult education, youth and community services. Part of the work involved pursuing the city's priorities for the area, but the main experimental focus was on community education. The CEDO saw himself as a catalyst in work with residents on self-help education programmes, the long term goal being to help people increase their self-confidence, esteem and awareness, leading to expressions of self-determination and control over their immediate environment. During the one year of his appointment the officer made considerable progress in exploring means by which community education could be developed locally, and indicated the particular opportunities offered by the new community school, due to open in September 1977. The lessons of the project are of both local and wider significance.

Alan Clawley,
Trinity Arts Playvan, DOE 1977.

The Playvan project was conceived in 1973 as a mobile play facility which could take stimulating forms of creative play to situations where little or none already existed. While mobile play facilities were not of themselves a new idea, Playvan's novelty was to bring these to children in Small Heath in a brightly coloured 'toybox on wheels'. The project was funded by BIAS for two years, during which time it became well known and very popular with children (and adults) in the area. Using parks, vacant sites, and any other available open space it provided a series of play 'events' using inflatable structures, art and craft materials, puppets, video-tape recorders, music amplifiers, etc. It undoubtedly has provided a valued and valuable supplement to the limited permanent play facilities in the area, and its work is to continue.

Helen Morley and Peter Walding,
Pre-School Community Worker, Not yet published.

This project was another attempt to bridge the gap between home and school, this time at the level of the nursery school, by the appointment of a teacher-counsellor to work on an area basis. Work within the community, outside the realm of the individual school, was emphasised. Initially the worker was attached to a nursery school, but then transferred to an independent, detached base. The work centred on mothers' needs to better understand and participate in the educational development of their children, and yielded some encouraging results. However, as with other BIAS home-school liaison work, the project revealed the necessity for a substantial change of attitude within some schools if parental interest in education is to develop into involvement with the school.

Helen Morley and Alan Clawley,
Pre-School Playgroup Development Officer, Not yet published.

Concern over the shortage of facilities for pre-school children in Small Heath and in inner areas generally provided the initial impetus for this project. The city council provides advice to playgroups, but is not involved with setting them up. The experimental appointment of a playgroup development officer (attached to the social services department) was specifically to initiate new groups within a particular area. During the one year of the appointment, two new groups were set up and there would seem to be a strong case for the local authority adopting a developmental rather than advisory approach to playgroup provision in inner areas.

Elizabeth Crowther-Hunt,
Self-Help Pre-School Centre, Not yet published.

The Small Heath Self-Help Pre-School Centre developed from a playgroup started and run by local mothers, using an annex of the Old Wyndcliff School, Little Green. Experience had emphasised a pressing need for a local day care centre, and the existence of suitable premises and a competent caring non-professional organiser (the original instigator of the playgroup) offered an opportunity to develop a flexible pre-school centre responding to the needs of children, mothers and childminders in an area where formal provision is low. Inner Area Study funds were provided for the low-cost conversion of the annex, and salary of the project leader, child care assistants, cook and cleaner. A great deal of hard work and commitment have produced a well-run and highly valued centre providing both care for children and much-needed support and guidance for many mothers in difficult circumstances.

Nobby Clark,
Consultative Committee on the Under-Fives, Not yet published.

One of the well-recognised problems associated with securing adequate pre-school provision is the division of functional responsibilities between a number of statutory and voluntary agencies. In order to see how far improved coordination at the local level could improve provision in Small Heath, the Inner Area Study set up a consultative committee comprised of representatives from the various departments and agencies involved in the care and development of under-fives in the area. For a number of reasons, this project had a very late start, and while there was undoubtedly the potential for further development of the committee's role, a number of questions raised by the project remain unanswered.

Community development

Alan Clawley,
Family Service Unit 435 *Neighbourhood Centre*, DOE 1977.

The Family Service Unit is a national voluntary social service organisation which provides intensive supportive social work for families facing severe problems in coping with their lives. The BIAS-sponsored project was an extension of FSU's traditional family casework approach into a 'group' or 'neighbourhood' approach to the severe social problems in many redevelopment areas, and comprised a combined play centre, community work and advice centre based in a converted off-licence in the Bolton Road/Cooksey Road clearance area. The centre provided considerable support for residents, notably in terms of advice and advocacy work. The project demonstrated the need for special support in similar areas, where problems of a decayed and often hazardous physical environment are compounded by uncertainty over clearance and relocation and the high incidence of severe personal and family problems.

336

Nobby Clark and Peter Walding,
Community Advice Centre, Not yet published, 1977.

The purpose of this project was to experiment with a 'one-stop' comprehensive information and advice service, accessible to all residents in Small Heath. The service, staffed by two workers attached to the urban renewal section, was run from a central location on the Coventry Road, in a building which also accommodated the social services family advice service, the BIAS-sponsored community relations fieldworker and BYV youthworker, and the community federation. The project, which ran for only one year, revealed considerable need both for general advice and for specialist housing advice in the area. While it demonstrated some of the benefits of running this type of service from centrally placed multi-use premises, it also pointed the need for a clearer local authority policy on the role and function of advice centres in the city.

Trevor Fisher,
Small Heath Community Federation: A Study in Local Influence, DOE 1977.

The third item of the Inner Area Study brief was an instruction to look at the advantages of greater coordination of local services, and at the implications for the city concerned. The BIAS team interpreted this as meaning not just approaches to 'management' reforms, but also 'community development' approaches. To this end, funds were allocated to enable the establishment of a community federation of residents' groups, whose broad objectives were to represent the interests of all residents in the area in matters relating to the physical, social and economic environment, to improve residents' standard of living and living conditions by liaising with the local authority and by promoting residents' associations and voluntary organisations dedicated to the same broad objectives.

In a little over two years the federation has become well established, and its experience and achievements have shown that within one of Birmingham's poorest areas there is a significant pool of talent for community organisation and activity. It has also shown that, if problems of alienation and decline in inner areas are to be tackled effectively, improved 'communication' between residents and local authority, welcome and desirable as it is, will only have any meaning if it results in action.

Nobby Clark and Alan Clawley,
Community Relations Council: Small Heath Fieldworker, Not yet published.

This action project, set up for one year, was directed towards the achievement locally of the Community Relations Council's overall objective of 'promoting harmonious community relations'. The post was experimental in that it was an attempt to clarify the role of the CRC field officer, and test the validity of a small area appointment. The fieldworker was involved in four major fields of activity: advice-giving; social/cultural activities; assisting other agencies; and community development. The project demonstrated both the very real need for the kinds of skill possessed by the CRC fieldworker in an area like Small Heath and the potential for providing a sensitive effective response to local situations and needs, so taking up the message of the White Paper on Race Relations that a more positive and determined effort is required by local and national organisations if the aims of eradicating racial discrimination and the promotion of good community relations are ever to be achieved.

Note:

During the course of the study the Department of the Environment has also published a number of the team's reports to their steering committee. These comprised essentially reviews of progress and proposals for future project work. Also published (in 1975) was an Interim Review, which represented a brief summary of the team's emerging conclusions and recommendations after the first full year of research and action on the ground. A full list and copies of individual reports may be obtained from the Department of the Environment, 2 Marsham Street, London, SW1 (Room P2/127).

Appendix C

BIAS Team

Practice management

Walter Bor, CBE *Partner in charge*
Francis Tibbalds *Head of Planning*

Core team

Peter Walding *Project director*
Paula Jones *Assistant project director*
Anne Apgar
Nobby Clark
Alan Clawley
Elizabeth Crowther-Hunt
Trevor Fisher

John Freeman
Derek Kerr
Matthew Melliar-Smith
Jon Stevens
Laura Stieg
Peter Wickenden

Temporary placements and specialist inputs

Rex Bird
Linda Darke
Sharon Fingland
Claire Glasspoole
Bryan Helm
Nigel Holt
Loretta Bristow *Secretarial*
Ann Flynn *Secretarial*
Lin Keating *Secretarial*
Margaret Rowe *Secretarial*
Eileen Pollard *Office manager (Birmingham)*

Gordon King
John Lloyd
Helen Morley
Martin Pinder
Bill Wicksteed

Sarah Andrew *Editor*
Graham Blake *Graphics*
Marilyn Gillespie *Graphics*

Consultants to the team

David Eversley *Centre for Studies in Social Policy*
Barbara Smith *Centre for Urban & Regional Studies*

Appendix D

Acknowledgments

It would be impossible to mention by name everyone who participated in projects initiated or sponsored by BIAS. Our apologies to the many whose efforts go unacknowledged. We should like, however, to thank in particular:

Zora Adam	Jill Keegan
Lee Allane	Roland Lewis
Ivy Beddall	David McDiarmid
Lorna Bell	Barry Martin
Geoff Boyle	Mike Martin
Gavin Brown	Dave Mason
Marie Buchanan	Mandy Okoosi
Linda Buckley	Bob Pike
Barry Coleman	Salim Rafiqi
Roger Coward	Gill Revitt
Bill Dixon	Fran Ridley
Jennifer Dixon	Lakhi Rihal
Julian Dunn	Carolyn Sikorski
Joyce Farley	Evadne Stevens
John Fitzmaurice	Dave Swingle
Carol Flanagan	Val Thomas
Claire Henderson	Frances Viner
Keith Henderson	Tyna Wagner
John Homer	Nick Wigg
Mike Jones	Joanne Worsdall

We are grateful, too, to members and officers of Birmingham City Council who gave their time, help and encouragement, to officers of the Department of the Environment for their patience and understanding, and to all others who made the study possible.

Finally, we would dedicate this report to the people of Small Heath. We hope they will benefit.

Printed in England for Her Majesty's Stationery Office
by Oyez Press Limited
Dd. 587495 K28 6/77